Conjugal Rights

NEW AFRICAN HISTORIES SERIES

SERIES EDITORS: JEAN ALLMAN AND ALLEN ISAACMAN
AND DEREK R. PETERSON

Books in this series are published with support from the Ohio University National Resource Center for African Studies.

David William Cohen and E. S. Atieno Odhiambo, *The Risks of Knowledge: Investigations into the Death of the Hon. Minister John Robert Ouko in Kenya*, 1990

Belinda Bozzoli, *Theatres of Struggle and the End of Apartheid*

Gary Kynoch, *We Are Fighting the World: A History of Marashea Gangs in South Africa, 1947–1999*

Stephanie Newell, *The Forger's Tale: The Search for Odeziaku*

Jacob A. Tropp, *Natures of Colonial Change: Environmental Relations in the Making of the Transkei*

Jan Bender Shetler, *Imagining Serengeti: A History of Landscape Memory in Tanzania from Earliest Times to the Present*

Cheikh Anta Babou, *Fighting the Greater Jihad: Amadu Bamba and the Founding of the Muridiyya in Senegal, 1853–1913*

Marc Epprecht, *Heterosexual Africa? The History of an Idea from the Age of Exploration to the Age of AIDS*

Marissa J. Moorman, *Intonations: A Social History of Music and Nation in Luanda, Angola, from 1945 to Recent Times*

Karen E. Flint, *Healing Traditions: African Medicine, Cultural Exchange, and Competition in South Africa, 1820–1948*

Derek R. Peterson and Giacomo Macola, editors, *Recasting the Past: History Writing and Political Work in Modern Africa*

Moses Ochonu, *Colonial Meltdown: Northern Nigeria in the Great Depression*

Emily Burrill, Richard Roberts, and Elizabeth Thornberry, editors, *Domestic Violence and the Law in Colonial and Postcolonial Africa*

Daniel R. Magaziner, *The Law and the Prophets: Black Consciousness in South Africa, 1968–1977*

Emily Lynn Osborn, *Our New Husbands Are Here: Households, Gender, and Politics in a West African State from the Slave Trade to Colonial Rule*

Robert Trent Vinson, *The Americans Are Coming! Dreams of African American Liberation in Segregationist South Africa*

James R. Brennan, *Taifa: Making Nation and Race in Urban Tanzania*

Benjamin N. Lawrance and Richard L. Roberts, editors, *Trafficking in Slavery's Wake: Law and the Experience of Women and Children*

David M. Gordon, *Invisible Agents: Spirits in a Central African History*

Allen F. Isaacman and Barbara S. Isaacman, *Dams, Displacement, and the Delusion of Development: Cahora Bassa and Its Legacies in Mozambique, 1965–2007*

Stephanie Newell, *The Power to Name: A History of Anonymity in Colonial West Africa*

Gibril R. Cole, *The Krio of West Africa: Islam, Culture, Creolization, and Colonialism in the Nineteenth Century*

Matthew M. Heaton, *Black Skin, White Coats: Nigerian Psychiatrists, Decolonization, and the Globalization of Psychiatry*

Meredith Terretta, *Nation of Outlaws, State of Violence: Nationalism, Grassfields Tradition, and State-Building in Cameroon*

Paolo Israel, *In Step with the Times: Mapiko Masquerades of Mozambique*

Michelle R. Moyd, *Violent Intermediaries: African Soldiers, Conquest, and Everyday Colonialism in German East Africa*

Abosede A. George, *Making Modern Girls: A History of Girlhood, Labor, and Social Development in Colonial Lagos*

Alicia C. Decker, *In Idi Amin's Shadow: Women, Gender, and Militarism in Uganda*

Rachel Jean-Baptiste, *Conjugal Rights: Marriage, Sexuality, and Urban Life in Colonial Libreville, Gabon*

Shobana Shankar, *Who Shall Enter Paradise? Christian Origins in Muslim Northern Nigeria, c. 1890–1975*

Conjugal Rights

*Marriage, Sexuality, and Urban Life
in Colonial Libreville, Gabon*

Rachel Jean-Baptiste

OHIO UNIVERSITY PRESS ᔕ ATHENS

Ohio University Press, Athens, Ohio 45701
ohioswallow.com
© 2014 by Ohio University Press

Printed in the United States of America
Ohio University Press books are printed on acid-free paper.∞

20 19 18 17 16 15 14   5 4 3 2 1

Library of Congress Cataloging-in-Publication Data

Jean-Baptiste, Rachel, author.
 Conjugal rights : marriage, sexuality, and urban life in colonial Libreville, Gabon / Rachel Jean-Baptiste.
  pages cm. — (New African histories)
 Includes bibliographical references and index.
 ISBN 978-0-8214-2119-2 (hc : alk. paper) — ISBN 978-0-8214-2120-8 (pb : alk. paper) — ISBN 978-0-8214-4503-7 (pdf)
 1. Marriage—Gabon—Libreville—History. 2. Divorce—Gabon—Libreville—History. 3. Sex—Gabon—Libreville—History. 4. Customary law—Gabon—Libreville—History. 5. Gabon—History—1839–1960. I. Title. II. Series: New African histories series.
 HQ694.9.J43 2014
 306.8096721—dc23

                                            2014014964

*In memory of Lumen and Emanuel Georges and
Melanie and Pierre Jean-Baptiste*

Contents

Illustrations

PHOTOGRAPHS

Acknowledgments

I received tremendous financial, intellectual, and emotional support from varied institutions and people in completing this book. Fellowships from the Andrew W. Mellon Foundation, the Department of Education's Foreign Language and Area Studies Program, and the Fulbright Program supported fieldwork and writing of the dissertation from which this book sprang. The Mellon Mays Fellowship Program has funded varied stages of research, writing, and a sabbatical year. An Individual Development Award Grant from the United University Professions at the State University of New York at Albany funded follow-up research in Gabon and Senegal. The University of Chicago's Social Science Division provided a year of leave and funding for further research trips to France and to Italy. The office of the Dean of Social Sciences provided funding for the stage of final production.

While a graduate student at Stanford, I was fortunate to be part of a dynamic community of faculty and peers. The indefatigable Richard Roberts has been a generous adviser and mentor for more than a decade. The late Kennel Jackson conveyed his love of African cultural and art history. Mary Louise Roberts taught me to not be afraid of theory, and Estelle Freedman taught me to think critically about how gender matters. Fellow graduate students Shelley Lee, Carol Pal, Lise Sedrez, and Matthew Booker read nearly every word of every chapter and continue to provide a sustained friendship. I have also benefited from commentary by Kim Warren, Cecilia Tsu, Shana Bernstein, Shira Robinson, and Amy Robinson, as well as Emily Burrill, Benjamin Lawrence, and Rachel Petrocelli. Abosede George has provided invaluable feedback along the entire road from dissertation to book.

At the University of Chicago, I found myself amid a remarkable intellectual community of scholars. I thank Adrienne Brown, Tianna Paschel, Micere Keels, and Gina Samuels for reading several chapters in a critical moment of transition and for their friendship that knew no bounds. Leora Auslander's keen discernment propelled me in new directions, as did the insights on the changing meanings of race provided by Julie Saville, Kathy

Cohen, and Daniel Desormaux. Linda Zerilli and affiliated faculty and students of the Center for the Study of Gender and Sexuality commented on several chapters. Ralph Austen, Jennifer Cole, Jean Comaroff, John Comaroff, Keisha Fikes, Cécile Fromont, Emily Osborn, Francois Richard, and graduate students who participated in the African Studies Workshop formed a tremendous gathering of Africanists. Research assistants Deirdre Lyons, Brittany McGee, and Jennifer Amos tracked down numerous leads. I learned much from undergraduate and graduate students in the classroom.

Many individuals beyond these institutions generously gave of their time and intellectual capital. I thank Jean Allman for meticulous criticism and probing questions. Gillian Berchowitz supported this project with patience and encouragement. Two anonymous reviewers provided valuable critiques. Carina Ray and Kahleen Sheldon read several chapters in varied stages. The book benefited tremendously from Michelle Beckett's close reading and editorial suggestions and Nora Titone's sharp eye for detail. Hilary Jones and Lorelle Semeley have conversed with me innumerable times about our mutual interest in historical change in Francophone Africa. The small community of scholars who work on Equatorial Africa—including Florence Bernault, Phyllis Martin, Jeremy Rich, John Cinnamon, Marissa Moorman, Meredith Terretta, and Kairn Klieman—has provided me with immeasurable assistance in obtaining access to archives, people, and institutions. In France, Pascale Barthélémy, Anne Hugon, Odile Goerg, and Catherine Coquery-Vidrovitch have been generous colleagues. At the State University of New York at Albany, conversations with Patricia Pinho, Glyne Griffith, and Lisa Thompson pushed me to think more critically about the analysis of race, and I have benefited greatly from Iris Berger's insights and mentorship.

I am grateful to and profoundly thank the men and women in Gabon who generously shared the most intimate details of their lives and hosted me in their worksites, homes, and sacred spaces. Jean-Emile Mbot and the Laboratoire Universitaire des Traditions Orales at the University of Gabon Omar Bongo provided me with institutional affiliation. Soeur Marie Sidonie and Soeur Maria Cruz of the Congrégation de l'Imaculée de Castres assisted me with transportation and introductions to social networks. Guy Rossatanga-Rignault and the Fondation Raponda-Walker pour la Science et la Culture also facilitated access to key documents and people. Patrick Cellier shared his treasure trove of historical postcards. The staff of the National Archives unearthed uncataloged documents and photographs. The company of Brigitte Meyo, Achille de Jean, Judy Knight, and many Haitian expatriates helped to make Libreville a home away from home.

I thank my family and friends for their love, patience, and encouragement during this long journey. Marsha Figaro and Erica Olmsted have been tremendous friends. My parents, Christie and the late Aramus Jean-Baptiste, and Ari, Sara, Pria, and Noah Jean-Baptiste provided me with sustenance beyond life in the academy. Cassandra Jean-Baptiste, whose life has unfolded within the shadow of writing this book, and Glenn Hoffmann formed the emotional community that nurtured the completion of this project.

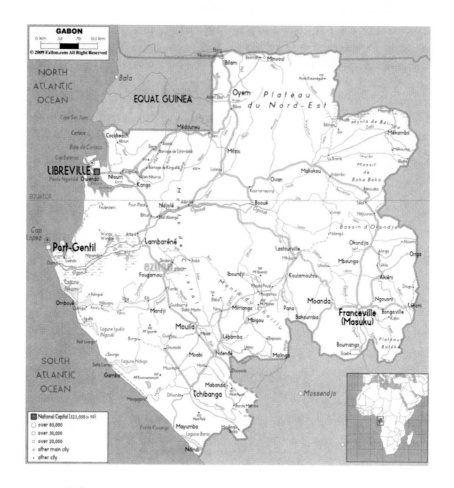

MAP I.I. Gabon

Introduction
Narrating a History of Domestic Life, Sexuality, Being, and Feeling in Urban Africa

→ AFFECTIVE HISTORY?

LOCATED ON THE GABON ESTUARY along the Atlantic coast, Libreville (Free Town) was founded in 1849 by the French on land that political leaders of Mpongwé ethno-language communities, who had lived there for centuries, ceded via a series of treaties. The French populated the new settlement with a contingent of slaves they had intercepted from a vessel traveling from Angola toward the Americas.[1] Fifty-two former captives — twenty-seven men, twenty-three women, and two children of unidentified Central African origins — disembarked at the Gabon Estuary in February 1849.[2] The skeletal staff of the French administration, comprising a handful of naval personnel, alongside Catholic missionaries, pledged to each of the former slave men a hut and a parcel of land to begin their new lives. Yet, within months, a number of these men expressed their discontent with the "freed" lives that the French envisioned for them. In September, French naval reports relay, ten to sixteen men ran away into the forest and carried out attacks on Estuary communities.[3] They stole arms, kidnapped women, and threatened to launch further attacks. The rebels issued a singular demand: they wanted wives. The mutineers had begun kidnapping women with the goal of making them their wives, and they threatened to inflict further terror upon Estuary residents unless they were given access to more women.[4]

The aspirations of these newly settled men to build a new present and future necessitated not just land and roofs over their heads, but also wives with whom to form households and ensure social and biological reproduction. Perhaps the rebels also conceived of wives as providing companionship and emotional attachment, factors that could provide them with a sense of belonging in their new home. These were poor men from distant places who had limited means to accumulate the imported goods that could constitute bridewealth payments to facilitate marriage. Bridewealth, a bundle of goods that a groom gave to a bride's family, was a primary legal and social marker across Africa that made a relationship a marriage. These men also lacked the social capital that could have facilitated interpersonal relationships, and therefore marriage, in the Mpongwé communities of the Estuary region.

Marriage conferred dignity and the capacity to articulate social, legal, and economic rights to shape one's personhood and status in society. If the men remained unmarried, they would be perpetual minors and socially dead, failing to establish adulthood and manhood.[5] Not only had being uprooted from their natal homes separated them from their ancestors, to whom they owed offerings in order to prosper in their present life, but their unmarried status would not produce the children who would honor them when they died and perpetuate their lineages. In making the claim to marriage as a universal right for men to establish selfhood in the emerging settlement of Libreville, these men asserted a conception of the basic necessities of town life in terms unimagined by the French.

By October, the rebels had been killed, captured, or rejoined the settlement and pardoned. Fearing further mischief, a meeting involving the chief of the former slaves, the French doctor, and the naval commander convened to consider "the urgency of marriage" for Libreville's new residents. Navy officers precipitously sought the approval of Catholic missionaries to bless en masse marriages of fifteen couples, fearing "very dangerous liaisons if they were left unmarried."[6] In alluding to the "dangerous liasons" that could develop if men and women among the former slaves remained unmarried, Catholic missionaries were also referring to the commonplace nature of interracial sexual relationships between African women and European men along the Gabon Estuary. In facilitating these marriages, the French acknowledged the rebels' claims of marriage as a right. However, the French sought to consecrate marriage in rites intelligible to French norms, civil and Christian. Written records and memory are silent as to the actions and subjectivities of the women who were historical actors in these events at the town's emergence. However, throughout the history of colonial Libreville, populations of women exceeded or nearly equaled those of men, and women's claims to make the city "home" through varied articulations of sex and marriage also deeply shaped urban life.

More than anything else, the (marriage mutiny of 1849) illuminates the importance of questions and contestations of how, not if, men *and* women would constitute self and sociality in Libreville through relationships with each other. This episode was the first and but one of a multitude of struggles to articulate the contours of domestic life and being in Libreville that would unfold in the century to follow. *Conjugal Rights: Marriage, Sexuality, and Urban Life in Colonial Libreville, Gabon,* tells the story of the *longue durée* of such questions, narrating a social history of heterosexual relationships as lived and a cultural history of the meanings of such relationships. This book thereby links three important processes of historical change in late nineteenth- and twentieth-century Africa: (1) transformations in conjugal and sexual relationships; (2) meanings of gender; and (3) urbanism.

I periodize such dynamics as early as the nineteenth-century years of the Estuary region's standing as a way station in transatlantic trade routes, but the greater part of this story centers on 1930 through 1960. These were years of tremendous social, political, and economic change in Libreville and its rural suburbs as the town grew through immigration and the export of timber came to be the colony's primary economic activity. Disembarking via oceans, rivers, and overland, a population of about fifty Central African ethnolanguage groups, West Africans, and Europeans converged to transform the equatorial forest located along the Atlantic coast into a town in which they could establish homes and achieve fortune. I focus principally on the conjugal and sexual careers of the Mpongwé, inhabitants at the time of Libreville's founding, and the Fang, whose migration toward the Estuary transformed the region and who would come to represent a large proportion of the city's population over the course of the twentieth century. During this same period, conjugality and sexuality in the Estuary region also involved the persistence of interracial relationships between Mpongwé women and white men of varied nationalities even as the colonial state sought to demarcate rigid racial boundaries. Engaging the call of scholars who have argued that the study of households and gender needs to take center stage in African history, I argue that Libreville's residents lived and contested meanings of urban life according to shifting mores of sexual economy.[7] In defining the term "sexual," I conceive of two meanings: practices and conceptions of what it meant to be male and female, as well as practices and meanings of sexuality. In conceptualizing the term "economy," I am inspired by Alfred Marshall's definition of economics as the study of humans "in the ordinary business of life."[8] Thus, "sexual economy" in this book means the transactions and relationships of everyday life around the meanings and lived experiences of gender identities and sexual relationships. Historical actors engaged in, had aspirations toward, and debated sexual economy based on changing emotional, social, political, and economic vectors. Ideas and lived experiences of sexual economy changed over time and shaped the very material and conceptual fabric of urban life.

Changing articulations and negotiations of sexual economy were motors of historical change that shaped the unfolding of key aspects of urban life: money and its use, distribution, and social value in the form of bridewealth (chap. 4); the law, legal systems, and jurisprudence (chap. 5); moral and social order and human and spatial geography (chap. 6); and racial and ethnic differentiation (chap. 7). Town life engendered an unprecedented circulation of people, material, and ideas in this Equatorial African locale. Taking advantage of the unparalleled opportunities and mitigating the risks required new forms of male-female partnerships. Heterosexual relationships changed as the city itself changed, presenting new kinds of social, cultural, and economic possibilities. The varied African and varied French communities understood sexual relationships to be the key to social, cultural, and economic goals, but in a variety of configurations that often resulted in contestation as well as convergence.

Colonial rule sparked the creation of Libreville, and the French sought to mold the lives of its African inhabitants into their own models. However, in examining the interstices of everyday affective life and institutional governance, I contend that African women and men were not accidental visitors to the colonial town. The loves, passion, breakups, makeups, courting, and jealousies of historical actors laid bare political and legal claim-making to belonging in the town. These processes shaped the very meaning of urbanism. African women and men in Libreville made urban life according to their own changing logics and sentience in ways that were touched by and sometimes circumscribed but never fully controlled by the colonial state, African political leaders, or church representatives. On the contrary, Libreville's inhabitants made choices about if and how to marry, if and how to divorce, whom to love, and with whom to have sex that changed government policies and caused the colonial state to perpetually scramble to maintain social control. Such contestations did not stop with the end of formal colonial rule. As Libreville became the capital of independent Gabon in 1960, marriage and sex occupied the forefront of ideas about modern urban life, governance, and nation.

In addition to material concerns, historical actors in Libreville married, divorced, and had sexual relationships based on emotional aspirations of love, fear, pleasure, pain, and belonging, sentient factors. As argued by historian of medieval Europe Barbara Rosenwein, the study of emotion should also guide historical inquiry and analysis. People across time and space, Rosenwein argues, have lived in "emotional communities," forms of grouping that are the same as social communities such as families and neighborhoods.[9] However, what makes emotional communities distinct from social communities are systems of feeling: "what these communities (and the individuals within them) define and assess as valuable or harmful to them; the evaluations that they make about others' emotions; the nature of the affective bonds between people that they recognize; and the modes of emotional expression that they expect, encourage, tolerate, and deplore."[10] Analyzing how "systems of feeling" in heterosexual relationships also shaped historical actors' negotiations of urban life opens a new window into the complex articulations of historical change and continuity in colonial-era West-Central Africa. Following the conjugal and sexual lives of Libreville's inhabitants and institutions offers a fresh perspective into the anxieties, hopes, disappointments, and unintended contingencies of city life. The varied articulations of sexual and conjugal comportment over time and space by varied African and French actors in Libreville reflected significant social, political, and economic change over the course of the twentieth century. *Conjugal Rights* engages three important historiographical themes of African studies: (1) urban history; (2) the history of women and gender; and (3) the history of sexuality. In foregrounding the history of sexuality, *Conjugal Rights* expands our understanding of this little-studied theme in research on Africa and reveals the linkages between shifting articulations of eros and social, political, and economic change.

URBAN AFRICA

This sexual-conjugal biography of Libreville in the precolonial and early colonial nineteenth century contributes to research that decenters colonial imperatives at the origins of urbanism in Africa.[11] As argued by John Parker of locations such as Accra that were urban prior to colonial conquest, "The transition from precolonial city-state to colonial city was not about the creation of new urban identities and institutions but the reconfiguration of old ones."[12] By identifying how marriage and sex were important currents in the Estuary in the nineteenth century, before the consolidation of French colonial rule, I demonstrate the continuities in how Africans conceptualized town life into the twentieth century.

In an important current in African urban studies, researchers have challenged the very concept of "urbanization" as a linear process that automatically results in a standard set of structural changes. James Ferguson has critiqued the manner in which modernization theorists have interchangeably used the term "urbanization" and the terms "modernization," "monetization," "proletarianization," and "detribalization," a slippage in language that he calls "teleologies of social change."[13] Similar to Ferguson, historians of Africa emphasized African agency in determining what urban life looks like. Town dwellers forwarded their own conceptions of modernity and directed their leisure time and sartorial makeup.[14] Wage laborers countered European bosses' conception of work time and offered alternative visions of wage labor.[15] After World War II, urban men were at the forefront of nationalist and anticolonial politics.[16]

However, in keeping the term "urbanization" as an analytical category, we have narrowed the possible terrains on which Africans conceptualized town life and have posited the source of transformations in city life to the very teleologies we seek to disrupt. In his research on four cities across sub-Saharan Africa, AbdouMaliq Simone contests the very term "urbanization" as the cognitive framework through which researchers analyze urban African history. Simone exhorts scholars to examine how specific actors "reach and extend themselves across a larger world and enact these possibilities of urban becoming."[17] Moreover, Simone contends, "particular modalities of organization, long rooted in different African histories, are resuscitated for new objectives and with new resiliency."[18]

Conjugal Rights traces "urban becoming" rather than "urbanization" in Libreville in order to encompass the multiplicities of processes through which individuals created and gave meaning to urban life. In correlating the themes of sexuality, marriage, and transformations in how to be male and female through the interpretive lens of urban becoming, this book offers a fresh perspective to understandings of African urban history.

There is a rich collection of histories of women in urban Africa, but this scholarship has not often resulted in the gendering of urban African studies. When discussing African urbanites, general overviews of African urban history often talk about only African men — the African city has been gendered male. The normative urban African character, the person with agency to shape meaning and experience of life on the Copperbelt, in Johannesburg, Mombasa, the Witwatersrand, and Dakar, the mine, the factory, and the street, is male.[19] In tracing the uneven and changing gendering of Libreville as male *and* female, this book centers the historiographical and epistemological paradigms of women's and gender history on urban African history.

WOMEN AND GENDER IN AFRICAN HISTORY

In a landmark 1996 edited volume on urban women in Africa, Kathleen Sheldon wrote, "Women and gender have rarely held center stage in accounts of urban analytic issues."[20] Since then, a number of books have been published on African women in cities. Countering earlier publications that posited African women as "passive rural widows," historians have demonstrated how women, like their male counterparts, migrated to cities in search of economic opportunities.[21] Women usually worked on the margins of the colonial wage-labor economy, as beer brewers, sex workers, and hawkers. Focusing primarily on Southern and Eastern Africa and on colonies in which there were large numbers of European settlers, this research has argued that though small in numbers, women shaped the political economies of cities and rural regions from which they originated, as well maintained the social reproduction of African societies.[22]

Several decades of research have yielded a commonly accepted chronology of African women's twentieth-century colonial history as marked by both opportunities and limitations. Dorothy Hodgson and Sheryl McCurdy have argued that the onset of colonial conquest and rule in the early twentieth century "intensified struggles over normative gender relations." "Wicked women," women who acted in ways outside the normative ideas of proper female comportment in urban areas across the continent, were at the forefront of historical change.[23] The early colonial period, for the most part, ushered in openings for women of increased autonomy as officials created legal institutions and wrote legislation in attempts to make African societies legible.[24] An unintended consequence was that women near European enterprises and colonial administrative centers brought marital disputes before officials, bypassing chiefs, who had been the "traditional" arbiters, and more easily obtained divorces.[25]

By the 1920s and 1930s, many scholars concur, colonial states and elder African men sought to enact control over women's labor, marriage options, and mobility by applying new varied regimes of indirect rule. In settler colonies in East and Southern Africa, land alienation and the expansion of male migrant labor fixed women in rural areas under the adjudication of chiefs and newly articulated bodies of customary laws that rigidified the control of senior men over women.[26] However, some researchers have countered, women's status in rural areas was not so bleak, with young men and women contesting the control of senior men.[27] Moreover, codification did not evenly occur, nor did it inevitably result in the "crystallization" of senior men's power over women and junior men.[28] Furthermore, scholars have demonstrated that the closing off of town life to women after the 1920s was not so categorical, showing that some women from Nairobi to Harare created niches for economic opportunity and social reproduction.[29]

During and in the aftermath of World War II, migration to cities increased across the continent, and British and French colonial officials turned their attention to creating a stable urban population composed of African men *and* women. From the Copperbelt to Harare to Lagos, elite Africans invoked politics of respectability to argue that African town life incorporate married couples and their children into permanent housing.[30] After World War II, Africans surged to cities across Africa, even in apartheid South Africa, with redefined pass controls. As colonial officials in settler colonies viewed the presence of African women in towns with less approbation, they sought to encourage monogamous households of wage-earning men and women trained in European domestic arts. In towns such as Harare and Nairobi, an increased number of women circulated through cities, including wives joining their wage-laborer husbands for part of the year in town through "marital migrancy" and individual women working as small-scale traders.[31]

Research on women in West Africa, which included African societies with precolonial urban traditions and fewer European settlements, has demonstrated that restrictions on women's and girls' movement in urban areas and socioeconomic mobility were not so unilateral.[32] Jean Allman and Victoria Tashjian have shown that in 1930s Asante, Ghana women had possibilities for economic autonomy through cash cropping on their own farms, instead of husbands' farms, in rural frontiers that bordered towns.[33] That some women were able to maintain control over land and cash proceeds facilitated their control over their sexuality and choice in marital status. In spite of the consolidation of indirect rule and the codification of customary law in the 1930s, some customs remained fluid and others rigid, resulting in a "shifting customary terrain" in which men and women reconfigured the meanings of customary marriage law in colonial courts.[34] Nevertheless, the dominant paradigm in the literature across East, West, and Southern Africa is that women did decline in economic, social, and legal status in the 1930s as chiefs, elder men, and colonial officials strove to limit their economic autonomy and ability to determine their marital lives and sexuality.

Research in women's history in Francophone Africa, published in English or French, remains embryonic. In 1997, Catherine Coquery-Vidrovitch wrote that the history of African women was "almost unrecognized in French historiography."[35] Since then a few edited volumes and essays have indicated some momentum toward this research theme.[36] Yet, by 2010, Pascale Barthélémy lamented the "as of yet little tread research path in France on the history of women and gender in Africa."[37]

The small body of research on women in French-speaking West and Central Africa has called into question some generalizations in the historiography on colonial Africa. For example, as argued by Frederick Cooper, in the minds of British and French colonial personnel, "the gendering of the African worker [as male] was so profound it was barely discussed."[38] However, as demonstrated by Lisa Lindsay in her research on towns in southwest Nigeria, the ideal of "the male breadwinner" was not normative, but expanded in the 1950s and 1960s amid the debates of Nigerian men, women, colonial government officials, and employers about the intersections of wage labor and family life in an era of rapid change.[39] Additionally, Pascale Barthélémy's book on the twelve hundred–odd women from throughout West Africa who received formal education and diplomas in Dakar as nurses and midwives between 1918 and 1956 demonstrates how African women entered professional and salaried labor.[40] Thus, the gender of the African worker, of the quintessential town dweller, and of the African city was not always normatively male. The work of Barbara Cooper on Maradi, Niger, and that of Phyllis Martin on Brazzaville, Congo, demonstrated how indelibly women, family life, and men's and women's marital aspirations were woven into processes of urban becoming well before the 1930s.[41] Several factors contributed to the greater presence of women in towns in Francophone Africa versus Anglophone Africa. First, urbanism predated the implantation of colonial rule in some regions that became part of French West and Equatorial Africa. Second, the French weren't as concerned as their British counterparts with impeding women from migrating to towns.[42] In focusing on the intersections of the sexual economy and wage labor in Libreville, *Conjugal Rights* demonstrates that how to be male and how to be female were very much in question and shaped the true fabric of urban African life and modes of "urban becoming" in the years of colonial rule.

Conjugal Rights contributes to women's history, but also seeks to engender central historiographical questions in African studies. In doing so, I follow Allman, Geiger, and Musisi's call for "foregrounding women as historical actors," with attention to "women as historical subjects in gendered colonial worlds."[43] Yet I also heed Joan Scott's critique that "gender" has become synonymous with "women" and her call for scholars to conceptualize gender as changing constructions of what it meant to be male and female.[44] The historiography of urban colonial Africa has detailed that colonial officials, African chiefs and elite men, and church personnel gendered colonial cities male. Yet this appears to be more ambiguous in Libreville. I trace the processes through which historical actors contested how men and women could occupy and interact with one another in the emerging cityscapes of streets, markets, homes, and rural suburbs. What constituted "feminine" and "masculine," "public" and "private" space, and who could legitimately occupy such spaces in Libreville was not fixed, but fluid.

Examining the gendered processes of urban becoming in Libreville contributes to an emerging body of research that challenges the idea of patriarchal power and masculinity as monolithic in twentieth-century Africa. Twenty years after Luise White's call for African history to "gender men," a small but important number of monographs and articles on men and configurations of masculinity in twentieth-century Africa has demonstrated the contradictory and changing ways in which societies conceived of and performed male gender. Researchers examining gender as something that men have done in changing forms in twentieth-century Africa have focused on the themes of wage labor, generation, and ideas of land ownership, classic themes of African social history.[45] As argued by Lisa Lindsay in her study of men and wage labor in late colonial southwestern Nigeria, gender is not necessarily something that people *have*, but something that people *do* in various ways. Male rail workers in cities such as Lagos and Ibadan navigated practices and ideas of adult masculinity in a context in which men, their family members, employers, and government officials fashioned multiple ideas about how to be "men."[46] Stephan Miescher's work on colonial and postcolonial Ghana has analyzed the interplay of changing notions of masculinity with men's self-representations and subjective experiences over the course of their life cycles, demonstrating that no single dominant notion of masculinity emerged over a generation that witnessed profound historical change.[47]

In conversation with the emerging literature that genders men, I call into question the category of "men" as a normative social collectivity to outline how differentiation in ethnicity, religious affiliation, wealth, and age resulted in competing practices and ideas of how to be a man. In focusing on both men and women in relation to marriage and sexuality, I show the intersectionalities of intimate matters, political economy, and politics. In Libreville, defining ideas and practices about marriage and sex involved struggles to define masculinity as well as femininity. Conflicts erupted not only between husbands and wives, but also between men competing for rights and access to the same woman, thereby demonstrating the cracks in the patriarchal edifice. Status and generational tension between senior and junior men, men with ready access to cash and those without, and men who had received formal educations in French schools and those who were illiterate reveal the contested and slippery nature of male power.

The gendered history of Libreville reorders our understanding of how urban spaces and selves unfolded in colonial-era Africa. Exploration of these questions in Libreville causes us to rethink some central concepts and time lines of African historiography, both of African urban history and of African gender history. First, let us reconsider the understanding of labor agitation and unions as a watershed in constituting the possibility of permanent urban settlement. As argued by Frederick Cooper, before the wave of strikes by male African workers in the 1930s and 1940s, British and French alike thought of a sociology of Africa that divided its populations into peasants and educated elites and treated everyone else as residual "detribalized Africans" or a "floating population." Only in the aftermath of this labor agitation did French colonial officials think about "more complex realities in African cities."[48] However, the marriage revolt at the mid-nineteenth-century founding of Libreville points to an earlier time in which African men drew attention to the questions of conjugal households, of social and biological reproduction, and of relationships with women as constitutive of lives in town. Libreville's newest inhabitants claimed that domestic life was part and parcel of urban life, compelling French representatives to perpetually renegotiate the very contours of colonial policy. Furthermore, many Gabonese men of varied ethnicities disavowed agricultural labor in favor of trade as early as the mid- to late nineteenth century. By the 1920s, men from throughout Gabon migrated to work in timber camps or other forms of wage labor, configuring Libreville and the Estuary region as a place of permanent settlement. Entire lineages of men, women, and children moved into the region, and men who settled without wives struggled to marry and build households. Farming became a low-status occupation, one in which women and some men of ethnic groups from Gabon's interior labored in plots kilometers away from Libreville. Mirroring what Tsuneo Yoshikuni found in 1920s Harare, urban life in Libreville included "dual participation in wage employment and agricultural production," with some women growing the food that fed the critical mass of wage laborers.[49] By the mid-1920s, the reality of an Estuary region in which many men were wage laborers, and in which women reached near parity or superseded the number of men, compelled colonial officials, missionaries, and African political leaders to grapple with the question of permanent African settlement in urban areas.

As was the case elsewhere in Africa, the 1930s in Gabon did usher in the attempts of colonial officials and some chiefs to work in concert to limit the autonomy of African women in marriage choices and sexuality. However, the patriarchy-state alliance was not unilateral. The category of "elder African men" in Libreville was differentiated by ethnicity, social and economic status, and individual interests. No single codified version of customary law emerged, but rather multiple articulations. Mirroring the "shifting customary terrain" in post-1930s Ghana, in the Estuary region litigants articulated varied definitions of customary marriage in colonial courts. After

World War II, when Libreville experienced increased immigration and expansion, public debates over the male and the female spaces and sexual respectability erupted in the streets and legislative halls.

Some scholars have criticized the emphasis on urban women in African women's history and the dearth of research on women in rural areas.[50] However, we have barely begun to scratch the surface of uncovering the complexities of women's and gender history and urban history in Africa. In recent publications on music, dress and fashion, and sexual politics in late colonial and postcolonial Luanda and Dar es Salaam, Marissa Moorman and Andrew Ivaska, respectively, demonstrate how male and female urbanites constructed their understandings of nation and culture.[51] This body of work has highlighted the improvisational and fluid dynamics of demarcating gender, generation, wealth, and culture in African towns from the 1950s into recent times. We need to further complicate our understanding of gender in African cities in the years of colonialism as well, unpacking the complex processes of social change in African societies, and understanding the multifaceted strategies of men and women for migrating to and creating lives in towns.

SEXUALITY AND AFFECT

In tracing the history of sexuality as imagined and practiced by Gabonese, this book expands an emerging body of research that challenges the dominant paradigm of sexuality in Africa as "other" in comparison to Europe or within the context of research of AIDS.[52] In challenging this paradigm, historians of sexuality in Africa have focused primarily on two themes: political economy and reproductive rights and circumcision. In her seminal book on prostitution in Nairobi, Luise White has shown that prostitutes and the domestic and sexual services they provided for African men in Nairobi were key to maintaining social reproduction of Kenyan societies under British colonial rule. Women's cash earnings from their labor maintained rural households, supported migrant men in negotiating harsh and racist labor conditions, and permitted women to purchase property in the city.[53] Lynn Thomas has shown how "the politics of the womb," female excision, pregnancy, birth, and abortion, occupied the center of how Meru women, girls, elder men and young men, and British colonial officials, missionaries, and feminists sought to configure political power and moral order in twentieth-century colonial Kenya.[54]

In an edited volume urging scholars to "re-think" sexualities in Africa, Signe Arnfred argues that European imaginaries of African sexuality have oscillated from ideas of the exotic and the noble and depraved savage, yet have been continually "other" in comparison to the norm of European sexuality.[55] Historians have analyzed European discourses of African sexualities as more fraught than Arnfred portrays.[56] Megan Vaughan's work on biomedical discourses in colonial British Central and East Africa and Diana Jeater's book on colonial moralist conceptions of African sexuality in early colonial Southern Rhodesia demonstrate that no dominant, hegemonic colonial discourse emerged, but rather a range of discourses. Megan Vaughan underlines how colonial representatives expressed anxieties about African women's sexuality in urban areas in particular and associated African women's sexuality with disease and social breakdown. Vaughan traces how state-employed doctors and medical missionaries conceptualized and debated the mechanisms of syphilis vaccination campaigns to construct governable African subjects.[57] In analyzing changing discourses of biomedicine, Vaughan's analysis demonstrates the persistent import of controlling African women's bodies by the apparatuses of colonial rule. Diana Jeater also demonstrates the multivalent nature of European ideas of African sexuality and how efforts to regulate sexuality were central to colonial rule. Jeater analyzes European discourses to argue that the colonial encounter profoundly altered ideas about and practices of sexuality. Between 1910 and 1930s colonial Rhodesia, Jeater argues, Christianity and migration to towns produced the idea of individual responsibility and "sin," as well as the idea that sexuality could take place outside of the sanction of family groups.[58] By focusing primarily on colonial discourses, we have not been fully able to understand the meanings of sexuality and the complexities with which African historical actors thought of and embodied their sexuality. Furthermore, how did ideas about sexuality intersect with praxes of sexuality?

I heed the arguments and engage the threads of previous works on the history of sexuality in Africa, that sex inherently shapes and is shaped by political economy, that contestations over sexuality were about the contours of generation, gender, and the state, that attention to shifting colonial discourses about African sexualities reveals the fissures of colonial rule, and that colonialism profoundly shaped the landscape of practices and ideas about sexuality. However, analyses of the history of sexuality in Africa have insufficiently considered that sexual expression is also about emotions—such as desire, pleasure, yearning, and pain. I argue for the need to step back from deterministic analyses of sexuality and also analyze the subjective and interpersonal realms in which historical actors engaged in and conceived of sex. Analyzing the varied sexual landscapes and relationships in Libreville and historical actors' often simultaneous expressions and experiences of the physical, emotional, and pragmatic offers a new window into the changing meanings and praxes of sexualities in African history.

Marriage was a primary relationship through which African men and women in Libreville articulated and experienced sexuality. A critical mass of books has chronicled social and economic change in Africa through the lens of marriage.[59] As this body of scholars, including Brett Shadle, has shown, "nowhere in colonial Africa was marital stability a foregone conclusion."[60] In the region that became Libreville, men and women engaged in varied forms of extramarital sexual relationships prior to the colonial encounter, and over the course of the decades of colonial rule new forms of extramarital sexual relationships developed. However, in spite of marital instability, there was a persistence with which Libreville's residents used changing forms of conjugal relationships as a metaphor in conceptualizing sexuality. As argued by Stephanie Newell, scholarship on marriage in Africa has emphasized "economic and social power rather than . . . desire and pleasure or coercion."[61] Furthermore, Jennifer Cole and Lynn Thomas contend that love, "the sentiments of attachment and affiliation that bind people to one another—in sexual, predominantly heterosexual, relationships," is a neglected lens of research in African studies.[62] I take seriously notions of sexual desire and love as units of analysis. Yet, following historical actors' conceptions of heterosexual relationships as also mediating economic mobility, I engage the recent literature on love and money in contemporary Africa that demonstrates how people viewed well-being in relationships according to both material and emotional fulfillment.[63]

By analyzing a multiplicity of ways in which historical actors experienced their heterosexual relationships—as material well-being, deprivation, honor, respectability, desire, violence, pleasure, biological or social reproduction, criminality, legality—I seek to demonstrate the multivalent meanings of sexuality in this urban, West-Central African context. Scholars have debated the definition of *sexuality* as a unit of analysis, drawing a line between sexuality as ideology ("what ought to be") and sexuality in behavior ("what was").[64] Historical actors in Libreville debated sexuality both as actualized and in discourse. Thus, I combine two definitions to analyze the history of sexuality in Libreville: Michel Foucault's conception of sexuality as "a field of mobile power relations," and Robert A. Padgug's definition of sexuality as "praxis, a group of social relations, of human interactions."[65]

I did not assume heterosexuality as normative when embarking upon research on the history of sexuality in Gabon. I was attuned to the multidisciplinary literature of queer theory, as well as emerging work on same-sex relationships and desire in African history that has disrupted ideas of heteronormativity.[66] I mined documentary sources for and asked interviewees about same-sex desire. Informants vehemently denied same-sex desire as manifesting in Gabon; nor could I find traces of homosocial sexualities in colonial reports. I questioned interviewees on the ideas of homosexuality as "un-African" that some expressed. However, I also began to realize that there has been relatively little scholarly attention to the history of heterosexuality in Africa. In tracing the changing practices and meanings of heterosexuality, this book does heed the call of queer theory to call into question the idea that sexual and gender identities are normative.[67]

SOURCES AND METHODS

This book draws on historical, ethnographic, and cultural studies methodologies and text-based and oral source materials. I followed AbdouMaliq Simone's formulation of "systematic social research" as the path to "immerse myself in various settings under whatever conditions and rubrics were possible" and for "multiple engagements as methodology."[68] I have utilized archival sources such as political reports, correspondence, legislation, policy debates, and ethnographies by colonial bureaucrats and military officers, as well as the correspondence of private French citizens with colonial officials and newspaper articles and editorials. Furthermore, the records of French Catholic and American Protestant missionaries are an important body of source materials, particularly for the nineteenth century.

Literary discourse analysis is a useful tool for demystifying the aura of "fact" that surrounds colonial and missionary documents. Literary theorist David Spurr argues that documents of imperial administrations involve some level of representations. Rather than reading colonial documents as only conveying history as it occurred, "scholars should consider these texts as snapshots of how [a] Western writer constructed a coherent representation out of the strange and often incomprehensible (to the writer) realities confronted in the non-Western world."[69] This interpretive lens allows the excavation of the anxieties and contradictions of colonial societies.

Though few registers have survived (only for scattered years in the 1930s through the 1950s), civil and criminal colonial court records housed at Gabon's national archives are a particularly precious body of sources that allow a view into interior recesses of Gabonese households. Customary law, aptly defined by Martin Chanock as the laws and practices recognized by European and African political leaders in the colonial period as "tradition," has been a crucial theme of African social historical inquiry since the 1980s.[70] Richard Roberts and Kristin Mann's 1991 edited volume, *Law in Colonial*

Africa, advocated for the critical use of neglected colonial court cases to illustrate transformations in African social history.[71] Since then, scholars have utilized the records of colonial courts, under the adjudication of Europeans, chiefs, and imams, to trace the transformations in the meanings of marriage, land rights, inheritance, and the end of slavery across Africa.[72] Court records, however, have their limitations. Court records tend to reify conflict as normative.[73] Furthermore, colonial court records may overstate the role of state institutions in people's daily lives.[74] Another limitation of court records stems from the question of language and translation. Though deliberations may have taken place in an African language, an African interpreter, with his own interests in presenting particular renderings of the case to a French judge, translates and writes the transcript into French, flattening out the nuances of orality and body language.[75]

Court records, nevertheless, remain an invaluable source material that permits the periodization and analysis of fundamental transformations in marriage and sex in the Estuary region. Contrary to elsewhere in British and French Africa, customary law was not decisively codified in colonial Gabon, and, thus, colonial courts remained an important arena in which litigants reworked legal and social understandings of the law. Colonial court records surviving in the Gabon national archives range from long-form summaries of testimony and biographical information about litigants to one- or two-sentence summaries of the conflict without identification of the litigants. The "option of the judicial path," as one female defendant phrased it in a 1950 Libreville court case, was an option that many Libreville and Estuary residents strategically sought out to adjucaticate domestic conflict.[76] Furthermore, the varied expressions of reconciliation, betrayal, disappointment, hope, and possibility that litigants conveyed have provided insight into the interior recesses of households. Courts presided over by chiefs in Estuary villages and Libreville neighborhoods were scattered across the region, and residents petitioned them—often bypassing the authority of elder kin—to attempt to obtain a desired outcome. Furthermore, over the course of the twentieth century, Libreville residents also increasingly brought problems of marital disagreement before French colonial officials, electing "to go before the white man," often overwhelming the capacity of colonial personnel to hear cases.

I have contextualized court records, framing the interpersonal conflicts presented in testimony with questions of social, cultural, economic, and political changes occurring in the time period. As argued by Sally Falk Moore in her study of customary courts in 1960s and 1970s Tanzania, small-scale "legal events . . . bear the imprints of the complex, large-scale transformations."[77] Tracing the dialectical relationships between small-scale legal events in colonial court records and large-scale transformations entails contextualizing court records within broader currents of historical change. Furthermore, I followed the methodology articulated by Richard Roberts in his analysis of court cases in early twentieth-century Mali. Roberts urges researchers to identify the "trouble spots" of conflict that emerge in individual court cases, to illustrate "the detail of these general patterns," and to track trends in aggregate data.[78] I mined extant criminal and civil court registries to identify the nature of the conflict that brought people to court. I categorized cases according to the various "trouble spots" of disagreement as articulated by litigants—divorce, adultery, wife-kidnapping, bridewealth, levirate marriage, child custody, and abandonment of the conjugal home. I have analyzed the terms of disagreements, outcomes desired by litigants, and, when available, the decisions of judges to chart transformations in praxes of marriage and sexual relationships.

The analysis of texts written by Gabonese opens a window into the discursive arenas in which elite African men, chiefs, and, on occasion, poor African men employed the French language and writing to claim rights in marriage and sex. Scholars such as Nancy Rose Hunt have critiqued methodologies of Africanist scholarship that emphasize "to Africa for voices, to Europe for texts."[79] In this paradigm, historians research European perspectives in archives and create "authentic" African historical records in gathering oral interviews in indigenous languages during fieldwork. In Libreville, French was the lingua franca of Africans, and access to basic education in mission schools meant that literacy in French was a symbol of status that many sought. As such, documents authored by Africans—correspondence to colonial officials, letters to newspapers in other colonies in French Equatorial Africa (FEA) and in France, ethnographies, and proposals of laws and policies—are another important body of source materials for this book.

Other types of documents I had hoped to find in my archival research in Gabon, France, Italy, and the United States proved to be nonexistent. Scholars of African history often navigate significant lacunae in source materials, yet Gabon and all of FEA are particularly challenging. Few oral or written sources exist to document the history of Gabon before the mid-nineteenth century.[80] The gaps continue into the colonial period. The political, economic, and social dislocation in the period of concessionary rule from 1899 to 1909 has made this period little-documented.[81] Catherine Coquery-Vidrovitch summed up the period of 1900 to 1920 as marked by the "poverty of the bibliography," with little documentary and oral evidence available.[82] The entire federation of FEA perpetually lacked funding and staffing that

issue of methodology

would promote systematic record keeping, and scholars refer to Gabon as the "Cinderella" of French Africa.[83] Moreover, the entire body of documentary archives of the municipality of Libreville, which may have included police reports, detailed censuses, and the mayor's reports, has disappeared from the archives in Gabon.[84] Another potentially rich source of documents, the local records of the two Catholic parishes of Sainte Marie and Sainte Pierre in Libreville, are unavailable to researchers. Documentary records of the Soeurs Bleues in their archives in Rome and Libreville are threadbare. No newspapers were produced in Gabon over the course of about one hundred years of French colonial rule. The postcolonial state of Gabon has been particularly autocratic, with one-man party rule over several decades, resulting in the virtual absence of documentation since 1960 in the national archives. Thus, my research on Gabon focused on creating historical records, in the form of oral histories, as much as mining existing historical sources.

The field of African history was founded on the commitment to use African sources, oral sources, given that few sub-Saharan African societies had written languages, as a means to pursue the accompanying commitment to demonstrate African agency. Yet as researchers began to set the methodological and epistemological parameters of using oral sources, debates about which types of oral sources were empirically sound abounded. Jan Vansina's publications stood as foundational texts that argued for the validity and accuracy of oral traditions as evidence for the reconstruction of the African past. Vansina specified that oral traditions were spoken, sung, or instrumental renditions of verbal messages originating at least one generation removed from the informant who relayed them. If analyzed according to a set of rules of evidence, history as what really happened could be parsed out from any embellishments or untruths that later generations may have added to the original messages.[85] Subsequent scholars unearthed the limita-tions of oral traditions in that they reflected the viewpoint of the powerful in African societies and represented normative accounts of social order.[86] Historians of colonial Africa turned to oral history, interviews of informants that yielded narratives about events in living memory or a person's lifetime, to elucidate the histories of the less powerful. Life histories, a particular form of oral history, encompassed an interviewee's entire life span. Many historians, particularly feminist scholars, publishing research in the 1980s and 1990s, used the words of women, peasants, and other marginalized actors to narrate everyday experiences of colonialism and emphasize African agency.[87] Oral histories, scholars argued, were "more authentic, and thus more objective than any colonial text could be," conveying the "truth" of historical experiences.[88]

Yet some scholars urged a more critical methodological and epistemological use of oral histories.[89] Belinda Bozzoli and Mmantho Nkotsoe, in their analysis of twentieth-century life histories of South Africans, forwarded a multifaceted reading of life histories as "documents, stories, histories, incoherent rumblings, interlinked fragments of consciousness, and conversations and/ or recital of facts," as well as a "product of the unique formal and informal exchanges between interviewer and interviewee."[90] Bozzoli and other scholars have called attention to the asymmetrical relationships of power between informants and interviewers and the need for self-reflexivity in how both parties shaped the content, form, and interpretation of oral history.[91] Perhaps the most trenchant reassessment of oral history came from Luise White, who in a 2004 article described her uncritical use of oral sources in *The Comforts of Home* as "perhaps the most arrogant defense of oral history ever written" in her assertion of their greater authority and truth compared to other sources.[92] White's words of caution call attention to how informants also play an active role in interpreting lives in the context of historical change and the figurative meanings of the accounts people give.

Oral histories are central to this book's analysis of how sojourners to Libreville lived in and framed their marital and sexual relationships. Between 1999 and 2005, I conducted and recorded about one hundred oral interviews with Gabonese men and women of varied ages and ethnic groups. Informants included individuals born from the late 1920s through the 1960s who lived in Libreville and peri-urban villages located along the Kango-Libreville road, people who made the Estuary region a place of permanent settlement. I conducted some interviews in Mpongwé and Fang languages with the aid of research assistants and translators Thanguy Obame and the late Edidie Nkolo. I conducted other interviews in French without interpreters. I recorded the interviews using directed questions, asking participants specific questions about their marital and conjugal careers, as well as allowing informants to discuss topics of importance to them. I and the men and women I interviewed were aware of my woeful ignorance about Gabon, and my interviewees sought to "school me" in the history of their lifetimes, often pushing back against the questions I asked and the assumptions embedded in them. As a woman, I sometimes faced reticence from male interviewees to talk with me, and, indeed, some men told me they would reveal only so much to me, since "women must not know men's secrets." I have changed the names of some of my interviewees per their requests, while others wished to be identified.

In critically utilizing these oral histories, I reject the binary of using oral sources either as history as lived or as representations of the past. Instead, I follow Stephan Miescher in "taking the middle road" by using oral histories to glean both data about the past as well as evidence of interviewees' conceptions of "how it should or could have been" and "a reflection of the past's meanings for the present and this reflection of a speaker's subjectivity."[93] The middle road allows for the uncovering of how the researcher and the interviewee produce history in the questions and conversations that unfold over the course of the interview, as well as the researcher's contextualization of oral sources with other sources and within broader historical processes. The middle road also heeds calls for critical distance from interviewees' words to explore how people give meaning to their lives and their places in their worlds. In endeavoring to critically analyze subjectivities in oral histories, I follow Corinne Kratz's suggestion that historians pay attention to how "narrators combine episodes in sequences based on particular notions of time, social relations, and self."[94] Building on Miescher and Katz, I have excavated the sexual and marital careers that narrators present in their interviews, their expectations, joys, and dismay, to analyze how historical actors have attempted to shape normative conceptions of order in their own lives and in relationship to strangers, neighbors, intimate partners, and kin in changing historical contexts.

PART I

⤶

From Atlantic Ocean Trading Post to Colonial Capital City, 1849–1929

PART 1 ANALYZES TRANSFORMATIONS in marriage and sex in Libreville prior to 1930. Chapter 1 explores Libreville's transformation from a small but strategic hub of Atlantic trade in slaves and forest and imported goods in the mid- to late nineteenth century to a nascent colonial capital city in 1910. I track the gendered dynamics of moving to and setting up homes in the emerging town and how the sexual economy shaped the political economy, legal infrastructures, and geographic layout. Chapter 2 picks up this thread from 1910 to 1929, years in which efforts by the French to consolidate colonial rule and direct the labor of Africans toward the colonial economy and timber production fundamentally altered daily life. I trace the unintended processes of women's sexual labor in generating cash and other forms of wealth and how worries about the sexual economy compelled transformations in French conceptualizations of customary law and governance. These two chapters set the stage for how the dynamics of conjugal and sexual relations demonstrate cracks in the edifice of colonial rule and spaces for Gabonese to shape the lived realities of urban life in the decades to come.

1 ⤳ Sexual Economy in the Era of Trade and Politics

The Founding of Libreville, 1849–1910

WRITING IN 1975, historian K. David Patterson observed, "The early history of Gabon has received almost no attention from scholars. . . . The whole region of Western Equatorial Africa remains something of a historiographical void."[1] Since Patterson wrote this, less than a handful of publications have filled the historiographical void. A few publications have focused on the period before European contact.[2] The few publications focusing on the nineteenth century can be characterized as the "trade and politics school," focusing on the end of the transatlantic slave trade, the exchange of Western and equatorial forest goods, and increasing French ambitions toward colonial rule and African resistance to French attempts at domination as motors of historical change.[3] Scholars have argued of marriage and family life as serving normative functions—to allow elder men to maintain political power and social control over women, slaves, and junior men that permitted them to control nodes of transatlantic trade in slaves and goods. Marriage was an important institution through which individuals achieved social adulthood and kin groups formed alliances. What is common in research on the nineteenth century is an absence of an analytical focus on women and gender, an empirical absence that has led to conceptual gaps in our understanding of historical change.

In chronicling how Libreville inhabitants negotiated dynamics of sexual economy over the course of the mid-nineteenth century to 1910, this chapter

[handwritten margin note: addressing gap in the literature]

23

demonstrates that questions of how marriage was to be consecrated and the forms of socially acceptable sexual relations and gender roles were very much under contestation preceding and at the moment of colonial encounters. As the Estuary region transformed from a precolonial Atlantic Ocean trading port to a fledgling colonial outpost, changing meanings of gender roles in heterosexual relationships shaped infrastructures of town life. The written texts of French military personnel, Catholic proselytizers, multinational traders and men on the spot, American missionaries, and the remembrances of Fang and Mpongwé chiefs that I recorded in oral interviews tend to convey an androcentric perspective. Nevertheless, in these extant sources lie fragments that indicate how contours of changing notions of how to be male and female shaped economic, social, and political life. Marriage was not a normative social system that regularized sexual unions and status of offspring and reinforced patriarchal power. Nineteenth- and early twentieth-century sexual and conjugal politics within Mpongwé and Fang societies revealed fluidity in determining how individuals and groups exercised power along the axis of gender. By the late nineteenth century, it was common for European traders and Mpongwé women to engage in relationships of long-term concubinage, often sealed with a bridewealth bundle of goods or cash payments from the European companion. An Mpongwé moral economy dictated the terms of interracial sex and incorporated European men into shifting conceptualizations of respectable female sexuality, bridewealth, and marriage.

Conjugal-sexual politics were central to how African communities and the French converged and diverged to build the town and their lives in these decades. Libreville had a relatively equal gender ratio from the time of its founding due to a combination of local and external factors. First, African households—men, women, and children, free and slave—already inhabited the space that later became the administrative center of the colony. As brokers of the lucrative transatlantic trade that began in the late fifteenth century, the Mpongwé served as middlemen between Europeans and interior African societies. Second, French imperial expansion in the 1840s and 1850s intersected with waves of African communities—who originated north of Gabon's modern-day borders—as they migrated toward the coast. Fang households that included men and women appeared near the Estuary in the 1840s. These new arrivals were to become the Estuary Fang, a group that would develop ways of life distinct from those of other members of their ethnolinguistic group in the interior. Third, the demographic fragility and sparse population density of the equatorial region meant that French state officials, missionaries, and private citizens were often eager to attract African populations, men and women alike, toward Libreville and other centers of colonial economic production.

The founding of Libreville and French efforts toward colonial rule created and intersected with a period of uncertainty, migration, and socioeconomic change within Gabon. Three historical turning points transformed the region: (1) the first of a series of treaties signed by Mpongwé political leaders in 1839 that ceded territory to the French and paved the way for French colonial rule and the "founding" of the town in 1849; (2) the parceling out of surrounding regions into concessionary control in 1898; and (3) the incorporation of the coastal town and interior regions into the more centralized colonial rule of French Equatorial Africa in 1910. Such political and economic changes were intimately tied to questions of the domestic lives of its inhabitants. As African and European strangers circulated through nineteenth-century Libreville, men and women strategized over how to ensure security, and weather the fluctuations of trade and politics, in formulating and reformulating their relationships with each other.

3 "TURNING POINTS" (handwritten margin note)

MPONGWÉ BEGINNINGS: THE GENDERED POLITICS OF SOCIETY, TRADE, AND EUROPEAN-AFRICAN ENCOUNTERS, 1600S TO 1840S

The equatorial climate and the environment—dense rain forests, lakes, rivers, and mountains—shaped the lives and livelihoods of Estuary inhabitants. Rain and humidity characterize the climate for most of the year, with seven to eight months of high humidity. The average temperature in a calendar year is twenty-six degrees Celsius. There are two rainy seasons, which result in rainfall for most of the year, with the longer season extending from January to May and the shorter one from September to December. In a normal season, about 2.5 meters of rain fall per year.[4] There are two dry seasons, the longer one during the period of May to September and a short dry season from December to January. Several types of topography mark Gabon. In the east, there is a small savannah region. A mountainous region extends north and to the west of Libreville across the center of Gabon and includes elevations up to eight hundred meters in the Monts de Cristal and Massif du Chaillu (named by European explorers in the nineteenth century). As far as three hundred kilometers from the Atlantic Ocean, the coastal plains are covered by dense rain forest, with trees as tall as twenty-sixty meters.[5] Rain forest is the dominant geographical feature, and it encompasses two-thirds of the region. Swampy regions next to the forested regions of the coast present an area of mangrove. The presence of tsetse flies and outbreaks of trypanosomiasis limit the possibilities of animal husbandry and the upkeep of many types of cattle. A French sociologist described Gabon as "a country of water."[6] A total of thirty-five hundred kilometers of rivers offer transportation routes, the longest of which is the Ogooué River at one thousand kilometers. These rivers provided transportation arteries foundational to economic transformations of the nineteenth and twentieth centuries. Lakes and lagoons dot the country, particularly in the Moyen-Ogooué.[7] Bounded by one thousand meters of the Atlantic Ocean along the south, a series of estuaries provide shelter. The northern coast, between the Bay of Rio Muni and the Fernan Vaz Lagoon, harbors one such estuary that became the site of Libreville.[8] Fed by the Como River, the Gabon Estuary is sixty-four kilometers long and fourteen kilometers wide at its mouth. It was this area, in mangroves surrounded by forests, that the Mpongwé would settle and that would come to be called the Estuary region. Europeans came to consider the Gabon Estuary "one of the best natural harbors on the coast of West Africa" after it was reached by the Portuguese in the 1470s.[9] It was this factor that contributed to the increased convergence of varied African and European communities in the Estuary in the nineteenth century and the founding of Libreville.

Most of present-day Gabon's fifty-two ethnic groups are of Bantu origins. By the seventeenth century, peoples of the Myènè ethnolinguistic group inhabited the northern and southern Gabon coasts.[10] It is not possible to determine a precise chronology of their migrations and settlements, but scholars date their movements toward the coast between 1600 and 1800.[11] The Myènè were composed of Orungu, Nkomi, Galoa, Enenga, and Adyumba matrilineal ethnic groups who concentrated along the Ogooué River in southern Gabon. The patrilineal Mpongwé concentrated along the right and left banks of the Gabon Estuary.[12] By the nineteenth century, Mpongwé clans were concentrated into approximately three politically dominant clans and fourteen less important ones.[13]

Mpongwé communities prospered from Atlantic Ocean trade in goods over the course of three centuries. Between the 1500s and 1600s, the Mpongwé received cloth and products made of iron, such as nails, knives, and axes, from Portuguese and Dutch traders in exchange for ivory, honey, and beeswax that they procured from African societies who lived farther inland. From the sixteenth century onward, the Estuary was a crucial docking station for Portuguese and other European ships that needed to restock food and water and undergo repairs as they headed to or from the former Loango and Kongo kingdoms for trade.[14] The Sékiani, who inhabited the area just beyond the Gabon River, and the Bakalai, who settled farther

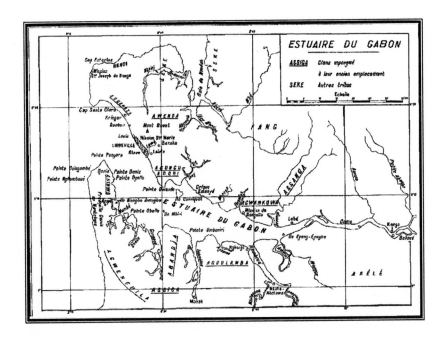

MAP 1.1. Mpongwé Settlement in the Gabon Estuary, Mid-Nineteenth Century. (Reproduced from André Raponda-Walker, *Notes d'histoire du Gabon*, with authorization from the Fondation Raponda-Walker pour la Science et la Culture.)

inland, encircled the Mpongwé. Until the Fang eclipsed them in the late nineteenth century, the Mpongwé represented the largest concentration of an African population in the Estuary region. The map below indicates the peopling of the Estuary circa the late nineteenth century, with several Mpongwé clans along the Estuary and the Fang in the Estuary's interior.

Early to mid-nineteenth-century Mpongwé were organized around several commercially, politically, and socially connected yet independent settlements. The political organization was composed of extended kin groups, among which "big men" emerged; these male leaders exerted a sphere of influence over a given geographic locale.[15] The basic unit of Mpongwé communities was a household headed by a male (*nago*), his wives and children, his sons, his sons' wives and their children, and other dependents. Several households combined into a clan, headed by the senior patriarch (*oga*), in which members followed exogamy. A few of the most powerful clan leaders or "kings" (*oga w'inongo*) exercised a degree of influence over several clans in a given region.[16] The most powerful clan heads, among which an *oga* was chosen, were also often affluent traders.[17]

Sexual Economy in the Era of Trade and Politics ⌐ 27

By the mid-nineteenth century, there were four principal Mpongwé political units, headed by "kings" Glass, Denis, Georges, and Quaben. European observers referred to each kingdom by the name of its king. Though European observers mistook the oga of an Mpongwé settlement as a centralized figure of authority, in reality, political, social, and economic power was decentralized.[18]

The period between 1698 and 1818 was an era of political change along the southern and northern coasts. Internecine wars took place between numerous clans, and gradual resettlement took place when newly arrived clans displaced those already settled. This period also witnessed efforts by powerful Orungu and Mpongwé oga to consolidate their power. Individual heads of household maintained their own spheres of influence and engaged in commercial activities with other African communities and Europeans without deferring to the ogas. By the 1880s, European observers estimated the Mpongwé population at between three and six thousand free inhabitants and slaves, men, women, and children.[19] The slave population ranged from one-third to one-half of the total population of Mpongwé villages. Nearly all households had at least one slave, and the wealthiest households had one hundred or more slaves.[20]

The expansion of the transatlantic trade in forest goods and slaves—which began in the 1500s and reached its height from 1815 to 1840 in the period of clandestine trade after many European nations had declared the slave trade illegal—profoundly altered Mpongwé societies.[21] By the beginning of the nineteenth century, the Mpongwé and other littoral Myènè societies had established themselves as middlemen to facilitate the trade of rubber, ivory, and slaves from interior peoples with European and American customers. It was the neighboring region of Loango that dominated the trade in slaves for this region of West-Central Africa, but Mpongwé middlemen trafficked in a smaller volume of slaves.[22] In 1788, the Estuary region and Cape Lopez, farther south along the Atlantic Ocean, exported 500 slaves, as compared to the 13,500 slaves leaving the coasts of Loango and Kongo. Following the legal decrees of some European countries to abolish the slave trade in the early nineteenth century, lesser-known and more clandestine trading ports off the Estuary expanded their slave-trading enterprises, but continued to be eclipsed by the volume of slaves emerging from Cape Lopez. Between 1815 and 1850, estimates are that a few thousand slaves were exported from both the Estuary and Cape Lopez. Estimates of the annual demographic loss due to slave exports within Gabon range from 1 to 4 percent.[23] European goods sought by Mpongwé included cloth, manufactured clothing, alcohol, metal objects, and weapons.

Europeans traveling in Gabon in the mid-1850s described Mpongwé traders as accomplished middlemen, enabling the transfer of goods from the inland to the coast through specialized trading networks based on the "trust" system.[24] Dutch, American, British, and French traders competed to profit from the trade as each nation sought to monopolize the commercial exchange along the coast. Over the course of the nineteenth century, wood and ivory were also among the products that Mpongwé traded to Europeans. It was common for an Mpongwé trader to speak French, Portuguese, and English; and skill in trade was "the epitome of manhood," argues Henry Bucher.[25] The Mpongwé affluent traders who had slaves and access to a large volume of goods from upriver societies were differentiated from the more numerous petty traders, who sold agricultural goods and fish to European ships and who worked as porters and provided other types of labor in expeditions.[26] By virtue of their geographical proximity to the Ogooué region, the most extensive slave-trading community in Gabon consisted of the Mpongwé on the left bank of the Estuary. Rivers connecting inland locations to the coast acted as highways, with a particular ethnic group specializing in and facilitating the transfer of specific goods from one branch of a river to another and extracting their commission. Mpongwé served as middlemen between African communities and Europeans, exclusively in control of direct trade with European representatives.[27]

The increase in trade as the primary economic activity of Mpongwé men, particularly young men, altered their roles within their communities.[28] As more Mpongwé men turned toward trade as their primary economic activity in the nineteenth century, their contributions to agricultural production and community labor decreased and the numbers of slaves increased.[29] Some free men continued to clear the fields during the dry season, while women and slaves planted, cultivated, and harvested plantations located several kilometers from the towns.[30] Crops included indigenous and imported produce such as cassava, plantains, sweet potatoes, pumpkins, and beans cultivated for subsistence and trade with local communities. Mpongwé also maintained small livestock such as goats and chickens, and men hunted and fished to add to their diets.[31] Historian K. David Patterson suggests that by the early nineteenth-century Mpongwé societies had achieved a prosperous way of life.

By the mid-nineteenth century, the region that was to become Libreville was cosmopolitan. The Mpongwé viewed their societies as superior to surrounding African communities due to their wealth in imported goods, their knowledge of white languages and cultures, and access to formal education. Americans established a Protestant mission in 1842, under the auspices of the American Board of Commissioners for Foreign Missions, in the area of King Glass that was also the center of German, American, and British commercial activity. Within two years the Catholic French Spiritan Fathers constructed the Saint Mary mission in the region of King Louis, and the Soeurs Bleues arrived to work with Gabonese women. Both missions included houses of worship and small medical dispensaries. Beginning in 1844, French missionaries operated a primary school, to which Mpongwé political leaders sent their sons for basic education in the French language and math. In 1850, the Soeurs Bleues opened a school for Mpongwé girls. Though families sent more sons than daughters to missionary schools, the daughters of wealthy families attended school. Nuns administered courses in the French language and domestic arts in addition to directing the girls' labor in growing manioc and other food staples to feed the mission. American Protestants also opened a school and taught in English in the village of Baraka. Protestant and Catholic missionaries struggled with each other to convert Libreville residents toward their respective faiths. By the end of the nineteenth century, a small group of literate elite—nearly all men, but including some women—Mpongwé existed.[32] That some Mpongwé women also received formal education in the mid- to late nineteenth century would set a precedent for girls of future generations to attend school and for the subsequent unfolding of renegotiations of gender, political influence, and wealth.

Women played key roles in constituting wealth and power in Mpongwé societies. There is no evidence that women held formal political roles or were active traders. However, women's agricultural production was crucial to the sustenance of Mpongwé communities and the increased numbers of foreigners living along the coast, as they were the primary farmers of manioc and other produce on plots located several kilometers from villages.[33] In more affluent households, nonslave women removed themselves from farming, labor undertaken by women of lower status and male and female slaves.[34]

Access to European goods was an indication of elite social status and wealth, but power in mid- to late nineteenth-century Equatorial Africa also depended on a person's wealth in *people*, including slaves and other dependents, but particularly in wives, both slave and free.[35] As outlined by Jan Vansina, in the political tradition of big men in West-Central Africa, to acquire honor and to become rich required having many wives.[36] Marriage, which was a crucial yet contested practice for nineteenth-century Mpongwé societies, established reciprocal obligations of assistance and networks of allies among affines that household heads could tap into for the purpose of strengthening social, commercial, and political status.[37] Since marriage conferred adult status, single men and women remained rare. An Mpongwé man seeking to crystallize alliances with a more powerful man could offer him a female dependent as a wife.[38] By the age of three or four, and sometimes at birth, some girls were already betrothed.[39] Prepubescent brides lived in their husbands' households, where they assisted and were raised by the mothers or senior wives of their husbands. Mothers could also play a key role in selecting their daughters' husbands. For women married at or after the age of puberty, some sources relay that the bride's consent was necessary, while other sources indicate that a father could marry his daughter with or without her consent.[40] A woman was at liberty to engage in sexual relations with chosen suitors until her family had entered into a marriage agreement for her and she left her birth family to live in her husband's household.

Contrary to functionalist interpretations of nineteenth-century marriage — the "trade and politics" paradigm that focuses on the "customary" use-value of sexual access to women — gender roles and sexual relationships were negotiated and renegotiated in the context of dynamic lived experiences.[41] Prior to the nineteenth century, marriage between Mpongwé took place by the exchange of women (*mipenda*) between two clan groups or by the groom's family remitting bridewealth consisting of iron bars (*ikwèliki*). But by the mid-nineteenth century, marriage by bridewealth was more prevalent than marriage by exchange and consisted almost entirely of imported goods. The incorporation of imported goods into bridewealth changed the universal attainability of marriage.[42] Bridewealth costs increased along the Gabon coast. Thus, heads of households could expand their wealth in goods in addition to their wealth in people through the marriage of female dependents. Bridewealth negotiations were a man's domain, and representatives from both parties debated the amount to be remitted based on the age, physical appearance, and work habits of the bride-to-be.[43] European observers recorded bridewealth transactions as including items such as liquor, guns, ammunition, knives, tobacco, china, cutlery, and European clothing, with a total value of 100–300 francs.[44] It is challenging to quantify what 100 francs was worth in the late nineteenth century, yet missionaries indicated that the amount was an astronomical sum that took a man many years to amass. Additionally, an Mpongwé fiancé had to furnish his bride with a dwelling and two years' worth of cloth.[45] Escalating bridewealth costs meant that some Mpongwé men delayed marriage well beyond postpuberty rites until they could collect enough goods.[46]

Marital ties could be tenuous. Husbands did not appear to exercise absolute power over their wives, nor was it certain that marriage severed ties between a woman and her family of origin. The most frequent node

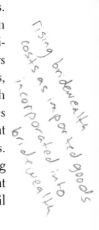

Change in exchange bridewealth

rising bridewealth costs as imported goods incorporated into bridewealth

of conjugal conflict was adultery, defined as the act of a married woman engaging in extramarital sex without her husband's authorization.[47] A wife's adultery could result in corporal punishment and public shaming. Armed conflicts between groups of Mpongwé men from different villages were often sparked by a dispute between two men over who had rights to a specific woman.[48] Married men could have lovers other than their wives with social and legal impunity. By all accounts, divorce occurred frequently. Either husbands or wives could initiate divorce proceedings, but wives did so more often.[49] A husband could repudiate his wife or demand a divorce if she failed to produce offspring or if she was too infirm to perform domestic tasks.[50]

Male and female kin and elder men assessed and made the final judgment on the validity of women's requests for divorce, thereby maintaining elders' social control over women's maneuverability in dissolving their marriages. A woman seeking to depart from her marriage would often take refuge with her family of origin to air her grievances and request a divorce.[51] Her husband would then approach her father or male guardian and request her return. If the woman's kin conceded, the husband would pay her father a penalty, usually in bottles of alcohol, to make amends for ill treatment.[52] If the woman's kin agreed to consider divorce, they convened a public discussion, presided over by clan elders, in which the husband and the wife's male representatives could both make their cases.[53]

Justifiable grounds for a divorce appeared to include the indication of ill-treatment between spouses or a physical ailment that hampered biological reproduction. Elders seem to have granted a divorce if a husband's drunkenness or physical abuse was excessive, and, following this decision, the husband and the wife's male kin debated over the reimbursement of bridewealth. At stake were both the reimbursement of goods and the custody of children. In cases in which the husband had not yet paid bridewealth, the woman's family retained custody of children born during their cohabitation. The reimbursement of bridewealth was not absolute. Under certain conditions, women's kin did not have to reimburse the bridewealth; for example, if children born during the marriage were to remain in the husband's custody or if the husband was found at fault for ill-treatment of his wife.[54] If a man's impotence was the grounds for divorce, then reimbursement by a woman's family was not necessary. If the elders judged that a man had repudiated his wife without cause, not only was her family exempt from reimbursing bridewealth, but they also retained custody of her children.[55]

With their husbands' approval, married women could have sexual relationships with men other than their husbands, and these extramarital sexual encounters were not considered to be adultery. In nineteenth-century

Mpongwé societies, men could accord to male visitors sexual access to Mpongwé women—their wives, slaves, and daughters—as a gesture of hospitality, in exchange for compensation, and to solidify commercial and political alliances.[56] While doing fieldwork in Gabon in 2001, I asked Mpongwé chiefs—individuals who self-identified as being knowledgeable about customs "before the time of the white man," which the Gabonese call the years prior to French rule—about these practices. Joseph Lasseny Ntchoveré, an Mpongwé chief, elaborated, "These were old systems which existed. Sometimes it occurred for security reasons, sometimes when one arrives at a friend's home in a foreign land, to avoid you having to go elsewhere, he would allow you to go with his wife, to ensure your well-being."[57] Husbands could also recognize a wife's lover as her legal lover (*nokndyè*) on the condition that the lover remitted the agreed-upon compensation to the husband.[58] These occurrences of married women engaging in extramarital sex with impunity could occur only if the husband granted permission. Husbands sanctioned their wives' extramarital sex within the context that the husband chose the lover and that the relationship would benefit his own material wealth or cultivate political or economic alliances.

Sexual and domestic relationships between Mpongwé women and white men of varied nationalities shaped sociality, economics, and politics in precolonial Gabon. Mpongwé women of varied statuses played a crucial role in facilitating the transatlantic trade via short- and long-term sexual-domestic relationships with European men. Historian Owen White argued that European men sought out "African women as companions from the earliest days of their presence" in Africa.[59] Yet African societies in Libreville also negotiated and benefited from interracial relationships. As African and European communities encountered each other along the coast, the Mpongwé adapted conjugal-sexual practices to incorporate interracial unions, and European men seeking partnerships with African women adapted to these conditions. As early as the 1600s, European traders docking in Gabon noted the commonplace occurrence of women from Mpongwé societies, who could have been slaves or other low-status women, boarding European vessels to engage in sex in exchange for goods.[60] Eighteenth- and nineteenth-century European visitors recorded that Mpongwé traders would offer wives, likely slave wives, as pawns to European traders for receiving a cargo of imported goods. European traders could have sexual access to female pawns until Mpongwé traders returned with the amount of forest goods that they had agreed to furnish in exchange for the European goods.[61]

By the late nineteenth century, it was common for European traders and Mpongwé women to engage in long-term relationships, often sealed with a bridewealth bundle of goods or a cash payment from the European companion. Unlike previous centuries in which Mpongwé women in relationships with European men were often low-status women, women in interracial relationships in the nineteenth century were often the daughters of elite families. Some Mpongwé and Europeans alike referred to these relationships as marriages.[62] European merchants trading along the coast could meet the bridewealth requests of Mpongwé households more readily than Mpongwé suitors. In Lambaréné, a European suitor might remit 600 francs' worth of cloth, guns, and alcohol to an Mpongwé companion's family.[63] Alternatively, European men in Libreville might have given anywhere from 15 to 25 francs per month to their Mpongwé wives, who would then transfer the money to their Mpongwé fathers or uncles.[64]

An Mpongwé moral economy dictated the terms of interracial sex and incorporated European men into normative conceptions of respectable female sexuality, bridewealth, and marriage. Moreover, the circulation of and sexual access to women solidified Mpongwé men's commercial and political alliances. European traders with Mpongwé wives held an advantage over those who were not married to an Mpongwé woman, as their marriages indicated acceptance into the "trust system" of trade along Gabon's coasts.[65] Interracial unions also consisted of short-term and episodic sexual relationships. Interracial sexual interactions were so commonplace in the Estuary region in the nineteenth century that missionaries referred to the area as "the Black Babylon."[66] French nuns groused in an 1860 report that not only did the roles of Mpongwé men change within the context of increased attention to trade, but a "certain emancipation modified in turn the Gabonese woman. Sly and prideful the *gabonaise*, used as a mistress by Europeans soon imposed on her male congeners the demands of her coquettishness, her nonchalance, and degradation."[67] It cannot be said that Mpongwé women voluntarily entered into intimate relationships with European men, in the same way that it cannot be said that marriage and sexual relationships between Mpongwé men and women did not involve some level of coercion. In eighteenth- and nineteenth-century Senegal, black and mixed-race women, often referred to as *signares*, who engaged in relationships with European merchants were able to amass wealth in property and slaves.[68] Unlike the *signares*, there is little indication that Mpongwé women involved in interracial unions established independent homes, trading networks, or amassed immense wealth.[69] As subsequent chapters will show, interracial domestic and sexual relationships between Mpongwé women and white men would continue to occur into the twentieth century, with some women accumulating independent wealth that would disrupt gender and generational hierarchies within Mpongwé communities.

Yet, to return to the story of Libreville in the nineteenth century, the mid-nineteenth century signaled a period of social dislocation, epidemic disease, economic change, and political flux along the coast in the Estuary region. It appears that by the 1840s the Mpongwé population had precipitously decreased. David Patterson cautions that demographic estimates for this period may reflect inaccuracies but indicates that it is probable that Mpongwé settlements experienced as much as a 50 percent decline in population between 1840 and 1860.[70] A series of smallpox and other disease epidemics undoubtedly caused many deaths. Yet, downplaying factors such as these, European observers attributed the population decline to alcohol consumption, abortion, and venereal diseases that spread through polygyny and the prostitution of Mpongwé women. French Catholic observers portrayed the Mpongwé as "drunken, promiscuous, dishonest, and effete, a people obsessed with the lure of trade wealth and willing to do almost anything for a profit," whose degeneration was due to their adoption of the vices of European civilization.[71] The Estuary region also experienced a decline in trading fortunes. By the turn of the century, Cape Lopez supplanted it as the principal port of commercial activity, and new commercial centers such as Lambaréné emerged as European fortune seekers followed new nodes of trade upcountry and sought to bypass Mpongwé middlemen. A series of nuanced localized and regional historical processes set in motion a movement of persons toward the coast. These demographic shifts—the presence of new arrivals and the lessening numbers of Mpongwé residents—facilitated the gradual but not inevitable transition to colonial rule.

MIGRATION, MARRIAGE AND GENDER, AND THE TRANSITING TO COLONIAL RULE, 1840s–1899

As Mpongwé and Europeans converged along the coast, the migration of the Fang toward the Estuary was a phenomenon that would alter the social, political, and economic landscape of the region. Over the course of the nineteenth century, the demographic and ethnic makeup of the Estuary region began to be reordered, as were commercial networks and exchanges.[72] How and why Fang groups migrated has been a topic of scholarly debate, yet most scholars agree that Fang migration commenced from the region of modern-day Cameroon.[73] Fang clans migrated along the Woleu and N'Tem Rivers, down the Ogooué, and into the Gabon Estuary.[74] Fang men who had previously hunted or procured forest goods that they transferred to Myènè middlemen now sought direct access to European traders. By the 1830s, the Fang appeared in the hinterlands of the Estuary region, near the Como River. Mpongwé kings, in turn, sought to protect their monopoly over direct access to European traders and consolidate their sphere of influence over smaller Mpongwé communities. Simultaneously, the French sought to overturn the dominance of British and German traders along the Gabon coast. Seeking to protect Mpongwé trading interests, King Denis signed a treaty in 1839 that granted the right to the French to construct "all buildings and fortifications" deemed necessary.[75] In 1843, King Louis also signed a treaty of alliance with the French that permitted the establishment of a naval post on the Estuary's right bank, paving the way for inland movement of French military personnel, traders, and missionaries.[76] Even as the French declared the name of Libreville in 1849, varied African and European parties jockeyed for ascendancy over lucrative trade and political power.

The aspirations of Fang and European traders to bypass Mpongwé middlemen and directly engage in commercial exchanges eroded the Mpongwé monopoly as trade brokers. By 1853, French adventurer Compiègne reported that Fang scouts had arrived at the coast; in 1857, an American missionary reported that Fang had erected housing settlements on the Como River.[77] European observers estimated the numbers of Fang who migrated over the course of the second half of the nineteenth century to be in the tens of thousands, but this was an exaggeration. Historians think the number was a maximum of a few thousand. French naval officers directed their aspirations for the imagined economic productivity of the nascent colony toward attracting Fang to locate villages near French posts and harnessing Fang labor. By the 1870s, European trading houses set up factories along inland fluvial systems, particularly along the Ogooué River, which facilitated the direct exchange of European and forest goods with Fang and other procurers. Many Mpongwé men now worked as managers of European factories that dotted the Ogooué or as traders who obtained European goods from the coast on credit and traveled inland to sell the goods in exchange for forest products.[78] Libreville became the center of trade, where multinational trading houses set up their headquarters, and where the French set up a fledgling government in an attempt to wrest control over the heterogeneous collection of Africans and Europeans who circulated through the region. Residents of Fang villages located near Libreville engaged in limited day-to-day interaction with Europeans and often battled in violent skirmishes with French officials and Senegalese militia well into the early decades of the twentieth century.

The intersectionalities of marriage and economic production of newly arriving Fang communities also indelibly shaped the fabric of Libreville's founding. The decentralization of political power, spatial dispersal of clans, and the mobility of villages were defining aspects of late nineteenth-century Fang sociopolitical organization.[79] The basic social, religious, military, and economic unit of Fang societies was a family unit called the *nda bôt*.[80] It included the founding patriarch, referred to as the *ésa*, his elderly relatives, his wives and children, his younger brothers, and his unmarried sisters and their illegitimate children. Each nda bôt was a self-sustaining economic and political unit, and members recognized only the authority of the ésa or other designated male leader.[81] Each nda bôt claimed membership to a clan (*ayon*) in which members shared a male ancestor. The ésa exercised ultimate authority and arbitrated conflicts between those who belonged in his nda bôt, though external arbiters could settle interclan conflicts. Affiliation with a clan did not entail territorial or political centralization, but exogamy was observed among members of the same ayon in the maternal and paternal lines.[82] Several nda bôt might inhabit a common geographical location that formed a village (*nlam*).

Among the ésa in a given village a leader would emerge, but there is no Fang term for a person who held permanent political power. "Chiefs" of given villages held temporary centralized power for purposes such as leading a group in war or to represent their interests in political or trade negotiations; another man could always assume leadership.[83] Key factors that determined which men would be selected as leaders were their oratory skills and wealth in people. Thus, the chief was often the person who was referred to as the rich man (*kouma*) or the orator (*nzôé*) in his community.[84]

Labor in the small and readily mobile Fang settlements was divided along gender lines. Mobile kin groups searched for fertile land, following the paths of elephants and hunting trails, and by the beginning of the mid-nineteenth century, sought direct access to European traders and bypassed Mpongwé middlemen. When the soil was exhausted, an entire village would relocate, a practice that resulted in only five to ten years being spent in a given location.[85] Once a clan decided upon a part of the forest to inhabit, during the dry season the men would clear the area of forest growth with machetes to make it habitable and agriculturally productive. Men were also responsible for defending the settlement, building the foundations of huts, doing the hunting, and, according to areas of specialization, forging iron or maintaining small livestock such as pigs and goats.[86] Fang men who lived near the Estuary and Ogooué regions traded ivory and rubber with European traders for guns, cloth, metal objects, and beads.[87] Women labored in shifting subsistence agriculture as they planted, maintained, and cultivated bananas, corn, peanuts, and the staple of manioc during the rainy seasons in plots located within walking distance from homesteads. Women might also maintain smaller gardens next to their homes in which they grew items such as tomatoes, yams, and eggplants.[88] By the 1890s, Fang were the primary producers of food for the Estuary region as fewer Mpongwé farmed. Fang women carried baskets of manioc and plantains to sell in Libreville. Written sources mention nothing about the distribution of income in Fang households from the sale of produce. Historian Jeremy Rich conducted oral interviews in 2000 with Fang male informants who relayed that wives had to give all proceeds to their husbands, yet he doubts the veracity of these claims as they may reflect contemporary gender tensions over control of wealth. [89] Women also fished and assisted in the construction of homes by using branches to cover huts built by their husbands. The Fang did not employ domestic slavery nor directly participate in the transatlantic slave trade, although they did sell war captives, criminals, and debtors to traders of other ethnolanguage groups.[90]

It is challenging to portray the interior architecture of Estuary Fang households of the nineteenth century and the transformations in domestic politics given the limited availability of firsthand accounts. As with the Mpongwé, it appears that the transference of women in marriage facilitated commercial and political alliances between Fang men and households and between the Fang and other African communities. Marriage (*aluk*) among Fang was to be negotiated by male kin of the bride and groom. A woman would leave her family of origin to live with her husband once he had made a good-faith deposit on the agreed-upon bridewealth (*nsua bikeng*), but this marriage was only provisionary until he paid the entire amount. *Nsua bikeng* literally means "bridewealth of iron"; the payment of *bikwela* (*ekwala* in the singular), about four pieces of iron held together, was the standard payment prior to the incorporation of European goods into bridewealth in the late nineteenth century.[91] This particular form of iron was not used for purposes other than a marriage payment. Gabonese historian A. Nguema Allogo underlines the value of iron for its rarity and that it symbolized the cohesion of two families joined by marriage, given that it could be procured only from collective labor.[92] Prior to the transference of bridewealth, a woman could engage in sexual relations with men of her choosing. Marriage conferred adulthood. A man older than sixteen years old who remained single was called a *nkoé*, a pejorative term meaning a boy.[93] Marriage transferred rights over a woman's labor, sexual access, and reproductive capacities to the husband's kin group, and through the practice of levirate, could become the wife of another man in her husband's family should he pass away. As with the Mpongwé, a Fang husband could authorize sexual access to his wife to another man—including a guest in his home, a neighbor with whom he hoped to establish a promise of mutual aid by exchanging wives for a period of time, or an unmarried man in the village—in exchange for some form of compensation.[94] As with the Mpongwé, a girl could be betrothed as early as infancy, though it was not usually until the age of seven or eight that she left her paternal house to become a part of her husband's household. Given the sex-segregated living quarters of Fang compounds (*abeng*), the child bride resided in the quarters with other women in the household. Expected practice was that a husband would not begin to have sexual relations with his young wife until after she had reached her first menstrual cycle (*ivoum*).

Though fathers had the final authority in contracting marriages, there was a variety of ways in which daughters and sons could influence or subvert their decisions. Sometimes a father submitted to his daughter's wishes if she refused a suitor.[95] Though a father usually selected a son's bride, a young man might approach his father and request a specific bride. Also, a young woman and man could undermine patriarchal authority through the practice of marriage by kidnapping (*abom*). The suitor would "kidnap" the woman, and her father or male guardian would then have to accept the bridewealth.[96] Having many wives and children represented wealth, but few men could obtain this status. It was mainly "chiefs" who had "harems" of five to twenty wives, as noted by European observers in the 1870s.[97] In fact, increased bridewealth expenses over the course of the nineteenth century made it difficult for many men to marry at all.

Escalating bridewealth expenses not only made it difficult for younger men to marry but also resulted in conflict between households if a husband proved unable to complete bridewealth payments after his wife had moved in with him. As was occurring in Mpongwé communities, imported goods displaced iron in the composition of bridewealth among Fang over the course of the nineteenth century. Moreover, bridewealth amounts among the Fang exceeded bridewealth costs in Mpongwé communities. For example, an 1875 bridewealth list for a Fang marriage in the Gabon Estuary consisted of one or two pieces of ivory, two or three goats or sheep, three or four baskets of spears, small Fang knives, small bars of iron, and indigenous salt, worth about 500 francs.[98] Bridewealth might also include *likis*, currency made of iron that circulated among only the Fang. For better-off Fang communities who resided near trade factories or missions, bridewealth was composed mainly of imported goods valued at around 770 francs.[99] Bridewealth payments could also include salt, cloth, tobacco, and gunpowder. Given the paucity of data about the costs of such goods, it is difficult to ascertain how much value this would hold if adjusted for inflation. However, commentary by European observers relays that Fang marriage payments of the era represented an enormous sum that would take young men years of labor in collecting rubber, ivory, or wood to exchange for the imported goods to compose bridewealth. Some armed skirmishes that broke out between villages near Libreville were the result of unpaid bridewealth. The wife's kin would attempt to kidnap her or an unmarried woman from the son-in-law's village as compensation if a husband defaulted on promised bridewealth. A French colonial administrator named Largeau recounted a particular outbreak of violence that resulted in fatalities among inhabitants of clashing villages in the 1890s. A husband had not completed the promised bridewealth ten years after his marriage. His wife was a prepubescent girl for whom an exorbitant bridewealth list had been demanded: 100 spears, 100 war knives, 50 trade knives, 20 mirrors, 30 small trade trunks, 3,000 iron links, 50 trade guns, 50 small barrels of gunpowder, 4 iron barrel covers, 40 earthen pots, 300 trade plates, 1 large canoe, 10 goats, 4 straw hats, 3 white trade shirts, 30 bunches of tobacco, 10 pieces of trade cloth, 12 bottles of liquor, and 4 dogs.[100]

Fang men, French missionaries argued, fought for, bartered, and sold women like chattel. Catholic missionaries and French observers described Fang women as "beasts of burden condemned to complete the most arduous work."[101] Having been "purchased" at a high cost, Fang women were subject to lives of servitude until their husbands abandoned them for younger wives once they reached old age and could no longer work or were postmenopausal.[102]

However, marriages in Fang communities were not static relationships that were purely commercial or political or functions of patriarchy, but tenuous social relations between individuals and groups that fluctuated between perpetuating and upsetting hierarchies of power. A husband's rights over his wife did not appear to be immutable but provisional, dependent upon his desire to remain in the marriage, his wife's desire to remain in or leave the marriage, and the volition of both kin groups. As was the case for Mpongwé women, even though Fang women appeared to be passive objects before groups of competing men, it was women's actions that precipitated the skirmishes. A wife's desertion of the conjugal home challenged the notion that she had been "sold" and could no longer negotiate rights in her person. A wife who was "kidnapped" by a lover was usually complicit in her displacement from her father's or husband's home. The wife's engagement in extramarital sex called into question the idea that her husband's remittance of bridewealth granted him control over her sexuality.

However, a husband could subject his wife to bodily harm in order to extract a confession if he suspected her of adultery or as a punishment if his suspicions turned out to be correct.[103] Over the course of the nineteenth century, Fang husbands could turn to violence against their wives' lovers to avenge ther wives' adultery and seek economic compensation as a public means of rectifying the offense. Should the lover be a man who lived in a different village, the adultery could lead to war between villages; it was not only the lover who was at fault, but his entire village. The husband could kidnap and hold hostage livestock, girls, married women, or men living in the lover's village until amends were made. This action frequently resulted in a series of fatal reprisals between villages.[104] A recorded payment for an instance of adultery in the 1870s was about 30 francs' worth of goods; for example, one trade gun, five portions of gunpowder, and a piece of cloth or livestock.[105]

DIVORCE

As among the Mpongwé, men and women alike could initiate divorce, and this could be resolved through multiple forums, though seeking a divorce was often a prolonged process. One option for a wife who could not or did not wish to leave her marriage, but sought to alter her husband's behavior, was to deliver a public curse on him. French observer Largeau emphasized the gravity of the curse—the husband would not be able to marry other wives nor succeed in any economic enterprises without having been publicly forgiven by his wife.[106] A man could repudiate his wife, send her back to her village (*a suu minga jan*) on grounds that she did not adhere to the behavior expected of a wife—perhaps she engaged in witchcraft, was disobedient or lacked respect for her husband, or was sterile.[107]

Like Mpongwé women, a Fang woman's success in obtaining a divorce depended on seeking refuge and support in her father's house. She needed to obtain the consent of the senior male family members—particularly the person who had received bridewealth (*nya ndômô*)—to represent her case for dissolution.[108] Women could claim divorce on grounds of excessive brutalization, witchcraft, or insult to her birth family by her husband or his kin. If the nya ndômô found another suitor to agree to reimburse the first husband's bridewealth, the marriage could be terminated more easily. If a father sent his daughter back to her husband and she fled again without anyone reimbursing her husband, a violent clash between villages could result. A husband sometimes attempted to exact revenge by killing a member of his wife's village, and the father of the wife in question was obligated to compensate the family members of those who had been killed.[109] Another avenue for a wife who wished to leave a marriage was to allow herself to be kidnapped by another man; her father was then responsible for reimbursing the first husband. Thus, it appears that Fang women had means at their disposal to rupture marital contracts or influence their rapport with their husbands.

The historical landscape of conjugal-sexual politics from the mid-nineteenth century through the turn of that century was neither a story of the unmitigated patriarchal hold of men over women nor a celebratory tale of women's social and economic autonomy prior to colonial rule. Rather, the portrait is one of a mobile terrain of relationships of power. Tracing the intersections of the town's founding, and trade and politics, with questions of sexual economy demonstrates the fluidity of how men and women formulated and reformulated their relationships with one another, a fluidity that would carry over well into the colonial period.

CONCLUSION

Fifteen years after the founding of Libreville, the French presence in the town had barely expanded. The underfunded and modest nature of the colonial presence in late nineteenth-century Libreville foreshadowed the uneven nature of colonial rule through the twentieth century.[110] In 1861, a British traveler described the colonial trading post (*comptoir*) as in a rather desultory state, noting a ship docked in the Estuary to provide defense; Fort d'Aumale, which housed naval officers and also served as the hospital; a few "wood huts" surrounding the fort that housed administrative personnel; and the Saint Mary Catholic mission and a convent for the Soeurs Bleues.[111] The French had not been able to establish either political or commercial ascendancy in the colony. A few feet away from Fort d'Aumale stood the trading houses of mainly German and British merchants. In 1875, the staff of colonial administration consisted of four people on a budget of 72,000 francs.[112]

In spite of the lack of a visible built environment of colonial society and state, colonial rule in Gabon was also marked by violence. In 1899, the French Congo was divided into about forty concession companies, with each land area roughly the size of France. The insolvent colony of Gabon was parceled into territories controlled by private concession companies. The brutal concessionary system unleashed further instability in a period already characterized by social fluctuation. In exchange for retaining exclusive rights over agricultural and industrial exploitation of their territories—mainly the exploitation of rubber and ivory—companies would give the state a percentage of their profits.[113] By the turn of the century, the brutalities inflicted upon African populations in the French Congo became public and created scandal internationally and in France.[114] The collection of rubber and other forest products under conditions of forced labor and violence resulted in tens of thousands of deaths, disease, and the decrease in agricultural production that contributed to massive food shortages and famine.

The creation of the French Equatorial Africa federation in 1910 signaled the attempt to enforce centralized colonial state control over Gabon's diverse African communities and European men on the spot. The paucity of documentation of the period of concessionary rule means that we can know little about domestic politics in the Estuary region in these years. Yet, as the French attempted to transition from colonial conquest to colonial rule, townspeople's shifting aspirations toward emerging forms of marriage and sexual relationships shaped transformations in political economy, and changes in politics and economics shaped domestic relationships in the next century of Libreville's existence.

2 ⤳ Planning, Protest, and Prostitution
Libreville in the Era of Timber, 1910–1929

FROM 1910 TO 1929, the Estuary region witnessed vast social, economic, and political upheaval. Libreville was transformed from a fledgling colonial outpost characterized by interdependent African and European exchanges to a colonial capital city. The French endeavored to expand and rationalize colonial rule; the town was to be the headquarters from which the French could broadcast political control over the colony. Beginning in the 1910s and reaching a height in the mid-1920s, global markets clamored for Gabon's okoumé wood, sparking the industry that was to become Gabon's primary economic activity through political independence from French colonial rule in 1960.[1] Greater numbers of Fang from northern Gabon migrated toward Libreville and other regions in southern Gabon to profit from the economic opportunities. Yet demographic decline and social disruption and dislocation brewed beneath the veneer of economic prosperity. Ecological disasters, food shortages, disease epidemics, and socioeconomic insecurity also arose.[2] The French extracted increased labor, raw products, and money from Estuary residents to fund the campaigns of World War I against Germans in bordering Cameroon.[3] In 1929, the global Depression made its way to Gabon, resulting in the near stoppage of timber production and a loss of work and money for Libreville residents. Through these fluctuations, a heterogeneous collection of African and European communities settled in, sojourned through, and departed from Libreville. Questions of urban planning regarding housing,

44

health and hygiene, tax collection, work, policing, and governance were on the minds of state personnel and new and old residents alike. Couched in such questions were the dynamics of sexuality and marriage, between African women and men and between African women and European men.

An unintended consequence of economic shifts and the circulation of people through Libreville between 1910 and 1929 was that women's sexuality provided paths for the generation of wealth in material goods and money. As had occurred in the nineteenth century, interracial sexual and domestic relationships between Mpongwé women and European men proliferated. Mpongwé men brokered such relationships for female dependents, often daughters who had received some formal French education. Some relationships were short-term sexual encounters and others long-term domestic and sexual relationships that Mpongwé societies viewed as marriages. These relationships occurred along local conjugal-sexual mores and were mutually beneficial for African and European societies. Some women accrued independent property and monetary wealth through interracial relationships, thereby disrupting hierarchies of gender and generation with elder kin and chiefs. Moreover, many Mpongwé women exercised a political voice, using their literacy to protest against colonial efforts to exact greater political and economic control over Libreville's African communities. By World War I and its aftermath, some groups of elite African men, chiefs, and colonial officials — made anxious by the social mobility that some black and mixed-race women involved in interracial unions achieved — sought to limit the occurrences of interracial unions. For some Fang women, compensation for having sexual relations with West African men and Fang migrant laborers provided a means for their husbands and male kin to obtain cash to meet colonial tax directives.

Over the course of these first two decades of the existence of French Equatorial Africa (FEA), Gabon continued to experience population decline, diminished birth rates, and increased mortality. French colonial state and society settled upon African women's sexual promiscuity and increased divorce as reflective of the "disorganization of the African family." In Libreville, regulating African sexuality, particularly that of African women, in order to populate and safeguard social and biological reproduction in the colony was to become a key and contested process of urban planning and state-building.

TIES OF DOMESTIC SPHERE TO STATE - BUILDING

POLITICAL AND ECONOMIC TRANSFORMATIONS: COLONIAL CONSOLIDATION AND OKOUMÉ, 1910–1929

Understanding the transformations in the manifestations of and anxieties about African women's sexuality involves tracing the transformations in politics, economics, and demography that swept through the Estuary region. Following the official "on-paper" creation of French Equatorial Africa in 1910, the French endeavored to place an infrastructure for colonial rule over the colony of Gabon and its capital city. These efforts encompassed four means: (1) to complete the task of military conquest; (2) to establish geographic boundaries and delineate where Africans could live; (3) to facilitate governance through appointing French and African personnel; and (4) to direct the economic activities of Gabon's population toward French profits. In the first ten years of FEA's existence, political control beyond the Estuary region was tenuous. French officers and Senegalese *tirailleurs* (colonial infantry) mounted numerous campaigns to temper varied insurgencies in the interior. While southern Gabon remained relatively free of armed resistance to colonial rule, it was not until 1925 that insurgent Fang populations in the northern region of Woleu-Ntem ceded to colonial governance.[4]

Following the task of military conquest, colonial officials endeavored to divide the colony into administrative units and set up a political hierarchy of French personnel and African chiefs and civil servants who were to be auxiliaries in military defense, civil governance, and economic mobilization.[5] The colony was divided into civil circumscriptions (*circonscriptions*), which were further divided into numerous subdivisions. The French subdivision heads reported to the circumscription leader, who then reported to the governor's Office of Political and Administrative Affairs. Libreville sat in the Gabon-Como Estuary circumscription and was both the capital city of the colony of Gabon and the principal administrative center of the Estuary circumscription. As in French Occidental (West) Africa (FOA), administrators could maintain political control through the *indigénat*, a policy that allowed the imprisonment or other punishment of Africans without any judicial proceedings.[6] By 1920, colonial personnel had put in place a system of African chieftaincy. In rural areas, French personnel appointed elder and often illiterate men to preside over administrative and territorial units classified in descending geographic territories called *canton, terre,* and *tribu*.[7] Chiefs' duties were ostensibly to conduct censuses, collect taxes, and recruit labor for colonial public works projects, and they had the authority to imprison those who failed to pay taxes or respond to forced-labor projects.[8] Administrators sought to make the French presence more felt throughout the colony, increasing the numbers of colonial officials who could undertake frequent tours around circumscriptions to persuade local chiefs' collaboration in these efforts.[9]

The infrastructure of governance in Libreville and its hinterlands was to reflect centralized political control in the colony's administrative capital. The Estuary circumscription was composed of the capital city of

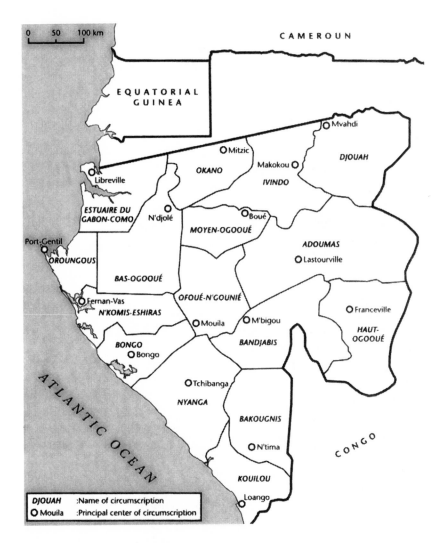

MAP 2.1. Administrative Division of Gabon, 1916. (Reproduced from Christopher Gray, *Colonial Rule and Crisis in Equatorial Africa*, 178.)

Libreville and rural areas within a few days' journey on foot or via riverways, Cocobeach to the west and Kango in the north. Libreville was governed by an administrator-mayor who was assisted by a commission of three French civil servants or private citizens plus one African.[10] However, echoing the rest of the colony, turnover of Libreville's French personnel was frequent.[11] As early as 1906, the military commander appointed five chiefs in Libreville to collect taxes and mediate civil conflicts among African communities.[12] African men who had received some basic French education, primarily Mpongwé, worked as civil servant clerks in varied administrative offices.[13]

Rocked by the insolvency of the concessionary period and suffering from tepid funding from mainland France, colonial officials sought to maximize the colony's local revenues.[14] By 1908, administrators required taxes to be paid in currency, not in kind, in an effort to compel Africans to work for wages in the colonial economy.[15] In 1910, the colonial state decreed that women in the Estuary region were also to pay taxes in addition to men; each woman was to pay 2 francs, while men were to pay 5 francs.[16] Only children, the elderly, the infirm, soldiers, and colonial clerks were exempt from the tax. By the end of World War I, the colonial currency of the franc was in circulation, and this was changed to CFA (Communauté Financière Africaine) franc coins and notes after 1945.[17] By 1920, individual tax rates had increased to 10 francs for Estuary residents, while tax rates remained at 3 to 5 francs elsewhere in the colony.[18] Another new policy was that of forced labor. Beginning in 1915, each able-bodied adult man was to give seven days of work per year on public works projects or could buy out his days of forced labor at the rate of one-half franc per day.[19]

The historiography of 1910s and 1920s Gabon has emphasized these decades as "the timber era."[20] The increased export of okoumé wood changed the colony and the Estuary region's fortunes, landscape, and peopling. The expansion of the timber industry had begun with the consolidation of FEA, with timber exports tripling between 1910 and 1913. The okoumé industry stagnated during World War I, when there was a near standstill in trade, but increased to unprecedented heights thereafter.[21] Africans and Europeans alike rushed to forests in southern Gabon to work in the timber industry, the moment of the okoumé rush that characterized the 1920s.

In the beginning years of the okoumé rush, the felling and transport of timber by African communities was an affair of kin, men and women alike, and involving entire villages. The years of 1920–1924 saw an era of African "free wood-cutters." Anyone with an ax could cut down okoumé trees to sell to European trading houses.[22] Colonial reports relay that Fang men were turning away from "traditional" labor in hunting, fishing, and cutting down brush to focus solely on lending services as tree fellers.[23] Taking about one month's worth of labor, a clan leader managed a workforce of kin—wives, children, nephews, brothers, and other dependents—and then floated the logs to European trading locations that began to dot Gabon's rivers.[24] Rivers were key to the okoumé economy, as the waterways provided an exit and transportation route for the trees to reach the coast for export. Free woodcutters could accept the purchasing price of a given European buyer or refuse it and try to sell to another.[25] In 1924, a head of a convoy of free woodcutters could earn the equivalent of 75–130 francs per person on his team for a period of work felling a tree.[26] In the regions of the Bas-Ogooué and Ogooué, but also in the Estuary region, where a confluence of forests and rivers existed, subdivision heads reported a veritable "okoumé fever," and that entire villages had abandoned their settlements in the bush and agricultural cultivation to work in felling timber.[27]

Historians Christopher Gray and Francois Ngolet have argued that the mid-1920s ushered in the decline of an economy in which Africans controlled their terms of engagement and work into an "economy of exploitation" in which African laborers lost the means to determine the nature, duration, and remuneration of their labor.[28] European forestry societies came to hold control over the timber industry.[29] Several factors contributed to this. First, the French more regularly implemented policies that required permits to cut wood and gain access to specific areas of forest plotted on maps.[30] Only French businesses with significant capital could afford the fees for permits of larger hectares. Furthermore, increased mechanization in cutting down and transporting wood resulted in the hiring of European workers to man machinery, while African laborers were hired to float logs along interior waterways toward the ocean, more manual and dangerous yet lower-paid work.[31] The amount of money that a wage laborer earned per month, 40 francs plus food rations, was lower than what a free woodcutter could earn for a month's labor, which was about 70 francs.[32]

In contrast to the era of free woodcutting that involved the labor of men and women linked by ties of affinity, timber production from the mid-1920s stimulated migrant labor of Fang men and other ethnic groups toward southern Gabon. Thousands of Gabonese men migrated from interior regions to timber yards looking for work and money. Though the lower Ogooué region and areas around Lambaréné were the hubs of the timber industry, the Estuary region was a key center of forestry as well, housing a number of timber concessions in its hinterlands. A new site of living and work occupied the landscape: the timber yard. One of the largest in the Estuary region employed forty Europeans and fifteen hundred Africans, and was composed of separate African and European villages, with stores selling durable goods, silos filled with rice, and fish and agricultural goods for purchase.[33] Libreville also housed the administrative headquarters of forestry and trading companies of varied European nationalities.

Historian Clotaire Messi Me Nang described the typical timber yard as a "monstrous devourer of men."[34] Work in timber camps was rough and dangerous—poor living and working conditions and little regulation contributed to the deaths of laborers, who were sometimes recruited through violence.[35] Workers frequently abandoned contracts with complaints of insufficient food rations, beatings to compel them to work, and long workdays of twelve hours or more. Few worksites employed medical personnel, and workers died from illnesses such as sleeping sickness, beriberi, leprosy, and dysentery.[36] In spite of these precarious conditions, okoumé wood continued to be king and was the sector of the colonial economy that employed the largest number of Gabonese laborers.[37]

By the end of the 1920s, nearly all economic production within African communities along the northern and southern Gabon coasts depended directly or indirectly on the timber industry.[38] The okoumé rush supported the growth of other types of enterprises, with some Africans self-employed as transporters or owners of bars.[39] Though few Mpongwé entered the industry as manual wage laborers, some Mpongwé men obtained new avenues of wage work as clerks, interpreters, and in finance. Though timber companies were owned by the French, the mid-1920s did appear to be a period of "extraordinary prosperity" for the state, French businessmen, and some Africans who worked in timber exploitation, as well as for the predominantly Fang village settlements near timber camps, who provided secondary services such as cultivating and selling agricultural products to feed the workers of timber camps.[40]

URBAN PLANNING AND THE HUMAN GEOGRAPHY OF LIBREVILLE, 1910–1929

Though the historiography of early twentieth-century Gabon has focused much attention on men and the expansion of the okoumé economy in the evolution of Libreville and the Estuary region, women were a key factor in the city's demographic and socioeconomic evolution in the timber era. As male migrants populated the timber yards of the Estuary region, the population of the city of Libreville and villages of the region reflected gender parity and included a critical mass of children. Figure 2.1 outlines available census data for the city of Libreville from 1912 to 1929. Records do not detail how colonial officials determined who counted as a child, man, woman, or elderly person, yet these numbers are useful for outlining a generational and gender portrait of the town's residents.

Census numbers suggest sharp increases and decreases in Libreville's population in the first two decades of FEA's existence. Through the fluctuations of Libreville's population, these numbers suggest that Libreville was

FIGURE 2.1. Population of the City of Libreville, 1912–1929[41]
-Statistics not available for this year

Year	Women	Men	Children	Elderly People	Total Population
1912	-	-	-	-	3,000
1916	1,083	1,244	1,550	200	4,077
1918	1,020	941	844	-	2,805
1920	-	-	-	-	2,400
1921	-	-	-	-	2,730
1922	922	935	846	-	2,703
1923	-	-	-	-	2,656
1924	1,082	730	769	-	2,581
1927	1155	900	825	-	2,880
1929	-	-	-	-	3,455

effectively a "city of women." African women equaled or outnumbered African men, with the exception of the years 1916 and 1922, in which there appeared to be nominally more men than women. From 1912 to 1916, the beginning of expansion years for the okoumé industry and its decline during World War I, the population of the city gradually increased and peaked at 4,077 people. Fang clans, made up of men, women, and kin linked by affinity in polygamous households, contributed to the population growth. It appears that children were a significant portion of Libreville's population, as high as about 30% in 1916.

As World War I continued and the French fought battles with Germans in neighboring Cameroon, economic constraints, disease, and food shortages decimated Libreville's population, which decreased by 31 percent from 1916 to 1918. The population whom the French counted as permanent residents remained at less than three thousand people for nearly a decade to come. Yet, between 1914 and 1916, two to four thousand conscripts from throughout the colony—porters, laborers, and soldiers—took up residence in camps immediately outside Libreville.[42] With the influx of people and the resulting demand for agricultural produce, food prices increased as farmers could not produce greater yields.[43] A series of food shortages that began in 1917 culminated in full-scale famine in 1918 and again in 1922.[44] Germany had been the main trading partner and recipient of Gabonese wood. The stoppage of trade with Germany and the reduction of ships in ports resulted in a near standstill in the export of timber and a shortage of goods available for purchase.[45] Prices increased dramatically for imported items such as salt, soap, tobacco, and pots that had become essential for quotidian existence.[46] In spite of this shortage of cash, the colonial state increased taxes from an individual rate of 3 francs in 1914 to 10 francs in 1918 or equivalent amounts of palm oil, rubber, or wood.[47] Furthermore, epidemics of sleeping sickness and men dying or fleeing from conscription and portage contributed to the population decrease. The most drastic demographic loss in Libreville's population seems to have been in terms of the numbers of children, the population of which was reduced by about 50 percent from 1916 to 1918.

After the war, the population only gradually increased, from 2,400 in 1920 to a little over 3,400 inhabitants in 1929. Drought and other ecological factors further diminished agricultural yields in the 1920s, and it was hard for residents to obtain food. From 1920 to 1921, the price for manioc nearly doubled, from 350 to 750 francs. Famine broke out again in 1922, further crippling population growth. With the exception of 1922, in which the numbers of men, women, and children were nearly equal, census figures suggest that women continued to dominate the town's population figures. Children and men each constituted about 30 percent of Libreville's population. Women represented about 40 percent of the town's population in 1924 and 1929, outnumbering men. This was most likely due to several factors. Alcoholism may have contributed to the death of some men. The okoumé rush may have resulted in the out-migration of men to forestry concessions. Moreover, it is probable that many of the Fang communities in the city limits were polygamous households. The Estuary-Como region, the immediate rural suburbs of Libreville in which Fang communities lived in villages, also reflected a greater number of women. Its total population grew from 8,561 men and women in 1910 to a population of 25,822 men and women in 1916. The average number of women in these rural regions exceeded the number of men by about 2,000.[48] The currents of historical change in early twentieth-century Libreville entailed the processes of women and men shaping the meaning of town life in the era of timber and the consolidation of colonial rule.

Implementing centralized political control, directing where Africans would live, and controlling labor and economic resources would prove challenging for colonial officials, in part because of the sheer diversity of African societies that belied French conceptions of a singular "African" colonial subject. Libreville's African population was a heterogeneous population with distinct cleavages in ethnicity, wealth, social status, and the degree to which they had adapted European mores. West Africans from Sierra Leone, Liberia, and Ghana worked as agents for various trading companies and as

PHOTO 2.1. Village of Louis, ca. 1900. (Reproduced from a postcard in the personal collection of Patrick Ceillier, Saint-Malo, France.)[49]

storekeepers, and hundreds of Senegalese tirailleurs circulated in and out of Libreville as they policed the colony. As at the founding of Libreville, the African population originating from Equatorial Africa within the city's boundaries was predominantly Myènè, particularly Mpongwé. Mpongwé viewed themselves as superior to Fang societies who lived on the outskirts of Libreville. In addition to educational offerings afforded by American Protestant and French Catholic missionaries, Mpongwé boys could attend the secular state-operated school that sought to train students in French and basic math in preparation for jobs as writers and clerks for the colonial government and French trading companies.[50]

Gabrielle Vassal, a French woman who was accompanying her civil servant husband to Brazzaville, stopped in Libreville for a few days in 1923. She was struck by the degree to which Libreville's residents, meaning the Mpongwé, had adopted European cultural norms, remarking that "all the natives seemed to speak and understand French," and that she found in "the natives of Libreville a veneer of civilization not to be found in the rest of Equatorial Africa nor in the hinterland of Gabon itself."[51] Libreville's residents readily adopted the sartorial accouterments of Europeans, with African men wearing pith helmets. Vassal noted, "Natives passing by politely took off their hats (their chief reason for desiring a hat is to be able to imitate the white man)."[52] Men wore shorts and shirts tailored from imported

Planning, Protest, and Prostitution ⇌ 53

cloth. Mpongwé lived in neighborhoods such as Louis and Glass (named after nineteenth-century kings). Townspeople constructed houses on stilts to offer protection from flooding. Local raffia palms provided the materials for the roofs and planks for the walls of the houses, which featured wraparound verandas.[53]

An Mpongwé girl divided her time between domestic tasks at home and small-scale agricultural production that supplemented families' diets. The daughters of elite families attended the school for girls that had been operated by the Soeurs Bleues since the late nineteenth century. Between 1916 and 1921, annual enrollment of boarding school pupils increased from 23 to 32 girls, and each year about 66 girls were day school students.[54] The curriculum included instruction in basic reading and writing in French, morality, hygiene, the domestic arts, housekeeping, and sewing, skills that supported the nuns' intention for the girls to be dutiful wives in monogamous marriages to Christian African men. Yet the Catholic efforts to mold a certain type of Mpongwé girl proved problematic. In a 1916 report, a nun characterized the typical student as follows: "The Gabonese student is talkative and vain. She has a difficult character and often sulks."[55] Many times girls' families withdrew them from school or girls walked out and returned home, likely due to the conditions of beatings and their forced labor in fields and in cleaning the mission.[56]

Mpongwé women were consummate purchasers of imported cloth and European adornment.[57] Vassal opined that "the native women with their gay-coloured cloths wound tightly round their supple bodies from breasts to knees had here a nonchalant, satisfied appearance which contrasted with the dreary impassive expressions we had seen in other ports."[58] British colonial civil servant Frederick Migeod, who traveled to Libreville in the early 1920s, described Mpongwé as "civilized," speaking multiple European languages, well-educated, and "clean," with the women often bathing themselves with soap several times a day.[59]

Libreville's African populations were avid consumers of imported goods. Articles off-loaded from ships and sold in stores operated by European trading companies (*factories*) included tobacco, sewing machines, knives, pots, beads, belts, cloth, and manufactured clothes—shirts, hats, men's boots, espadrilles, and women's shoes.[60] Townspeople readily incorporated European foodstuffs into their diets. Sugar, butter, rice, spirits and wine, preserves, and canned milk were part of daily intake.[61] A 1928 annual report recorded that there were at least a half dozen bakeries in the town, and Africans were the main customers.[62] Libreville residents viewed themselves as sophisticated and cosmopolitan, with men and women sporting European-style clothing

PHOTO 2.2. Maritime Boulevard, ca. 1927. (Reproduced from a postcard in the personal collection of Patrick Ceillier.)[63]

and parading their fashions in Sunday strolls along the Ocean Boulevard or at public Bastille Day celebrations.

The Estuary region's thin population density worried French colonial officials and businessmen, who were eager to increase Libreville's African population and harness the labor of Fang communities. Colonial personnel, who viewed Mpongwé as "lazy" people who refused to perform manual labor, looked toward African societies other than Mpongwé to populate the town. In a 1916 report, the governor outlined efforts to draw people from the interior regions to Libreville and receive primary education at the state school so that they could increase the number of African auxiliaries from Gabon's varied ethnic groups. He urged the subdivision heads from interior regions to send their most serious students to Libreville for schooling, where they would receive a scholarship.[64]

Officials worried about how to exact greater control over "elusive" Fang populations living in the forested suburbs of Libreville.[65] Fang populations circulated in and out of Libreville to sell agricultural products and fish, sell forest

PHOTO 2.3. Bastille Day celebration, 1929. (Reproduced from a postcard in the personal collection of Patrick Ceillier.)[66]

products for export, purchase imported goods, and to seek out medical services from the French, but often eluded French efforts to extract forced labor and taxes. Frederick Migeod traveled through some Fang Estuary villages and described the houses as composed of raffia palm and flattened bark; he also noted that everything was laid out in "perfectly straight lines," of houses, trees, and streets.[67] In comparing Fang to Mpongwé, Migeod viewed Fang as "a dirty race" whose women "make no pretention to ornamental dress," with some tattooing and red dye on their bodies and men sporting a cloth around their waists.[68] The few Fang men who worked as clerks or interpreters differentiated themselves from other Fang by wearing a European trouser and shirt.

Though they lived on the outskirts, Fang were essential to Libreville as they cultivated the agricultural produce that fed the city's African and European inhabitants. Fang women, the principal farmers, worked daily on individual cropland plots. In contrast to Mpongwé women, whom European observers described as independent and exhibiting a certain liberty, Fang women were portrayed as "beasts of burden" and "veritable slaves," who toiled in farming and then walked to town carrying thirty to forty kilograms of produce in baskets on their backs with a band around the forehead that helped stabilize the loads.[69] Fang women sold the produce in markets to African and European purchasers and reportedly gave their husbands the money. While Migeod and other European observers rarely recorded Mpongwé women carrying children, the Fang woman always had her child with her, with "the babies carried on the right hip. One woman I noticed with a big basket on her back, had a child too big to carry on her hip, so she had it astride her shoulders above the basket."[70] As hunters and fishermen, Fang men procured the little meat present in the diets of Estuary residents.[71] While most Estuary Fang communities lived outside of what colonial officials recognized as Libreville's boundaries, some clans did move within Libreville in the 1910s and 1920s, further fueling the concerns of French personnel about how to maintain social control over townspeople and manage Libreville's built environment.

French efforts to consolidate political power in Libreville involved attempts to expand European living, business, and administrative quarters. Executing this urban planning entailed displacing African communities who occupied land desired by the French. Mpongwé and Fang societies refuted French conceptions of urban planning on the grounds of gender, clan and ethnic differentiation, and rights to land and to construct their own housing. Early administrators sought to diminish Libreville's nineteenth-century landscape of Africans and Europeans living in close proximity. Between 1912 and 1913, military officers expelled Fang who had been living near the military fort in order to create the area named the "plateau" that was to serve as the segregated European administrative and residential neighborhood.[72] The French envisioned that they would segregate Africans into distinct neighborhoods by ethnicity and designated plots of land. Yet, in June 1912, a group of Fang men refused to move from the designated plateau area into a single area of the city that was to serve as the Fang neighborhood. In a letter to the mayor, these men refused on the grounds that Fang clans were not part of a single collectivity and were distinct from one another. Such close proximity to other Fang groups, the men argued, would encourage their wives' infidelity.[73] The mayor accused government-employed Fang of being at the head of the revolt and punished some of the protesters for their refusal.[74] Mpongwé communities also protested French urban-planning efforts to displace them from land on which they lived, as well as against new colonial restrictions on economic and educational privileges that they previously held. Parallel to protests by Fang men, a group of Mpongwé writers and clerks in the colonial service wrote letters to French officials against the 1912 urban plan, claiming that their descent from Mpongwé kings gave them ancestral rights to the land.[75]

Libreville's Mpongwé residents viewed themselves as equal to whites and chafed against French colonial efforts to categorize them as "natives" (*indigènes*), colonial subjects who had few economic and educational privileges. After the creation of FEA, administrators expelled the Saint Gabriel Fathers who had been providing secondary education to Mpongwé students. In 1918, some Mpongwé men founded a branch of the Ligue des Droits de l'Homme in Libreville. League members wrote letters to colonial officials asking for the return of the Saint Gabriel Fathers to provide secondary school education and for Gabon to be autonomous from the new FEA, which members viewed as a turning point in which new racialist attitudes of the French emerged.[76] That same year, a group called the Professional Association of African Native Employees, composed of West Africans and Myènès, lobbied against the lower salaries that African civil servants received in comparison to French employees.[77] While in exile in Senegal and France in the 1920s, discontented Mpongwé elite men published the newspaper *L'Echo Gabonais*, later called *La Voie Coloniale*, to decry increased colonial taxes and limitations on education.[78] The letter and newspaper campaigns against tax increases, reductions in educational opportunities, and low salaries, what the authors interpreted as racial discrimination, did little to stop such colonial directives. Nevertheless, these campaigns do demonstrate moments in which varied constituencies of Libreville's African residents coalesced to forward alternative visions of the town life imagined by the French.

Recalcitrance toward French urban-planning efforts continued into the 1920s, and the diagrams and maps created by several architects of what Libreville should look like went unimplemented.[79] Forecasting what other European observers would note later in the twentieth century, visitors in the 1920s described the city as dominated by the naturally occurring—rather than a built—environment.[80] Gabrielle Vassal's impressions of the town were of a sleepy seaside hamlet: "huge trees left standing, either isolated or in clusters about the town, the overgrown path, the spaces abandoned to the undergrowth of coarse grass and tangled bushes give a picturesque appearance to the town."[81] As his ship approached Libreville, Frederick Migeod summarized the view as, "the northern bank being hilly, though the hills were of no great height, while the southern bank was covered with mangroves. The town lies spread out three miles along the north side of the Estuary." He also noted that the town was "pretty," with palm, mango, coconut, and almond trees along its avenues.[82] He signaled, as would urban planners to come for several decades, that the town was swampy and needed better drainage. There was only one road of four miles along which the only car owned by a European could traverse. He repeated the perpetual complaint that Libreville was an unhealthy place for Europeans, noting the low availability of meat, and because there was "no real segregation from the natives," which resulted in whites' being diseased.[83] Africans lived in a variety of huts constructed of materials ranging from straw and bark to cloth. Libreville remained a rather unplanned city.

Though the French endeavored to consolidate colonial rule, hegemony was on a shoestring in Libreville in the first decade of FEA's existence.[84] A lack of colonial personnel, poor infrastructure, low population density, and the topography of dense forests and winding waterways provided shelter for Fang communities who wished to escape colonial control and enter into and leave Libreville at will.[85] Furthermore, townspeople, insisting upon differentiation by clan, gender, ethnicity, and social status, claimed rights to housing and to shape the physical geography of the town, as well as to retain control over the wealth that their labor generated. Nevertheless, the expansion of colonial control was transformative, adding new political power brokers such as chiefs, diminishing some of the prestige that Mpongwé male elites held, and bringing about new economic opportunities and constraints with the export of Gabonese timber to global markets. These political and economic transformations shaped gender, marriage, and sexual relationships, and Estuary residents shaped the contours of historical change in their interpersonal relationships.

INTERRACIAL RELATIONSHIPS, PROSTITUTION, AND PROTEST: GENDER AND GENERATIONAL HIERARCHIES REORDERED

As Libreville was transformed from a nineteenth-century trading port to a colonial capital city, interracial sexual relationships, variably referred to by historical actors as "prostitution," "debauchery," or "marriage," continued. Though the numbers of French women in colonies elsewhere in the French Empire increased after World War I, few traveled to FEA. In 1900, of 130 whites in Libreville, only 28 were women.[86] By 1910, the European population of Libreville slowly grew to 200 people and remained at that level for the next twenty years. By 1931, about 1,300 Europeans lived throughout the colony, but white women represented only 29 percent of this population.[87] The French cited disease epidemics, inadequate supplies of potable water and electricity, a lack of roads, and the small number of colonial personnel as making FEA unsuitable for women and children. Interracial relationships were prevalent in urban centers—Libreville, Lambaréné, and Port-Gentil—where European adventurers, traders, and government personnel converged.[88] Myènè peoples, particularly the Mpongwé, established a monopoly in sexual-domestic unions with Europeans.

It is challenging to quantify the extent of interracial relationships. According to early twentieth-century missionary and colonial records, nearly every Mpongwé family sent their daughters to engage in relationships with European men. A 1914 letter by the governor of Gabon to the governor-general of FEA indicated that attached was a sixty-nine-page report listing the names of women engaged in interracial relationships and the names and ages of their mixed-race children. But the referenced report is missing from the archives.[89] Interracial relationships of Mpongwé women and European men continued beyond Gabon's borders. As French soldiers traveled toward Cameroon to fight Germans during World War I, Mpongwé women followed them. In a 1914 report, the governor complained that women native to Libreville were clandestinely leaving to carry out a "licentious life."[90] In a 1915 letter to superiors in France, a Catholic priest stationed in Libreville bemoaned the difficulty of cultivating monogamous Christian marriages among the region's African communities, as well as among the European residents. Father Matrou, from the Sainte Marie missionary station, conveyed in his letter that "the presence of Europeans in Libreville and their dubious morality has introduced the commonplace existence of temporary unions between blacks and whites; this [is a] pernicious example."[91] Citing a 1918 colonial political report (the document is now missing from the archives), Georges Balandier wrote that of the 935 African women of marriageable age, as many as 400 remained single. Of these single women, 65 "cohabited with European men" and 100 lived by "prostitution."[92] Balandier did not detail if those categorized as living by prostitution engaged with white or African men or perhaps both. However, given the disdain that Mpongwé expressed toward Fang, it is likely that the women's clients were Europeans and, if African, originated from West Africa. That about one-half of Mpongwé women were not married in 1918 is a vast change from Mpongwé women of the previous generation, for whom normative societal expectations were of universal marriage for men and women. Several factors likely diminished the possibility of Mpongwé women marrying Mpongwé men: mores of consanguinity that limited the available pool of marriage partners, the diminished numbers of Mpongwé men, and the presence of European men unaccompanied by European women.[93] Gabrielle Vassal maintained that Libreville women "exercise a charm on Europeans" and "they are quite unlike all other native women throughout this vast colony, who admire and envy them."[94] It does not appear that every Mpongwé woman was in an interracial union, but that interracial domestic and sexual relationships between Mpongwé women and white men were commonplace.

Mpongwé and some Europeans described interracial sexual and domestic relationships that lasted over the course of months or years as "marriages." It appears that women's engagements in interracial relationships were family affairs. Male kin—fathers, uncles, or brothers—often initiated, sanctioned, and brokered Mpongwé women's relationships. Missionaries noted that it was sometimes mothers who incited their daughters to enter interracial unions, which was in keeping with Mpongwé practices in which a woman's mother had some influence in determining whom and when her daughter married.[95] Many women's families required that European men give them bridewealth, the jural and social confirmation of a relationship as a marriage in Mpongwé customary practice. Simone Agnoret Iwenga St. Denis, an Mpongwé woman with a mixed-race father, recounted the setting up of her grandmother's union: "We demanded from the Norwegian white man to give bridewealth. He did this. It's only following this that my grandmother began to regularly go to the man's house."[96]

MOTHER'S INFLUENCE

Based on interviews with French businessmen and colonial personnel who had traveled to Gabon after World War I, French journalist France Renucci published a fictionalized account of an interracial relationship in Libreville. In the book *Souvenirs de femmes*, a newly disembarked French banker in 1920s Libreville accompanied colleagues to the home of his potential wife and her family, declaring his desire to marry "in the Gabonese way."[97] The young woman's father initially refused the Frenchman's request, needing to first consult with his wife. The mother responded with her demands for bridewealth: a demijohn of wine, a colored umbrella, bags of rice, packets of sugar, a dog, and 500 francs.[98] This list represented a combination of luxury items, such as the umbrella and sugar, and basic items, such as the rice, which supplemented the family's diet in times of low harvest.[99] It would have taken an Mpongwé man several years to amass such a bundle of goods and currency.

In living with and/or maintaining the homes of European men, Mpongwé women completed the quotidian tasks of wives, of housekeeping and sexual labor, sustaining colonial manhood. Women's care provided the "comforts of home" to European men.[100] European travel narratives and fiction of the 1910s and 1920s convey that nearly all white men stationed in Libreville, from the governor-general to subordinate civil servants, from managers to lower-skilled laborers in the timber industry and trading companies, encompassing European men of high social status to those of lower social status, engaged a "mistress" or "native wife."[101] Joseph Blache, a sailor who sojourned in and out of Gabon in the 1920s, described the wife of a French colleague (or perhaps his own) as a "housekeeper, tailor, laundress, unrolling her mat

"Mpongwé wives sustained 'colonial manhood'"

in the bedroom of the white, each night!"[102] However, Blache qualified, many a "black marriage of Gabon" involved only sex as Mpongwé women lived in their family homes in Mpongwé villages by day and came to their European husbands' houses only at night. The care of métis children fell to Mpongwé kin. As children grew beyond infancy, their white fathers, or more commonly Mpongwé mothers and kin, often conferred métis boys or girls respectively to Catholic priests or nuns at the mission station of Sainte Marie for rearing and education.[103]

Interracial relationships brought material and monetary wealth to women's families, prompting critiques by Catholic missionaries and some European observers of the prostitution of women that benefited Mpongwé men. Some women's families gained a monthly monetary payment from their female dependents' European lovers, bringing about a relationship that a study funded by the Anti-Slavery Society described as "a rental contract."[104] Others portrayed Mpongwé male intermediaries as "pimps." French journalist Albert Londres, visiting Gabon in 1928, relayed that as he arrived in the port he witnessed, "a Gabonese woman, followed by a *nègre* who appeared to want to offer her to the newly disembarked, walked along on high heels, her black legs in yellow silk hose, swaying in a rose dress a body for rent, if not for sale."[105]

Women's sexual labor permitted some Mpongwé families to maintain their elite social status as fortunes changed in Libreville's shifting economic currents and the colonial state sought to curtail African economic autonomy. In the early twentieth century, a Catholic missionary stationed in Libreville reflected that women acquired money, linens, dishes, canned goods, and rice during the time with their European husbands. Once the European men left Gabon, the missionary concluded, "they return to their parental home and the family struggles with a difficult problem: how to live comfortably without having done anything."[106] In the new era of colonial restrictions on African social and economic ascendency, Mpongwé women facilitated the continued flow of imported prestige goods. Women's labor also brought in cash, of increasing necessity in Libreville. In instituting a head tax, colonial officials hoped to compel African men to work for European enterprises or in agricultural labor producing cash crops. However, daughters' sexual labor allowed some Mpongwé men to avoid such colonial directives.

Mpongwé women also used their wealth and literacy to claim economic rights for all of Libreville's African residents. For some women, the provision of sexual and domestic services to European men also resulted in their ownership of property. After departing from Gabon, some European men left the cement homes in which they had lived to their Mpongwé wives.

This made some Mpongwé women among the most wealthy of Libreville's African inhabitants. Women's independent wealth paved the way for them to have a political voice alongside Mpongwé men in efforts to assert African economic rights in face of colonial tax increases. In November 1919, Angélique Bouyé, an Mpongwé woman, wrote a letter to French officials complaining that the amount of poll tax to be paid had increased in the past year from 3 to 5 francs.[107] Bouyé claimed to be writing on behalf of Libreville residents, and the inspector of colonies to whom she addressed the letter referred to her as the spokesperson for the city's African residents. Bouyé requested that colonial officials cease in instituting further tax increases. Moreover, Bouyé's letter included specific requests on behalf of women in Libreville. She complained that African soldiers collecting taxes wrongfully arrested African women on the pretext that they had not paid taxes.[108] Bouyé concluded the letter with the request that female property owners who paid the land tax be exempt from the poll tax.

While French colonial personnel expressed anxiety about women's sexual promiscuity and prostitution in Libreville, colonial economic policies set in motion the very currents in which women's sexual labor was a viable path for earning money. Fang communities could also make money from women's sexual labor, with African men of Equatorial African or West African origins.[109] In a 1913 annual report, the governor of Gabon opined that the social ills of Mpongwé men's laziness and their reliance on women's sexual labor to make money had spread to other ethnic groups migrating to Libreville. The governor surmised, "Whatever the origin of the [native] inhabitant of Libreville, his mentality quickly becomes that of a Gabonese. The prostitution of women is elevated to the level of an institution; as a result the poll tax is an illusory obligation."[110] The governor's words illuminate how cash had become the method of obtaining sex and how the money earned permitted some Fang men to pay the new and perpetually increasing tax requirements. Some Fang husbands in polygynous marriages consented for their wives to have sexual relationships for a certain number of nights with African laborers who had migrated to the Estuary region's timber camps in search of work.[111] The migrant men could travel with the women to another location and would return the wives after the stipulated amount of time and remit the agreed-upon payments of cash or goods to the husbands. In 1918, an inspector's report of the Estuary region noted that tirailleurs would set up temporary unions with married or unmarried women in Fang villages in which they were sent to enforce the collection of taxes. Fathers or husbands would consent for sexual relationships with female dependents to occur. The soldiers would pay a "bridewealth" fee for sexual access to a woman, and the husband or father would in turn remit the money given by the tirailleur to the village chief as the tax payment.[112] Turning to these relationships did not appear to be motivated by efforts of husbands or fathers to become wealthy, but was rather a desperate act to meet tax obligations when families didn't have enough money.

As interracial unions continued to occur in early twentieth-century colonial Gabon, African and French societies shifted in their ideas about the desirability of interracial unions and of the respectability of women involved in such relationships. On a day-to-day basis, African women and European men engaged openly in domestic-sexual relationships, with little censure from French and African political figures. Yet, in moments of socioeconomic and political crisis, "native wives" appeared in public records as persons that impeded governance and contributed to a decline in moral and social order in Libreville. Particularly in moments of economic and food crisis that occurred in waves following World War I, some Myènè men sought to restrict Mpongwé women's social, economic, and political mobility.

Some women who engaged in interracial unions held a privileged status, allowing them to escape colonial regulation of African communities, which resulted in the ire of African men. This especially was true when colonial officials extracted forced labor or increased taxes from African populations after World War I, yet seemed to exempt some Mpongwé women. In efforts to rationalize the production of timber toward the benefit of French interests, officials attempted to limit the autonomy of Myènè men who had managed to obtain permits for large forestry concessions and become wealthy from exporting timber. In 1921, a letter signed "The Inhabitants of Lambaréné" arrived on the desk of the lieutenant governor in Libreville. Since 1918, the colonial state had required male and female subjects to perform ten days of labor per year. However, a provision had allowed wealthy Gabonese, usually male Myènè *forestiers* (timber industry exploiters), to pay cash rather than serving forced labor. Yet a 1921 law took away this option, ordering that "all native forestiers are required to perform forced labor. . . . None among them will be allowed to pay cash in lieu of their days of obligatory labor."[113] The letter writers signaled the hypocrisy of this law, since European forestiers who did business in the same manner as African forestiers did not have to perform labor. They protested the existence of two systems of laws regulating forestiers: one for Europeans, the other for Africans.

Gabonese women's relationships with European men allowed them to attain higher status in the new colonial order compared to Gabonese men, thereby disrupting an imagined gender relationship of women's political and economic subjugation. The letter writers remonstrated that female lovers of Europeans occupied a privileged status that allowed them to escape the new racialized forced-labor requirements: "In enforcing this law, is the circumscription commissioner going to make his native wife, his domestic servant work! And the women who live in debauchery with Europeans, will he make them work or even have to buy out their days of obligatory labor? If he intends to execute orders as received, why apply regulations to some and not to all?"[114] As implied in this letter, in the new colonial differentiation between Africans and Europeans, black and white, the woman lover of a European man occupied the status of "European." The letter writers' social status had declined. Reordering former hierarchies of men's greater access to wealth, female lovers and live-in domestic companions to European men could now rise to a status of privilege formerly granted to Myènè men. The categorization of interracial relationships as "debauchery" also implied condemnation of these women as morally suspect, living outside normative sexual relationships that benefited male heads of households. No longer did a woman's relationship with a European benefit an entire community, but it individually placed her at a level above other "natives."

While Mpongwé women's family members might have brokered, approved, or acquiesced to their unions with European men, involvement in these relations did reorder power relationships within Mpongwé communities. Conflict over property could sometimes escalate among kin, as represented in a story recounted by French journalist Albert Londres of his voyage to Libreville in the late 1920s. En route on a ship, Londres encountered a European man named Rass who said that he had lived with a woman whom he identified as "ma Gabonaise" in Libreville for seven years. Her aunts had poisoned and killed her, Rass claimed, in order to gain control of her clothing and the hut (*case*) that he had left to her after he departed.[115] Poisoning was a common manifestation in Mpongwé communities to control recalcitrant members of society or to exact justice over a disagreement, and some older women were the most skilled practitioners.[116] When Rass arrived with Londres at the house in which he and his wife had lived, Rass was shocked to find that the aunts whom he said poisoned her now lived in the case. He accused the aunts of killing her because with her death they inherited all of her property. The unnamed woman's individual ownership of the house and clothing, and her unwillingness to allow her aunts to access this wealth, challenged the authority of senior women over junior women.

generational conflict control

Mpongwé women's independent accumulation of wealth through interracial relationships also provided a pathway to question the authority of Mpongwé chiefs, who claimed political control over residents, and of colonial officials, who sought to direct how women earned and spent their money. In earlier years of colonial rule, colonial projects had attempted to turn Mpongwé men into peasant producers of foodstuffs and cash crops or laborers on European plantations.[117] Amid the food shortages of the 1920s, colonial officials blamed the shortages on the supposed laziness of Mpongwé populations and their lack of participation in agricultural production. Officials turned to Mpongwé chiefs in an effort to compel Mpongwé women to farm, as did women of other ethnicities, to produce more food for the town's population. Yet a chief testified to a 1922 commission of inquiry on the availability of food: "He [the mayor of Libreville] advised us to work in food cultivation like in other countries, that those who put in real efforts would be compensated. We responded that this was good! But it is you others, Europeans, who prevent our women from working because they earn too much with you."[118] The chief relayed that the cash and material resources that European men gave their Mpongwé wives provided women with enough earnings to refuse agricultural work. Another chief argued, "In the past, our women worked on the land, but today they no longer want to and they no longer listen to us!"[119] Mpongwé patriarchs could not fully control Mpongwé women's labor or how Mpongwé women would participate in the colonial economy.

On a January morning in 1922, a group of sixty mainly Mpongwé women, some holding children in their arms, mounted a cacophonous demonstration at the town hall before the mayor, his deputy, and the police commissioner.[120] The group of women arrived at the mayor's office in response to a rumor. Officials had allegedly announced the day before that all farmers, mainly Fang inhabitants of Libreville's hinterlands, were to bring produce to city hall, where colonial officials would purchase their products at preset prices, instead of to the public market, where Fang farmers could control the prices. Colonial officials would then ration and distribute food to the city's African and European inhabitants. The investigative report following the women's protest summarized the assembled women as "Mpongwé, without a profession or living in concubinage with Europeans; three or four among them claimed to be seamstresses or washerwomen who have found themselves to be without work or money, although they were luxuriously dressed and well shod."[121] The report characterized the women as "lazy," refusing to work in agricultural labor that would have yielded produce to relieve the shortage of food. Rather, the women would arrive at the market early and purchase large quantities of food, leaving nothing for wage laborers, who could not reach the market until the end of their workday.

Libreville's colonial officials reacted angrily to the women's demonstrations, noting that they had asked the women to present themselves individually, not in a group, and that a committee of male Mpongwé notables had already convened earlier in the week to address native concerns over food rationing. It was the male chiefs, not this ad hoc gathering of women, whom officials viewed as the authorized intermediaries with the colonial state. Though the women were asked to leave the premises, some refused, and four were arrested in an attempt to compel those who remained to disband.

This gathering of an all-female Mpongwé delegation asserted that women could claim a political voice and directly address the colonial state without African men as intermediaries.[122] The Mpongwé women gathered at city hall challenged Mpongwé gender and colonial stratifications—thereby proving to be "dangerous" women, as seen by colonial officials and elder Mpongwé men. Women's provision of sexual and domestic services to European men simultaneously circulated colonial capital into African communities, yet threatened colonial plans for socioeconomic and political management. As alluded to in the summary of the encounter, many of these women were currently or had been previously engaged in relationships with European men. They invoked their visible positions as taxed property owners and conspicuous consumers with money to protest state attempts to restrict their purchasing power and redirect their labor into agricultural production. Carrying children in their arms, some perhaps the métis children of colonial officials, the women cited their roles as mothers and caretakers of children as justification for their privileged access to food. Unlike the Igbo women's protests in 1929 Nigeria, Mpongwé women did not protest in order to reclaim roles of the precolonial past.[123] Mpongwé women were protesting in order to maintain the privileged existence that they had gained within the transition to colonial rule. The investigation concluded that other African inhabitants of Libreville applauded the women's arrests. The approbation of townspeople at the women's imprisonment indicates how less-affluent African urbanites might have resented the privileged status that the women sought to retain as others went hungry and felt the impact of colonial efforts to increase their labor and constrain the money that they could make.

Amid the political, social, and economic upheavals, colonial and health personnel assessing demographic data in the first two decades of the twentieth century determined that African populations throughout the colony were decreasing.[124] By the 1920s, French medical officials and missionaries reported the disappearances of entire villages that they had visited in the early years of the twentieth century.[125] In a 1920 article, a French doctor who headed the colony's health service described Gabon as "a sick country" with a diminishing population, insufficient food supply, elevated rates of morbidity, and reduced fertility.[126] By 1929, a colonial medical report estimated that the population of the entire colony was 334,000 inhabitants, reduced from estimates of 403,000 people in 1924.[127] Furthermore, the document conveyed, 10 percent of women in some villages were sterile, and the infant mortality rate was about 50 percent. Colonial states and societies in the Belgian Congo, Kenya, and Malawi reported similar anxieties regarding population stagnation or decrease.[128] Among the factors of communicable disease epidemics, forced labor, and food shortages that contributed to demographic decline and mortality in Gabon, colonial state and society settled upon African marital and sexual practices, transformed by colonial rule, as the principal culprit.

A chorus of colonial health personnel, colonial officials, and Christian missionaries settled upon the reduced fertility and morbidity as primarily caused by the prevalence of African women's extramarital sexuality, particularly in the coastal regions of southern Gabon such as the Estuary region. A 1930 publication on marriage and sexual practices, commissioned by an antislavery society and based on written surveys completed by colonial administrators in the 1910s and 1920s throughout French-controlled Africa, encapsulates these views. Written by West African colonial administrator Maurice Delafosse, the monseigneur for French Africa Le Roy, and a medical professional identified as Dr. Poutrin, the introduction argued that colonial rule thwarted the establishment of stable marriages and fecund families by making women into commodities. First, African women's sexual promiscuity with African and European men spread sexually transmitted diseases that compromised male and female fertility and were often passed on to children.[129] Second, the expansion of the timber economy and the circulation of money had resulted in increased bridewealth prices. Delafosse, Poutrin, and Le Roy reported that the 1910 bridewealth list for the marriage of a Fang woman and a man of unspecified ages in the Estuary region was

3,000 francs' worth of goods: 15 stone guns, 80 small barrels of gunpowder, 20 pieces of cloth, 10 machetes, 8 crates, 5 bags of salt, 1 vest, and 1 mutton or dog.[130] By the 1920s, bridewealth in coastal regions ranged from 1,000 to 3,000 francs, the same worth of goods as in the 1910s, but it was now composed of 70 percent cash, a large sum that made marriage difficult for young men.[131]

Customary practices already allowed for divorce, but women and their families increasingly sought out divorce in order to earn the higher bridewealth amounts paid by new suitors. To save the colony and ensure the biological reproduction of African societies would require the regulation of African women's and men's bodies, French colonial state and society and Catholic representatives would argue. As noted by Lynn Thomas, European states exhibited great interest in questions of "regulating sexual behavior and promoting the growth of national populations" in the early twentieth century, and "colonial rule in Asia and Africa fueled these reproductive concerns by situating the definition of and maintenance of racial, cultural, and sexual boundaries as important state projects."[132]

With the view toward forming African families that would buttress the colony's demographic growth, the French argued for the need to codify and regulate marital and conjugal relationships in Gabon. Between 1918 and 1925, state and Catholic personnel launched the first efforts toward codifying customary laws. Such efforts came later than elsewhere in colonial-era Africa. By the late nineteenth and early twentieth centuries in French West Africa, colonial administrators, armchair ethnologists, and missionaries had compiled customary practices of many African societies.[133] By the 1920s, codified versions of customary law existed in many British colonies.[134] The 1921 eleven-member customary law commission in Gabon included mostly Frenchmen: medical and administrative civil servants, representatives from Protestant and Catholic missions, and the president of the Planter, Businessmen, and Settler Association. The two African members, one a Fang and the other an Mpongwé, were civil servants of the colonial state. The governor's annual report summarized the committee's mandate to "reorganize the native family" through facilitating marriage for young people by decreasing bridewealth amounts, limiting adultery and the prostitution of wives by husbands, making divorce more difficult, and prohibiting the marriage of prepubescent girls.[135] The commission was charged with producing a set of laws that would serve as a blueprint for local administrators and African auxiliaries in enforcing social order. Documents do not detail the opinions of the African members of the committee. However, a report by member Monsignor Matrou encapsulated the common goal of state and church members of the commission, which was to establish immutable written laws to ensure that all African men could find a wife and to make marriages last. Stable marriages, in turn, would increase birth rates.[136]

The various drafts of customary marriage law that emerged from 1922 to 1925 reveal the conflict between church and state regarding which institutions had the authority to determine what types of marriages would be allowable. Catholic officials viewed marriage as a spiritual contract, of monogamous men and women, consecrated by priests who were intermediaries between humans and God. Colonial bureaucrats viewed marriage as a civil contract, to be consecrated and recorded before those appointed by the colonial state. Church officials argued that polygamy should be discouraged and eventually made illegal. The church sought to add "liberty of consciousness" as grounds for divorce—women could leave a polygamous marriage in order to enter a monogamous one.[137] Colonial administrators viewed polygamy as ingrained in African practice and feared that efforts to abolish polygamy could result in revolt against the colonial state. Church officials also argued that bridewealth was equivalent to the sale of women and argued for strict limits on bridewealth.[138] Yet some colonial administrators viewed the monetization of bridewealth payments as a transformation that benefited the colonial economy, given that the need for bridewealth cash provided incentive for African men to participate in wage labor. Bridewealth amounts should, the governor argued, fluctuate according to wages. Colonial officials did worry that elder men with female dependents would ask for high cash payments in order to tap into the cash earnings of young men.[139] However, the governor concluded that the need to alleviate the acute labor shortage for French enterprises was a greater imperative.

Drafts emerging from the commission recognized the state, not the church, as the arbiter of African marriages. Initial drafts specified that all marriages between Africans were to be consecrated and recorded in a register maintained by the subdivision administrator of the bride's village of origin in order to be considered legal.[140] The 1922 draft sent to the governor-general subsequently erased the requirement that administrators witness all marriages, explaining that it was too cumbersome.[141] The final version completed in 1925 defined marriage as a relationship consensually entered into by men and women who had reached puberty, with established rules for consecrating marriages and regulating divorce. Bridewealth was to be paid in cash instead of goods and be limited to between 250 and 400 francs for matrilineal and patrilineal groups in certain regions.[142] Reflecting that African societies along the coast had more cash than those in the interior, bridewealth limits were higher in coastal regions.[143] Modifying the practice of levirate marriage, the proposal allowed that a widow could choose whether she wanted to remain in her husband's family or return to her own after reimbursing the portion of bridewealth deemed just by a French administrator. The parameters within which husbands could divorce their wives were limited to instances of adultery, repeated absences from the conjugal home, crimes committed, and "bad behavior."[144] Grounds on which wives could request a divorce were limited to instances in which the husband gave her a communicable disease, refused to provide for material needs, was excessively physically abusive, or had committed a crime. It was not disagreement between church and state that resulted in the failure of the first codification efforts, but the resistance of higher levels of administration to consider codifying customary law.

Responding to initial calls of Gabon's governor to codify laws in 1921, FEA Governor-General Alfassa urged him to act with "extreme prudence," for fear that African societies could mutiny against the state's efforts to modify customs. Alfassa also cautioned that efforts toward codification required careful and long-term research to ensure that the gathered information about customary practice was accurate. Furthermore, codifying customary law risked delaying African societies in their evolution. Rather than creating bodies of law, the governor-general agreed for administrators to gather ethnographic data in the forms of reports and monographs about the customs of varied "tribes."[145] In 1925, Gabon's governor sent a final proposal codifying customary marriage law to the governor-general. In a terse response, the governor-general rejected the document altogether, arguing, "This question of the reorganization of the native family is particularly delicate. . . . We cannot resolve such a problem in a one and a half page document."[146] At the local level of governance in Gabon, the French were zealous to enact social change, struggling between church and state to determine the parameters of the civilizing mission. Church and state alike sought not only to weaken the power of senior men to determine when and to whom women and junior men would be married, but also to ensure that African women's sexuality would be contained within marriages. However, higher-level administrators were hesitant to legislate marriage and sexual practices.

CONCLUSION

The era of timber ushered in intersecting paths of economic opportunity and loss, migration toward and movement out of Libreville, and social dislocation and consolidation. Converging with the okoumé rush, townspeople participated in a sexual economy of women's extramarital sexual labor to generate cash and goods to maneuver their social status, meet tax obligations, and provide basic needs. Material benefits from the sexual economy benefited the husbands, fathers, and other male kin of women to stabilize or increase their economic status through the fluctuations of the timber market and the consolidation of colonial rule. At times, the sexual economy provided openings for women who were able to accumulate independent wealth, allowing them to claim political rights against colonial directives that would limit the autonomy of Africans to direct their labor, time, and money. Marital relationships among Africans were affected by social, political, and economic instability, which resulted in the increased unaffordability of bridewealth payments for many African men and greater opportunity for African women to extract themselves from undesired marriages. In differentiated ways, these sexual maneuvers worried colonial officials, missionaries, elite African men, and a new generation of chiefs, who were vying to enact social and political control over the colonial capital city. No concrete policy directives to regulate marriage and sex emerged from these decades, yet the contestations and debates reveal the fluidity of efforts to define and control Libreville's sexual and conjugal landscape that would continue for decades to come.

PART II

⮑

Libreville's Growth, 1930–1960

PART 2 ENCOMPASSES 1930 through 1960, years of tremendous migration and spatial expansion of Libreville, and concludes with the end point of decolonization. Chapter 3 lays out the chronological context of demographic, spatial, economic, and political change in these decades that are the heart of this book. Chapters 4–7 synchronistically analyze a particular theme of contestation and convergence of sexual economy and how praxes and discourses changed over these decades. Chapter 4 traces the impact of the expansion of a monetary economy on the significance of bridewealth, a foundational marker of marriage and a contested social, legal, and economic exchange. The emergence of what I call the bridewealth economy reflected the reconfiguration of ideas concerning what constituted marriage, masculinity, and the elasticity of precolonial concepts of wealth in people to shape the expansion of a capitalist economy.

Chapter 5 turns to the themes of urban landscapes and the social, affective, and legal geography of how men and women navigated sexual experiences within Libreville and its rural suburbs. Utilizing criminal and civil court records, oral histories, and ethnographies, the chapter analyzes negotiations of the hopes for and perils of the good life through sex. The chapter argues that shifting understandings of desire, material well-being, disease, and ideals of respectability informed the very human geography of the town. Chapter 6 analyzes the varied legal pathways of negotiating varied forms of relationship conflict via state, chief, and religious courts of justice. What constituted customary and civil law, and therefore the parameters of marriage, was highly contested. In staking claims to the control over property, money, and custody of children, Libreville's inhabitants outlined a multiplicity of conceptualizations of moral, social, and economic rights of and in marriage. Chapter 7 investigates interracial sexual and domestic unions between Gabonese women, continuing to be predominantly of Mpongwé ethnicity, and white men of varied national origins. African women traversing racialized sexual boundaries also destabilized social orderings of gender, seniority, and wealth within African communities. Individual African women utilized such relationships to negotiate tenuous avenues toward social, economic, and legal mobility.

3 ↬ Migration and Governance
The Expansion of Libreville

BETWEEN 1930 AND 1960, Libreville became a pole of attraction for thousands of migrants from throughout the colony, and the city's borders expanded to incorporate Estuary hinterlands.[1] The hope for a better life shaped the decision of many to migrate. The town's ethnic makeup changed, from a town of primarily Mpongwé residents to one that reflected the multiplicity of Equatorial African ethnolanguage groups. Having money was of crucial necessity, and residents negotiated how to pursue wealth and status in the midst of booms and busts of the timber economy and ethnic differentiation about who was and who wasn't a true city person. Matters of urban planning and the spatial organization of Libreville continued to be tense, as newly arrived residents struggled to build sustainable living conditions and colonial personnel sought to maintain oversight over a town that grew with little government planning. With the circulation of increased numbers of people into, out of, and through the town, colonial administrators worried about how to maintain political control, social order, collect taxes, and direct residents' labor capacities. In the 1930s, African chiefs emerged as principal intermediaries of the colonial state and maintained day-to-day administration of Libreville's neighborhoods and Estuary villages. Yet, after World War II, elite, Christian, and literate African men competed to maintain control over governance and policy making in Libreville and broadcast their legitimacy to the rest of the colony and the broader French Empire. Converging with these changes in politics and economics were transformations in Libreville's

gender landscape. As in the first two decades of the twentieth century, there were more female than male residents in Libreville and the Estuary region for much of the 1930s. After World War II, a gender imbalance of more male than female residents for many ethnic groups took hold, a transformation that generated and was shaped by political and economic changes and that shaped residents' aspirations of urban becoming.

ATTRACTION IN THE MIDST OF BUST AND BOOM: MIGRATION AND POLITICAL CONTROL, 1930–1939

From 1930 to 1931, the okoumé boom that had reshaped southern Gabon over the course of the 1920s came to a crashing halt. Overspeculation and overproduction, as well as a decrease in the global demand for timber caused by the Depression, led to a catastrophic stoppage of the industry.[2] Okoumé exports decreased by 41 percent, from 381,774 tons to 224,379 tons.[3] A number of Gabon's timber industries went bankrupt and European employers were unable to pay their African laborers. The crash of the timber industry was catastrophic for Estuary residents, closing off the primary avenue through which people earned cash.[4] Though residents had little money, prices for imported goods and food only increased.[5]

Despite the precariousness of life in the administrative capital, Fang clans migrated toward the coast in increasing numbers in the 1930s.[6] The population of the subdivision of Libreville, the rural hinterlands of the city, reached seven thousand inhabitants by 1936. This growth in population was in stark contrast to the earlier decades of the century, in which census records indicated a population decline. A combination of push-and-pull factors drew Fang migrants. As timber camps let their workers go during the slowdown, timber companies decreased their purchases of foodstuffs from Fang farming communities, who moved closer to Libreville in search of ways to earn cash.[7] Wage workers previously employed in timber camps also moved to Libreville in search of work opportunities.[8] A 1934 report conjectured that the population increase was also due to the return of men who had previously been working as wage laborers in the timber industry in other parts of the colony. These men did not return alone but were accompanied by women they had married in the regions where they had worked.[9]

Okoumé exports rebounded in the later years of the 1930s to surpass pre-Depression levels, sparking another wave in immigration. As timber production began to increase, young men from interior regions migrated south to tap into economic opportunities, searching for cash, which was in rare circulation in rural areas.[10] New roads linking Libreville to northern regions predominantly populated by Fang groups made travel easier.[11] In 1937 the governor stated in a political report, "Finally Libreville is playing her role as a center of attraction."[12] The population of Libreville and its neighboring villages changed as the numbers of Fang surpassed the numbers of formerly predominant Mpongwé and other Myènè groups. One official reported that there were about one thousand Mpongwé remaining in the entire Estuary region from a total population of about thirty thousand inhabitants.[13] A 1938 political report by an Estuary administrator relayed that Mpongwé, Benga, Sékiani, and Akélé communities near Libreville were being "slowly surrounded by Pahouins."[14] Though other administrators countered that the reported decline of the Mpongwé was exaggerated, colonial personnel consistently reported that Fang communities appeared in greater numbers. Fang communities proliferating in villages remained wary of contact with the French. Village residents stayed in mobile settlements, entering the city only to engage in trade or sale of agricultural produce, and fleeing into the forest to escape colonial tax and forced-labor obligations. Yet other Fang communities also settled closer to the city's boundaries. By the end of the 1930s, the French expanded the city's boundaries to incorporate some of these villages as neighborhoods.

Libreville's port lacked the deep water necessary to support large freight ships, and thus the town of Port-Gentil surpassed Libreville in maritime traffic and became the center of industrial production.[15] However, wage-earning opportunities in the timber industry of the Estuary region were abundant, and the capital city remained a key hub of economic production and allure for African migrants.[16] In 1937, a colonial report stated that forestry companies employed 13,000 men across the colony, with an additional population of 4,000 women and 1,400 children living in timber yards.[17] About half of Gabon's forestry workers were in the Estuary department— 6,500 men were engaged in yearlong and short-term contracts in forestry and mining enterprises, and about 2,100 women and 723 children also lived in these timber yards.[18] The number of laborers working under contract in 1937 had increased fivefold since 1932.[19] The vastness of the numbers of wage laborers for private companies is striking, considering Gabon's sparse population, in comparison with more densely populated colonies in French Occidental (West) Africa (FOA). In comparison, 20,880 men in Ivory Coast, with a total population that far surpassed that of Gabon, worked for private enterprises in 1935.[20] While able-bodied men sought work as timber fellers (*coupers de bois*), agricultural cultivation by women continued, and to feed their employees, companies purchased the manioc and other crops Fang women cultivated.[21]

FIGURE 3.1. Population of the City of Libreville, 1931–1938[22]
-Statistics not reported for this year

Year	Women	Men	Children	Percentage of Adult Women/Men/Children	Total Population
1931	1,763	1,877	1,958	31/34/35	5,598
1932	1,981	1,816	2,404	32/29/39	6,201
1933	1,666	1,384	1,234	39/32/29	4,284
1935	-	-	-	-	5,426
1936	2,212	1,987	1,651	38/34/28	5,850
1937	2,232	1,997	1,661	38/34/24	5,890
1938	-	-	-	-	6,673

In the 1930s, Colonial personnel began census keeping for the subdivision of Libreville (the rural region surrounding Libreville) in addition to tallies on women, men, and children of the city Libreville. Throughout this decade, census records indicate that the population of women in Libreville and its hinterlands continued to nearly equal or exceed that of men. The recorded numbers reflect the dramatic increase in the number of Libreville's inhabitants from the previous decade (Figure 3.1). The city's population nearly doubled from 1930 to 1932, surging to more than 6,000 people. In his 1932 report, the governor attributed the population increase to "vagabonds" and "roaming populations," male wage laborers who had deserted the timber camps following the shutdown and moved to Libreville rather than going back to their regions of origin farther into the interior.[24] Amid the continued economic slowdown, the population decreased by nearly 2,000 people in 1933, only to increase by more than 1,100 people the next year and steadily increase to about 7,000 people by 1938. Population statistics for the rural subdivision of Libreville appear in the records for the first time in 1930, indicating a steady population of 7,000, give or take a few hundred people, over the course of the decade (Figure 3.2). For many years in the 1930s prior to World War II, the number of women surpassed that of men in both the city and the subdivision of Libreville. The governor noted in 1933 that the number of women surpassed that of men by about 4,000 for the entire Estuary circumscription.[25] As had been the case in the first two decades of the twentieth century, the population numbers for children suggest that not every woman gave birth. The numbers of children declined or remained stagnant in relation to the increases in male and female residents

FIGURE 3.2. Population of the Subdivision of Libreville
(does not include the city of Libreville) 1931–1938[23]
-Statistics not reported for this year

Year	Women	Men	Children	Percentage of Adult Women/Men/Children	Total Population
1931	2,728	2,919	1,450	38/41/21	7,097
1932	2,719	2,824	1,437	39/40/21	6,980
1933	3,211	2,301	1,460	46/33/21	6,972
1934	3,208	2,256	1,556	46/32/22	7, 020
1936	3,065	2,543	998	42/35/23	7,339
1937	3,177	2,436	902	44/34/22	7,190
1938	-	-	-	-	6,884

in the mid- to late 1930s. The birth rate appeared to be particularly low in the subdivision of Libreville, for which there was one child for every three women in 1937 and 1938.

Though the town's population increased through migration, the stagnation in birth rates and the numbers of children troubled colonial administrators. As Fang moved within Libreville, colonial officials argued, these communities experienced the rapid evolution toward a money economy without a commensurate system of moral and social order. The Estuary's residents rejected "customary laws" and the social and political control of the senior men who would enforce them. In the 1932 annual report, the governor wrote, "For Gabon, it is necessary to distinguish between the population of the interior that is strongly tied to their old customs . . . and the populations of Lambaréné, Libreville, and Port Gentil, evolved too quickly in a bad sense of the word, who have been freed from all ties to custom except for witchcraft. Among these people living as they please, to marry and remarry, the family is gradually losing its true shape."[26] Colonial administrators in Gabon looked to African chiefs to assist in the delineation and implementation of customary laws among populations in urban centers.

Colonial officials who were worried about how to maintain social and political control as the city's population increased, and who sought to enforce indirect rule and the power of chiefs, appointed men in Estuary villages and in town who would maintain order as auxiliaries of the colonial state.[27] Bolstering the authority of chiefs, the governor of Gabon argued in a 1932 report, would "reinforce the social armor of marriage and family."[28] In 1932 chiefs were appointed as judge-arbiters who would adjudicate litigation in newly reconfigured colonial courts under the supervision of French administrators.[29] Recognizing that recent migrants had formed new communities, administrators expanded city limits in 1934 to incorporate new villages and divided Libreville into twenty-five neighborhoods (*quartiers*), each with its own chief assisted by two or three advisers (*conseilleurs*).[30] Furthermore, administrators divided rural areas into fifteen *cantons* (administrative units), each assigned a chief. In addition to presiding over courts, chiefs held the duties of signaling the arrival in and departure of inhabitants from their neighborhoods to the colonial mayor's office, collecting taxes, and administering a census. Concurrent with the changes to chieftaincy in the 1930s, the French also renamed territorial administrative units from circumscriptions into departments (*départements*.) The head of each was a French administrator who was to manage chiefs within the department.

The idea that African societies were inherently organized around ethnic identity was at the core of how colonial officers viewed the infrastructure of indirect rule. In 1938, administrators appointed five group chiefs (*chefs de groupe*) for each of the major ethnolinguistic communities in the Estuary region. Colonial representatives scrambled to find leaders among the Fang and other populations to serve as appointed chiefs. Each group chief was to "be the designated representative of the administration in his sector and the liaison between the administration and the neighborhood chief."[31] The lieutenant governor also created regional councils of notables, composed of mainly elder men and a few young men.[32] Chiefs of varied ranks, advisers, and those appointed to councils were to act as the principal intermediaries between African populations and the colonial state.

Recruiting and expanding the duties of chiefs for groups other than Mpongwé was challenging; few of the ethnic groups who were newly arriving in Libreville spoke French, and few administrators spoke a Gabonese language.[33] Thus, administrators also sought to educate the sons of chiefs and looked toward younger men who had been educated in French mission schools as a new generation of chiefs. One such product of this effort was a Fang man named Léon Mba, the future prime minister of independent Gabon, who was educated in a Catholic mission station in the Estuary circumscription and appointed as a canton chief in the 1920s. Mba wrote and spoke French and authored essays on Fang history and customs that would shape jurisprudence in colonial courts after World War II.[34] These political infrastructures of 1930s Libreville, however, would be reconfigured after World War II, and transformations wrought by changing historical contexts.

Just as the First World War changed the relationship between France and its colonies, the Second World War reordered relations between the colonial state and its African "subjects." Along with the vast majority of the French Empire around the world, all the colonies in FOA decided to follow the Vichy regime.[35] Under the governorship of Félix Éboué, a black colonial official from French Guiana, Chad made the decision to align itself with the Free French Forces, which seized control of all of French Equatorial Africa (FEA).

Conditions of life were harsh for those who lived along the Gabon Estuary during World War II. Given internecine conflict between the French and the halt in international trade, the okoumé market stagnated.[36] Furthermore, the severing of ties with the metropole meant there was no money coming in to fund the colony. A majority of forestry societies were forced to liberate employees and stop all activity. Workers chose to stay in the Estuary region rather than return to their places of origin since they hoped that work would begin again. Wage laborers who once worked in timber yards throughout the colony streamed into Libreville as they searched for money, food, and resources.

To fuel the war effort, colonial officials compelled forced labor for road construction and the collection of rubber and palm kernels; taxes were also increased.[37] Foodstuffs of daily necessity, including sugar, milk, flour, bread, and meat, were rare and expensive. When meat and fish were available, crowds queued early in the morning, and there was not enough available for all the customers who sought the products. Colonial officials were alarmed at the massive rural exodus that was occurring, the large numbers of villages left with only women and old people, the crops not planted or harvested, and the possibility of famine breaking out again. The price of manioc doubled from 2 francs in 1938 to 4 francs in 1941. Farmers from villages close to Libreville redirected the sale of their produce to the town rather than to the few functioning timber yards, because people in town paid higher prices. West African Hausa immigrants who operated stores that sold soap, oil, and flour prospered. Colonial officials tried to set limits on prices for food and goods, but inflation was rampant.[38]

After the war timber production surged again, and the Estuary became the primary site of timber exploitation as forests elsewhere in Gabon were depleted. By 1943, the Estuary department housed nearly 50 percent of the wage laborers in the entire colony.[39] Reflective of the greater availability of cash, the French raised taxes in the city of Libreville and other urban centers such as Port-Gentil and Lambaréné, while residents in northern regions paid reduced rates.[40]

Free French forces during World War II placed this previously neglected region at the center stage of French colonial governance. An invigorated attention to "the development" of African communities led to a number of new policies intended to shape labor and social and family life.[41] Creating such policies necessitated new forms of knowledge about African societies to replace those furnished in previous decades by the subdivision-head ethnographer or missionary ethnographer. The Institute for Central African Studies was founded in Brazzaville in 1947 and staffed with social scientists to conduct research on FEA milieus under changing social conditions, which could lead to more effective social and economic development policies.[42] The theme of urbanization in FEA was of particular interest in these new paths of social science research and thought. Along with Georges Balandier, sociologist Guy Lasserre was at the leading edge. In 1958, Lasserre wrote a book on urban planning in Libreville and transformations in the town's human and physical geography, the only such analysis of colonial-era urbanism in Gabon.[43] The studies of Balandier and Lasserre provide some precious glimpses into the changing fabric of life and topography in the town during the 1940s and 1950s, filling in the evidentiary gaps created by the inexistence of municipal archives. Yet, as argued by Henrietta Moore and Megan Vaughan in their study of changing gender relations and agricultural production in nineteenth- and twentieth-century Zambia, colonial-era ethnographies should be used critically as source materials for African history. Moore and Vaughan urge scholars to use anthropological texts as "both a record and an interpretation."[44] As such, I glean data about changing forms of urbanisms from the ethnographies of Balandier and Lasserre, but with the careful contextualization and critical assessment of the breakdown model of African societies that framed their interpretations.

In the midst of and after World War II, a sustained rural exodus from interior regions toward Libreville resulted in unprecedented growth and a reordering of the town's human and economic geography. The 1940s witnessed the massive desertion of Gabon's rural areas in the northeast and western regions. Ethnic groups previously nonresident or existing only in small numbers in the region of the Gabon Estuary increasingly appeared. Peoples from Ngounié, Haut-Ogooué, Nyanga, Moyen-Ogooué, and Ogooué-Ivindo departments arrived, first settling in Kango or Estuary forests and then heading to Libreville. Walking by foot for several weeks or traversing rivers in pirogues, migrants came carrying their meager possessions. Gabonese historian Léon Modest Nnang Ndong argues that the relative poverty of rural areas in the interior pushed people out of those regions.[45] Fang clans that formerly resided in the rural outreaches of the Estuary department also moved within Libreville's limits. A wave of Fang migration occurred from 1945 to 1946, after elephants destroyed villages and farms on the left bank of the Estuary.[46] The resurgence of the timber industry attracted people who hoped for work and social elevation. Many newcomers found initial refuge and housing with relatives who had already established themselves in the town.[47] A 1961 demographic survey of Libreville demonstrates the extent to which the post–World War II surge of people marked the city: only 21 percent of the population claimed to be native to Libreville; 26 percent had arrived before 1946, but 53 percent arrived between 1946 and 1961.[48]

No single group could claim majority, and Libreville was ethnically diverse. By 1948, the ethnic makeup of the city had changed. Colonial censuses estimated that Libreville was 35.5 percent Fang and 14.5 percent Mpongwé, with the remaining 50 percent representing various populations from Gabon's fifty-three ethnic groups, including the Akélé, Ouroungou, Bapunou, Nkomi, Benga, Sékiani, Galoa, Boulou, Eschira, and Nzebi.[49] By 1953, the Fang had grown to an estimated 43 percent of the population and the Mpongwé to 18 percent.[50] A French missionary passing through Libreville in 1948 remarked on the wide range of African residents he saw in the city: "A heterogeneous crowd of the country's tribes traverse the city's paths of red earth; there is even the inevitable sighting of the blue *bou bou* of a Muslim."[51] Africans from elsewhere in French Africa and Anglophone West Africa represented a significant portion of the population, about 14 percent, or 2,200 people, according to the 1953 census.[52] Given the ethnolinguistic diversity, French was the lingua franca on the streets of Libreville, and speaking French was an indication of status.

The gendered demographics of Libreville and its rural suburbs during and following World War II reveal a dramatic shift in comparison to prior years—men now outnumbered women. Analyzing the gender demographics of Libreville's African population is challenging for the post–World War II period. Many of the annual reports for the years after 1942, which may have contained census records, are missing from archives in Gabon and France. However, the newly constituted health department tracked some gendered population data as the French attempted to manage the question of biological reproduction. The following tables present the recorded population of the Libreville region after 1939, with some years missing due to gaps in census records.

FIGURE 3.3. Population of the City of Libreville, 1939–1960[53]
-Statistics not reported for this year

Year	Women	Men	Girls	Boys	Children	Total Population
1939	2,292	1,957	-	-	1,508	5,757
1941	2,706	2,870	209	208	-	5,993
1943	3,454	4,212	960	1,211	-	9,837
1945	-	-	-	-	-	11,866
1946	5,698	7,237	1,825	2,184	-	16,944
1947	-	-	-	-	-	11,152
1950	-	-	-	-	-	11,432
1951	-	-	-	-	-	18,230
1953	6,369	8,834	-	-	-	15,203
1955	-	-	-	-	-	15,255
1956	6,226	7,280	2,767	2840	-	19,133
1960	-	-	-	-	-	27,400

Due to several factors, including how French officials determined who was a resident, these numbers cannot be said to provide an exact recording of Libreville's population. Some years the count was based on who had a *carte d'identité* and other years included "the floating population," those who did not have such a card.[55] In 1936, colonial laws required Africans to obtain a pass from their home province to travel to Libreville and to carry the pass in an identity card, but Africans irregularly applied for the cards and the measure remained unimplemented for the most part.[56] Undoubtedly, some townsmen absconded to the forests at census-taking time in order to avoid tax collection. These statistics are useful, however, in indicating broad shifts that occurred in the town's makeup. The populations of the town and its rural surroundings increased dramatically from 1939 to 1960, an increase of nearly 400 percent.[57] By 1956, the city of Libreville housed 40 percent of the population of the Estuary department.[58]

An aspect of the accelerated wave of migration that began during World War II in Libreville and other towns was that a significant proportion of new migrants to the city limits were young men, single or unaccompanied by wives. In Lambaréné, only about one-third of migrant laborers were accompanied by their wives.[59] This imbalance appears to have been similar in Libreville. The above table indicates that in Libreville from 1942 onward,

FIGURE 3.4. Population of the Subdivision of Libreville
(does not include the city of Libreville), 1939–1955[54]
-Statistics not reported for this year

Year	Women	Men	Girls	Boys	Children	Total Population
1939	3,097	2,428	-	-	1,715	7,240
1942	3,150	2,547	871	1,082		7,650
1945	3,106	2,256	-	-		5,362
1947	3,481	4,069	1195	1415		10,160
1948	3, 640	4,367	-	-		8,007
1955						43,488

men were recorded to have outnumbered women by a few hundred. In the subdivision of Libreville from 1947 onward, these numbers relay that men outnumbered women by about a thousand. A 1955 survey recorded that for every 100 women who were fifteen years of age and older, there were 134 men in the city and subdivision of Libreville. This gender imbalance was higher than that of other cities in Gabon. In the city and subdivision of Port-Gentil, for every 100 women there were 120 men, and in the city of Lambaréné, there were 114 men for every 100 women.[60]

In Libreville, the ratio of women to men varied according to neighborhood and whether the inhabitants were relatively recent migrants or had lived in the city prior to 1939. The number of women and men remained nearly equal in a neighborhood such as Glass—composed of Mpongwé and Fang who had settled in the city prior to World War II. In neighborhoods of newly arrived migrants, the dominant population was men. For example, a 1958 survey indicates that the neighborhood of Nombakélé was composed of 2,600 residents, mainly newly arrived single young Fan men who had been laborers in Estuary forest camps. Per 1,000 men between the marriageable ages of fifteen and forty-five, there were only about 522 women—nearly two men for each woman residing in the neighborhood.[61] The oversupply of men to women was an occurrence not just in the city, but in the entire subdivision. A 1957 demographic survey detailed the subdivision of Libreville's sex ratio over the preceding twenty years. The ratio of women to men gradually improved but remained skewed. Between 1938 and 1942, there were 803 women per 1,000 men, while by the years 1953–1957, there were 920 women per 1,000 men.[62] The male-to-female ratio in Libreville was better than that of other cities in FEA, such as Brazzaville, which had an average of about 760 women per 1,000 men in 1957.[63] Yet the 1960 census revealed continued gender disparity, with a recorded population of 56 men for every 44 women.[64]

Though the overall population of adult men and women increased in the post–World War II years, the percentage of children in Libreville remained steady at 24 to 25 percent of the population. The small population of children had better access to French education than elsewhere in French Africa. Lasserre estimated that the number of children going to school was one of the highest on the entire continent, with 90 percent of children in Libreville attending at least a few years of primary school, just enough time to learn how to speak French, read, write, and count. Though gender disparities in schooling existed—girls accounted for 32 percent of primary school pupils and 19 percent of (the equivalent of) junior high pupils—these numbers still represent a relatively elevated number of African girls attending school.[65] Libreville residents widely professed to be Catholic, with a 1958 church report relaying that 90 percent of the city's population were "so-called" and "superficial" members of the church.[66] The colonial state operated a few secular schools, but it was Catholic schools that educated about 60 percent of students throughout Gabon.[67]

Anxieties about how gender ratios in cities resulted in population decline reached a crescendo during the post–World War II period, validated by new social-scientific and statistical studies. In spite of census records that indicated the population of the Estuary region increased fivefold between 1939 and 1959, a decrease in the birth rate and high infant mortality relayed demographic decline. In a 1944 report for the entire Estuary department, a health official warned, "The demographic situation is only getting worse." The official estimated that for the year, there were only 148 children born in the city of Libreville and 70 born in the subdivision.[68] In a 1947 report, the head of the subdivision of Libreville reported that there was only one child for every three adults in that year's census.[69] A 1950 law decreed that demographic studies were to be completed in the largest towns throughout Overseas France, including a focus on the distribution of sexes and "the sex-ratio problem."[70] A 1956 FEA-wide census recorded the average size of an African family in Libreville as 2.6 people, compared to 4.3 people in rural areas.[71]

As in previous decades, the French viewed the problem of decreased fertility and demographic growth in the heart of the colony's most populous center as being the result of "the marriage crisis." The post-1939 marriage crisis, as articulated by colonial officials and missionaries, was a decline in marriage rates. Lasserre encapsulated French worries of how

FIGURE 3.5. Marital Status by Ethnicity and Gender of Inhabitants of Libreville, 1944[74]

Ethnic Group	Not Married	
	Men	Women
Fang	32.1%	28.5%
Sékiani	40%	42.5%
Mpongwé	54.3%	38.5%

the sex-ratio problem led to the "valorization" of women and "the dissolution of morals, prostitution and a slowing down of the birth rate."[72] When referring to the "valorization" of women, Lasserre meant that the limited number of women held tremendous social and economic value. Bridewealth costs were spiraling. Marriage was increasingly unattainable for young men. Colonial officials worried that prostitution provided an avenue for women to be economically independent and refuse to marry. Health officials conjectured that high rates of infertility in women and sterility in men were due to venereal diseases caused by women's sexual promiscuity.[73] These ideals of marriage as a normative relationship, essential to the "functioning" of African societies, were also espoused by Libreville's male and female residents and African political leaders. Yet this "norm" did not appear to be a lived reality for most of Libreville's inhabitants. The 1944 census recorded statistics on marriage rates, along with the annual demographic data for the three most populous ethnic groups: Fang, Mpongwé, and Sékiani (Figure 3.5).

These results indicate that the ideal of every man and woman of marriageable age being married was not universally actualized. Almost one-third of Fang men over the age of fifteen remained unmarried, and the rate for women was comparable at 28 percent. Marriage rates were much lower for the small ethnolanguage group Sékiani, with the percentage of unmarried women at 42 percent and men at 40 percent. For the Mpongwé, the marriage rate was sharply distinct by gender. Almost 55 percent of men were single, compared to 40 percent of women. Though post–World War II Libreville's population reflected all of Gabon's varied ethnic groups, few people intermarried, and antagonisms between different ethnic groups abounded.[75] As the gender and ethnic makeup of the city changed, questions about where people would live, how they would make a living, and how they would differentiate themselves were also part of the processes of urban becoming.

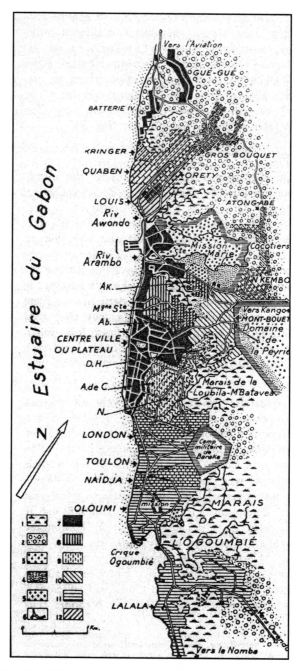

MAP 3.1. Libreville's African Neighborhoods, ca. 1957. (Reproduced from Guy Lasserre, *Libreville: La ville et sa région*, 30.)

Where Africans lived within the city reflected some ethnic self-segregation. By the 1950s Libreville was composed of twelve African neighborhoods, which were further divided into twenty-two villages. Colonial officials incorporated villages that they had considered hinterlands within Libreville's borders. Lasserre recorded that an Mpongwé informant characterized the Fang as "not really city people," engaging in nonurban labor, with men fishing and women smoking and selling fish.[76] Furthermore, Fang who had lived along the Gabon Estuary for a few generations regarded the new arrivals as less civilized.[77] New arrivals were concentrated in the periphery of the city's borders, and Mpongwé remained closer to the plateau in the neighborhoods of Louis and Glass. Fang communities that originated from the rural areas on the left bank of the Estuary settled in the neighborhoods of Lalala, Antong-Abé, Nkembo, and Cocotiers. Fang communities from elsewhere in Gabon and other ethnic groups scattered throughout the city. The area of Nombakélé, close to the center of the city, was inhabited mainly by new arrivals of varied ethnic groups and by Africans from other regions, such as Hausa from Nigeria or Senegalese.[78] By 1961 there were close to thirty neighborhoods. The rural suburbs continued to be "the bread basket of Libreville," composed of farming communities of varied ethnicities.[79]

Although they welcomed the population surge, officials sought to enforce strict boundaries between the European plateau and both the newly forming and the already established African neighborhoods. A 1939 urban plan was to rationalize and control the growth of the physical space of Libreville. Seeking to keep Africans out of areas designated for whites, the mayor hired a team of urban planners to create a plan that divided the city into lots. Provisions included that African residents be required to ask for a property title for the land on which they lived and to pay a new property tax. As in response to colonial efforts at urban planning in previous decades, the 1939 plan incensed Mpongwé inhabitants of the Glass and Louis neighborhoods, who insisted that they had ancestral rights to the land and refused to abide by the requirement for a title.[80] In 1947, the administration settled Mpongwé land claims, which had plagued previous efforts to expand European areas, by compensating Mpongwé communities 20 million francs for the buyout of some land. Yet the French were not able to establish the total segregation of European neighborhoods from African neighborhoods. Mpongwé maintained their neighborhoods—Glass and Louis—of cement houses in close proximity to the plateau. The above map of 1957 Libreville reveals that African neighborhoods enclosed the plateau. Commissions drafted urban plans in 1946, 1950, and 1955 to direct where African neighborhoods could be located and to determine the extension of electrical and sanitation services to these areas, but none of these plans seem to have been implemented.[81]

Rather than Libreville expanding as a city planned by the French, Africans built and created neighborhoods and colonial officials scrambled to provide sanitation services as a critical mass of inhabitants appeared. During slumps in the timber industry, officials were especially worried about the numbers of "vagabonds," unemployed men with no fixed housing.[82] Men without wage-labor contracts were not paying taxes, were living off of others, and were sporadically sent to jail for vagrancy. Fang communities also struggled with French efforts to direct their housing. The 1955 Urban Plan of Libreville proposed a project that would displace the inhabitants of Lalala to a new neighborhood. The new site was to be in Batavia, a quarter closer to the center of the city and an area that a French urban planner deemed "safer for habitation."[83] Lalala existed on a swamp, making it a breeding ground for mosquitoes. The plan proposed to drain the swampy area of Batavia, fill it in, construct concrete housing, and have one thousand residents of Lalala move in.[84] Records do not indicate why, but the plan was never implemented. It is possible that Fang communities refused to move or perhaps city administrators lacked the funding. Lasserre compared the "disorderly" nature of African settlements in Libreville with the planned communities in other cities of Equatorial French Africa. He emphasized that though Brazzaville and Pointe Noire had larger populations than Libreville, these cities had one and two African neighborhoods respectively.[85] Urban planners continued to be confounded by the environmental features of the Estuary department, surrounded by rivers and composed of swamplands, in which illnesses such as malaria and yellow fever proliferated. Health officials endeavored to reduce epidemics through sporadically spraying African quarters with insecticides and through vaccination campaigns.[86]

Colonial administrators spent more money on Libreville's built environment after World War II. Most of the efforts were concentrated on areas in which whites lived. The French managed to expand the plateau by five kilometers, constructing new housing and government buildings and paving the streets.[87] Between 1942 and 1947, the French extended the road network throughout the colony from 512 kilometers to 2,331 kilometers of primary roads and 8,000 kilometers of secondary roads, the largest infrastructural investment in Gabon.[88] In the late 1940s and 1950s, the government enlarged the port to accommodate larger ships, built a radio tower, and expanded the hospital to accommodate more African patients.[89]

Libreville's African residents shaped the city's built environment, constructing homes, creating and tending gardens, and carving out passageways to move about the town. European visitors described the town as more of a rural space than a city. Balandier characterized French colonial capital cities such as Dakar, Abidjan, and Douala as "modern," with great bursts of construction, while "only Libreville remains languid among its coconut and palm trees, old fashioned and so typically colonial."[90] Furthermore, Balandier decried Libreville as a "remote administrative seat, unused sham port, the city seems to endure only to affirm its loyalty to a past full of still glorious memories."[91] Lasserre described the overall look of Libreville as quaint, resembling a nineteenth-century trading post, in contrast to the urban decay in quarters such as the medina of Dakar, Treichville in Abidjan, or New Bell in Douala.[92] Cars were in rare sight, nearly exclusively driven by and used by Europeans, and there was one bus service with a limited route. Walking remained the major mode of transportation to travel from one part of town to another. To use the term "neighborhoods," he offered, was a misnomer since the urban landscape ended at the borders of the plateau. With banana and mango trees dotted between huts and small gardens, the town's African inhabitants lived in "African villages."[93] Streets in African neighborhoods were footpaths of dirt and sand, following the twists and turns of where houses were located with no apparent logic. The locations of homes did not correspond to colonial cadaster surveys that depicted African neighborhoods as divided into neat grids of lots.[94] In theory, Africans were to apply for a certain lot at the cadaster department before constructing a residence. Applicants were to be issued a permit of occupation for a fee of 3,000 francs and could receive a deed of property after two years of living on the property if no one else claimed it. Few such applications were submitted or permits obtained.

Libreville homes encompassed a wide variety of building materials and degrees of durability. By the 1940s, empty land on which to build a home was scarce. Newer arrivals constructed *cases* on less-desirable terrains, the slopes of valleys, rocky spurs, and swamplands, where the lack of soil stability often resulted in flooding during the rainy seasons.[95] All houses in Libreville were rectangular, although materials used in their construction varied. Poorer inhabitants built their *cases* themselves, from "irregular" materials that they could salvage from ports or what was thrown away by stores, ranging from cardboard and barrels to remnants of crates still bearing the names of products such as whiskey, beer, or concentrated milk.[96] The homes of Fang communities in the city's periphery were *cases en "poto-potos,"* a name for a type of house made of earth similar to those found throughout Brazzaville; or houses made of tree bark, thin squares of which were merged together to construct walls. Residents with more money hired professional carpenters who constructed homes with planks of varied qualities of wood from surrounding sawmills. Many homes in Glass and Louis, elite Mpongwé neighborhoods, were made of cement and sat on stilts to weather flooding from heavy rains, though persons of other ethnicities in varied neighborhoods who worked as civil servants also had similar homes.[97] Mpongwé earned revenue by renting out homes to Europeans.[98] The roofs of modest houses were usually made of raffia fibers or straw and the floors were packed earth. Those with more money generally had houses with iron roofs and cement floors. A single neighborhood could contain all of these types of housing, with office workers and specialized wage laborers occupying houses of more durable materials, domestic servants and less-skilled workers in houses of earth and bark, and the newly arrived and poor in salvaged materials.[99]

Living conditions in Libreville provided a stark portrait of differing conditions for the haves and have-nots, those who had lived in the town for a few generations and recent arrivals, as well as along lines of ethnic differentiation. A mark of "civilized" status was eating imported food, available for purchase from small stores called *boutiques* owned by Africans selling items such as cans of tomatoes, sardines, and sugar. Residents purchased more expensive items such as jams, cigarettes, and household goods from European-owned stores.[100] A 1961 survey of living conditions in Libreville provides a vivid snapshot of the material and hygiene conditions that may have been present in the 1950s as well. Most of Libreville's residents obtained their water for drinking and washing from a public spigot (*robinet*) or well located in a concession, but inhabitants of poorer neighborhoods obtained water from ponds, while a small number of elites had private water faucets in their homes.[101] Some Mpongwé homes had interior kitchens and gas ovens, but it was more often the case that kitchens were outdoor spaces in which women cooked meals over fires. Electricity was rare, found in only 12 percent of Libreville's homes.[102] Sanitary facilities were also rare, with 27–29 percent of households equipped with indoor showers and toilets, mainly the homes of Mpongwé or office workers of other ethnicities. Furniture was also an indication of wealth, with more prosperous households equipped with beds, chairs, and sofas. Sewing machines, radios, record players, and bicycles were desired objects, and possessing such items was an indication of high status.[103]

In keeping with previous decades, European modes of dress were de rigueur in Libreville. Men wore shorts or pants and shirts as daily attire,

PHOTO 3.1. House on stilts, ca. 1950s. (Reproduced from a postcard in the personal collection of Patrick Ceillier.)[104]

and those with more money wore shoes. As did European visitors in prior decades, Lasserre expressed surprise at the sight of female residents of Libreville who spoke perfect French and sported cotton dresses, skirts, and blouses tailored in European styles, in contrast to cities in FEA such as Bangui or Brazzaville, in which women wore cloth wrapped around their bodies and few spoke French.[105] Newly arrived inhabitants could easily be distinguished in that they wore cloth wrapped around their bodies instead of tailored or ready-made clothing.

African women who lived in the Libreville region engaged in a variety of economic activities to earn cash. A small number of women worked in offices or as midwives, teachers, and store clerks, predominantly Mpongwé women. Lasserre estimated that 80 percent of women in Libreville maintained a small plantation on the outskirts of town within a few hours' walking distance. Elite Mpongwé women had plots of land maintained by other female kin.[106] In particular, women of Nzebi and Fang ethnicities engaged in agricultural cultivation as their primary day-to-day work. These farmers grew the staple of manioc and other items such as corn and sweet potatoes. They spent a majority of their day several times a week on their plantations, covering the distance with their children on their backs. Women farmers also cut down and transported wood for cooking to the town. Women of varied ethnicities maintained small gardens behind their homes as well, where they grew items such as spinach and eggplant for family consumption.[107] Women's agricultural labor continued to be crucial not only for sustenance of family members but also for cash income from proceeds of the sale of manioc to individual consumers and timber camps. The Estuary region continued to be plagued by high food prices, as the production of manioc, plantains, and yams was barely enough to feed the population.[108] By the 1940s and 1950s, some Fang women also took in sewing and tailoring jobs, sold prepared food from their homes, or worked as housekeepers in the homes of more elite Africans.[109]

Though the timber industry drew the greatest number of workers, Libreville's male inhabitants participated in other forms of wage labor. French schemes for men to become farmers and grow products such as peanuts, rice, or coffee floundered, though the numbers of cacao growers in the northern region of Woleu-Ntem did flourish in the 1940s and 1950s.[110] In a publication that assessed Gabon's economic prospects, French author François Charbonnier relayed that there were many more salaried workers in Gabon compared to other areas of French Equatorial Africa, with 8.2 percent of men working in wage labor, compared to 5.1 percent in Congo, 4.3 percent in Oubangui, and .08 percent in Chad.[111] Charbonnier further assessed that unlike other African cities, in which three-fourths of newly arrived immigrants from rural areas were unemployed, opportunities for wage labor abounded in Libreville, and unemployment should have been relatively low.[112] Desired work for men included jobs in the areas of domestic service, construction, and transportation. Literate men could work as clerks and writers in state and private enterprise. As in other regions of Africa, men were engaged in domestic service for Europeans in larger numbers than women, a particular manifestation of the gendered division of wage labor.[113] Sojourning through Libreville in 1956, British travel writer Russell Howe mentioned "the ballet of uniformed boys at noon" he witnessed traversing the streets.[114] Small business operators included owners of boutiques and also carpenters who managed teams of salaried employees.[115] Desired occupations with the highest salaries for men in Libreville included becoming a civil servant or the profitable venture of owning a beverage boutique, selling sodas and beer.

Colonial officials perpetually expressed frustration at not being able to recruit as many laborers as they needed. In 1956, Laurent Bastiani, the head of the Department of Statistics and Mechanization, bemoaned the meager population density in FEA as potentially necessitating the importation of

CACAO

Africans from outside of FEA as workers.[116] Particularly disturbing to him were "idle populations" of men who refused to work, instead depending upon kin who were wage earners for food and housing. Unlike the railways of Dakar, the docks of Nairobi, or the mines of Ghana, in which labor strikes erupted in the course of the 1930s and 1940s, labor unions remained embryonic with few members in Gabon. While the rest of Francophone Africa erupted in labor union protests and campaigns after 1945, such agitation remained sporadic in Gabon's urban centers. The French tightly monitored and restricted the formation of African labor organizations.[117] Labor union activity in Libreville consisted primarily of organizations of civil servants. The Professional Association of African Native Employees that was founded in the 1910s became the Association of Civil Servants after World War II. In 1946, the organization joined a Brazzaville union in mounting a two-day strike calling for higher wages and promotions of African civil servants, the only manifestation of strikes similar to those elsewhere in Africa in this decade.[118]

Though the post–World War II period witnessed the explosion of political parties and mass political mobilization toward greater self-governance by Africans across the continent, such efforts were tepid in Gabon. Political scientist John A. Ballard attributed this lack of political mobilization in Gabon as due to the following: "The absence of a bourgeoisie capable of accumulating capital meant that no Africans in FEA were able to finance a newspaper or send children to France for schooling, none who could contribute large funds to political parities, and, at least in Bangui and Libreville, not one who owned a truck or automobile that could be used for political purposes."[119]

At the famous 1946 Congress in Bamako that included African political leaders who were later to become the first generation of leaders of independent nations, no Gabonese delegate was present. Though political parties in Libreville had elected three delegates to attend, when they arrived at the airport, French officials told them that their airplane reservations could not be honored.[120] Ballard argues that while elsewhere in French-speaking Africa numerous political parties and conflict among varied factions arose, Gabon was "a relatively quiet backwater of mild personal and regional feuds among Africans and Europeans."[121] However, to understand what constituted "politics" as only agitation pertaining to parties and questions of independence obfuscates the immense tides of political activity in Gabon. Struggles to regulate the hearts and bodies of Librevilleois, through the social relations of conjugality and sexuality, formed the very substance of negotiating status, influence, wealth, and governance.

CONCLUSION

As the 1930s ushered in increased migration to Libreville, the French faced the dilemma of how to transform migratory groups into sedentary wage laborers, mobile social and familial groups into docile subjects in the colonial capital city. French colonial officials set out to impose a rationalized and geometric grid on an urban geography marked by twisting alleys, blurred boundaries of land tenure, and seemingly illogical architectural designs. Colonial officials created institutions and documents—laws, maps, and plans—that painted the illusion of a rational and legible city. Looking at the domestic and emotional lives of Libreville's African inhabitants, the French employed the same metaphors of anarchy and chaos that urban planners used when describing the town's physical layout. African political power brokers—through colonial service, the Catholic Church, legislatures, colonial courts, and chief and clan-based organizations of elder men—sought to enforce apparatuses of control over the intimate lives of the city's inhabitants. Amid these transformations, men and women configured new ways of loving and living with each other, spurring renewed formulations of what marriage, sex, and family should look like in the expanding town.

4 ⤻ The Bridewealth Economy
Money and Relationships of Affinity

IN 1935 A MAN NAMED Emane Ekong was sentenced to twenty years in prison and ten years' prohibition of residence in Libreville by the criminal court of the Estuary department for the murder of Nse Meyo, his brother-in-law's wife.[1] Relaying only Ekong's testimony, the case summary presented his confession of committing the murder with forethought and without remorse. However, he qualified, though he deliberately aimed the gun with the intention of killing her, she was not his original target. Some time before, Ekong had decided that he was going to kill either his wife or his brother-in-law, and he had warned them that he would do so. Days before the murder, Ekong borrowed the gun from his French boss on the pretext that he needed to go hunting. Traveling to his wife's family's village, he first spotted his wife and her brother, but they were among a crowd and therefore too difficult to target. However, he happened upon his brother-in-law's wife in a vulnerable position, alone in her hut, and he shot her.

Ekong's testimony painted him as a reasonable man with reasonable expectations. He agreed to the initial bridewealth amount that Miko's brothers requested when he expressed the wish to marry her five years earlier, and so he expected her to be present in their marital home and for her priority to be the care of her husband. Instead, avaricious in-laws and his wife blackmailed him for money and drove him to murder. Ekong summarized his motive for killing his brother-in-law's wife as vengeance: "She was a stand-in for her husband. He and his brothers deprived me of my wife. I took vengeance by

97

depriving him of his own. It is my brothers-in-law who got it into my wife's head that she had to separate herself from me because I did not give in to their incessant demands for money. This is why I wanted to take my vengeance upon them."[2]

Over the course of their marriage, his wife, Miko, spent an increasing amount of time visiting her relatives and was otherwise absent from her husband's home. Each time, her brothers refused to allow her to return to Ekong unless he paid supplemental bridewealth payments to them. He ceded to these demands for money, giving a little bit here and a little bit there. Yet, on one occasion, his in-laws drove him too far and he took matters into his own hands to reassert his manhood.

At the end of August 1935, Ekong had just paid cash to his brother-in-law to facilitate Miko's return when his boss ordered that he go elsewhere in the colony for work. His wife relayed that she was going to stay at her brother's home during his absence. Ekong told her no and beat her for her insolence. He testified that he would have stabbed her to death in that moment if it were not for their neighbors who separated them. When Ekong left, she went to her brother's home, and when he went to retrieve her to return to their marital home, Miko said that she wanted a divorce. Her brother told him that he could have his wife back for 500 francs. Ekong responded that he would not pay anything more and demanded that the brothers reimburse to him all that he had paid in initial bridewealth and supplemental payments, a sum that now totaled 2,000 francs. Ekong viewed this amount that he paid in total as the equivalent of "two bridewealth." However, he warned, if she did indeed divorce him, he would kill her or one of her brothers. What made him decide to act upon his threat was one final slight that was simply too much for him to bear. Ekong fell ill and asked his wife to come care for him. She refused. At wit's end because his wife would not even nurse him, he decided "to place his threat into execution at the first moment that presented itself."[3]

This court document is problematic. Domestic violence of husbands upon wives appears to have been common in this period in Gabon. Sociologist Honorine Ngou has conceptualized marriage as being "a field of violence in which a wife was subjected to varied types of abuse and bullying" by her husband.[4] However, the spectacular theatricality of this case of murder is extreme; conflicts over bridewealth with this degree of violence are rare in court records.[5] Nevertheless, this case is illustrative of the contested understandings of bridewealth that abounded and the varying expectations of the rights in and of marriage that such payments facilitated. This court case reveals the landscape of the claims of varied individuals about how bridewealth in the form of money brokered or broke relationships of affinity, and emotional and social rapport within such relationships.

Each of the persons in this case acted according to his or her normative expectations of how the flow of money facilitated relationships between a wife and her husband, a wife and her natal family, and a husband and his in-laws. At an unspecified time, Ekong happened upon a woman whom he wanted to marry and who ostensibly wanted to marry him. Though Miko was already married, he reimbursed the first husband's bridewealth, which finalized the divorce, and then sought to build a home with his wife. Ekong did not appear to mind his brother-in law's requests for contingent payments of bridewealth in the first few years. Written sources by African political leaders, French missionaries and colonial personnel, and oral history interviews that I conducted indicate that payments of money by husbands to in-laws beyond the initially agreed-upon bridewealth were normative practice.[6] A good husband was one who continued to give gifts of money when the in-laws requested it and on occasions such as the birth of a child. For a husband to not give money was a slight, an act of disrespect toward his in-laws. At a certain point, however, Ekong felt that their demands were exigent and that the balance had tipped precipitously. Playing by the normative script, he was making payments, yet he was not receiving the reciprocity of his wife's presence in the conjugal home. It is not clear why the brother requested the money and what he did with it. In Ekong's testimony, his brother-in-law viewed his sister's husband as a source of income. Why wouldn't Ekong just concede to divorce? Divorce was a long process in Libreville, entailing years of negotiations, and it was likely that Miko's family would not have fully or even partially reimbursed him. Though Ekong's profession was not specified in the record, he earned wages from a white employer and his work entailed some mobility away from his *case*, complicating the possibility that Ekong would marry again.

Miko did not appear to be a passive observer in the events. At times, she returned to her husband even though he had not paid her brother, and at other times, she stayed at her brother's home until Ekong gave cash. Ekong's threats when they first married that he would kill her if she ever left him, the beating, and the subsequent murder indicate that he was a jealous and violent man. Miko may have absconded to her brother's home for refuge after Ekong assaulted her, only to return, either with the hope that her husband's treatment would improve or at her family's behest to stay with her husband since they could not afford to reimburse his bridewealth or for other unspecified reasons. Miko's family may have requested money from Ekong in compensation for having physically abused Miko. When a wife took refuge with her natal family on claims of her husband's mistreatment, a council among the kin and compensation from the husband to his in-laws could facilitate her return.[7] In the end, Miko may have convinced her natal family to support her in pursuing a divorce. When the possibility of divorce was in the air, Ekong viewed all of the money that he had given over the years as constitutive of bridewealth and therefore felt that his wife's family needed to reimburse him in order to terminate the marriage.

Though the topic of conversation that led to the tensions among husband, wife, and affines was about money, at heart were questions of "the tense and tender" ties of interpersonal relationships.[8] As the case of Ekong, his wife, Miko, and his affines reveals, varied understandings about the interplay of marriage and money entailed incoherence and unintended consequences as well as attempts to make sense of the changing world and establish the boundaries of affinity. Such debates were prevalent within households, villages and neighborhoods, mission stations and churches, legislatures, and colonial administrative offices in Libreville, Brazzaville, and Paris from the late 1920s to 1960.

What unfolded in Libreville in these decades was what I call "the bridewealth economy," disbursements of primarily cash, but also goods and labor, that facilitated the consecration or rupture of relationships of affinity. Bridewealth was a motor of African economic activity in colonial Libreville, a credit-based economy in which men and women promised, earned, borrowed, transferred, and absconded with money to facilitate interpersonal relationships. Over the course of the twentieth century, Libreville's residents fundamentally incorporated the monetary economy into bridewealth payments. By the mid-1920s, the height of the okoumé rush, the composition of bridewealth had changed from a combination of indigenous and imported goods to almost exclusively cash. As the monetization of bridewealth took hold through the decline and expansion of the timber industry, varied political constituents—African chiefs, elite African men, colonial personnel, and missionaries—decried that bridewealth inflation was rampant and reflected social and moral decay. In varied projects, political leaders from Libreville, Brazzaville, and Paris tried to regulate bridewealth payments and to mold the bridewealth economy into legible orderings of political and moral economy, yet rarely arrived at a consensus to pass laws that would limit marriage payments.

The monetization of bridewealth reveals the deep insertion of colonial and global capital into African societies, but in ways unintended by colonial interests and, in the end, not completely controlled by African political leaders, colonial society, or the very participants in Libreville's bridewealth economy. Libreville inhabitants variably viewed bridewealth as a source of income and a vehicle for the accumulation of wealth, a legal and social marker of whether a relationship was a marriage and the rights of persons within the relationship, a yardstick revealing the degree of "civilization" of a given ethnic group, and an indication of adult manhood and womanhood. Bridewealth payments, or promises to pay, were longitudinal negotiations over the course of men's and women's marital careers that reordered relationships among affines along the axis of generation, ethnicity, gender, and wealth.

Wives, husbands, the betrothed, lovers, strangers, neighbors, brothers, uncles, fathers, and sisters debated the prestation of bridewealth payments and the linkages between the circulation of cash, goods, and people. Bridewealth was not only a man's domain of negotiation; women increasingly participated in the determination and distribution of bridewealth payments on their own behalf and facilitated their divorces by accessing the cash reserves of kin, lovers, and their own reserves. Furthermore, Libreville residents of varied ethnicities measured how civilized one ethnic group was versus another based on the monetary amounts of marriage payments. It is such general practice to assess the degree to which the colonial monetary economy transformed African societies that the subject of how African appropriations of money transformed colonial policies is rarely considered. The unfolding of a bridewealth loan fund subsidized by colonial budgets after World War II demonstrated how African uses of money compelled the colonial state to conform to African logics of the use value and circulation of colonial currency.

BRIDEWEALTH IN AFRICA:
ANTHROPOLOGICAL AND HISTORICAL RESEARCH

Bridewealth is a theme that has been studied in some depth by scholars of twentieth-century colonial Africa, particularly in the area of anthropological research. The transfer of goods, labor, livestock, or varied forms of wealth primarily from the groom to the bride's family was central to legitimizing a relationship between a man and a woman as a marriage in varied societies across the continent.[9] Bridewealth varied in form according to "the dominant resource and main economic activity" across time and space.[10] As analyzed by John Comaroff, scholars have interpreted the meaning of bridewealth within three frameworks: structural functionalist methodologies, jural interpretations, and Marxist analyses.[11] The limitation of these frameworks, as Comaroff argues, lies in the mechanical way scholars equate the remittance of bridewealth with resulting normative relationships of affinity. Comaroff urges that scholars pay attention to the symbolic significance of bridewealth as both "a constitutive order" and the dialectical relationship with the "lived-in everyday context that represents itself in individuals and groups in a repertoire of values and contradictions, rules and relationships, interests and ideologies."[12] Historians such as Barbara Cooper have focused on the changing everyday context of bridewealth, demonstrating how in twentieth-century colonial Niger exchanges of wealth between the bride's and groom's families were reciprocal and how the bride brought along her own wealth into the marriage that remained in her possession.[13] Following Comaroff's call, I analyze the meaning of bridewealth both as an organizing structure of social order and as lived experience, while heeding Cooper's attention to changing historical contexts.

Historical and historically minded anthropological research has elucidated some key transformations that monetization wrought in practices of bridewealth in 1920s–1960 West, East, and Southern Africa. That African men entered into migrant wage labor as early as the 1920s to earn money for bridewealth payments to marry women in their rural villages has been documented in historical and anthropological studies ranging from colonial Southern Africa to Kenya to Cameroon.[14] The demands of colonial taxation increased male participation in migrant wage labor and cash-cropping endeavors and resulted in new infusions of wealth. When men with cash returned to rural areas, they converted their cash into cattle to meet the increased bridewealth demanded by fathers with daughters in colonies ranging from rural Gusiiland in Kenya to cocoa-farming regions in Cameroon.[15] Cattle remained the primary form of bridewealth payments in rural areas in Kenya and across Southern Africa, where most of the research on bridewealth has been situated, well into contemporary times.[16] Some urban communities in West Africa seem to have incorporated money into bridewealth payments. In certain Ashanti areas in Ghana as early as the 1920s, a cash payment instead of or in addition to drinks was common in marriage payments; by the 1950s bridewealth was composed entirely of cash.[17] In the city of Maradi, Niger, residents began to constitute bridewealth in the form of French-issued currencies rather than goods, or indigenous currency such as cowries, by the 1950s and 1960s.[18] Marriage payments pegged to cash income often exceeded the annual income of individuals.[19] Beginning in the 1920s and particularly after World War II, the concern of colonial officials and African political leaders that bridewealth costs were increasing to the extent that young men could not afford to marry was common in many regions in Africa.[20]

Of note is the totality with which colonial currency became the dominant form of bridewealth payments along the Gabon Estuary by the 1920s, much earlier than elsewhere in Africa.[21] Estuary residents needed cash, French-issued francs, to constitute bridewealth payments in the city and its rural suburbs, where money was of daily necessity and an indication of status. As argued by Lynn Schler in her study of immigration and community in colonial Douala, Cameroon, "it is true that the introduction of colonial money led to a reorganization of economic and social life. But once in circulation, the cultural value and impact of colonial money was largely determined by social relations and hierarchies of power deeply imbedded in African society."[22] Furthermore, Schler argues, "social alliances remained of primary significance in the lives of immigrants to the city, and were often the impetus behind efforts to accumulate cash." She goes on to advise that scholars need to consider local, global, and "intimate household dynamics" to understand the "social meaning of money."[23] Estuary residents invested a significant portion of their cash reserves to facilitate marriage. Money as a means to facilitate relationships of affinity demonstrates the ways in which Gabonese adapted precolonial practices of wealth in people to changing historical milieus.[24] However, this adaptation involved change as well as continuity. As Jane Guyer cautions in her study of the monetization of bridewealth payments in twentieth-century colonial Cameroon, scholars should not assume that "terms and practices" of marriage payments carry over seamlessly from one era to the next. Guyer argues that the study of bridewealth does not yield "a narrative history of a single, coherent institution," but "entailed whirlpools of debate, incoherence and unintended consequences," and understanding the complexities of marriage payments "can be established only by empirical historical study."[25] Analysis of changing forms, practices, and conceptualizations of bridewealth in Gabon opens a new window in our understanding of the history of bridewealth in Africa.

BRIDEWEALTH AND CHANGING CONCEPTS OF MARRIAGE AND INTERPERSONAL RELATIONSHIPS, LATE 1920S–1960

The analysis of bridewealth and money raises some fundamental questions about the meaning of marriage: What constituted marriage? Why did people get married and what did they expect from marriage? What roles did affines play in determining the processes and meanings of marriage? What set of normative beliefs and laws would guide such questions and answers? My oldest informants were about seventy-five years of age when I interviewed them in 2001 and 2005. They were born between 1925 and 1930, the first years of the okoumé rush, and reached pubescent age in the late 1930s and early 1940s, years of economic difficulty. Through these years, women and men of this generation sought marriage, and men also aspired to amass resources to constitute bridewealth. I interviewed people of a younger generation as well, those who reached puberty in the 1950s. When I asked how universal the aspiration to marry was, people of both generations answered that marriage was the marker of social adulthood and that a perpetually unmarried man or woman was unheard of.[26]

Men and women of all ethnicities and through the two generations articulated that marriage conferred respectability. As articulated by Fang interviewee Thérèse Biloghe, "for women, marriage brought respect, and to be a respectful woman, you had to be married."[27] Moise Meyo Mobiang exclaimed, "How can someone be a man if he is not married? Marriage brings everything. You are considered rich when you have several wives and several children."[28] However, as noted in chapter 3, a 1944 colonial survey showed that one-third to a little more than one-half of men and women resident in Libreville were not married. There appeared to be just as many Libreville residents of marriageable age who were not married as were married. Informants' memory of marriage as universal is paradoxical to statistics from colonial documents that not every adult married. Rather than dismissing this disjuncture between memory and documents as the failure of memory or faulty statistics, I argue that it reveals the degree to which Libreville's inhabitants conceived of marriage as a metaphor for well-being, security, and status in the city. Yet what made a relationship a marriage? Interviewees stressed marriage payments as the central feature, not only in the transference of money and goods, but in facilitating the relations of trust, mutual aid, and attachment between the bride's and the groom's kin that negotiations over payments entailed.

In the era of French colonial rule, few Libreville inhabitants of any ethnic identification entertained the idea of marrying without bridewealth. Marriage by bridewealth, which informants referred to as "customary" marriage, was the legitimate form of marriage over Catholic or civil modes of marriage. As Jane Guyer found in colonial Cameroun, marriage payments in Gabon did not decline "as modernization theories expected."[29] Though the vast majority of the Estuary region's inhabitants identified themselves as Catholic, few married in a church ceremony, and even the most avowed Catholics identified the church's prohibitions against divorce and polygamy as troublesome.[30] Catholic missionaries perpetually bemoaned that so few adherents consecrated their marriages in the church, assessing that

Christianity was "insufficiently anchored" in African mores.[31] Those who did marry in the Catholic Church were mainly Mpongwé, who viewed such ceremonies as indicative of their elite status, and persons of other ethnicities who married in the church in their elder years, when they were sure that they would never seek a divorce. The lack of colonial record keeping of African civil marriages makes it difficult to quantify how many of such unions took place, but political reports indicate that the numbers were low. Fang interviewees who married in a civil ceremony did so for pragmatic reasons.[32] After World War II, the colonial state began to give family grants (*allocations familiales*), travel and housing subsidies for the wife and children of African men employed as civil servants. Some Mpongwé men who married Mpongwé women completed all three marriage ceremonies.[33] However, couples of any ethnicity who married in the Catholic Church, civil unions, or both did not reject customary marriage altogether, but married in three forums: customary marriage, a civil ceremony, and a church wedding. As outlined by a Fang woman named Marie Bidang, who got married in all three forums, she did so "for respect of custom, because I was a committed Christian, and so that the state would also subsidize me during my husband's numerous transfers."[34] As expressed by an Mpongwé man named Myènè Avekaza, and repeated by informants of all ethnic groups, "a civil marriage is only a process of filling out papers. The real marriage is the customary marriage."[35] Yet what was a customary marriage?

As Tabitha Kanogo has argued for twentieth-century colonial Kenya, so it was in Gabon that "marriage was part of a cultural process, rather than an institution which was created in a one-time action at a registrar's office, or in a church."[36] The endeavors of the groom and his kinsmen in approaching the bride's male kin with his request to marry, subsequent negotiations over marriage payments, and a public ceremony and celebration in which the groom's kin made the agreed-upon prestations was foundational in establishing affinity. Furthermore, the negotiations created a series of interactions in which both families researched and became familiar with each other and conferred legitimacy to the union. These rituals gave the marriage social and jural recognition. Joseph Lasseny Ntchoveré, an Mpongwé neighborhood chief, reflected on the importance of bridewealth negotiations as told to him by elders when he was a youth in the 1950s: "When a man did not fulfill these formalities, the woman does not have value in the mind of the family, even if they are married in a civil union. There is a distance between the two families because they do not know each other. On the man's side, people say, 'She is here, but we don't even know why she is there since they haven't yet had the formalities of the customary marriage.' It is a clandestine marriage."[37] The rites of bridewealth negotiations were to be a constitutive order that brought together a network of persons who were obligated to aid one another and whom the bride and groom could turn to in times of trouble.

A woman interviewee nostalgically reflected upon the purpose of bridewealth payments made in goods in the 1920s on the occasion of her mother's wedding. While the composition of bridewealth for Fang in the Estuary region increasingly consisted of francs, goods and indigenous currency still remained of use by some in the rural suburbs. The conceptualization of bridewealth payments as increasing women's capacities for social reproduction is revealed in the story of a Fang woman named Thérèse Biloghe, whom I interviewed in Libreville in 2002. Biloghe married twice, first when she was sixteen years old in 1945 and again when she was thirty years old in 1955 after a divorce. She contrasted the meaning of bridewealth for her and her mother's marriages:

> In my mother's time, my mother, she did not get married for money. It is us who went into marriage for money. In my mother's age, people asked for extra-large pots. They called these pots "our mother-in-laws are smiling." People added to this tools, machetes, hoes, and axes. The money that they used in this time period was called *bière* or *suso*, pieces of wood that had holes in them. At that period, marriage was not an affair completed with money. It was an affair involving bags of salt, limes, soap made with bananas.[38]

At the time of her birth, Biloghe's parents lived in Libreville's rural suburbs, laboring as farmers and fishermen. Biloghe accounted for bridewealth payments in goods in her mother's time of marriage as meant to provide the bride's female relatives with day-to-day necessities for taking care of their families along the lines of a gendered division of labor. The pots, objects used by women to cook food, and the hoes that aided women's agricultural labor reflect that the mothers of brides could also have benefited from marriage payments. The machetes and axes were for men to clear brush. Additionally, the salt, limes, and soap were luxury goods that increased the family's daily quality of life. The wooden indigenous money, the *bière* or *suso* that Biloghe mentions, could be used to purchase imported goods from other Fang clans. The content and meanings of bridewealth in relation to women's value is a matter of ethnocentric comparison and debate among Libreville residents.

Into the 1930s, cash payments were a relatively small part of most Mpongwé marriage payments; the goods that the groom purchased and gave to the bride's family were of greater significance. An Mpongwé woman interviewee interpreted that bridewealth payment in goods in their culture was of symbolic import that revealed the social value of brides and their mothers. "Unlike our Fang compatriots," a woman named Madame Messani recounted, "the amount of bridewealth is truly at the minimum. Bridewealth is symbolic, but carries much value."[39] The symbolic value of bridewealth, elaborated Messani (who first married before puberty sometime in the 1930s), could be seen in the objects that "represented compensation for the suffering of mothers for their children." Messani elaborated that bridewealth in her time was money and a few objects such as beverages, tobacco, a machete, and pipes. The items that the fiancé's family gave to the woman's family went to the mother of the bride: "All of these objects were symbolic. The soap signified the bathing that the mother did to her daughter over the years and the mosquito net, the numbers of mosquitoes that bit the mother all the nights while she cared for her baby. All of these things represented compensation for the suffering that the mother endured."[40] In a public ceremony attended by invited guests, with the groom's kin sitting on one side and the bride's kin on another, the groom's male kin would bring out the objects and deposit them before the bride's male kin. The bride's male kin would give some of the goods to her mother. These objects had "value" in demonstrating to the groom, bride, and those gathered to witness the ceremony the important role that the mother had played in raising the bride. In receiving the goods, the mother also received public recognition of her person.

By the mid-1920s, customary marriage, meaning a relationship sealed by bridewealth payments, became the dominant form of legitimate marriage for Estuary residents. As new possibilities of Christian and civil marriages emerged, marriage by bridewealth remained "the real marriage." Yet as money became a more important factor of bridewealth, either in monetary payments or cash needed to buy goods, Libreville residents began to debate the unintended consequences in the use and meaning of money to constitute marriage. Benoit Messani, who was married to Madame Messani (quoted above as saying that bridewealth payments were symbolic of women's social value), countered his wife's use of the term "symbolic." In our 2002 oral interview he qualified, "It is true that it [bridewealth] is a symbol; the gifts that we give to in-laws are symbolic. But to obtain them, you have to have the means. To collect the marriage gifts means to go in search of a lot of money."[41] The search for a lot of money and how a lot of money shaped marriage aspirations entailed new configurations of kith and kin relations, generational hierarchies, gender roles, and modes of labor.

Even as some Myènè did incorporate more cash into bridewealth payments in the 1930s, some wives themselves seem to have benefited from a portion of the bridewealth. Completing her studies at a Catholic mission in Libreville in 1938, Marie Appia Remondo married a Myènè man who was also a student when she was twenty-one years old. Remondo and her husband were from Port-Gentil, and they married in the church at Libreville's Sainte Pierre parish. They had no kin in Libreville to negotiate bridewealth payments, nor to attend their wedding. Her husband gave the bridewealth payment to a missionary, who gave Remondo the money. She then traveled to Port-Gentil to see her relatives and distribute a portion of the bridewealth to them.[42] She kept a portion of the bridewealth money to pay for school fees. Jane Guyer has noticed a similar increased importance of women receiving a portion of marriage payments in postcolonial Cameroon. In the late 1960s, marriage payments included a lump sum of cash for the bride's mother, and the wives selected for themselves the best containers of wine from the offerings given by the groom's kin at the marriage ceremony.[43] That women played an increasingly important role in the circulation of marriage payments, and sometimes received a portion of direct proceeds, was also evident in other African communities in Libreville.

Among Fang communities, bridewealth was an affair not only of men, as a number of women participated in bridewealth negotiations at the time of marriage. In migrating to Libreville, many men and women lived away from their families of birth. Some women indicated that living away from natal kin meant that they chose their own husbands and then presented their suitors to their fathers to negotiate the bridewealth amount after the couple had already discussed the matter and agreed upon what they thought was a sufficient payment. Albertine Ntsame Ndong, who selected her husband, traveled back and forth between the village of Okolassi, where she lived and labored as a farmer, and Libreville to sell manioc. Of her marriage process she relayed, "I loved my husband, and he me," and then she presented him to her father after she and her fiancé had already decided upon what the appropriate bridewealth payment should be. Her father accepted her suitor's payment in 1951: 2,000 francs, pots, and other objects.[44]

Léotine Nseghe, who lived in Libreville away from her Fang father's village near Cocobeach to attend the Catholic school at Sainte Marie, met the man who became her husband in 1952. She had finished her schooling and decided to stay in Libreville, making a living selling fish in the market and living at the home of an uncle. She and her suitor decided they would marry, she moved to his *case*, and then he visited her father's home to offer and pay the bridewealth. Her father did not want her to marry. That his daughter spoke French made her of great value in their home; she could explain what white men were saying when they came to the village requiring something from residents. Her father refused to allow the marriage to take place. Her father took her away from her fiancé's home, but the fiancé "kidnapped" her from her father's home and took her back to his. This time her father accepted the bridewealth. That her suitor was able to pay a high bridewealth amount afforded Nseghe the leeway to choose her husband over her father's objections. Nseghe remembered that her bridewealth amount once they married in 1956 was an astronomical sum since she had a primary school education: "150,000 francs, 10 pieces of cloth, a bag of rice, and other small items."[45] A white government official, she remembered, had decreed that all homes in her father's village get a new roof, and her father was hard-pressed to refuse her bridewealth that would provide him with money to fulfill this directive.

Marriage payments continued to be a process, often incremental and supplemental payments of cash that husbands and in-laws alike sought to quantify and qualify over the course of a marriage. Elder men with daughters and men with sisters benefited from these increments of money. Bernadette Angone recounts that in her six-year marriage, the initial sum of 15,000 francs that her husband had given to her father had "grown considerably" to 100,000 francs.[46] Married when she was six years old in 1950, she recounted that she went "innocently" to live in her new home with her in-laws, not quite knowing what being married meant at first, and soon considering her mother-in-law as her mother. By age twelve, after consummating her marriage, she grew to realize what bridewealth meant. In running away to her father's house after an argument with her husband, she learned that "my father did not cease to go to my husband's house each time he had a problem and needed money. And in this way the bridewealth amount increased. Each time my relatives came to my husband, he gave them money." The "problems" for which her father, a cash-poor fisherman, sought money from his son-in-law included the annual tax payments, bridewealth payments for his sons' marriages, and the fees for consulting a nurse at the medical dispensary in Kango. The flow of money from his son-in-law, facilitated by the marriage of his daughter, allowed him to pay for day-to-day necessities and afford extraordinary, higher-status expenses such as biomedical health care.[47]

In oral interviews, African men who attempted the search for bridewealth money in the 1940s and 1950s lamented that it was difficult to accumulate enough money to pay the high bridewealth payments that fathers requested for their daughters. The monetization of bridewealth impeded their expectations of self-realization and adulthood through marriage and parenthood. An Mpongwé man named Myènè Avekaza, who considered marriage as early as 1946 when he was eighteen years old and had finished primary school in Libreville, summarized his youth as a series of "failures."[48] Long bouts of unemployment and illness prevented him from earning wages. By his thirties, he had three children with the same woman, and he wished to marry her and claim his children. Yet he did not have the money for the marriage payment bundle of the wedding ceremony and the bed, chairs, and other furnishings for a conjugal home that elder men told him were requisite. He did not marry until later in life, around the age of fifty, and then to another woman since the mother of his children had married another man years prior.[49] A Fang man named Moise Meyo Mobiang, who aspired to marriage in the 1950s, reflected, "At the time, bridewealth was a veritable struggle. This is why certain men died single, for lack of bridewealth. They had children with women, but they could not claim the children since, with us, there is a proverb that the child belongs to whoever had paid bridewealth, and not to who was the real father."[50] By "real father," Mobiang meant the biological father. In the money economy, bridewealth established a man as the social and legal father, who had control over education and child rearing and the receipt of bridewealth payments of daughters. The accounts by Avekaza, Mobiang, and other men of their years of singlehood reveal the anxieties young men felt in earning and saving money and of the multiple and tenuous avenues men accessed to earn cash in the bridewealth economy.

While in theory young men were free to select their own spouses, few could independently raise enough money to marry, in spite of indications that there was no shortage of wage-labor opportunities for men in the 1940s and 1950s. Some men depended on money received from elder male and female kin, who in turn held some level of control over men's marital options. The question of whether a young man had a choice in deciding on a wife was determined by the degree to which he was dependent upon kin to give him the money necessary to get married.[51] Mothers could also play the key role in collecting money and paying for bridewealth and selecting their sons' spouses. For example, Emmanuel Ongone Bikeigne, who fought in the French army during World War II, said, "My mother picked and married [me to] my first wife, and this was in my absence, without needing my opinion. Upon my return, I just accepted this, without arguing."[52] His mother sold the manioc she cultivated to neighboring timber camps, which allowed her to slowly save money.

The viability of a man's marital aspirations, particularly for Fang men, greatly depended upon his sister's conjugal status. Pulling together the cash resources of elder kin alone did not suffice. Sylvain Mba, who attended school in Libreville, returned to his father's Estuary village in 1957 to find that his father had chosen a wife for him and negotiated the bridewealth amount. However, the marriage did not even last a year because his father was unable to raise enough cash to pay the bridewealth asked by the father-in-law and Mba himself had few resources.[53] Mba's father-in-law took his daughter back. After his father's death, Mba was able to give away his younger sister in marriage, and her bridewealth allowed him to select a wife and in turn pay the amount requested by his bride's kin. Strategies for a cash-poor father to actualize his son's marital aspirations included finding a husband for his daughter and transferring his daughter's bridewealth money to the male kin of the intended daughter-in-law.[54] Bridewealth gained by a woman's family for her marriage could facilitate the marriage of a number of male dependents in her natal family. Emilie Minkue, a woman who was married and moved to her husband's village of Okolassi shortly after she reached puberty in the 1940s, recounted that the 1,500 francs and ten pieces of cloth that her husband gave to her family for her hand in turn permitted her brother to marry. Her marriage benefited her natal family, Minkue emphasized, given that many children were born from the union of her brother and his wife.[55]

In the face of insufficient money reserves of social and kin, wage labor remained a path of long and last resort. As David Edou Ntoutoume, who married in 1957, recounted:

> I did not come to know women quickly. I had to wait. I was older than twenty years. There was the problem of financial means. I needed to gather bridewealth money, about 15,000 CFA. By this time, the amount required for bridewealth had increased a lot. It had gone beyond the 3,000 CFA from the time of my parents to 15,000–20,000 CFA. For bridewealth problems, there are two solutions. Some came to be married due to the fact that they had sisters, and when their sisters left for marriage, they recuperated that bridewealth and it was with this that they married in their turn. Others like me were obliged to count upon our own efforts, because we did not have sisters to give away in marriage. We had to find jobs in order to procure bridewealth, which is why we got married very late.[56]

Men like Ntoutoume who did not have sisters were at a disadvantage in being able to accumulate bridewealth cash. He viewed wage labor as a much slower path to accruing cash. Ntoutoume received a certificate of training in carpentry at the Sainte Marie mission in his twenties, but it was at a timber camp where he found work. He speculated that after five years of work, with two weeks of rest each year to return to Libreville to visit aging parents, he had enough money to marry.

All of the paths to accumulate money had their limitations. A man's sister's marriage was a tenuous source of bridewealth money. Her husband may not have been able to remit the promised amount to her family. If the sister divorced, this would precipitate a crisis whereby her brother would have to marshal his cash reserves to contribute to her bridewealth reimbursement. Furthermore, some men disagreed with their fathers about whom they would marry, yet were limited in protesting in that their fathers held the purse. Male interviewees such as Ntoutoume expressed seeing wage labor as a temporary endeavor. Minimum wages increased by slight amounts and could often only cover living expenses. These conversations about money and marriage occurring at interpersonal and community levels reached colony-wide stages to encompass African and French political leaders and their attempts to manage African marriages through the regulation of bridewealth payments.

BRIDEWEALTH INFLATION AND REGULATION IN THE 1930S

In July 1931, Félicien Endamne, chief of an Estuary department village, wrote a letter to the administrator of the Estuary circumscription arguing that he witnessed great perturbations among those he governed concerning questions of bridewealth, the difficulty of reimbursing bridewealth in instances of divorce, and the challenge of gathering enough money to facilitate new marriages.[57] At the time, southern Gabon was reeling from the full brunt of the global Depression, with the export of timber at a virtual standstill and opportunities to work and earn money limited. Endamne wrote that the families of women who were in the process of divorce had a hard time scraping together enough money to reimburse the husbands. Marriages that had taken place in the 1920s period of prosperity had required thousands of francs, an amount of money that was now virtually impossible to gather. Ignoring the new reality of the scarcity of cash, families with unmarried women continued to demand bridewealth amounts of the previous decades from men wishing to marry. Endamne proposed caps on bridewealth for new marriages and on the reimbursement of bridewealth in instances of divorce. In the case of a divorce, the wife would reimburse a maximum of

1,000 francs to the husband, no matter what the original amount of bride-wealth may have been. In cases of newly contracted marriages, bridewealth could not exceed 500 francs. Endamne proposed that these caps would be made to all Estuary subdivisions and that chiefs would be the enforcers.[58]

In September 1931, the French administrator of Endamne's subdivision wrote a letter to the head of the Estuary circumscription strongly support-ing the proposal, noting that it was a matter of particularly heightened importance in Fang communities. He cautioned against completely out-lawing bridewealth to be paid in cash, but suggested reducing bridewealth amounts to a level commensurate with the diminished cash resources that were the new reality.[59] Endamne's proposal made its way up the colonial hierarchy to reach the desk of the governor-general of French Equatorial Africa (FEA). He cautioned that limits in cases of divorce should not be retroactive and that a woman could be divorced only if the amount of bridewealth that had been paid at the time of her marriage was reim-bursed.[60] He agreed that bridewealth costs had been so inflated during "the period of prosperity" that young men could not marry. Rejecting ef-forts to limit the amount of bridewealth to be reimbursed in instances of divorce to a certain sum, the governor-general approved only the recom-mendation that bridewealth for new marriages be limited to 1,000 francs. This reform, he hoped, would have the impact of allowing young men to more quickly find wives and found households, thus bringing "a certain measure of relief to the demographic problem."[61] The 1932 annual report of the colony of Gabon relayed that in a meeting of the council of elder and younger notables in the Estuary department, attendees unanimously approved the limits on bridewealth for new marriages.[62] Chiefs and no-tables in other wood-producing areas such as Lambaréné also urged that limits be placed on bridewealth amounts.[63]

This policy that limited bridewealth to 1,000 francs was sporadically fol-lowed and enforced. By the end of 1932, the administrator of the Estuary circumscription noted that on the subject of "eternal women palavers," the effort to reduce bridewealth to more reasonable amounts had been fruitful. He stated that the fixed amount of 1,000 francs had been volun-tarily accepted and practiced by villagers, especially younger men, who could more readily obtain wives as a result.[64] Yet it is not clear just how voluntarily the Estuary residents were following the new limits. Attached to the 1932 annual report were the summaries of two court cases in which two Fang men were sentenced to ten to eleven days in prison for matters relating to bridewealth. The men, who requested bridewealth payments of 2,000 francs for their daughters rather than the 1,000-franc sum fixed by the governor, were convicted of the crime of "creating disorder."[65] In spite of the policy directives of chiefs and colonial administrators to place limits on bridewealth, some men with female dependents continued to ask for bridewealth amounts beyond the decreed sums, and men seeking to marry paid these amounts.

The monetization of marriage payments worried Myènè political leaders as well. It was not the expenditure of bridewealth paid to the bride's family that Mpongwé men disparaged, but rather money for the expenses of the *noce*, the wedding reception. A lavish celebratory party, in which attendees were well fed and there was a copious amount of alcohol, demonstrated the status of the groom and his esteem for his wife and her family. An Mpongwé author who identified himself as Gilbert Obembe wrote a letter in the early 1930s that appeared in a newspaper in Brazzaville. Obembe qualified his letter as a response to claims that elder Mpongwé men had apparently made regarding male youth of his generation (that they were bandits who were causing societal disorder by refusing to marry).[66] Obembe retorted that expectations that the groom give one to two bottles of liquor to the girl's family when asking to marry her were excessive. In addition to this initial gift, a man's prospective in-laws expected the groom to provide 12 bottles of liquor, 20 liters of red wine, a case of beer, and 4,000–5,000 francs for the expenses of the noce. Young men of his generation wanted to marry, he insisted, but were hampered by the initial expenses, and often two or three months after a marriage, the wife subsequently requested a divorce. Obembe ended the article by asking colonial authorities and notables to intervene to make marriage less expensive.

In June 1932, a Galoa man named Michel Julien Faguinovery, who identified himself as a forester, wrote a letter to the governor of Gabon to suggest that bridewealth be abolished.[67] Faguinovery argued that bridewealth as practiced had been corrupted from the original intent and was the source of many misunderstandings in Galoa homes. Faguinovery relayed that marriages of yesteryear were based on love. He recounted the origins of bridewealth to an unspecified period in the distant past and to a man named Fevarweekant, a man who was physically repulsive and whose name meant "If ugliness was a sickness." Fevarweekant pursued a woman of rare beauty to be his wife. They married, but in the fear she would leave him, he gave his in-laws empty bottles, items rare and highly valued at the time, as insurance for the marriage to last. In current times, Faguinovery complained, wives left their husbands "as often as they changed dresses" on their families' counsel to obtain higher bridewealth from suitors. The larger problem with the monetization of bridewealth, Faguinovery continued, was that men were hostages to their in-laws and husbands had little power to direct their wives. The solution was the suppression of bridewealth as the legal marker that made a relationship a marriage, which would give conjugal and paternal authority to a man over his wife and children. The Galoas, he concluded, were a civilized group, and the colonial administration should implement such a radical change beginning with Galoas; this would serve as an example for the other ethnic groups.[68] As had the Fang chief Endamne, Faguinovery's and Obembe's letters directly beseeched colonial personnel to intervene in regulating this most fundamental aspect of African households.

By the 1930s, French and African political leaders—chiefs, mission-educated African men, colonial civil servants, and Catholic missionaries—concurred on decrying "the bridewealth problem." For French missionaries, increased bridewealth costs in money represented a moral danger: the degradation of women as families "sold" them to the highest bidder, and the degradation of marriage as the relationship became a means to make money. Marriage became a form of prostitution.[69] Colonial administrators concurred that bridewealth inflation was also a problem, but emphasized the problem of demographic and economic loss. As young men could not afford and thus delayed marriage in the years of their prime reproductive capacities, marriages of younger women and older men resulted in fewer births.[70] Elite African male political leaders and chiefs proclaimed that the constitutive order of bridewealth as social glue had fundamentally been altered. Escalating costs of bridewealth cultivated a culture of divorce, prevented young men from marrying, and reinforced the power of women's in-laws over the households of their sons-in-law, brewing instability. High bridewealth costs threatened the social and biological reproduction of African communities.

The bridewealth problem, according to all of these constituencies, was one of bridewealth inflation. From 1930 to 1935, years in which the timber industry was nonexistent or limped along, bridewealth amounts remained at the pre-Depression levels, consisting of 1,000–3,000 francs nearly exclusively in cash.[71] In the post–World War II period, bridewealth payments in the Estuary department varied widely, ranging from a recorded payment of 3,000 francs in 1946 to a payment of 150,000 francs for a marriage in 1956.[72] Although bridewealth payments by these years consisted nearly exclusively of cash, goods such as mutton, goats, cloth and clothing, and alcohol continued to be part of the bridewealth payment bundle. These numbers seem to convey that there indeed was bridewealth inflation.

Was bridewealth inflation occurring continually from the mid- to late 1920s, through the period of independence? In other words, was there a

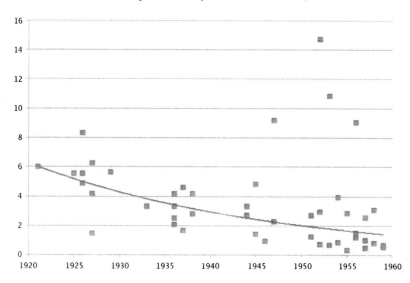

steady rise in the price of bridewealth? Did the purchasing power of men, and therefore their ability to earn money and marry, diminish over these decades? Comparing bridewealth prices with wage-labor earnings presents a more complicated picture than a seamless narrative of bridewealth infla-tion. Calibrating bridewealth payments and wages by year can be a chal-lenging endeavor, given the fragmentary evidence of bridewealth payments in written records and human memory. Additionally, sources differ on if bridewealth was only the amount that women and men's kin agreed to at the time of marriage or also "gifts" of money that a husband made to his wife's family over the course of their marriage. I was able to periodize bride-wealth payments by collecting evidence by year from an array of sources, including missionary and colonial documents and oral interviews.[73] I was not able to find records of bridewealth payments for every year and for every ethnolanguage group; most of the available data was for the Fang. Figure 4.1 illustrates the number of years it would have taken a man to work to obtain the varied bridewealth amounts recorded by year. The salary data are the minimum monthly salaries for unskilled laborers in timber camps, the larg-est sector of wage employment for African men.[74]

This chart indicates a downward trajectory from 1921 to 1960 in the num-ber of years it would have taken for a man to earn enough cash to make recorded bridewealth payments. In 1921, it would have taken a man about six years of wage labor to earn the 1,000 francs needed for a bridewealth payment. In the years of the okoumé rush in the mid-1920s, bridewealth inflation is apparent, particularly for 1926 and 1927, as it could have taken a man as many as six to eight years of wage labor to earn enough money for a bridewealth payment. Over the course of the Depression of the 1930s, bridewealth costs appear to have decreased. It would have taken a man from as little as two and a half years to just over four years to earn sufficient wages, a decrease in the number of years of work in comparison with the previous decade. This decrease in bridewealth costs mirrored what was happening in Cameroon as well, as recorded by Jane Guyer. There, bridewealth payments decreased in the mid-1930s from the high costs of the 1920s.[75] In Gabon, given the virtual stoppage of the timber industry, with most wage laborers unemployed (and thus with little to no cash), few men were likely able to afford to get married. With the post–World War II resurgence of the timber industry and increased wage-labor opportunities, men's purchasing power of bridewealth dramatically increased as bridewealth prices decreased in relation to wages. Between 1951 and 1960, it would have taken most men one to two years to earn bridewealth payments. Hence, at first glance, there appears to have been a bridewealth deflation after the 1930s.

However, from 1945 onward there is more variability between high and low bridewealth payments than in previous decades. For example, an astronomical bridewealth amount recorded for 1952 entailed nearly fifteen years of labor, while another reported bridewealth amount that same year entailed a little more than a year of labor. Rather than bridewealth inflation, bridewealth speculation seems to have been rampant. That some bridewealth payments in 1947 and 1953 required from ten to fifteen years of labor reveals the amount of leverage that families with female dependents held over men seeking to marry. Individual fathers, perhaps those with daughters who had some primary school education or whose fertility had been proven because they had already born children, may have asked higher bridewealth payments than a neighbor who also had daughters of marriageable age. The variability of marriage payments reveals that some men seeking to marry were willing to pay such higher rates. A similar trend in unprecedented rises in individual cases of bridewealth costs occurred in post–World War II rural Kenya as many fathers asked for amounts of cattle that poor men could not afford.[76] Calculating the median amounts of bridewealth payments made in a given year in comparison with wage-labor salaries also reveals a more complex picture than the unmediated narrative of bridewealth inflation of African and French political leaders.

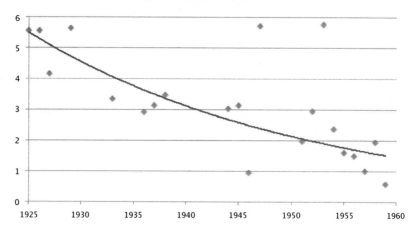

FIGURE 4.2. Median Fang Bridewealth in Years of Timber Laborer Salary. (Chart produced by Glenn Hofmann.)

Figure 4.2 suggests that the number of years a man had to work to make median marriage payments decreased from five and one-half to two years between 1925 and 1959. From the high of four to six years of wage labor from 1925 to 1930, bridewealth prices seem to have decreased over the course of the slump in the timber industry in the 1930s, when men would have had to work from three to three and one-half years. Even with the resurgence of the timber industry after World War II, bridewealth prices appear to have dropped as the number of years a man would have had to work to earn money for bridewealth continued to decrease. Though this data may demonstrate that the years of wage labor in relation to bridewealth payments decreased, the real costs of living in the Estuary department, expenses such as taxes, housing, and food, meant that earning enough money to accumulate marriage payments constituted considerable effort over a man's lifetime.[77] Moreover, after 1945, there were anomalies in median bridewealth payments. In 1944, 1945, and 1954, bridewealth payments required about three years of labor; a high of six years of labor was required in 1946 and 1952. Bridewealth amounts appear to have varied sharply in the 1940s and 1950s. As in the 1930s, getting married after World War II was speculative and could be expensive. Varied iterations of colonial policies and moments of contestation and collaboration between African and French political leaders around the question of regulating the bridewealth economy shaped the contours of governance in the late colonial period.

BRIDEWEALTH REFORM AND POLITICAL POWER, 1941–1952

World War II ushered in the marked interest of high-level administrators in France and throughout French Africa in policies that would regulate African marriage practices, concerns that local officials in Gabon had been voicing for decades. In a 1941 circular titled *Native Social Policy*, Félix Éboué outlined a new era of French colonial governance. In the circular sent to each governor of FEA's colonies, Éboué proposed a series of reforms with the objective of improving standards of living and addressing the "instability of native families." He envisioned the colonial state as the facilitator of monogamous and fecund marriages through legislation and social programs.[78] Éboué's first priority was to encourage marriage by limiting bridewealth amounts. Unlike predecessors who had relied primarily on chiefs, Éboué looked toward emerging numbers of literate, Western-educated African men to act as intermediaries in shaping colonial governance.[79] Male Gabonese *évolués* had grown up in the colony's towns—Libreville, Port-Gentil, and Lambaréné—and worked as wage laborers for private French or state enterprises as civil servants, teachers, clerks, and accountants. Such men were voted in by a limited African electorate to serve in the newly constituted legislative body named the Territorial Assembly or appointed to colonial commissions in Libreville, Brazzaville, or Paris.

Elite Gabonese political leaders called for increased African autonomy in governance, and regulating bridewealth was an important theme in this process of political mobilization. Few of the policy initiatives proposed to regulate bridewealth payments were ever passed or applied by colonial officials. The Territorial Assembly could suggest but not impose legislation.[80] However, as argued by Frederick Cooper in his study of unimplemented colonial labor policies in post–World War II British and French Africa, "the very processes of imagining and codifying framed problems for some time to come, and even if the consequent policy did not resolve basic social and economic problems."[81] The interpretations, debates, and proposed solutions to "the bridewealth problem" of African political leaders reveals the multiple stories of how African historical actors sought to define social relations, reproduce households, and demarcate power in an era of new opportunities.

As Frederick Cooper and Lisa Lindsay have argued, a wave of strikes across British and French Occidental (West) Africa (FOA) from the mid-1930s to the late 1940s compelled colonial officials to conceive of free-labor, wage-earning men living in urban areas with a wife and children as the foundation of a revamped colonial economy.[82] In the minds of colonial policy makers, the "industrial man" and the "male breadwinner" was to be a "predictable, known being who could make Africa into the orderly, productive, controllable society that seemed viable in the post-War."[83] However, what if the "male breadwinner" imagined in varied forms by African activists and colonial personnel did not even have a family to care for because he could not afford to marry, for lack of the resources to pay the bridewealth? Such was the worry commonly expressed by African and French political leaders in Gabon, but disagreements about how to address the problem of high bridewealth and who should address it reveal the incomplete project of regulating gender roles, family life, and how people earned money and what they did with it in the colonial city. Analyzing the history of post–World War II policy debates about bridewealth also underscores the centrality of the social engineering of marriage and family life to late colonial African political mobilization.

African elite political leaders in Gabon advocated for local and African solutions to the regulation of bridewealth payments. Jean-Hilaire Aubame, a Fang and an adviser to Governor Éboué during the war and to his successor Bayardelle in 1944, was elected as Gabon's deputy to the National Assembly in France in 1946. Subsequently stationed in Paris as the delegate and member of the Commission of Overseas Territories, Aubame used this platform to amplify social problems he saw as troubling Gabon and to propose solutions. In a 1949 letter addressed to Governor-General Soucadaux of FEA, Aubame highlighted the problems of bridewealth in "black marriage." Aubame saw bridewealth not as a custom to be abolished but as a custom that had been corrupted by the colonial encounter and needed to be reformed. For Aubame, bridewealth was neither the sale of a woman nor a loss of her rights as argued by French politicians, but functioned as "a deed or official document in the form of the obligation to give an object that certified that a relationship was a marriage." Thus, the European term "bridewealth" was a misnomer. He argued that Europeans were incorrect to emphasize the economic aspect of bridewealth; the purpose of bridewealth was jural given that "marriage, like all contracts among blacks, is sanctioned by the transmission of an object, a tool that is evidence of the agreement."[84] Supplemental bridewealth payments by husbands were "appending deeds," gifts for specific occasions such as the birth of a child or the visit of a member of the bride's family. However foundational and sound bridewealth was, it had been corrupted by money, and its primary purpose as the title deed of marriage had lost its function. Like many previous attempts at legislation of the 1930s, Aubame proposed that bridewealth be limited to 1,000 francs. This amount would return bridewealth to what he viewed as its original juridical purpose. Solving the bridewealth problem would solve the divorce problem. It is hard to tell if Aubame's specific recommendations gained any traction. There is no response to his letter from the governor-general in the archives. But the question of bridewealth across French Africa would be at the forefront of colonial policy a few years later. Many of Aubame's proposals would circulate again.

In 1951, the Ministry of Overseas France authorized a Customs Commission composed of African and French delegates across French Africa to study the regulation of bridewealth amounts.[85] The delegate for Gabon, a man identified as Autin, signaled that the problem of bridewealth inflation was more acute there than elsewhere in Overseas France.[86] It became clear that not all commission members agreed on what policies should emerge. Some French and the few African commission members cautioned that to summarily make bridewealth illegal would draw widespread protest in all colonies. Other commission members argued that limiting bridewealth amounts would create problems that had not previously existed. Autin advised that local notables were unanimously in favor of legislating limits of bridewealth at the time of marriage, but such limits were not to be applied at the time of divorce. No husband at the time of divorce would accept being reimbursed only the official amount; he would fight to prove that he had paid a certain amount over several years and would demand to be reimbursed that entire amount. The only solution, he proposed, was for local assemblies to establish limits on how much bridewealth could be paid both at the time of marriage and at the time of divorce.[87] Solutions to the bridewealth problems were not to come from the minister of Overseas France, but from within the local legislative bodies in each territory. The final recommendation of the commission was that each colony, in consultation with local councils of notables, should determine the maximum bridewealth amount for their locality.[88]

Preempting the recommendations of local legislative bodies in the colonies to demarcate bridewealth limits, the colonial ministry passed the Jacquinot Decree of 1951, whose purpose was to facilitate the marriage of young men and women across all of French Africa.[89] Couples were to register their marriages with colonial authorities. The decree allowed couples to marry without their families' consent if parents made "excessive demands" for bridewealth. Furthermore, a woman's family could not retake possession of her, nor could she abandon the conjugal home on the grounds that her husband had not yet completed bridewealth payments.[90] This decree sought to make marriage the decision of the nuclear couple and to diminish the power of a woman's family to determine her marital aspirations.

In 1952, Governor-General Reste of FEA charged the newly convened Territorial Assemblies to set maximum bridewealth amounts in each colony. Debates raged among varied Gabonese delegates in an appointed subcommission for studying "the problem of bridewealth and fixing a bridewealth amount."[91] Most agreed that maximum bridewealth amounts were to be set, but some argued for the commission to also establish minimum bridewealth amounts in order to encourage young men to work for wages. Now serving as the Woleu-Ntem delegate to the assembly, Aubame insisted that maximum and minimum bridewealth amounts vary from region to region. People living in the Estuary department had greater access to wage-labor opportunities and money than those in a rural department such as Adouma, Aubame argued. Legislation that set minimum and maximum bridewealth according to the relative access to cash would return bridewealth to its juridical purpose.[92]

A central challenge in codifying bridewealth limits was that even touching upon the question of bridewealth by legislators immediately sparked questions of what marriage was more generally and the roles and rights of wives and husbands in relation to each other. Some delegates saw several problems with setting bridewealth limits. Mpongwé delegate Paul Gondjout said his colleagues were getting ahead of themselves.[93] First, there was still no civil code that codified marriage, family, and inheritance law. As long as what constituted "marriage" had not been well defined, regulating bridewealth would not solve anything. Léon Mba asked if the object of fixing bridewealth amounts was to consolidate marriage or prevent divorces. He saw these as two separate issues, but argued that divorce was the "greatest difficulty troubling Gabon." Codifying bridewealth, he explained, would not prevent divorces. Not having reached a consensus, the delegates voted to put this question aside.[94] The next week, the full gathering of the Territorial Assembly met to vote on the subcommission's proposed limitations on bridewealth. The commission changed their original proposal of graduated bridewealth minimums and maximums and instead proposed that there be a bridewealth limit of 5,000 francs for all of Gabon. To enforce this, the obligatory declaration of all marriages before state authorities would be required, and the bride and groom were to sign a marriage certificate. On the question of divorce for marriages that had taken place before the law was passed, women's families would reimburse the original amount that they paid even if it exceeded the new limit of 5,000 francs.[95]

Fellow delegates who opposed the bill raised several objections. Aubame again argued that the fixed amount of 5,000 francs was too high for some people and that this would not encourage marriage; those who could not amass enough money would remain unmarried. The debate turned to what Mba had argued, that high bridewealth was but a symptom of the real problem of African marriages, which was instability or divorce caused by women's "debauchery." A delegate named Mossot summarized this sentiment with the following: "We cannot vote on fixing bridewealth amounts without definitively regulating African marriage." Delegates elaborated upon how the colonial administration needed to intervene to stop women's debauchery because some women currently were able to reimburse their own bridewealth, without actually needing assistance from their families, destroying the family and diminishing the colony's birth rate. Rather than concentrating on bridewealth, some delegates echoed Mba in calling for a study on the regulation of divorce. However, Aubame contested, they had not consulted any women in their attempts to formulate bridewealth policy. Delegates again tabled the vote on bridewealth limits, this time in favor of a study on the codification of marriage; bridewealth reform needed to occur in conjunction with a comprehensive body of law that regulated all aspects of marriage.[96] The next week the delegates convened again, yet moved on beyond the question of bridewealth to debate various proposals about punishing adultery and limiting divorce. Delegates could not come to a definitive decision and did not vote on the matter of establishing bridewealth amounts.[97]

The inability of African elite men and French colonial officials to regulate bridewealth in Gabon was in keeping with the failure of similar attempts across Africa in the period of colonial rule. Noncompliance with bridewealth regulation mandated by the Jacquinot Decree was evident not only in Gabon but in other colonies across French-speaking Africa.[98] Since few Africans registered their marriages in colonial civil registries, the state had limited capacities to apply directives. Though the cost of marriage was of high importance to the French colonial government, Barbara Cooper argues, colonial policies failed to take into account the immense local variations of form, content, and significance of bridewealth, as well as the variations in payment amounts based on the status, age, and wealth of the family of the bride.[99] In Kenya, chiefs and British colonial personnel also made wartime and postwar efforts to limit bridewealth payments.[100] As in Kenya, bridewealth regulation policies in Gabon failed due to noncompliance by communities and individuals and the inability of African and colonial political leaders to enforce the very limits that they had set.

Attempts at bridewealth policy reveal the conflicts of interest and the contestations among African men of differing generations, wealth, and ethnicity about access to money and the shifting terrain of defining adult manhood

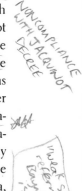

through marriage in urban areas. The debates of African political figures in the Gabonese assembly about the regulation of bridewealth costs reveal anxieties that the circulation of colonial currency opened up avenues for women to exercise extramarital control over their sexuality and persons. The discourses that correlated increased bridewealth payments with the increased occurrences of the unattainability of marriage (in that young men could not afford marriage), and instability of marriage (in that wives more frequently divorced or engaged in adultery), reveal that the determinants of masculinity were shifting. If men could not marry, a central measure of reaching male adulthood was no longer a possibility. Rather than regulating the bridewealth economy, the colonial state would enter into it and validate bridewealth payments through providing loans in cash to African men to marry.

THE BRIDEWEALTH LOAN FUND, 1941–1952

Beginning in 1941, African men in FEA could, in theory, take advantage of a new arena of earning money for bridewealth: the marriage loan fund for FEA decreed in 1940 by Charles de Gaulle's Free French government. With the sole purpose of subsidizing African men's bridewealth expenses, de Gaulle's administration established the special fund of 100,000 francs that was to be shared among colonies in Free France.[101] Documentary evidence of the loan project is fragmentary and does not reveal the genealogy of this fund. It is probable that it was Félix Éboué, with his emphasis on colonial policies that forwarded the social development of African societies, who was at the helm of developing this program. In a letter dated August 1941, Éboué introduced the loan fund to the governors of the colonies of FEA.[102] That this fund was being launched in the midst of World War II was symbolic for Free France in their efforts to project de Gaulle as the legitimate ruler. In contrast to Vichy-led FOA, which retracted the rights of African colonial subjects and increased the manifestation of racism, FEA was to invest in its African populations.[103] In 1942, the central administration in Brazzaville allocated an additional 200,000 francs specifically to the Gabon bridewealth fund.[104] African employees of the colonial state of any level, as well as wage laborers of private European enterprises, were eligible to apply. Called "marriage loans," these disbursements of cash were meant to assist men in marrying by subsidizing their bridewealth payments. Loans were to be made only for monogamous marriages, and applicants were to have signed a document that renounced polygamy. The men would repay the colonial state in monthly installments determined by local administrators. By 1950, the line item for the marriage loans became a part of the individual budget of each colony, the amount for which was to be set by the colony legislatures.[105] This allowed each colony to decide how much would be set aside for the loans, the amounts that would be granted, the modalities for lending out the funds, and the modes of repayment.

Varied levels of the colonial administration in FEA, from the governor-general to subdivision administrators, took a great interest in the application and administration of the loan program. At the end of 1941, the governor-general of FEA inquired as to how the program was unfolding in Gabon, and the governor subsequently inquired to circumscription administrators in the colony.[106] The governor of Gabon replied that over the course of his tours around the colony, African men reacted with enthusiasm about the availability of cash for bridewealth. However, potential applicants persistently thought that the money was in the form of a grant, an outright gift rather than a loan that needed to be paid back. He indicated that it was an uphill battle to explain that it was a loan, and this misinterpretation would result in a delay to get the bridewealth loan program off the ground. Governor Valentin-Smith hoped to work in collaboration with some French managers of mines and timber camps who were willing to cooperate with the administration in disbursing advances in the form of loans to their workers. At first it seemed the program was not attracting as many men as administrators had hoped for, and the governor urged subdivision administrators to solicit applicants.

In 1942, the governor established a committee that would oversee the applications, ensure the reimbursement process, and keep the fund liquid in the hopes that the fund would be "for the population, a living reality and institution that little by little would achieve the goal of sustaining young marriage-minded men in the transactions of haggling to establish a family."[107] Gabonese men who were of "native status" could apply for the loan, whether their brides were natives or French citizens, but men who were French citizens could not apply for the loan. Men who requested loans were to submit typed forms and provide required documentation to local officials in their region of residence. Applicants were required to furnish documents that specified both the groom's and the bride's ethnicities, the chief who would witness that the payment of bridewealth abided by the customary law of the particular ethnic group, a written statement to identify the fiancée and her consent for the marriage, and a document to certify the total amount of bridewealth. This had to be the applicant's first marriage and he could not be polygamous. Local officials would forward the documentation and their assessments of the applicants to the governor of Gabon or the mayor of Libreville for final veto or approval of the application.[108] In some years it was the mayor who had final say over which applications to decline or fund; in other years, the governor of Gabon. Officials anticipated that applicants would request from 2,000 to 3,000 francs and that they would repay the state in monthly installments of 200 francs.

By the end of 1942, local officials in Gabon assessed the efficacy of the program and emphasized the distinct nature of the bridewealth problem in Libreville compared to rural areas that made up the vast majority of the colony. The governor had allocated different amounts for each of the colony's departments. For the Ngounié department, only 6,105 francs of the budget of 16,105 francs had been disbursed. Not 1 franc had been spent in the rural Nyanga and Djouah departments, where there appeared to be "little enthusiasm in the population for marriage loans."[109] The administrator of the department of Djouah responded to the governor's remonstration that he had not reached enough applicants. The administrator replied that suggested loan amounts of 2,000 to 3,000 francs were more than anyone in his department, primarily of the Bakota ethnic group, who engaged in small-scale subsistence farming, had the opportunity to earn and save. The department had no timber camps and therefore no opportunities for Gabonese men to engage in wage labor and earn cash. The administrator was hopeful that the recent opening of gold excavating sites and a public works project for building a road might provide young men the opportunity to earn wages in cash and therefore be able to take advantage of the loan program.[110] Bridewealth payments in the area averaged 500–600 francs, half of which was in cash and the other half in goats and objects such as native iron hammers, leather bracelets, and blocks of iron. Although bridewealth payments were not as high as in Libreville, the administrator did qualify that rates had increased over the years; the current rates were still too much for most young men to afford. As a result, one-third of young men remained single, while older men who could afford bridewealth payments had polygamous households.[111] Making marriage affordable, the department's administrator intimated, was not about offering money through loans, but about providing jobs to earn wages in cash, to create the male breadwinner.

Qualifying for the marriage loan depended on one's sustained employment in wage labor. In March 1948, Djouah received money for a road-building project, from which the governor hoped that the administrator could find "dignified" laborers whose marital projects the fund could support. Moreover, the governor wrote, he also saw no problem if the administrator

FIGURE 4.3. Marriage Loans from the De Gaulle Marriage Loan Fund[114]

Year	Number of Applicants	Region or City	Total Amount Requested from All Applicants (Francs)	Number of Grantees	Total Amount Disbursed (Francs)
1941	Not indicated	Estuary	5,000	3	7,500 (two loans of 3,000, one of 1,500)
		Ogouée-Maritime	4,500	1	3,000 (one loan of 3,000)
		Woleu-N'tem	3,000	3	4,500 (three loans of 1,500 each)
1942	1	Libreville	2,000	0	0
1943	Not indicated	Libreville	Not indicated	7	7,500 (Six applicants given 1,000, one given 1,500)
	"	Moyen-Ogouée	"	Not indicated	5,000
	"	Ngounié	"	"	5,000
	"	Woleu-N'tem	"	"	2,500
	"	Nyanga	"	"	2,500
	"	Ogouée-Maritime	"	"	2,500
1944	1	Libreville	1,000	1	1,000
1945	2	Libreville	2,000 (each applicant requested 1,000)	2	2,000 (Each applicant granted 1,000)
1946	3	Libreville	5,500 (one applicant requested 3,500, the second 2,000, the third not indicated)	1	3,500
1947	1	Mouilla	Not detailed	1	Not indicated
	2	Woleu-N'tem	"	2	"
	2	Ogouée-Maritime	"	2	"
	1	Lambaréné	"	1	"
	10	Libreville	Not detailed for all the applications (1 applicant requested 5,000, another 6,000)	9	" Not indicated (extant documents reveal 5,000 given to 1 applicant, another 6,000)
1952	2	Libreville	Not detailed	2	15,000 (5,000 francs given to 1 applicant, 10,000 francs to another)
Total					72,500

saw fit to divert some of the money earmarked for building roads to instead offer a free gift to the hardest-working laborers so that they could more easily meet the bridewealth demands of prospective in-laws.[112] In contrast, the administrator of Nyanga, where young men had opportunities to work in mines, eagerly wrote to the governor-general upon learning that Gabon had been given more funds for bridewealth loans to inquire if people from his department would be eligible to apply.[113]

Figure 4.3 lists extant applications received for the bridewealth loan in varied regions. Few of the applications of African men to the bridewealth loan fund have survived in the archives, yet the existing records hint at the steady stream of requests and loans granted in the Estuary department. It is not clear how many African men in total applied for these loans each year. That so few applications have survived in the archives belies the indication by colonial personnel in Gabon that the loan fund's budget could not meet the demands. The applications of only some successful candidates are in the archives. More men could have inquired about the loans but never completed all of the documentation. It is also not possible to calculate the finite amount disbursed from the marriage loan fund, given that records are missing for certain years. By 1952, records of the marriage loan fund stop appearing in the archives. It is not clear how and why funding for this program ended; there is no mention in legislative debates or correspondence about how and if the bridewealth loan was no longer funded. However, the existing documentation does provide some glimpse into the modalities and strategies of African men to gain cash for bridewealth payments and the ways in which the colonial state sought to regulate African marriages through subsidizing bridewealth.

Although there were few to zero applicants in some rural subdivisions of the Estuary department, it appears that the overall demand outweighed the resources and the bridewealth fund was often depleted. In February 1942, Governor Valentin-Smith of Gabon forwarded two dossiers of applicants from the Estuary department to the governor-general of FEA in Brazzaville. He indicated that although Gabon had already distributed all of its allocated 25,000 francs of bridewealth loans, he hoped that the governor-general would consider dipping into other funds in his budget to respond favorably to these additional requests.[115] In an undated letter, the governor-general of FEA remarked that after several years of the program's being in place, "unfortunately, it is evident that the only beneficiaries of this social measure are African civil servants residing in the colonial centers and not those in the bush."[116] The bridewealth fund did not increase the numbers of wage laborers, but provided new avenues to augment the cash holdings of men already employed, primarily in the Estuary department. African men who had served in the army or worked as teachers, laborers, or civil servants constituted the pool of successful applicants.

For a vast majority of applicants for whom documentation is extant, administrators approved their requests, with individual loans ranging from 1,000 to 3,000 francs in 1942. Given that median bridewealth payments were about 3,000 francs in 1942 (see fig. 4.1 on page 116), the loan likely subsidized about one-third of the applicants' bridewealth. By 1952, approved bridewealth loan amounts ranged from 5,000 to 10,000 francs. Recorded bridewealth payments that year spanned 7,500–30,000 francs. Thus, the bridewealth loan seems to have provided as much as 75 percent of the cash that some men required for bridewealth payments.[117] Loan recipients from throughout Gabon tended to be men who worked in elite wage-labor jobs, such as accountants, telephone clerks, and teachers, or men who worked independently and had access to money, such as foresters. Additionally, some grantees in the Woleu-Ntem department listed themselves as planters, likely owners of cocoa farms, an emerging avenue of wealth in the north. Loan recipients in the Estuary department included both Myènè and Fang men.[118]

The bridewealth loan fund as it evolved facilitated the marriage of wage-earning and likely literate African men, middling to elite men who could constitute stable urban family lives. Colonial administrators assessed the creditworthiness of applicants and their ability to repay the loans based on their current salaries. Applications included letters from bosses and police personnel reporting on applicants' general conduct, any criminal history, and a sound financial past. Full documentation about the process of applying and being granted a bridewealth loan for individual applicants is sparse, yet there are extant documents for some applicants in 1943, 1946, and 1947. The existing documents from several successful applicants illustrate that the process of applying for the loan could take from three months to one year. A successful applicant was required to engage varied levels of the colonial administration and had to be literate in French or be aligned with French-speaking Africans who could author correspondence on their behalf.

Applicants had to furnish varied forms of documentation, but the morality test of applicants as assessed by administrators could make a key difference in loan requests' being denied or approved. In 1946, the administrator of the Estuary department denied and the governor of Gabon confirmed the denial of the request for 2,000 francs for a man named Philipe Okongo, who was an auxiliary agent for the public works department.[119] The administrator recorded that investigations into Okongo's life revealed him to be "an individual of doubtful morality"; he had been implicated in two incidents involving theft earlier that year. In contrast, a 1946 application by a man named Toussaint Etoughe, exercising the same profession as Okong, was approved for 3,500 francs. The primary factor of his approval was his "good morality and sound associations." Unnamed persons that administrators questioned about Etoughe testified to his honesty. Furthermore, he was the owner of his residence, a small wood hut.

Fraud, defined as the possibility of men borrowing the money for purposes other than to pay bridewealth or to marry a woman who was already married, was another reason for denial. In 1942, the secretary of the governor-general of FEA wrote a letter to the governor of Gabon requesting information about a Gabonese applicant named Michel Biteghe, who was working as an artist for the education department in Pointe-Noire, Brazzaville. The fiancée of record, a woman named Thérèse Afanbélé, resided in Libreville and was supposedly an orphan who had been raised at the Sainte Marie mission. The secretary wanted to know if the aunt with whom Ms. Afanbélé lived consented to the marriage, the bridewealth amount, and verification of her ethnic group. Governor Assier de Pompignan responded that she was indeed an orphan, but that he had tracked down her brother, who was the titular head of the family. According to her brother, she was already married, since 1939, to a man named Joseph Obiang Adane of Libreville, who had given him 1,500 francs in bridewealth for his sister's marriage.[120] In 1946, the mayor of Libreville wrote to the governor of the colony that he had denied an applicant because investigations revealed that he had already paid bridewealth for the bride listed on his application.[121]

The bridewealth loan documents reveal the efforts of the French to create monogamous, consent-based African marriages of wage laborers in Libreville through controlling the purse. For decades, the French had endeavored to create African marriages that accorded with French mores through regulating bridewealth payments. Attempts to limit bridewealth payments had failed. The bridewealth loan program opened a new possibility for the French to encourage certain modes of marriage. First, the man applying for the loan had to state that he renounced polygamy. A document signed by the woman indicating her consent was also necessary for a successful application. Furthermore, the brides had to be beyond puberty. The French wanted to assure that women were not child brides and were embarking on marriages of choice. However, in assuring that women's families consented to the marriage and that the brides had not decided to marry against their parents' wishes, colonial officials wished to direct that women were to be married with the endorsement of their elder matriarchs and patriarchs. The goal was to allow younger women some measure of individual determination, but not too much. A monogamous marriage of consenting adult men and women, approved by their kin and sealed with a codified bridewealth amount, was thought to ensure a long-lasting relationship devoid of conflict and the possibility of divorce.

The trail of documents for the successful application of Henri Ango, an Mpongwé man who worked as a draftsman-topographer aide for public works, is revealing of the form of marriage the French sought to facilitate within African societies. The process of Ango's marriage that emerges from the documents is one of a rationalized relationship achieved by mutual agreement between consenting adults, acknowledged by their kin, consecrated by chiefs, and partially funded by and registered with the colonial state. In February 1947, Henri wrote a letter requesting a loan of 4,000 francs and offering to repay the amount in monthly installments of 200 francs.[122] In August of that year Mr. Ango addressed yet another letter to the head of public works, asking after the status of his request as he had yet to hear back.[123] One month later, the governor replied to the head of public works that he was returning Mr. Ango's application, requiring that Mr. Ango furnish the following documents: a certificate of the ethnic group of the person receiving the bridewealth payment, a certificate of the fiancée's consent, a certificate indicating the amount of bridewealth, and a document indicating that the applicant was single and had renounced polygamy. Once the dossier was complete with all of this information, the head of public works was to attach his assessment of the applicant and forward the dossier to the mayor of Libreville, who would pass it on to the governor.[124] The French employers of many applicants wrote the cover letter for the application and facilitated communication between the candidate and colonial administrators.

Over subsequent months, Ango's file accumulated the requested documents. A document dated September 23 and signed by Henri Ango attested that he was single and had renounced polygamy. On September 26, his fiancée, Odette Mengue, signed an attestation that her parents did not oppose her marriage. A man named Obame, identifying himself as the head of Odette's family, signed a document consenting that the two could marry and numerating the bridewealth amount as 2,000 francs and an additional 2,000 for "various expenses." Bernard Mba, the chief of the neighborhood of Mont-Bouet, declaring that to his knowledge there was no reason to oppose the marriage, signed a document titled "Attestation of Group Chief."

On October 22, the head of public works forwarded the application and supporting documentation to the governor and indicated his support for Mr. Ango's request.[125] On November 3, 1947, the governor signed a decision that granted Henri Ango a loan of 6,000 francs and stated that repayment would begin on the first of December, with twenty monthly payments of 200 francs. It is not clear why an additional 2,000 francs came to be added to the original 4,000 requested by Ango. The letter approving the loan qualified that he was to reimburse the state the entire amount at once if he became a polygamist.[126] By providing a new avenue for gaining access to cash, the bridewealth loan program, in part, legitimatized the very bridewealth payments that were protested as too high by African men seeking to marry and by African and French political leaders.

CONCLUSION

The emergence of and transformations in the bridewealth economy in twentieth-century colonial Libreville reveal how bridewealth practices were contested negotiations and not a closed system.[127] By the first decade of the twentieth century, residents of Libreville incorporated money into bridewealth practices, and bridewealth money circulated as debt, wealth to purchase goods and services, credit, loans, and interest, subject to the booms and busts and inflation and deflation of the colonial economy. However, the bridewealth economy operated along the logic of attempts to create personal relationships of affinity that were to provide support and establish personhood—parenthood, emotional attachment, care in times of illness, allegiance, and trust—in colonial Libreville. Though the colonial state and African political leaders attempted to set limits on bridewealth expenditures, consumers largely ignored these regulations. Capitalism did not completely reorganize the meaning of bridewealth and the monetization of bridewealth did not result in the breakdown of social relationships. Rather, historical actors folded and reordered the economic and social value of money into changing processes and practices of conjugality and the quotidian relations of kith and kin.

At the heart of contestations over bridewealth was the definition of marriage, under what terms arrangements between men and women could be recognized as social and legal marriages, and the parameters within which marriages could be ruptured. Anxieties about bridewealth money centered upon the attainability of marriage and marrying well, and how money facilitated or called into question rights to as well as in marriage. The inability to marry was high on the anxiety list of Libreville inhabitants, yet equally fraught was the question of the instability of marriage, the question of divorce. This question was also of great importance to African and French political leaders, who sought to define customary law and shape a colonial court system to maintain marriages.

5 ⤳ Jurisprudence
Marriage and Divorce Law

(

FROM 1930 TO 1960, colonial courts emerged as central venues that
Libreville residents sought out to adjudicate marital conflict. In these decades,
a host of husbands, French colonial officials, elite African men, and some
chiefs decried "divorce debauchery" and an increased number of "fickle"
wives in the Estuary department who demanded divorces for "frivolous" reasons.[1] Political figures and Libreville residents debated conceptualizations,
policies, and applications of marriage and divorce law and the adjudication of
marital conflict in colonial courts. What constituted justifiable grounds and
processes for divorce in colonial courts and courts of public opinion was very
much up for debate. Areas of disagreement unfolded along questions of what
husbands, wives, and affines viewed as the benefits and rights that marriage
should be accorded and their conceptualization of restorative justice to re-
dress social and material wrongs. Litigants came to courts seeking or trying to
preclude divorce or to air grievances in the hopes of reconciliation. In negotiating divorce, parties sought to settle upon terms of child custody, whether
a child would legally and socially belong to the father's or the mother's lineage, the care of children, and monetary payments such as the reimbursement
of bridewealth and the payment of court fees or fines. Widows and heirs of
deceased husbands sought to determine the boundaries of levirate marriage,
whether a woman could "divorce" her dead husband's family.

Such legal contestations raised multiple questions: What were the expectations of marriage of spouses and their kin? Under what grounds could

a marriage be terminated? Who would ensure the care and physical custody of children? Who had the authority to adjudicate instances of marital conflict? What set of laws would guide efforts at reaching an agreement? These were uneasy, tense questions that permeated the varied fora of colonial courts under the purview of African chiefs and assessors and French colonial officials. Such questions were particularly fraught with tension in that African and French political and religious leaders continually sought to codify customary marriage and divorce law, yet invariably offered differing interpretations of marital law.

In theory, the codified customary marriage laws of individual ethnicities were meant to render clear the answers to these questions for African and French adjudicators in colonial courts. In the 1930s, through independence, varied African and French political and religious constituencies endeavored to codify customary marriage law in order to provide preventive and curative parameters to reduce divorce rates. Codification projects included efforts to reform the legal and social processes of marrying in order to preempt conflict that provided catalysts for spouses, most frequently women, to request a divorce. Additionally, codified customary laws that delineated clear and restricted grounds for divorce and were applied in a rational court system were intended to reduce divorce rates. Colonial arguments about the necessity of codifying customary marriage law in the post–World War II years centered on the perception that African populations had too quickly adapted to living in urban areas.[2] Migration and money had reordered gender, generational, and political hierarchies of power. Administrators and missionaries argued that the African family cell, particularly among the Fang, had disintegrated.[3] Africans living in or near urban areas had been "detribalized"—urbanization, contact with the colonial state and the church, and wage labor had resulted in African communities that no longer lived according to customs.[4] Elite African men also worried that women increasingly engaged in libertinage—on numerous occasions married women committed adultery and divorced to remarry other men. African political leaders argued that the result, particularly among the Fang, was a serious problem of demographic and socioeconomic crisis.[5] Establishing social order meant controlling women's sexuality and conjugal fluidity and limiting divorce.

However, customary marriage law in colonial Gabon was never codified. There was no unified French or African opinion. Catholic Church representatives expressed concern over increasing divorce rates, yet sought to establish conversion to Christianity as a justifiable reason for divorce. Colonial administrators were hesitant to downright hostile toward the Catholic

ETHNIC DIVERSITY AS A FACTOR

change in power brokers after WW2

Church's regulating marriage. Additionally, administrators vacillated between wishing to facilitate African women's individual freedom in choosing marriage options and wishing to control women's conjugal mobility.[6] Furthermore, concurrent courts operated to adjudicate marital conflict and were presided over by state, chief, and church personnel. Libreville's ethnic diversity resulted in varied understandings of the social and legal parameters of marriage being forwarded by residents and chiefs. Some chiefs tended to more readily grant wives' requests for divorce, censoring individual husbands who sought to maintain their marriages. After World War II, young African men elected to local legislatures emerged as new political power brokers who sought to regulate marriage and divorce according to varied logics of African and French best practices. Colonial courts were frontiers along which litigants offered multiple understandings of social and legal order, just comportment between husbands, wives, and affines, and what constituted "marriage" in these decades of immense historical change.

LEGAL PLURALITY: MARRIAGE LAW AND LEGAL SYSTEMS IN THEORY, CA. 1925–1936

In setting up a system of courts to adjudicate civil conflict within African societies, the French colonial intention was to create an orderly process of adjudication and establish legal and social order.[7] The French attempted to establish the architecture of a streamlined colonial court system in the first decade of the twentieth century. Each subdivision was to have a native court, to be presided over by the highest-ranking military commander or civil officer. The subdivision head was to mediate *all* civil, commercial, and criminal conflicts between African subjects. French personnel who presided over courts had little to no training or expertise in jurisprudence. At his discretion, one European assessor and one native assessor assisted in rendering verdicts. By the first decade of the twentieth century, African communities of the Estuary brought their conflicts before colonial authorities.

Questions concerning marriage emerged as a focal point of disputes brought before colonial courts.[8] Though no written records of this early decade have survived in the archives, colonial administrators wrote in quarterly reports that the numbers of marriage-related cases they oversaw overwhelmed their day-to-day administrative responsibilities.[9] The governor of Gabon relayed in the 1912 annual report, "If it was obligatory to settle all disputes between natives by a judicial channel (numerous repetitions of bridewealth, reimbursement of money, abandonment of the conjugal home, etc.), all of the *circonscription* commander's time would be taken up

FIGURE 5.1. Colonial Native Court System, 1927–1939

Homologation Court
- Appeals from second-degree court
- French judge headquartered in Brazzaville

Second-Degree Court
- Judgment of felonies and appeals from the first-degree court
- French judge assisted by two African assessors

First-Degree Court
- Judgment of civil disputes if agreement had not been reached in conciliation, divorce, and misdemeanors.
- French judge assisted by two African assessors

Conciliation Court
- Subrogation of civil disputes, except divorce
- African judge-arbitrators

by the role of civil judge."[10] Historian Silvère Ngoundos Idourah argued that by the mid-twentieth century, the colonial state had succeeded in co-opting the administration of native justice away from indigenous representatives and that individual colonial administrators were endowed with the roles of judge, jury, and sentencer.[11] However, French control over the rule of law was not so categorical.

By the 1920s, a series of decrees incorporated elements of indirect rule and African chiefs into the colonial legal system. Subsequent reforms over the course of the 1930s delineated a multitiered colonial court system (Figure 5.1). Chiefs were to serve as a firewall that reduced litigation brought before French judges, colonial personnel who also usually worked as the head of a subdivision or other administrative unit.[12] Appointed African chiefs were assigned the role of judge-arbiter (*juge-conciliateur*) with the power to reconcile civil conflicts.[13] It was mandatory that disagreeing parties first present

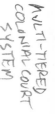

their cases before African judge-arbiters, usually a neighborhood, village, or canton chief, for an attempt at reconciliation before petitioning French administrators.[14] Litigants were to act upon the oral agreements facilitated by chiefs in these conciliation hearings. In theory, chiefs were to maintain a written record of proceedings and agreements reached. If parties could not reconcile their differences, it was only then that they could submit a written petition to request a hearing before the first-degree court in each subdivision headed by French personnel. The next level in the colonial court system, the second-degree court manned by French personnel who could consult with African assessors, could decide upon appeals of decisions from the first-degree court and any criminal infractions. Chiefs could reconcile parties, but could not declare divorce. To declare a marriage null and void was the reserve of a French judge. Decrees establishing the native court system vaguely outlined that courts should follow "local customs, unless they proved contrary to principles of French civilization." Yet what was "custom" in colonial twentieth-century Gabon? What customs did the French administration deem to be contrary to French civilization and therefore refuse to recognize in legal proceedings?

As analyzed in chapter 2, the project of codifying customary law in Gabon in the first decades of colonial rule did not come to fruition. Across much of colonial-era Africa by the 1930s, there was ostensibly one body of law based on "native customs" for Africans who were colonial subjects and another body of European law for white settlers and the few Africans who achieved European citizenship. Scholars have described this system of law as a form of "legal pluralism."[15] The unfolding of customary law in Gabon was a form of legal pluralism, but different from elsewhere in colonial Africa. The nature of legal pluralism in Gabon was of multiple conceptualizations of customary law. The processes of codification in Gabon—how African men and Frenchmen conceptualized and debated what constituted customary marriage law—reveal that colonial society and African patriarchy were not monolithic constituencies. Rather, among African and French political leaders there were conflicting and competing interests, and control and matters of jurisprudence operated along a disjunctured continuum. In Gabon, "elder men" did not constitute a uniform political block that held unwavering political power, nor were junior and senior men always in direct opposition.

In the 1930s, colonial officials again endeavored to codify customary marriage law, utilizing the knowledge and indirect rule of chiefs as the vehicle for enforcement. In 1932, the current governor urged, "If elaborated, debated, and adopted by the chiefs, there is more of a chance that these new customs will be accepted by the population."[16] Distinguishing the populations of Libreville and other towns such as Lambaréné from African societies in rural regions, the governor opined that the problem of customary law in towns was of communities who had rejected customs. City life, he argued, "had accelerated women's freedom in a negative sense." With ever-increasing bridewealth rates and the possibility of earning money from sex with unmarried men, women were tremendous generators of money for their uncles and fathers, who perpetually facilitated the marriage, divorce, and remarriage in search of cash. As many husbands and wives moved to Libreville without kin, some women sought out divorce of their free will, without the involvement of male kin who may have brokered their marriages. In his assessment of the frequency with which women in the colony's urban centers brought requests for divorce before chiefs and colonial administrators, the governor surmised in a quarterly 1932 report, "Without extended family members present, these individuals were free to live as they liked, to marry and divorce, engage in prostitution to the extent that from day to day the family loses its true physiognomy."[17]

Codified customary marriage law was to reflect modifications of "traditional" practices. These documents were to serve as a blueprint for chiefs, subdivision administrators, and other colonial representatives in officiating marriages and settling marital conflicts. The European composition of these commissions ranged from colonial bureaucrats, Protestant and Catholic missionaries, and court officials, to doctors and public health officials, private businessmen, and colonial court judges. African men—chiefs and interpreters—also served on these commissions, in contrast to the attempts to codify customary law in the 1920s (which did not include African members). Backed by the colonial state, chiefs were to decide upon the modalities of marriage, mediate conflict, and declare or deny divorces.

In 1933, Gabon's governor forwarded the document "Galoas, Pahouin, and Akélais Customs," a text that codified customary marriage laws among these ethnic groups, to the governor-general of French Equatorial Africa (FEA) in Brazzaville.[18] The text resulted from meetings with hundreds of chiefs of varied ethnic groups and was to ensure uniformity in how chiefs viewed conjugal law. A group chief was to witness the exchange of bridewealth, record the amount in a register, and issue a certificate of marriage. The remittance of bridewealth—limited to 1,000 francs for all ethnic groups—was but one component of a relationship's being legally recognized as marriage. In addition to a bridewealth payment from the groom's kin to the bride's kin, both the fiancé and the fiancée were to consent to the marriage. Girls who had not yet reached puberty could not be married. Only a

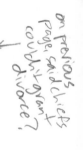

husband or wife, not their kin, could request a divorce. Divorce would be granted only in cases of abandonment or adultery by either party, debilitating physical abuse, refusal to provide food and lodging, and serious cases of incompatibility.[19] In addition to censuring unfaithful wives, the law was to preclude husbands who sought divorce because they wished to be rid of an aging wife in favor of a younger one. A husband lost the reimbursement of his bridewealth if he was at fault, and the wife was subject to prison in addition to reimbursement of bridewealth if at fault.

A 1936 codification document specifically for Fang populations duplicated the directives of the 1932 document, but further reduced bridewealth to 500 francs.[20] Levirate marriage as an automatic course was abolished. A widow was free to choose whether she wanted to marry someone within her deceased husband's family or choose to divorce the family by reimbursing a proportion of her bridewealth. A man and woman who wished to divorce would first be heard by the judge-conciliator, who was an auxiliary of the first-degree court. If conciliation was not possible, the judge-conciliator, under the approbation of the French head of the subdivision, could pronounce a divorce. Gabon's governor did not seek the formal approval of superiors in Brazzaville before circulating the document to subordinate administrators, instructing that the document serve as a rubric for French personnel and chiefs to mediate litigation in colonial courts.[21] Chiefs would be the centralized authority to oversee the consecration of marriages and the facilitation of divorces. As discussed in chapter 4, efforts to regulate bridewealth payments proved ineffectual, but what about efforts to standardize customary divorce law and the authority of chiefs to enforce such directives?

Chiefs who were to exercise centralized control over the conjugal practices of the communities to which they were appointed competed for control with men who were the senior members of extended kin groups. Colonial administrators selected chiefs from among senior men of varied ethnic groups. Establishing a chief's authority involved reducing the power of individual senior men who were heads of extended families.[22] Senior men were not a unified block. Heads of families sought to preserve final say over whom female dependents married in order to maintain children born within their lineages and to maximize bridewealth money. Codification projects of the 1930s were intended to create marriages entered into by consenting men and women and regulated by a legible body of laws. Yet it does not appear that chiefs universally applied all colonial directives, and husbands living within chiefs' jurisdictions called their authority into question.

In August 1936, a letter signed by "The Married Native Population of Libreville" arrived at the desk of the governor of Gabon.[23] The anonymous signatories complained about the manner in which chiefs in their Estuary village managed divorce proceedings. First, the letter writers complained that once chiefs ruled for a divorce, husbands were awarded only about half of the bridewealth payments they had remitted to brides' families. Not only did husbands receive only half of bridewealth monies due to them, they also had to pay chiefs a fee of 100 francs. Additionally, the letter outlined, chiefs gave refuge to wives in the process of divorce much longer than necessary. Chiefs delayed ruling on divorce proceedings in order to use the women as laborers for their own farms.

Though the letter writers began by complaining about corrupt practices by chiefs, they solicited the governor not to rein in chiefs, but to rein in their wives and their wives' lovers who waited in the wings to marry them. The ultimate goal of the aggrieved husbands was to retain their wives and maintain their marriages. The married men asked that if a woman's lover failed to fully reimburse a husband's bridewealth within a week, the husband retained whatever little bridewealth money the suitor had paid as damages and interest and the wife was to return to the conjugal home. If she refused to return, she was to be imprisoned for an entire week, until she "came to her senses" and returned to her husband. They ended the letter by emphasizing that they greatly depended upon women's labor to earn a livelihood and asked how people expected them to survive in such circumstances when deprived of their wives.

This letter sparked an investigation by the French into the adjudication of civil disputes by chiefs of Estuary villages and reveals debate among Africans as to who—the couples themselves with the assistance of chiefs or the heads of families—had the power to negotiate the dissolution of a marriage. The inquiry resulted in nearly one hundred complaints, some of which were transcribed in short paragraphs in the investigative report, and portrays the widespread discontent among Fang husbands with chiefs' mediation of marital differences.[24] Rather than declaring that wives had to return to their husbands, chiefs often sided with women's requests for divorce, the complainants protested. Instead of sanctioning unruly wives, chiefs' courts provided a harbor for women seeking divorce. A resident of the village of Aléné noted, "The village chief does not look after men's complaints. [He] pushes women to divorce and imposes his individual will instead of reconciling natives."[25] A resident of Asie stated, "Divorces are pronounced on the demand of the woman."[26] Another resident in a village named Anza relayed, "When a wife has a dispute with her husband, she takes refuge at the chief's [house] who, instead of giving her good advice to return to the conjugal home, pronounces the divorce without the husband's agreement. The chief is a judge without the possibility of appeal."[27] Rather than reinforcing control of husbands over wives as husbands had hoped, chiefs frequently judged in favor of wives' requests for divorce.

It was nearly always women who initiated requests for divorce. Many husbands requested that chiefs harbor their wives in the instance of divorce. A husband feared that if his wife resided with her kin while they settled the question of divorce, he would never have his bridewealth reimbursed. Estuary chiefs responded that they harbored women in the instance of divorce on their property until the husband and wife's family reached an accord and the woman's family or lover reimbursed the bridewealth to the husband or the disputing couple settled their differences.[28] In a 1939 letter, a canton chief based in Ntoum explained the purpose of wives taking refuge with a chief as being to ensure "good security, to prevent palavers that could result in death." He elaborated a possible scenario that could take place if a chief were to give the woman back to her family before the bridewealth had been paid: she would just go commit adultery with another man and then there would be three parties involved, which could potentially lead to an outbreak of violence.[29] In oral interviews, residents of Estuary villages remembered the role of chiefs as intermediaries in marital conflict as normative. One interviewee interpreted that the chief acted in the role of "a father" in these instances.[30] The chief would convene the women's fathers and brothers to reimburse the husbands' bridewealth and reestablish a sense of peace and mutual accord. Yet, as the husbands' letter of 1936 and the subsequent investigation into the operation of colonial courts revealed, divergences between chiefs and husbands demonstrate struggles and renegotiation among differentiated groups of men over the control over women. Protests over chiefs' ruling of marital disputes reflected contestations within Fang communities regarding the centralized authority of chiefs and the implementation of indirect rule.

Husbands expected chiefs to confirm their marriages by dismissing women's claims and forcing wives to return to their husbands' homes, yet the opposite was true. Why would village chiefs easily grant divorces? Wouldn't granting women's requests weaken patriarchal control over women? What would chiefs have to gain? One motivation to promote marital conflict was immediate material gain. Chiefs extracted a fee for even presiding over a dispute, pocketed a percentage of bridewealth reimbursements, and forced women under their care to labor in their fields. Because many women married another suitor soon after divorce, the chief acted as an intermediary for the new marriage and received a portion of the bridewealth paid by the new husband to the woman's family.[31] Another motivation for chiefs to readily grant divorces was that they themselves could then marry some of the women among the increased pool of unattached women. Their role as intermediaries to the colonial state already afforded chiefs access to land, money, and labor that made them wealthy individuals. Increasing their number of wives would only further their wealth in people, thereby also increasing their wealth in cash and goods.[32] Chiefs appointed by the colonial state became principal negotiators and arbiters of divorce proceedings. Judge-arbiters declared divorces and permitted women or women's lovers to reimburse husbands their bridewealth without heads of families present.[33] In a 1936 report, the French head of the first-degree court relayed, "In regards to obtaining the consent of heads of families in matters of marriage or divorce as outlined by custom the Fang of Libreville at least, take no notice of this with relative ease."[34] Chiefs sought to capitalize on their partnership with the colonial state to establish themselves as big men, but these efforts to establish centralized political authority over other potentially powerful men unintentionally provided avenues for women seeking divorce.

In contrast to what Sean Hawkins found for 1930s northern Ghana, where women were characterized by "their almost complete absence as litigants" and were "denied an active voice in courts,"[35] women in Libreville were prevalent as litigants and their voices reverberated in colonial court records. Colonial blueprints for the administration of native justice in Libreville envisioned appointed neighborhood chiefs serving as judges for conflicts within their particular ethnic groups. However, the city's ethnic diversity added greater fluidity in determining the boundaries of conjugality in Libreville. At the time of investigation in November 1936, there were eight Fang women pursuing divorce before two Mpongwé neighborhood chiefs in Libreville.[36] Of these eight women, three had abandoned their marital homes in nearby Estuary rural villages to seek refuge with chiefs in the town, and the others resided in Libreville. Five of the eight women had previously been married and divorced at least twice.[37] Fang husbands accused the Mpongwé chiefs of ceding to their wives' unfounded requests for divorce. Chiefs Massamba and Ndende responded to the charges leveled against them by the husbands and defended their judgments of divorce: "On the subject of palavers relating to Fang marriages, that unfortunately occur too frequently, women come to us who often and in spite of our advice do not want to rejoin the marital home."[38] Unlike more common instances in which husbands placed wives in the custody of chiefs, Massamba and Ndende emphasized that it was the wives who approached them to arbitrate their requests for divorce.

Massamba and Ndende defended their rulings of divorce as morally and legally justifiable. The chiefs argued that the women under their care sought divorce in order to escape the brutalities typical of Fang husbands. Massamba and Ndende insisted, "It is true that the husband is sometimes wrong! And this is the cause of the unhappiness of our Pahouin. Speaking frankly, [the husbands] complain about us, [but they] think the woman is an animal! They never admit that they could be wrong sometimes."[39] These Mpongwé chiefs, who viewed themselves as civilized individuals, looked upon Fang men as savages who treated women as less than human. Massamba and Ndende countered that they were elevating the status of Fang wives by allowing them to leave marriages in which they were mistreated. Rights to divorce, in their view, were an indication of the degree to which a particular society had evolved.

The 1936 letter and subsequent investigation unearthed the unregulated and irregular nature of the colonial legal system. In theory, chiefs were to maintain written registers of conciliation hearings, yet most chiefs were not literate and did not have the resources to employ a secretary to transcribe proceedings.[40] The French subdivision head was to review the proceedings of conciliatory courts, reverse the decisions of chiefs when he deemed necessary, and ensure that chiefs were following "custom." Yet, as the aforementioned disagreements between chiefs and their constituencies reveal, Estuary residents offered varied interpretations of what constituted custom. Furthermore, the 1936 investigation revealed that administrators remained largely removed from the proceedings and outcomes of conciliation courts. The independent investigator critiqued that no registers existed and that colonial personnel rarely oversaw what occurred in chiefs' courts. Record keeping in first-degree courts presided over by French judges was also nonexistent. Following the investigation, French personnel were required by law to maintain court registers. Local administrators were unhappy with the new record-keeping requirements and requested the appointment of a specialist whose sole duty was managing native justice.[41] Nevertheless, presiding over colonial courts remained part of the quotidian duties of administrative personnel. Questions about customary marriage law, divorce, and the organization of native courts would continue into World War II and beyond, and reflect further shifts of French and African ideas.

LEGAL PLURALITY: CUSTOMARY MARRIAGE
AND DIVORCE LAW IN THEORY AFTER WORLD WAR II

While colonial officials viewed limitations to divorce as a matter of great importance, missionaries and colonial personnel also felt that the lack of choice African women had in choosing husbands contributed to marital instability and greater divorce rates. The question of African women's freedom and consent in choosing their husbands had long haunted the French. In 1939, the French Senate passed the Mandel Decree, which was to be applied in FEA (French Equatorial Africa) and FOA (French Occidental [West] Africa). The decree mandated the minimum age for a woman to marry as sixteen, made the consent of both the bride and the groom mandatory, and allowed that a widow could choose to refuse levirate marriage. How the decree was to be applied remained vague, and, as Barbara Cooper has argued for French West Africa, the changes to marriage outlined in the decree remained rather ineffectual.[42] The question of levirate marriage in the Mandel Decree did result in its practical application in Gabon and sparked questions about the parameters of women's marital choice. As the chapter will address later, Estuary colonial courts commonly ruled to allow a widow who refused to become the wife of her deceased husband's male kin to "divorce" her in-laws by reimbursing her bridewealth payment.

Within his wartime and post–World War II governorship of FEA, Félix Éboué sought to endow Africans with some measures of self-governance by arguing that native judges, not Frenchmen, should be formally invested with the authority in the colonial court system to decide on "the state of persons—marriage, divorce, adultery, the conferring of natural children, inheritance—to be settled in the first instance by native judges alone."[43] Furthermore, Éboué proposed the creation of new customary courts to be presided over by appointed judges of various ethnic groups who would handle questions of states of person.[44] Senior administrators appointed after Éboué were less keen to invest African judges with such final authority in questions of conjugal rights in persons and property and modified Éboué's conception of customary courts. In July 1944, senior French administrators in Brazzaville added the new layer of customary courts, also known as courts of common law, to the colonial court system of FEA. They were to be staffed exclusively by Africans and were to preside over civil and commercial disputes according to customary law.[45]

According to the letter of the law, customary courts presided over by African judges were charged with settling noncriminal litigation between African populations *except* cases relating to "the state of persons, the family, child custody, marriage and divorce." Legal rulings of marriage and family law would remain under the jurisdiction of first-degree courts presided over by a French judge, who would consult with native assessors in making rulings.[46] In a 1946 letter to the governors of individual colonies, governor-general of FEA Bayardelle cautioned administrators to ensure that "customary judges are frequently and attentively controlled." Bayardelle also urged first-degree courts administered by French judges to assume the role of "guarantor and guardian of the institution of marriage" by ruling for divorces only in limited circumstances. Bayardelle outlined the justifiable grounds for divorce as sterility, congenital malformation, incurable disease, brutal violence, and "traditional" unpardonable insults. Bayardelle closed the letter by asking the governors to respond right away to his recommendations, without the need to consult with "native collaborators."[47]

In this new configuration, the multilayered colonial legal system was to be an arena in which the stability of African marriages was maintained. Conciliation courts, manned primarily by chiefs, remained the first level of the colonial legal system in which litigants in civil disputes were given the opportunity to arbitrate and come to common agreements. If parties did not reach agreement there, they could petition the newly created customary courts presided over by African assessors for further efforts of reconciliation. Since neither conciliation nor customary courts, in theory, could declare divorces, litigants who wished to divorce after failing to reach reconciliation could then approach the first-degree court presided over by a French judge.

In day-to-day practice in Gabon, the newly reorganized colonial court system outlined by the French for FEA was a fiction. The adjudication of conjugal conflict in Libreville ran along a network of multiple sites of dispute resolution. In a 1948 letter to the governors of FEA colonies, Governor-General Luizet signaled that conciliation courts operated on an ad hoc basis, without colonial personnel knowing the dates on which hearings were to be held and without the presence of state-appointed African assessors; furthermore, no written records of the proceedings were kept. Chiefs presiding over the multitude of courts in Libreville neighborhoods and Estuary villages issued rulings of divorce and judgments of child custody, questions that exceeded the mandate laid out by the colonial legal system.[48] The governor-general underlined that subdivision and circumscription administrators were to complete a monthly inspection of courts presided over by chiefs and to reinforce that only first- and second-degree courts presided over by French judges were to decide upon rulings of divorce. In Gabon, such inspections were rare, and colonial personnel relied on African intermediaries to manage the numerous conjugal disputes. Local colonial employees sought to maintain rather than detract from the authority of chiefs in settling civil household disputes.[49]

According to the French, all colonial courts were to operate according to customary law, but what constituted the customary law that African and French court personnel were to apply remained ambiguous. Léon Mba would prove to be influential in the question of the codification of customary law in Gabon. Historian Gaston Rapotchombo wrote that Mba, an Estuary chief of an area encompassing hundreds of kilometers, was respected as well as feared by members of the community over which he governed from 1926 to 1931.[50] Having earned tremendous wealth from trade in timber, the cultivation of cacao and coffee, and the ownership of several boutiques, Mba owned a typewriter, had a car and driver, and preferred imported bread and cheese to the locally produced manioc of his constituencies. Convicted on dubious charges of embezzlement of tax revenues in 1931, Mba was imprisoned and exiled to Chad from 1931 to 1946.

While in exile, he wrote the 1936 article "Essay on Fang Customary Law," which was published in the *Bulletin de la Société des recherches congolaises*, a journal that rarely featured African authors.[51] In the essay he stated, "The Fang woman had no legal power."[52] Mba outlined that a Fang woman, "assisted by he who had received bridewealth, is authorized by custom to ask for a divorce against her husband" in specific instances.[53] A woman could ask for a divorce if her husband lacked respect, refused to aid, or caused bodily harm to her kin, inflicted grave bodily harm on her, or if he committed adultery with a woman in her family. The essay outlined that a woman could not ask for a divorce in case of her husband's sterility. Men, however, had more extensive grounds for divorce: "a wife's repeated adultery, inveterate laziness in carrying out work dictated by custom, incurable disease caught as a result of relations with someone other than her husband, witchcraft, and abortion."[54] With his reentry into Gabon in 1946, historian Florence Bernault wrote that this essay became the accepted guide to Fang customary law employed in colonial courts.[55] Yet, as legal scholar Dominique Etoughe states, "we know nothing about the interpretation of the laws summarized in Mba's essay by judges."[56] Mba's essay was not the only written version of Fang customary marriage law that gained currency in post–World War II Gabon.

Other versions of customary law included more expansive parameters for women to request divorce, in contrast with Mba's essay, while simultaneously seeking to reduce the rate of divorce. In 1942, at the behest of Gabon's governor, Catholic missionaries and nearly seventy Fang chiefs met in the Estuary town of Donghila, the site of one of the largest mission stations in the colony, to codify customary marriage laws for the Fang. The question of whether or not to allow women to divorce for reasons of "consciousness," meaning their adherence to Christianity, had long been an area of conflict between Catholic missionaries and colonial officials.[57] Over the course of the 1920s and 1930s, there were a few instances in which Catholic missionaries of Sainte Marie

differing versions/ opinions on customary law

in Libreville and at Donghila harbored and tried to facilitate the divorce of female converts in polygamous marriages, on the grounds that such marriages violated Catholic doctrines of monogamy.[58] Yet colonial officials denied the requests for divorce on these grounds and maintained that polygamy was recognized by customary law and not contrary to tenets of French civilization. Colonial officials ordered women to return to their conjugal homes. The 1942 document of customary law gave women who converted to Christianity the right to divorce husbands who were not Christian.[59] Furthermore, a second or third wife in a polygamous marriage could ask for a divorce for "serious and proven motives," defined as the desire to marry a single man, or if she had been married prior to puberty, or if she wanted to be baptized. A woman could also solicit a divorce if she was subject to cruelty and severe ill treatment in her marriage.[60] The document defined "severe ill-treatment" of a wife by her husband as excessive, prolonged, and unmotivated abandonment. Relatives or other third parties who encouraged women's requests for divorce and women who deserted their husbands outside of the approved parameters were subject to an undefined "severe punishment." Yet the colonial state and Catholic missionaries continued to clash. State officials were not wont to view conversion to Christianity as legitimate grounds for divorce and, at times, sought to support codification projects that did not involve representatives of the Catholic Church.

With a view toward cultivating candidates and sowing political cohesion for upcoming Territorial Assembly elections, in 1946 the governor of FEA directed each colony to organize meetings of chiefs of each ethnicity, to name one head of each ethnic group, and to have these heads meet to study and decide on customs for their groups.[61] In February 1947, Fang delegates convened the Pahouin Congress in the town of Mitzic, located in the northern Fang province of Woleu-Ntem.[62] This eclectic group reflected the competition among Fang political leaders for political authority. More than fifty delegates—chiefs, members of councils of notables, timber exploiters, civil servants, and cacao planters—convened. Fang delegates articulated that the demographic crisis was particularly perceptible in their society, as women were not giving birth to enough children; they conceived of the codification of customary law as vital to the survival of their societies. Mba emerged as the leader. The delegation produced a pamphlet codifying Fang customary marriage law that reflected Mba's view that customary law should incorporate Fang and French aspects. The summary emphasized that the customs they outlined were not practices that dated from time immemorial but were reforms to custom in keeping with transformations Fang societies had undergone through contact with the French.

The recommended customary laws listed in the brochure reflected the idea of *la réforme de la coutume* (the revision of custom).[63] Canton chiefs were to possess the authority to consecrate customary marriage; all customary marriages needed to be declared to canton chiefs, who would record them in a register.[64] Though the document attempts to encourage new marriages by placing limits on bridewealth, the main aims of customary law as defined were to buttress marriages once legally legitimized by bridewealth, to curtail divorce, and to protect the rights of husbands in the case of divorce. As argued by Georges Balandier, the Congress's document on customary law was "essentially concerned to protect the husband's rights with regard to his in-laws."[65] As a modification of the Mandel Decree, it outlined that a widow was free to divorce, but only if she reimbursed her husband's family's bridewealth.[66] The children of divorced women could stay in their mother's care until they were six years old, when she had to return them to her ex-husband.[67] The Mitzic document was not the final word on customary law. Rather, the Pahouin Congress ignited further debates among African male leaders about conceptualization of customary marriage law.

From 1950 to 1952, the elected body of African political leaders in the Territorial Assembly took up the question of divorce and customary marriage law. Gabonese legislators proposed numerous pieces of legislation and debated measures proposed by colonial authorities in Brazzaville. Delegates criticized chiefs as illiterate, atavistic individuals who prevented their societies from evolving by hanging on to outmoded notions of customary law.[68] In a 1952 speech, Jean-Hilaire Aubame argued, "These are not questions to be decided upon in the villages, but by us" and that "we [should take on the role of] leading the masses and reforming custom."[69] This younger generation sought to establish their own interpretations of customary laws that benefited their visions of modern African families and that chiefs would follow.[70]

In another session that year, Aubame argued that a written study on African marriage formulated by the assembly could then serve as the text that chiefs would follow in adjudicating marital conflict.[71] A week later the commission proposed a resolution that would meet the demands of delegates for a more comprehensive document that regulated marriage.[72] The proposal addressed three items: the registration of customary marriages, the limitations on divorce, and the penalties for adultery. Echoing the Pahouin Congress, all marriages were to be witnessed by the canton chief in order to be legally binding. First, in an effort to centralize governance, the resolution proposed that all village chiefs be required to present couples before the canton chief, who would record all marriages in a register. Second, the resolution asked that the governor put measures in place to make divorces less frequent. In an attempt to undermine fathers whose pursuit of the highest bridewealth for their daughters was the catalyst for divorce, delegates proposed that such efforts be prosecuted under the criminal charge of fraud. Heads of families who requested high bridewealth, future husbands who agreed to pay such elevated bridewealth, and village chiefs who facilitated the fraud were all to be equally pursued. Finally, it was proposed that adultery fines normally paid to husbands be distributed to social organizations such as churches, schools, and cultural centers. The resolution sought to make marriage a relationship recorded and regulated by a set of rules that would limit the possibility of divorce.

 These 1952 debates over the codification of customary marriage law in Gabon became a platform on which to question the authority of the colonial state. Delegate Gondjout raised an objection to the proposal that chiefs be punished for encouraging divorce.[73] Gondjout argued that village and canton chiefs used to have the authority to pronounce divorce, but that the French had inserted themselves in the place of chiefs. Delegates then turned to the question of whether the colonial state even had the authority to regulate customary marriage. A man identified as Owanga asked, "Why is the administration involving itself in questions about women, our affairs?"[74] Another elected man named Mossot questioned the sudden French interest in such matters and asked why the French had not intervened sooner to stop the long-standing problems of divorce, adultery, and prostitution. Delegates argued that as the elite, they should be the ones to take the responsibility in directing the country, in leading the masses in reforming customary law and practices. Nevertheless, there is no evidence that any of these measures were accepted by the governing body in Brazzaville, and if they were, that they were effectively implemented.

 Though none of the post–World War II marriage law codification projects in the Territorial Assembly became the law of the land, these efforts illuminate the sheer diversity of African conceptualizations of what constituted customary marriage law and how such conceptualizations shaped late colonial legal ideas of jurisprudence. Customary law remained as contested and fluid as before colonial rule. Moreover, the delegates emphasized not just the codification, but the reform of customary practices. These men forwarded conceptions of customary law that incorporated how Africans had adopted and adapted some French ideas of rights in marriage. Disjunctured articulations of customary law did not always fall along the lines of colonizer versus colonized but also reflected contestations among and between the French church and state, among African men of varied status (chiefs and *évolués*), and among évolués along lines of ethnicity. As such, the sociopolitical apparatuses of the colonial state and indirect rule were irresolute and on shifting foundations. Customary marriage law in Gabon was not codified through a coalition of elder African men and colonial officials. As a result, customary marriage law was in a state of flux in which marriage and divorce law could be debated in homes, on the street, and—as many Libreville residents chose the option of the judicial path—in colonial courts.

MARRIAGE AND DIVORCE LAW IN CIVIL COURTS

The question of the jurisprudence exercised by courts in Gabon after World War II has been yet to be analyzed in a published study, in French or English. The summaries of civil court cases provide a valuable portrait of dynamics among Libreville's residents in what they sought out, disagreed over, and were willing to concede in negotiating the parameters of marriage and divorce. There are numerous gaps in court records that have survived in the archives. Registers for Estuary department colonial courts are extant only for the years of 1950–1961 and only for the conciliation, customary, and second-degree courts.[75] Case summaries usually list the names of plaintiffs and defendants, sometimes their professions, and little other biographical information about the litigants. The majority of plaintiffs were men, while the majority of defendants were women, their kin, and their lovers. Some of the documentation provides a more detailed account of the testimony by litigants, the deliberations of judges and assessors, and explanations for their decisions. Yet most of the documentation includes just a few sentences that summarize the claims of each party and the decision reached by the courts. In many of the hearings, records indicate that the litigants presented their cases in French, without the assistance of interpreters of various Gabonese languages.

Who approached the colonial legal system and why? Litigants before the colonial courts were of middling and elite echelons of Libreville's African society. The parties before the court reflected the ethnic diversity of the town. The majority of plaintiffs and defendants were Fang, but also included Mpongwé and other Myènè communities, as well as Africans from other Francophone colonies. Many male litigants were employed in wage labor by the colonial state or private European enterprises. Their professions ranged from domestic workers—gardeners, cooks, and drivers—to masons, carpenters, clerks, teachers, catechists, and typists. Some were self-employed as cultivators, fishermen, bakers, and foresters. Most women were listed as "without profession," but some were identified as maids and midwives. Though not listed as a profession in court documents, many women

FIGURE 5.2. Categories of Legal Complaints in Divorce Disputes[77]

	1950	1951	1952	1953	1954	1955	1956	1957	1958	1959	1960	1961
Divorce	1	10	9	9	10	3	35	5	7	8	11	2
Levirate	0	5	6	2	2	0	0	1	0	0	0	1
Bridewealth	1	10	9	9	10	3	25	3	6	8	11	2
Abandonment	0	4	4	2	1	6	11	0	3	3	3	1
Wife Kidnaping	0	3	3	8	6	3	11	0	0	0	0	0
Adultery	1	3	3	8	4	0	11	1	2	3	3	2
Child Custody	0	1	0	0	1	0	7	4	3	1	5	2

litigants were likely farmers. Libreville residents appear to have rarely approached colonial courts as a first recourse to resolve marital conflicts, but instead convened family councils of kin in an attempt to reach a point of agreement, and then considered the conciliation and customary courts presided over by African arbitrators if the family councils did not result in a solution to which all parties could agree.[76] First- and second-degree courts presided over by French judges appeared to have been the last resort of parties who had been in conflict for several years.

Figure 5.2 summarizes the categories of legal complaints that litigants presented in divorce proceedings between 1950 and 1961. Extant records reveal that the courts presided over 110 cases that involved the question of divorce. Each legal case to determine a ruling of divorce involved multiple legal complaints. I categorized each complaint according to the language used in the court records by litigants and judges.

The question of divorce illuminates the complex social, emotional, and economic meanings of marriage. Of the 110 rulings of the varied levels of courts, judges ruled for a divorce in 56 cases, just shy of 50 percent of the judgments they made. That half of the cases resulted in a ruling of divorce reveals that even with the efforts of political leaders to limit such rulings, the dissolution of marriage remained a probable outcome in colonial courts over the course of the 1950s and 1960s.

Husbands rarely brought suits seeking divorce against their wives. Men brought complaints of adultery, abandonment, and wife kidnapping before the customary court and primarily sought the return of their wives who were taking refuge with kin or lovers. Husbands sought for the court to confirm and maintain their marriages. Over one-third of the suits involved litigation between husbands and their in-laws and another two-thirds between husbands and their wives' lovers or men who claimed to be married to the same woman. Adultery and wife kidnapping alike involved complaints by husbands that their wives had engaged in extramarital sex. In adultery cases, the wife may have returned to the conjugal home, while in wife kidnapping cases, she no longer resided in the conjugal home and refused to return. The charge of abandonment, defined as the act of a wife who deserted her husband without just cause, was a civil infraction for which husbands sought the return of their wives or for the wives to be found at fault and fined. Similar to Gabon, colonial courts and husbands in Mali sought to temper women's conjugal mobility. Marie Rodet has documented the invention of wives' desertion of their marriages as a criminal act, which led to the possibility of imprisonment for women who refused to return to their husbands.[78] In Gabon, a husband also attempted to compel his wife to return with the petition that his in-laws reimburse his bridewealth, often a sum that had grown exponentially over the years of the marriage. In such cases, husbands gave their wives the option that they would drop the proceedings if their wives would return to the conjugal homes.[79] Hearings on levirate marriage involved disputes between two men who each claimed to be the rightful heir to become the husband of a widow or disputes of widows who refused to marry the heirs of their deceased husbands. While husbands often sought to retain their marriages, wives initiated 80 percent of cases requesting an outright divorce.

Cases brought before the second-degree court involved litigants appealing the terms of settlement that the lower first-degree court had made in a judgment for a divorce. While the first-degree court records have not survived, second-degree court records do provide a summary list of the legal decisions of the lower court. Litigants before the second-degree court contested the judgments on their divorce cases—questions of fault, monetary compensation between litigants or punitive fees levied by the court, and the terms of child custody and the financial care of children. In all, husbands were the plaintiffs in 55 percent of the cases, while wives and their lovers or male kin were the plaintiffs in 45 percent of court cases.

For some spouses, the court hearings presented a platform on which to address grievances in their marriages and arrive at reconciliation, rather than to achieve a divorce. Such was the case of Marie Lucienne Nzé, whose husband, Jean Bernard Ngoua, brought a complaint of abandonment before the conciliation court in 1957. Jean Bernard emphasized that he and his wife had children together, the youngest of whom was five months old, when she left him and their children to take refuge at her older sister's home. He maintained that "in spite of certain domestic disputes [*scenes de ménages*] which has separated us from time," he did not want to divorce, and he asked that his wife return to the marital home. Marie Lucienne replied that she took refuge at her sister's home because of the physical abuse her husband inflicted on her. Her husband beat her because she was often absent from their conjugal home, going to town to visit people she knew. She complained that he went so far as to take away the children and give them to his mother for fear that she would abscond with them. She conceded that she did not want a divorce, but wished that he would "[improve] his character and appear before a family council to settle their differences."[80] Records indicate that her husband agreed to withdraw the petition and that she agreed to return to their marital home.[81]

Even before courts could assess whether or not to grant a divorce, the question of whether a relationship was a legal marriage was one that often proved to be a conundrum. The factors of what made a relationship a legal marriage could be answered along a shifting continuum of whether goods and money exchanged constituted bridewealth, intent, consent of the bride or of her family, and residency. In one 1949 court interpretation of Mpongwé customary law, the ruling outlined that a man and woman were married not at the point in which the groom's family transferred bridewealth to the bride's family, but at a preceding moment in which the two families publicly met and agreed upon the marriage. As such, the payment of bridewealth alone did not legitimize a marriage. Therefore, among the Mpongwé, the reimbursement of bridewealth was not required for a divorce to be finalized; a couple could agree to divorce without the reimbursement of bridewealth.[82]

In cases involving Fang couples, interpretations of what constituted a legitimate marriage in Fang customary law, and therefore divorce, proved to be more variable. A 1939 first-degree court proceeding interpreted a legal marriage in Fang custom as constituting two elements—the completion of bridewealth payments and the cohabitation of the wife and husband in the husband's residence or in a residence that he had built for her.[83] It could take a man several years to complete payment of the promised bridewealth amounts. Though a woman and a man might cohabit and people might refer to them as "husband" and "wife," according to this interpretation the relationship remained concubinage until the final payment was concluded *and* the man and the woman in question cohabited in the same home. However, Léon Mba's essay emphasized, "the initial payment of bridewealth to a woman's family assures the definitive possession of the woman. Custom permits the payment of bridewealth in several payments."[84] Once two families had agreed on the promise for a man and woman to marry (*dzanghan*), the fiancé began to remit the agreed-upon bridewealth amount in increments. According to Mba, the first payment of bridewealth transformed the relationship into a legal marriage. Mba's definition also outlined that when parties divorced, kitchen utensils and household objects that a husband had given to his wife were the wife's personal property. Any objects or money that he had given to his wife's kin over the course of their marriage, though, constituted bridewealth and was to be repaid before a divorce could be finalized. The requirement was meant to temper the number of divorces. However, in 1942, the governor-general of FEA stated in a letter to the governor of Gabon that a husband's supplemental payments to his in-laws were separate from bridewealth and that a wife's family did not have to reimburse these payments in the case of divorce. The supplements, he argued, "which are greedily demanded from the husband are gifts, and sometimes represent penalties."[85] The summaries of court cases for Fang couples do not provide enough detail to be able to analyze which of these competing understandings of bridewealth were commonly applied.

The line was often blurred around the question of monetary payments that men made in heterosexual relationships. Money could be bridewealth that formalized a relationship as a marriage, gifts that reflected the efforts of a suitor to gain the favor of his prospective bride and in-laws, or compensation of a lover to his concubine for the domestic and sexual services she rendered. It was this movable boundary that set the parameters within which African and French judges determined whether a relationship was a legitimate marriage, an engagement, or concubinage, and therefore decided upon the question of divorce. The 1958 case of Augustin Mougangue versus his former lover Pauline Babina involved such a quandary.[86] Mougangue appealed the decision of the first-degree court that denied his request for the reimbursement of bridewealth in his separation from Babina. Mougangue contended that he and Babina had been legitimately married, and the cash he had given to her family constituted bridewealth. The first-degree court denied his claim for reimbursement of 35,975 francs and stated that she was his concubine, not his wife. Concubinage did not include an agreement to marry, thus, any gifts given to a woman or her family by her lover were compensation for the sexual and domestic services she rendered. She did not have to reimburse him. However, the second-degree court reversed this decision and determined that Mougangue had given 11,700 francs to Babina's family and that this constituted bridewealth.[87] The court pronounced a divorce between the two and ordered Babina to reimburse Mougangue his bridewealth, consisting of 10,000 francs, a thermos, and household objects.[88] Money and goods given by Mougangue and accepted by Babina's family, the court determined, were payments that sealed their relationship as a legal marriage.

The cooperation of male kin who had negotiated and accepted bridewealth from a woman's current husband—father, brothers, or uncles— or a lover who was willing to reimburse the first husband's bridewealth was crucial to the outcome of a woman's claims for divorce in customary court. The February 1952 proceedings involving a husband named Emane Bekale, his wife, Assengone Meyo, and her brother Mba Nkile are representative of many cases involving abandonment. As was a normative expectation when one's wife went to her family of origin to air conjugal grievances, Emane Bekale pursued Assengone Meyo in an effort to reconcile. After she refused to return with him and asked for a divorce, he sued her brother Mba Nkile. Yet the court allowed the divorce, along with the reimbursement of Emane Bekale's 25,000 francs in bridewealth, because Mba Nkile "consented to the dissolution of his sister's marriage."[89]

Judges also apparently decided to grant or deny a divorce based on a woman's consent and volition in choosing her husband. At the heart of complaints involving wife kidnapping and levirate marriage was the question of whether or not women could choose their own husbands. The term "wife kidnapping" was often a misnomer, since women were usually complicit in absconding with their lovers. Gabonese assessors Andre Bolo and Bernard Mba, assisting in a 1941 case in which a man was charged with kidnapping a widow, stated, "Fang custom commands the reimbursement of bridewealth if the woman had voluntarily followed her ravisher."[90] Women's deliberate pursuit of extramarital sexual relationships in order to find a new husband proved crucial in the court's granting a divorce. In 75 percent of cases in which a husband levied a charge of kidnapping, the court ruled for divorce if the wife indicated a wish to remarry her lover instead.

Judges' rulings for divorce sought to ensure that the wife in question would be transferred into a conjugal arrangement that garnered less discord. Husbands claimed that their remittance of bridewealth to the bride's family meant that the marriage was binding. However, the court's ruling for divorce signified that a wife could request a divorce if she had aligned herself with a suitor able to reimburse her first husband's bridewealth. Even while African and French judges affirmed that a marriage could be dissolved if a woman wished to leave a current husband for another, judges did not declare divorce with impunity. In 47 percent of cases in which the court declared a divorce between the wife and her first husband, the court also ordered the defendant to pay the husband a fine for adultery or wife kidnapping ranging from 2,500 to 5,000 francs.[91]

Disagreements over monetary compensation propelled both husbands and wives to appeal divorce judgments made by the first-degree court before the second-degree court. Husbands appealed decisions on the grounds that the bridewealth amounts were actually higher than what the lower court had determined or to expunge expenses such as the travel costs to repatriate ex-wives who originated from colonies other than Gabon.[92] In 1950s Ghana, Jean Allman and Victoria Tashjian found the "manifestations of monetized conjugal relations" in the adjudication of divorce cases in Ashanti courts as husbands resorted to "inflated claims for marriage expenses to recoup their investment in a marriage or as a tool for some other desired end."[93] In Libreville also husbands sought maximum repayment, as they desired to recuperate monies and goods they had dispensed to their affines over the course of the entire marriage and worried about paying a new bridewealth sum in order to remarry in the speculative bridewealth economy. In contrast, wives facing divorce deflated the amount that husbands had made as marriage payments. For women, divorce was costly due to bridewealth reimbursement and potentially unattainable if their male kin or lovers could not ultimately reimburse their husbands. Women, their lovers, or family members appealed judgments for divorce on the grounds that former husbands had inflated bridewealth amounts and that the amounts to be reimbursed should be lower. Women also contested additional fines that the lower court assessed for adultery or abandonment. In instances in which the lower court found women at fault for these reasons, settlements also included fines of from 5,000 francs to an astronomical 30,000 francs owed to the ex-husband. In ten cases between 1957 and 1960, women and their kin or lovers appealed the finding of fault, the adultery fee, or sought a lower bridewealth reimbursement. In nine out of ten of these appeals, the court maintained or increased the amounts of the fines or reimbursements assessed by the lower court. In one ruling, the court assessed a late fee of 20,000 francs to chastise the ex-wife for having not yet paid the lower court's bridewealth judgment three years after the initial decision.[94]

Money was also a factor of contention in the adjudication of divorce cases involving widows. Rather than the Mandel Decree, which stated that widows could refuse levirate marriage but made no provisions for the reimbursement of bridewealth, the amendment of the Pahouin Congress, which stated that widows could refuse levirate marriage only if they reimbursed their deceased husbands' heirs, seemed to be applied in court rulings. In 75 percent of cases in which men claimed the right of levirate marriage, the court allowed the widow to divorce from the family of her deceased husband and marry the man of her choice.[95] The case of Evoung Nzogo, the heir of a deceased husband, versus Mbembang Minko, the lover of the widow, illustrates the common manner in which the court decided the question of who was legally the husband. The customary court made its ruling based on the following: "The widow in question categorically refuses to marry into the family of her deceased husband."[96] Following this indication of will from the widow, the customary court settled the suit by ordering the lover to reimburse the husband's family the original bridewealth payment, thereby paving the way for the widow to enter into a new marriage. Disagreements over bridewealth amounts in divorce proceedings were not only about how monetary compensation finalized a divorce, but also about the rights to children.

The most contentious aspect of settling a divorce remained that of child custody. In theory, accounts of customary law rendered the matter of child custody after the dissolution of a relationship routine. In a 1948 second-degree court hearing involving a Fang man and woman claiming custody of a child, the judge and assessors cited Mba's essay as their guidebook.[97] In discussing the question of children, Mba quoted the Fang proverb: "*Mone asse mona mbiè, mone ane mona biki*" (A child does not belong to whomever is the biological father, but to whomever gave the bridewealth). This proverb established that a man who had begun to pay bridewealth was legally married and established rights over his wife's progeny. For the patrilineal Mpongwé, common opinion in court rulings seemed to be that in order to exercise paternal rights over a child, a man was required to have paid the entire agreed-upon bridewealth.[98] For all ethnic groups, a man who had not remitted any marriage payments had no rights to his child. However, such a man could gain legal paternity by marrying the mother through bridewealth payments after the child's birth and paying an additional fine to her family.[99] If a marriage was recognized as having been consecrated by bridewealth according to these varied understandings, men retained physical and legal custody of children after a divorce. Mothers could see their children and have a say over decisions in their upbringing only at the behest of their fathers. This tenet held true not only among the Fang, but among other Gabonese ethnicities as well. In patrilineal societies, in cases in which a relationship was not a marriage, a woman's father would retain legal custody and affiliation of the child, while a woman's uncle would do so in a matrilineal society.[100]

Men and women who struggled for custody of children bolstered the legitimacy of their appeals based on the question of whether monies and goods from a man to a woman's kin had indeed been bridewealth. In cases before the second-degree court in which women proved that their children were born during relationships that had not been legitimated as marriage with the payment of bridewealth, the court granted custody of children to the women's families.[101] In cases in which the higher court determined that men had paid bridewealth, child custody went to the fathers.[102] However, the idea of what constituted bridewealth, and therefore marriage itself, was continually in flux, thereby providing room for maneuverability in determining child custody.

The case of Joseph Ngoua versus Marie-Thérèse Betoe is particularly illustrative of how malleable the definition of marriage by bridewealth, and therefore rights over children, could be in the various levels of the colonial court system. Records of this lawsuit exist in the registers of both the conciliation court for the city of Libreville and the second-degree court. In August 1956, Ngoua went before the conciliation court of the city of Libreville requesting that the court annul a decision made by the customary court of the neighborhood of Atong-Abé.[103] The customary court had denied him the custody of children born over the course of his relationship to Betoe. Ngoua argued that the customary court had superseded its mandate, since the court did not have the legal authority to decide upon questions of child filiation and custody. He argued that he and Betoe had been legitimately married and demanded custody of the two children born during the marriage and the reimbursement of 4,500 francs he paid as bridewealth in order to finalize their divorce. Betoe countered that "she did not acknowledge that she had ever been Joseph's wife; in consequence she unconditionally refuses to confer the children to him."[104]

The suit made its way to the first-degree court, where the judge annulled the customary court's decision. The judge ruled that Ngoua and Betoe had been married and recognized Ngoua's paternity. But, for reasons that are not stated in the case proceedings, the court did not order Betoe to return the children to him. Upon Ngoua's appeal of the decision, the secondary court recognized that paternal authority in Fang custom meant that Ngoua retained sole legal and physical custody of the children. The second-degree court ordered that the children be returned to his home.[105]

Determining that the flow of bridewealth determined child custody, the court divided the custody of individual children between their mother and their father based on when bridewealth had been paid. For example, in the suit of Paul Bekale versus his wife, Marie Louise Condja, the second-degree court determined that their first two children were born before they were legally married, that is, before the payment of bridewealth. Condja was to retain custody of these two children while the subsequent three children, born during their marriage, were to go to Bekale.[106]

Some women attempting to keep custody of their children after the dissolution of a marriage challenged the very custom that child custody was to be based on the transfer of bridewealth. Such was the case of Eyang Emane, who appealed a ruling of divorce from her husband, Philippe Mouloungui, in which the first-degree court awarded him "all the rights associated with paternal custody." Emane proposed a formulation of parental rights based on biology. She argued that Mouloungui was not the biological father, and her indisputable status as the mother of the child entitled her to legal custody. Emane asserted, "I ask the court to keep custody of the child. I was already pregnant by someone else when I married Mouloungui. The child belongs to me." However, the second-degree court confirmed the lower court's decision to grant custody to Mouloungui, affirming the tenet that custody of a child born in the instance of marriage would go to the man who was paying the bridewealth; the remittance of bridewealth conferred rights over offspring.[107]

However, by 1960, some of the second-degree court's decisions on child custody reflected more contextual decisions about who was awarded child custody, based on maternal care and the emotional attachment of the child. The question of physical custody and the best interests of children under five years old or still in their mothers' wombs posed a conundrum for the court. In 1960 rulings in cases involving children born under bridewealth, the second-degree court confirmed legal custody to fathers, but reflected that maternal care of infants was best. In three appeals, two made by women or women and their fathers, the second-degree court confirmed the first-degree court's decision to award legal custody of children to their fathers who had paid bridewealth, but with the condition that the children remain under maternal physical custody and care for a certain number of years. The infant children in question were to live with their mothers, who were presumably nursing, until they were two to five years old. Furthermore, ex-husbands were to pay their ex-wives 1,000 francs per month. The fathers could visit the children whenever they wanted, and after the age determined by the court was reached, children were to live with their fathers.[108]

Cases of divorce and child custody involving the question of levirate custom, in which the heir of a deceased husband claimed custody of a woman's children, resulted in yet another shift in how the court determined if the payment of bridewealth determined rights over children. Widows wishing to remarry husbands of their choice instead of their husbands' heirs seemed to receive special dispensation in child custody matters. Though their deceased husbands had paid bridewealth, the second-degree court ruled for child custody in favor of mothers and not to the heirs of the deceased husbands. With the reimbursement of bridewealth, both the widow and her children "divorced" her deceased husband's family.[109] In appeal cases before the second-degree court in the 1940s–1960s, the court ruled in favor of women's claims for custody of their children when the woman in question was a widow and it was the deceased husband's inheritor who sought custody of his male kin's children. In explaining its decision in one 1949 summary, the court acknowledged Fang customary law that children followed bridewealth, but argued, "It is contrary to public order and principles of civilization to confer rights in property of one individual over another." The children would remain in the custody of the woman whom they knew to be their mother, based on the care she had given to the children and not on the trajectory of bridewealth and legal conjugal status.[110]

CONCLUSION

Negotiating marital conflict, separation, and divorce in twentieth-century colonial Libreville required that men and women access a host of legal forums. While families and men and women in conflict looked toward kin as a first path to negotiate conjugal and sexual relationships, individuals sought out intervention from colonial courts when they did not receive the desired outcome from such networks. Participating in and observing conjugal dynamics in their own homes and communities, elite Gabonese men sought to define what constituted "custom," cobbling imagined pasts and changing currents of social and political order. Observing conjugal dynamics from a distance, colonial representatives attempted to implement a host of policy initiatives and legal institutions that would control the perceived household chaos.

Colonial courts were not mere apparatuses of a colonial-patriarchy alliance. Status and generational tension between senior and junior men, men with ready access to cash and those without, created spaces for women to demand more fluid definitions of marriage in a period in which those in power sought to restrict women's maneuverability. Many women seeking to leave their current marriages influenced their conjugal status through their relationships with their brothers, fathers, and in seeking out lovers. However, Gabonese and French judges allowed for divorce, provided that the husbands were duly compensated for their losses. The idea of women as property was mirrored elsewhere in 1940s and 1950s Africa in areas such as northern Ghana, where colonial courts awarded husbands monetary compensation for wives who had abandoned the conjugal homes.[111] At the heart of many conflicts were questions over sexual relationships within and outside of marriage, leading parties to consider the question of divorce. Pursuing this underlying thread, the next chapter analyzes sexuality.

6 ↪ "Faire Bon Ami"
(To Be Good Friends)
Sex, Pleasure, and Punishment

IN NOVEMBER 1944, one Bandjabi woman and seven men were tried before the colonial criminal court in Libreville on charges of rebellion and of assaulting some African guards at the timber camp in which the accused worked and lived. All of those who testified—the defendants, guards, other laborers, and the French management—confirmed that two violent encounters between the accused and the guards had occurred. On the first occasion, a verbal confrontation between the defendants, the guard, and the guard's wife resulted in a brawl that included punching, stabbing, and hurling pieces of wood. The following day, a crowd of Bandjabi sawmill workers laid down their tools in the middle of the workday, and several of them pummeled guards to prevent the arrest of one of the workers who had been at the previous evening's assault. All present singled out two of the defendants in particular—a laborer named Fidèle Ndongo and his wife, Pauline Tsiangani—as igniting the outbreaks of violence. In convicting the accused of the rebellion charges, the French and African officers of the colonial court focused on the question: Who threw the first punch, the accused or the guards? Yet, for Pauline and Fidèle, the problem of why and how violence had broken out focused on questions of the moral economy of sexual affront and material compensation.[1]

Pauline testified that, with Fidèle's consent, she had worked for one month as a cook for the Fang guard named Goyo. Over the course of her employment, she had sex with Goyo five times, in secret, in locations where no one saw them. She had not asked her husband, Fidèle, for consent to have sex with Goyo. When Goyo terminated her employment, he paid her wages of 25 francs for cooking meals. But he did not compensate her for her sexual work. Pauline confessed to Fidèle that she had sex with Goyo and that Goyo had not compensated her. Fidèle beat her, Pauline relayed, and commanded that they go to Goyo's house to request the adultery fee.[2] Pauline, Fidèle, and some Bandjabi male friends arrived at Goyo's house to request that Goyo compensate Fidèle for sexual access to Pauline. What inflamed the situation and led to the fight, Pauline contended, was when Goyo denied that he had sex with Pauline. Furthermore, Goyo's wife took her by the arm, led her to the side, rebuked her for causing such scandal in the wee hours of the night, and told them to leave. Contemplating the outbreak of violence that involved numerous personnel and the stoppage of work, the French manager mused that he had heard of the "quarrel that came about due to the sentimental relations [of the guard] with the Bandjabi woman. But I initially gave this matter the little importance that it deserved."[3] Yet the stakes of the quarrel were high.

At stake in the quarrel over "sentimental relations" in the triangle between a married woman, her husband, and her lover or ravisher were standards of sexual mores, access to material resources and status, and the gendered geography of male and female space and mobility in multiethnic Libreville. As the town, its rural suburbs, and surrounding timber camps became a destination of residency for increased numbers of people between 1930 and 1960, inhabitants struggled to shape the moral economy of having sex outside marriage. As discussed in the previous chapter, societal ideals across ethnic groups as people settled in the Libreville region carried over: marriage was the foundation of society, every man and woman past puberty was to be married, and procreative sex within marriages sealed by the exchange of bridewealth would perpetuate lineages. Yet there was a paradox between ideals and reality. Engagement in extramarital sex by husbands and wives, as well as increasing numbers of unmarried women and men, was prevalent. In different terms, ordinary citizens and figures of political and religious authority worried about the expression, restraint, and regulation of sex within and outside of marriage.

The social and economic setting of the timber camp created a thorny sexual landscape. The transcript of the court case focuses on the violence that broke out between the Bandjabi workers and Fang guards and offers little detail on the sexual exchanges between Pauline and Goyo. However, other sources permit the contextualization and analysis of this case. That

Fidèle consented for Pauline to work for Goyo demonstrated the precariousness of conditions in their household. Part of the wave of thousands who migrated to Libreville in the midst of World War II, Bandjabi were fairly new arrivals.[4] Few Bandjabi had access to formal education or spoke French, and they generally performed low-skilled jobs in the timber industry or farmed and were relatively poor. Workers in timber camps throughout the colony complained to colonial personnel that their employers had not paid them or given them food rations for months in these precarious years.[5] It is probable that Fidèle faced these same conditions of money and food deprivations. Earning cash, and the time spent outside of homes that it entailed, was a distinctly masculine affair. Reflecting on gender mores in the 1940s as he returned to Libreville from schooling in Brazzaville, an Mpongwé chief named Benoit Messani Nyangenyona relayed in an interview in 2002 that to permit one's wife to circulate outside the conjugal home, to work for other people, was to open up the possibility that other men would attempt to "go after her," or have sex with her, and thus increase the likelihood that one's wife would commit adultery.[6]

It is not clear if these sexual exchanges occurred voluntarily or were forced. Working for wages in Goyo's home meant opportunity as well as vulnerability for Pauline. As a relatively low-status woman of Bandjabi ethnicity, it is likely that Pauline had little volition in refusing sex to Goyo if he approached her. His position as a guard provided Goyo with an immense cloak of power. Charged with maintaining public order and overseeing workers, he could interact with the timber camp's varied African populations with virtual impunity. However, it is also probable that Pauline may have welcomed sexual relations with Goyo given that he was wealthier than her husband. Pauline may have hoped that Goyo would pay her in cash or kind for sex that could supplement her family's resources. Moreover, Pauline may have wished that the liaison would evolve into her becoming a wife to Goyo and divorced from Fidèle. Conflict among unattached laborers in timber camps and neighboring male villagers who lived with their wives occurred in other timber-producing areas in Gabon. Sometimes wives complained that laborers kidnapped them against their will and raped them. Other times, wives of neighboring villages left their husbands for the timber camp workers, refusing to return to their husbands and seeking divorce in order to remain with and marry their lovers.[7] A polygamous marriage to Goyo would have been an improvement in Pauline's social and material status. It is also possible that Fidèle may have been aware of the sexual relations between Pauline and Goyo as they were occurring and hoped to profit from the adultery fee.[8]

Furtive sexual exchanges that occurred between a woman and a man of differing ethnicities and social statuses in a timber camp—the central locale of colonial economic production—unleashed ripple effects that reached into several households, workplaces, courts of inquiry, and political institutions. Pauline's confession of sexual exchanges ignited the public airing of multiple conundrums: the boundaries of ethnic distinction in a heterogeneous setting; Fidèle's masculinity in his ability to manage sexual access to his wife; Pauline's dignity as a wife who maintained fidelity to her husband; Goyo's efficacy to retain his high-level employment and uphold public order; Goyo's unnamed wife's reputation in sustaining a respectable household in the face of scandal; and regulation by the colonial state in mediating the domestic quarrel that threatened political and economic order in the shadow of the colonial capital city. These conundrums encapsulate the themes of sex, the mobility of male and female bodies, space, repute, and regulation explored in this chapter.

Analyzing the quotidian sexual scenes of Libreville from 1930 to 1960 recasts our understanding of transformations in African urbanisms. As argued by Sarah Nuttall and Achille Mbembe, research on urban Africa often focuses on the material infrastructures of cities, ignoring that "the main infrastructural unit or building block is the human body."[9] Calling further attention to the body as a unit of analysis, anthropologist Mary Weismantel urges scholars to pay attention to "the gendered social geographies" of city life and how "bodies take on an almost architectonic function."[10] Nuttal, Mbembe, and Weismental's theories allow for the analysis of the bodies of Libreville's inhabitants as fundamental to transformations in the city's landscape. Yet what did bodies do? Urban becoming for Libreville residents entailed experiencing and responding to the erotic wants and needs of their bodies, as well as their minds and hearts. People's efforts to seek out pleasure, alleviate loneliness, facilitate biological and/or social reproduction, obtain daily bread, and demonstrate power often simultaneously fueled intimacies between male and female bodies. The notion of "geography of experience," as articulated by Frederick Cooper and Mamadou Diouf, encourages scholars to follow the threads of where historical actors went to attempt to tie together social linkages, and where such linkages were destroyed.[11]

Following the geographies of sexual experience, I focus on the actions, words, sentiments, and subjectivities men and women expressed in sexual relationships.[12] Sexual relations, and attempts to regulate sexuality, also shaped the physical geography of the city. The physical presence of women and men in Libreville called into question seemingly normative ideas about how to define male and female and public and domestic space in decades in which Libreville experienced tremendous growth. New conceptions of moral order emerged based on how men and women interacted with each other in heterosocial public and private spaces.

DEMOGRAPHY, MARRIAGE RATES, AND PUBLIC AND PRIVATE SPACES

Three factors of social and economic change altered conjugal sex in Libreville and the Estuary region from the mid-1920s through 1960. First, the speculative nature of the bridewealth economy resulted in marriage being less attainable. Second was the emergence of gender imbalance. Third, the density of persons in the city provided new spaces for men and women to interact and called into question the seemingly normative distinctions between male and female spaces. What was to distinguish married and single women from one another was that married women were to rarely circulate outside the conjugal home without their husbands as escorts. Reflecting on what he recalled of the lives of women who lived "before the white man came" (meaning before colonial rule), Fang chief Sylvain Mve Mba relayed in an interview: "Before, to see a Fang woman in the cour [public courtyard of a home or village] was a rarity. For example, if a male relative visited her and her husband, he barely said hello to his sister then went to join his brother-in-law in the corps du garde [public square for men]. Women had their own courtyard behind the house."[13] Male spaces were "public" spaces in which strangers and other visitors could gather. Women's spaces were "private," the inner recesses of homes, away from the eyes of strangers and men outside of their clan, and sites where only other women were present, such as the cooking areas behind houses and fields.[14] Respectable married women limited their mobility outside of their conjugal homes and traveled longer distances only in the company of their husbands.

The visibility of women in the public spaces of Libreville caused the dividing line between a woman who was married and one who was not married to be blurry. Married and unmarried women's visibility and mobility increased in twentieth-century colonial Libreville as they traversed the pathways of the city and its rural suburbs. Husbands were reluctant to permit their wives' engagement in income-generating activities that would require them to leave the home or have clients visit their homes.[15] Yet economic necessity, and wives' insistence on engaging in cash-generating activities, often resulted in wives' taking in sewing and tailoring jobs, selling prepared food from their homes, or working as housekeepers in the homes of more elite Africans.[16] Women's fields were located a long walk from Libreville. Guy

Lasserre observed of 1957 Libreville that men employed by the colonial state or private enterprises traveled back and forth between the *plateau* (city center) and African neighborhoods. He observed women, morning and night, "with baskets on their backs leave for or return from their plantations."[17] Husbands and wives often spent days, if not weeks, or months, in separate spaces.

Daily life in the post–World War II era through the 1960s necessitated that married women move in the presence of strangers, incurring negotiations of married women's movements outside the conjugal home and husbands' efforts to maintain control. Reflecting on her experiences and those of other married women friends in 1940s and 1950s Libreville, Biologhe Metou recounted, "If you moved too much in the presence of strangers, your husband would ask you 'What are you looking for?' and 'Are you the only woman in the *village?*' "[18] Metou's husband asked if she was not actually on the search for lovers or going to see a lover by being outside the home so often. Suspecting her of infidelity, he threatened that he could easily divorce her and find another wife among many other women in their neighborhood. Yet, given the shortage of women and anxieties about bridewealth inflation, the threat by Metou's husband was an empty one. Nevertheless, many women, both those who lived in Libreville and those who lived in surrounding villages, repeated the adage that a good wife refrained from *se promener*, which literally meant to go for a walk, but figuratively meant being outside the home or homestead for frivolous purposes.[19] The street, literally and figuratively, was a space of sexual danger for women. Men and women of varied ethnicities recounted that with her husband's permission or escort, a wife might travel to and from fields, transport food to sell in Libreville markets, or go to purchase food in the market. In keeping with Fang and Mpongwé customs that a man could maintain lovers other than his wife, but that a wife's infidelity was an affront, women relayed that their husbands kept close watch over their whereabouts and the company that they kept.[20]

Women of varied ethnicities described the intensity with which husbands kept track of their movements, and verbally reprimanded or beat them if they could not sufficiently account for their whereabouts, as "jealousy." A wife who greeted or talked to other men in public, or who was absent from the conjugal home without telling her husband beforehand of her whereabouts, was suspect.[21] Such representations of "jealousy" among husbands and wives convey that opportunities for sexual relations between women and men were ever omnipresent in any of a woman's quotidian actions, from walking to work in the fields to singing at a community function.

Remembrances of husbands' efforts to monitor and control their wives' mobility paint a picture of the city as occupied by men who were sexually insatiable and women who were equally sexually insatiable and who could not resist men's advances. Husbands' attempts to restrict the movement of their wives outside the conjugal home were to maintain social control of married women having extramarital sex. Yet, over the course of these years of immense demographic and spatial expansion of Libreville, wives, elders, and youth, as well as husbands, articulated that there was "a crisis" of extramarital sexual relationships. Representations of men and women engaging in sexual relations outside relationships of marriage illustrate the reconfiguration of multiple hierarchies of seniority in addition to those of gender.

"I HAD EATEN AN UNRIPE BANANA": YOUNG MEN, WOMEN PROSTITUTES, AND HAVING SEX WHEN UNMARRIED

Regulating the sexual engagements of unmarried men, the expression of men's sexuality in a period in which conjugality was often delayed until men were in their forties or later, was crucial for elder men across ethnicities. Many young men who came of age in the 1940s and 1950s conveyed that they were twenty years of age or older, much older than their fathers, when they first entered into sexual relations with women.[22] Their fathers recounted "the period before the white man," as a time in which men engaged in sexual relations after their respective puberty rites. Once a young man and woman engaged in sex on a regular basis with one other person, the relationship was to be formalized by the two kin groups into ébou ("concubinage" in Fang). Rites to establish concubinage resembled those of marriage. Mirroring bridewealth, the man gave labor, material goods, or money to the woman's family, and these payments or services were the marker that both families sanctioned the relationship.[23] Once this was done, lovers did not have to see each other in secret, but the man could openly come to the woman's family home to see her. Fang informants insisted that the man came to the woman's house and never the reverse in relationships of concubinage. For a woman to leave her house and go to the man's house meant that the couple was married.[24] Concubinage did not necessarily have to result in marriage, but would provide young men and women a framework within which to engage in sexual relations with the approbation of elder men and women.

Concubinage continued to be practiced in post-1939 Libreville, but interviewees reported that they expected these to be temporary relationships that youth engaged in until they had the monetary resources to marry. Albertine Andone Essono, who embarked upon a relationship of concubinage with an eighteen-year-old man she met when she was fifteen, relayed that he presented himself before her father and they reached an accord on the relationship. "In my day," she remembered when I interviewed her, "only the man had the right to come to your house, and this was only at a very precise time, not whenever he wanted."[25] Yet, as Raphaël Sala, in his twenties in the 1950s, recounted, youth of his generation did engage in long-term sexual relationships without the formal rites of concubinage, with men going in secret at night to the homes of young girls they fancied.[26]

Elder men in twentieth-century colonial Libreville counseled younger men to delay sexual exchanges because they had insufficient income and material resources. Benoit Messani Nyangenyona, an Mpongwé chief who reached his twenties in the 1950s, recounted that men of his generation often did not have sexual relations until twenty-five years of age, because "when I began to work, I said to myself, and well, now is the moment to know women. I was twenty-five years old then. If you do not have work, how will you take care of a woman?"[27] Jean Francois Mba Ntoutoume emphasized that a man's lack of financial resources to take care of a woman, as well as any children who may be born, required that "you restrain yourself, unlike the young people of today who have children when they are only fourteen or fifteen years old."[28] Young men did not necessarily expect for their first lovers to become their wives. However, men did measure their suitability to have a lover based on providing material resources, as a husband would for his wife. A yardstick for adult male sexual maturity in post–World War II Libreville was a sufficient amount of cash to provide basic necessities for one's lover—to subsidize her housing, food, clothing—and potentially pay bridewealth to turn a sexual relationship into a marriage and provide for a wife. In sum, to furnish a household with basic material necessities and to ensure the social and biological reproduction of one's lineage. Marriage, a relationship that ostensibly granted a husband control over his wife's sexuality and custody of the children that his wife bore, as a marker of adult manhood was in flux.

Sex with women before marriage was an initial signpost of maturity in post–World War II Libreville. A man in his twenties who had begun working and earning cash but was not yet having a sexual relationship with a woman was socially suspect and subject to ridicule. Raphaël Sala embarked upon sexual relationships much later than other men of his generation: "I began to know women very late; I was scared of women. At the time, to tell a woman that you liked her, that was a hard thing. We were scared and said to ourselves that she could be angry at you and cause you problems and such things. Young men waited a long time to approach women. I didn't know women until between twenty-six and twenty-seven years old. By that point people started teasing me and telling me all kinds of things; that I was chicken and impotent."[29] I asked Sala and other Fang and Mpongwé male interviewees if men gave sexual pleasure to each other in their youth, whereupon respondents said no, that such interactions did not occur. They replied that they had heterosexual extramarital sex, but within boundaries set out by elder men as socially acceptable, and no same-sex sexual acts. I asked men in interviews what they defined as sex acts, in terms of contact and penetration, but embarrassed looks and refusals to answer my questions greeted such inquiries.

Elder men of varied Myènè and Fang groups alike attempted to limit the sexual experimentation of young men who had not yet amassed enough resources to constitute bridewealth. Sex before men reached a certain age and material means was dangerous, older men warned younger men.[30] Elder men's portrayal of premature sexual exchanges as resulting in sexually transmitted diseases and perilous to bodily health was to maintain restraint over younger men's sexuality. Elder men warned younger men that women in Libreville were predatory and could physically overpower men and force them to have sex. Jean Francois Mba Ntoutoume remembered of growing up in the 1940s and 1950s that younger men rarely entered into sexual relations without the sanction of elder men: "It was not allowed, because first they talked to you about rape. They told us, 'You are a young man; if you go with women, you risk being raped [*violé*].' They told us myths like this."[31] Accounts of young men's sexual experiences as rape conveyed women as persons who physically coerced men into sex without their consent. The city woman was a sexual aggressor. An Mpongwé man, who did not wish to be identified, recounted his first sexual encounter as "having been raped." When he was in his twenties, he and some male and female friends would often go to the beach. He always made sure to be on his way home by dusk, yet: "One night, when I wanted to go home as usual, a young girl caught me at the beach. This is how I came to know women, without really wanting to. After this first adventure, I became sick. Everyone said that I was raped. I spent my time sleeping, I was always tired. Everyone made fun of me, saying that I had eaten an unripe banana. I had to get treatment. After this unfortunate experience, I waited three years without ever touching a woman."[32]

The metaphor of this first sexual encounter as "eating an unripe banana" depicted the young man as a greedy child who acted with little discernment, ingesting produce prematurely, thereby resulting in his illness. In making fun of him, peers of the young man chastised him for having failed in his masculinity, measured not by having sex, but by his restraint from having sex. Though it was the narrator who ingested the unripe food, it was the young girl who was blamed for accosting him and forcing him to have sex against his will. The young girl transmitted disease and threatened the young man's physical health. In this narrative, women in Libreville were morally suspect persons and predators who had tremendous power over men, particularly in the street and under the darkness of night.

Emerging moral codes of young men's masculinity and sex conveyed that men's discernment was necessary because of a particular type of woman inhabiting the city: the prostitute. Martin Nguema recounted of his upbringing in the 1940s and 1950s in Libreville and the neighboring village of Medoneau: "At twenty years old, you could begin to go with women from the neighboring village. But in Libreville, it is a mess! It is not like it is in the bush. I was scared of an illness called *dowé*. There are women in Libreville who are prostitutes. A woman can be with three men each day, while it is not like this in the bush."[33] Though dowé is not an illness recognized in biomedical lexicon, informants relayed that it was a disease sexually transmitted to men by women of ill repute. Sylvain Mba, who spent his adolescence in 1950s Libreville, recounted similar anxieties of the threat of women who had sex with several men and were carriers of sexually transmitted diseases. Remembering his days as a student, he relayed:

> In my time, there was an illness like AIDS today. You could not know easily that such or such woman was sick, even if she looked healthy. In that time the difference between a woman who was a prostitute and one who was not was not always evident, everyone was badly dressed. In order to know that a certain woman was or was not good, it's your brother who would tell you, thanks to the help of other women who are around her. If she was sick or if she had several different men, your sister would tell.[34]

Both Mba's and Nguema's accounts defined the prostitute as a figure distinctly inhabiting Libreville and not its rural suburbs. In their accounts, rural areas were not just a space, but took on the meaning of an imagined time period, the "old days" of sexual order. Mba and Nguema located their ideal of a woman who would be sexually monogamous in a rural space. They lamented that such "good" women were in short supply in Libreville. A prostitute was a woman who had sex with multiple men, in sexual relations not mediated by kin groups, for the purpose of amassing individual wealth. The prostitute was a dangerous figure who could transmit diseases that could kill or seriously debilitate men. Men seeking a lover sought a "good" woman, in the terms similar to the mores of concubinage or marriage. In the absence of extended kin to negotiate and sanction sexual relationships, men relied on fictive kinship of other male inhabitants and the women with whom they were familiar to inform them about their potential lovers' sexual health. Nguema's narrative indicated that men could not discern a "prostitute" by sight. Physical markers of disease were not always visible on women, and a diseased body could appear healthy. The relative poverty of Libreville's African inhabitants meant that everyone wore the same quality of clothing, making it further difficult to discern a good woman from a prostitute. The margins between "a woman who was a prostitute and one who was not" were complex and contested. Varied discourses about "prostitution" as a gendered term in 1920s–1950s Libreville reflected varied conceptualizations of women's sexuality, particularly around questions of the number of men with which women had sex and questions of the circulation of money and goods in sexual relationships.

Not only were historical actors talking about prostitution with their friends in bars, but French missionaries and colonial administrators also worried about prostitution and sought to temper the remittance of money for sex. On how to define prostitution, colonial administrators and French missionaries sometimes agreed. The primary factor, in their view, was the act of a woman, or her husband or other male patron, receiving compensation—monetary, material, or labor—from men with whom she had sex.[35] Colonial criminal laws across FEA (French Equatorial Africa) and FOA (French Occidental [West] Africa) listed prostitution as illegal. However, in 1928 a French civil servant in Gabon noted that colonial personnel did not police and regulate prostitution and that "prostitution" as practiced by Africans was "very different from our way." Women did not solicit clients in the street.[36] Rather, colonial officials and Christian missionaries decried various aspects of Gabonese conjugal and sexual mores as "prostitution." Husbands' receiving monetary restitution in the form of an adultery fee from their wives' lovers was a form of prostitution.

In a 1950 debate of a policy brief that would encourage the owners of timber camps to allow laborers to bring along their wives, a French legislator argued that particularly in the timber camps that increasingly dotted the Estuary department after World War II, husband-sanctioned prostitution was rampant.[37] In villages near timber camps, husbands in polygamous marriages knew that their wives were engaging in sexual relations with other men, yet permitted it to happen knowing that they could receive the adultery fee when they brought the lovers to court. Even if a pregnancy did result from the extramarital relationship, the husband would maintain the custody of the child, since having paid bridewealth granted him rights over any children his wife bore. The legislator characterized wives who engaged in sexual relations with lovers, with the knowledge and sanction of their husbands and for which lovers compensated their husbands with labor or money, as prostitutes. In a 1950 article on bridewealth, Pastor Jean Keller, a Protestant missionary, declared that the trafficking of married women by their families who encouraged them to divorce one man and marry another in order to receive higher bridewealth, a family inheriting a widow, as well as the practice of a husband or family loaning out a woman to a single man were all forms of prostitution that led to venereal diseases and abortion on a vast scale.[38]

Implicit in colonial and missionary definitions of prostitution were conceptions of degeneracy and the insatiable sexual capacity of African women. The mere act of a married woman living outside a conjugal home or an unmarried woman living outside a parental home could be enough to label her a prostitute. Single women who lived in timber camps, which were primarily populated by men, were prostitutes. Colonial officials also conflated women's "promiscuity"— women having sex with more than one man over a given period of time or maintaining several lovers at a time—as constituting prostitution. Gabonese men's and missionary and colonial state discourses about sexually predatory women also reveal anxieties that women's sexuality permitted economic opportunities in towns could sometimes earn them more cash than wage-laboring men. Sex provided a means for women to earn money and to be autonomous.

Yet Gabonese informants, particularly women, countered that the exchange of material resources for sex in and of itself was not prostitution. In fact, women of all ethnicities insisted that a "good" man was one who generously provided his lover with material goods and money.[39] Women who came of age in the first half of the twentieth century in Libreville expected the men with whom they engaged in sexual relations to give them gifts of either goods or cash. Flirting, the promise or a hint of sexual attraction, was reason alone for men to gift women. Reflecting on her youth in 1950s Libreville, Achey Oyeng reminisced, "I simply had to walk a short distance . . . before meeting several men trying to court me. The simple act of talking to a man allowed me to obtain about 3,000 francs without even having had sex."[40] Women relayed that men's sexual desire was a given and that men initiated the approach to let women know they were sexually attracted

"Faire Bon Ami" (To Be Good Friends) ⌐ 173

to them. A man was expected to provide money and material resources as gifts to actual or potential lovers, and, in fact, it was a sign of his masculinity to do so. Furthermore, Gabonese women emphasized that women's physical pleasure was key to their well-being and that women's "promiscuity" was not a matter of moral sanction. Women could have many lovers and still maintain the cloak of respectability. The fact that an unmarried woman was having sex with an unmarried man at a particular time was not a guarantee that he would be the only lover she maintained. Yet some men expected their *bonne amies* to be monogamous.

Raphaël Sala, who, like many other men of his generation, met a girl in a bar in the 1950s, recounted the story of his first sexual encounter when I interviewed him in 2002. He saw a girl whom he found attractive. He approached her, and over a Fanta, he first asked her if she was married and she asked him the same question. With the response of no, he embarked upon a sexual relationship with her for six months, coming to the home in which she lived with an uncle, and giving her money occasionally to purchase food and clothing. Yet six months later, he ended the relationship because he suspected that she also had another lover, given that "she lied to me regularly. For example, when I would arrange a meeting time with her, she didn't show up, but afterwards she would tell me all types of reasons about why she hadn't come. She was a liar and a crook."[41] Sala expected his lover to have sex only with him, yet she did not concur with his expectations of her monogamy. In his mind, her sleeping with him and accepting his money, but also having sex with other lovers, made her morally suspect and an undesirable lover.

A 1938 criminal case of physical assault illustrates the incongruent expectations surrounding monogamy and money between men and women. On December 29, 1938, a thirty-year-old mechanic identified as Lobi filed a complaint of assault against another man identified as Constantin before the first-degree court in criminal matters; he requested compensation of 500 francs for Constantin's hitting him on the head with a stick four days earlier. At the heart of the assault was that both men had carried out a sexual relationship with a woman named Ana. Lobi testified that he had sex with her on an occasion and gave her 50 francs. She told him that she couldn't see him again the next day because of a prior commitment. The next day and the following days, he tried to see her again, but he couldn't find her. One day, he ran into her on the street with the defendant. Lobi asked Ana if she would come back to him, she responded no, and he asked her to reimburse him the 50 francs he had given her. The defendant and Lobi got into a heated argument about the money, but in the end Lobi let the matter drop and went home. On December 24 Lobi went to a dance in the neighborhood of Pointe Marie, where he happened upon Ana and Constantin. Lobi said that he didn't talk with the couple and went to dance with other women. However, when the couple was leaving, Constantin called him outside. There Constantin asked Lobi why he had demanded from his "bon amie" Ana the return of 50 francs, given that she had allowed him to have sex with her (*accorder des faveurs*). Lobi concluded his testimony by saying that when he turned to walk away, Constantin hit him. Witnesses, including Ana, gave conflicting testimony about who hit whom first and started the fight, but it was Constantin who was convicted of assault.[42]

Of interest in this case, though, is not culpability in the assault, but the diverging expectations of sex and compensation between a man, his lover, and her other lover. Lobi had sex with Ana, gave her money, and expected fidelity and continued sexual relations. Ana had sex with Lobi, accepted the money, but exhibited no sense that this meant a repeat occurrence was obligatory and that this prevented her from being with other men. Constantin chastised Lobi, not for having been lovers with Ana, who was also his "bonne amie," but for asking her to reimburse the money. In Constantin's view, Ana's having had sex with Lobi entitled her to keep the money whether or not she had other lovers.

With amusement, Catherine Okili pondered that in their youth during the 1950s, women of her mother's generation could be "mischievous" and have two lovers at once, "one in plain view of everyone and the other hidden!" However, Okili continued, women's sexual conduct necessitated "a certain morality."[43] This particular morality entailed the public appearance of monogamy. If a woman did engage in sexual acts with several men, she was to do so in a manner so discrete that these multiple sexual relations did not become public knowledge.

Being labeled a prostitute meant crossing a fine line within Libreville's African communities. Engaging in sexual encounters with several men at one time could become "prostitution" if the woman publicly walked around with her lovers or went to a man's house for sex. The distinguishing factor that characterized a woman as a prostitute, a woman who engaged in degenerate sexual relationships with several men and gained wealth from them, was a woman who publicly solicited lovers, whom neighbors witnessed walking the streets beckoning men to come to her. Survival in Libreville entailed that women walk about publicly, traversing paths from home to fields, to markets, to work in people's homes, paths that placed them under the public gaze of men other than their husbands or kin. Women could transform the fleeting glances and flirtations with men whom they met on the street into sexual relationships. Many women interviewees argued that it was unseemly for a respectable woman, whether she was married or unmarried, to solicit a man. A man was to take the initiative of approaching a woman.[44]

For unmarried women well beyond the age of puberty, engaging in sexual relations entailed some circumspection in minimizing the potential of social ostracization and accusations of prostitution. Women who never married or remained unmarried after a divorce engaged in sexual and domestic relations with lovers that mirrored many aspects of marriage, but allowed women some measure of self-determination. Many women and men engaged in *unions libres* (free unions), monogamous live-in relationships with long-term lovers.[45] Agathe Iwenga, an Mpongwé woman, spent her twenties and thirties in serial concubinage with Mpongwé and West African men. Her father refused suitors who wanted to marry her because, as his only child, he wanted her to be available to take care of him in his old age. Iwenga maintained, "But I have always lived with men. In fact, if with these men it did not go well, it is because in part I have a personality that is difficult for men to put up with. I was very strong-headed, capricious, and wouldn't stand for people treating me badly."[46]

Simone Agnoret Iwenga St. Denis, also an Mpongwé woman, recounted that her father was an especially hard man who refused to allow any of her suitors to remit bridewealth and marry her. Though not married through bridewealth, civil, or Catholic rites, St. Denis referred to the men who fathered her children and with whom she shared a house as her "husbands." St. Denis maintained that she retained her respectability by living "in a married way":

> I did marry a man, without money, but we lived in a married way [*maritalement*]. I had four children with him. I also had a second man [and then a] third husband with whom I had two children. If luck does not smile upon you, you remain unhappily single. But you carry yourself like a married woman. And then no one would say bad things about you. With us, when you live maritalement with a man, even if you are not legally married, people talk of marriage. Even more so, when you have already had children, everyone knows that you are husband and wife. I can [also] have a lover, but without him ordering me, whether he comes to stay at my house or not, it does not matter. What is important here is that I must raise and provide for my children. I have a man's character.[47]

Both Iwenga and St. Denis alluded to their "male-like" characteristics of autonomy and economic wealth that made it difficult for them to accept the compromises that wives of their generation were expected to make. The two women negotiated two forms of male control over their lives, that of their fathers and that of their "husbands." The marital aspirations of both women were curtailed by their fathers' refusal to accept male suitors' requests to marry their daughters. In the women's choices to maintain lovers, they negotiated their lovers' efforts to control their persons. Iwenga worked as a seamstress in a European tailoring shop in the 1930s and then opened up several small stands (*boutiques*) selling canned foodstuffs in neighborhood markets. St. Denis worked as a teacher after graduating from Sainte Marie Mission School, the most elite educational institution for African women in Libreville. Married women, they conveyed, were subject to their husbands' will. Wives had to answer to their husbands about where they went, obtain permission to leave the house, could not work or retain independent control of their cash, and were subject to physical abuse. Iwenga's and St. Denis's ability to earn income allowed them to survive the vulnerable position of being a woman without a husband. St. Denis did, however, worry about neighbors who viewed her with disdain because she was not married. To be regarded as a respectable woman by one's neighbors and kin entailed the public appearance of a heterosexual and monogamous domestic household.

Maintaining respectability, to "live in a married way," in a sexual and domestic relationship with a man who was not one's husband entailed several factors. Sharon Marcus's conceptualization of homes in nineteenth-century Paris as "domestic theatre" is a useful concept for interpreting how Iwenga and St. Denis created respectable homes and selves.[48] Though they were not legally married according to customary, French colonial, or Christian laws, in their domestic theaters—their homes and neighborhoods—they played the roles of respectable women. The public face of monogamy was a key factor for respectability. St. Denis and Iwenga engaged in serial monogamy with a series of "husbands." Additionally, motherhood—exhibiting devotion to provide for one's children, maintaining a clean home, and raising children who were well-clothed and respectful to elders—provided another measure of respectability. Iwenga and St. Denis represented the statistically increasing number of women who never married or remained not married for a number of years over the course of their adult lives. Motherhood mitigated the questionable repute that their unmarried status placed on them. Informal urban marriage, such as that articulated by St. Denis, emerged elsewhere in urban Africa, from Harare to Kumasi and Bulawayo, much to the chagrin of colonial officials and African chiefs.[49] Yet, for most of

Libreville's female and male inhabitants, questions of sexuality and status coalesced over the course of their marital careers, around the sexual relationships in which they engaged with their husbands and wives and, for some, their extramarital lovers.

HE SAID, SHE SAID: HUSBANDS, WIVES, AND LOVERS

In their seventies when I interviewed them separately in 2001, husband and wife Maman Denise and Sylvain Mba reflected on their expectations when they got married a little over forty years ago. Both received the advice from male and female elders that the conjugal relationship was the foundation to establish fortune for themselves, their ancestors, and progeny. When she married her first and only husband, Sylvain, Maman Denise's female relatives advised her on how to be a good wife according to Fang custom.[50] This advice reflected commonly held expectations for women of her era across all ethnic groups: to obey and be sexually faithful to your husband, to maintain good relations with your husband's relatives, to have as many children as possible, to maintain a clean house and cook, and to not se promener excessively.[51] In addition to these expectations, women who lived in the rural suburbs, as well as those who lived in Libreville and had access to land within or outside city limits, were expected to grow food for their families to eat. Produce in excess of daily consumption could bring extra income.[52] When he married Denise, who was his second wife, having been divorced from the first a few years earlier, Sylvain Mba received advice from his uncle of what being a good husband entailed. He was to construct a house for Denise and possibly future wives, as well as provide basic necessities such as clothing, and to have as many children as possible.[53]

Both Sylvain and Denise relayed that they experienced the greatest marital discord around the discovery that their spouse engaged in extramarital sexual relations and their disagreement over the significance of these relations to their household. For Denise, that Sylvain had several girlfriends and gave them money and gifts signified an economic slight; there was less money circulating in their conjugal household. For Sylvain, Denise's yearlong tryst with a man who was a merchant at a market was a moral and social slight; once married, Denise should have sex only with the man whom she had married. Extramarital sex, by both husbands and wives, and differing views of it, reflected a reordering of gendered ideas of sexual desire and morality and the circulation of material resources in sexual exchanges. Conceptions and discussions about extramarital sex among husbands, wives, and co-wives reflected both gynocentric and androcentric logics.

Ethnic Group	Monogamous		Polygamous	
	Men	Women	Men	Women
Fang	46.7%	37.4%	21.2%	34.1%
Mpongwé	45.7%	61.5%	—	—
Sékiani	40 %	42.8%	11.1%	26.2%

As polygyny decreased among several ethnic groups in post–World War II Libreville, *la copine* (the girlfriend or informal wife) emerged as a figure. For Fang men of the postwar era, a polygynous household remained an indication of wealth, status, and prestige.[54] Multiple wives not only elevated the husband's status in the eyes of his community, but multiple wives added a sense of security to the maintenance of households. If one wife died, or the couple separated or divorced, the husband would still have other wives to take care of him.[55] Additionally, if one wife was sterile, there was the possibility of having children with another. However, given that many men could barely afford to marry for the first time until well beyond their twenties or thirties, expanding a household to more than one wife was challenging.[56] Figure 6.1 summarizes the estimates from a 1944 survey of monogamous and polygamous marriage within Libreville's three largest ethnic groups.

Reported rates of polygyny were nearly nonexistent among Mpongwé populations. Only about 25 percent of married Fang men were in polygamous households, a decrease from estimates in the previous decade that more than one-third of Fang households were polygamous.[58] Among the Sékiani, who immigrated to Libreville in increased numbers after World War II, rates of polygamy were lower than the Fang. However, the conceptualization of marriage, as defined in this census as legal categories of monogamy or polygamy, did not capture the realm of conjugal-like relationships that men married to one legal wife maintained with other women who were not legally their wives.

As polygamous marriage became more difficult, the ideal for many men in demonstrating masculinity, sexual virility, and wealth by the 1950s was to maintain a girlfriend. Few men or women expressed the expectation that married men would remain monogamous, but women and men did offer differing accounts of how men were to maintain other lovers in a way that was respectful to their wives. Most male informants were rather reluctant to discuss their extramarital relations with a female researcher; thus, the few

PHOTO 6.1. Simone Agnoret Iwenga St. Denis, husband, and child, ca. 1950s. (Reproduced from a photo in the personal collection of Simone Agnoret Iwenga St. Denis, Libreville.)

interviews in which informants were willing to discuss such themes were particularly informative. Sylvain Mba had several copines over the course of his younger years, and, for him, such relationships indicated youthful sexual virility.[59] Maintaining a girlfriend facilitated physical pleasure and fun in the face of the drudgeries of day-to-day life, Mba elaborated. There were distinctively separate spheres in terms of places a man visited and emotions he displayed with his wife versus his girlfriend. Sex with one's wife was primarily for purposes of procreation and did not leave men satiated. A husband attended family and children's school functions, and church if he was a pious Christian, with his wife and maintained a serious demeanor, rarely smiling or laughing in her company. A café (a bar), a location often consisting of a few benches and a radio erected under an awning at dusk, was a place where men drank alcohol, danced, and laughed. The café was a locale that men visited with their girlfriends.[60]

As they expected of their wives, married men also expected that their girlfriends would remain monogamous and engage in sexual relations only with them. When I asked about girlfriends who may have in fact had several boyfriends (amis), Mba countered, "If you suspected that your girlfriend was cheating on you and had another boyfriend in the bar where you were, all you had to do was tell her that you were leaving for a moment and in fact never return."[61] *Une copine* provided sexual pleasure, engaged in outings involving drinking and dancing, and cooked meals when their amis visited them. In return, the copine expected her ami to pay for their outings, to give her cash for the purchase of food, clothing, and housing, and also to give her gifts of material goods or luxuries. If a copine gave birth to a child, ostensibly the biological child of her ami, she expected money and material resources for the child's upbringing. The more generous a man was with gifts, the better ami he was. As elaborated by Jean Ebale Mba, "When you have a girlfriend, you had to satisfy her, to support her. At the end of the month, you had to give her something. If her mother was still alive, for example, you would give a piece of fabric [*pagne*] or food for her mother."[62]

Material resources that a man was to give to his copine were identical to the material resources that a husband was expected to provide for his wife and her kin. Yet, unlike a wife, with whom a husband's relationship was maintained through public acknowledgment, involving negotiations of a wider network of people, the copine inhabited a world in which her relationship with her ami was to remain a public secret. The copine went to the bar to visit her family with her married lover. The wife went to her husband's kin's functions and he to her kin's functions, but never together to a bar. Societal ideals and legal conceptions of adultery in customary law were distinctively gendered in that husbands could engage in extramarital sexual relations with legal and social impunity.

Yet, within conjugal households, wives and husbands negotiated a moral compass about the ways in which men were to engage in extramarital sex with "a certain morality." Wives expected that husbands would conduct their sexual liaisons with other women within boundaries of discretion, in a manner that maintained the public dignity of the conjugal home. For example, a married man was not to sleep with a woman who was not legally his wife in or near his wife's bed, but elsewhere. The testimony of a married woman named Mengue Me Ndong in a 1936 criminal court case, which examines a fight between her husband, a guard, and a male nurse in the village of Médouneu, illuminates one instance in which a woman thought she could express moral indignation at her husband's infidelity. Her husband, Bourobo Pambo, expressed his wish to have sex with an unmarried woman visiting their village and Mengue consented to this, but with the understanding that he knew where it was proper to sleep with the visitor. When Mengue suspected that her husband had slept with the woman in Mengue's own bed located in the kitchen, she exploded in anger, insulted her husband, and a violent fight between husband and wife unfolded that night. Bourobo Pambo expressed bewilderment that Mengue would be angry about his possible infidelity, but Mengue insisted the problem was not the sexual act, but that it took place in her bed, claiming it as a space in which her husband had no right to sleep with another woman.[63] Additionally, other women argued, a married man was not to spend the night at his lover's abode. Agathe Iwenga elaborated, "I think a married man can go out with other women, but in a respectful way. I don't think that men are meant to be with just one woman. If a man is with another woman, he should not pass the night sleeping outside [*découcher*], he should return home by three or four o'clock in the morning. There are some men who cheat on their wives only during the day, and at night, they are at home with their wives. The neighborhood [*entourage*] should not know what is going on. Especially, when he comes back from his double hit, don't bother me! But I also think that there are women who are too jealous, and that isn't a good thing either."[64] Husbands and wives were to mutually understand that the husband would indeed have lovers other than his wife. For such an accord to work, the husband was to interact with lovers in a way that maintained the repute of his marital home, to not stay overnight at his lover's home, and to return quietly to the marital home so as not to call attention to the neighbors nor his wife that he had been with other women.[65] A wife's jealousy was an inappropriate reaction that created unwarranted discord.

 Wives protested husbands' extramarital liaisons as disrespecting their conjugal homes, not due to the expectation of sexual fidelity, but on the issue of money and material resources. City life was expensive and precarious. Simone Agnoret Iwenga St. Denis emphasized that a man who began to sleep elsewhere and spend several days away from his residence was also likely to stop contributing money to the household budget for food, clothing, rent, and other necessities.[66] This was a particular danger, she emphasized, if the wife also earned money, as some men felt that their wives' money alone was enough for household and children's expenses and then stopped contributing altogether. Céline Ntoutoume Escola recounted that she accepted her husband's infidelity except for when "he would waste money, either his or mine, and this would cause us problems especially when he allowed himself to give the money to other women."[67] Women expressed that only the legal wife or wives were to receive a husband's wages, not his copine.

Who were the "other women"? No female informants indicated, or were willing to admit, that they had been a copine to a married man at some

PHOTO 6.2. A man and his copine, ca. 1950s. (Photograph from the personal collection of Marie France, Libreville.)

point in their lives. Married women conceived of copines as morally suspect women because they were more public women, parading in the sight of men and circulating in streets and bars, while respectable women (i.e., wives or women who had the potential to become wives), spent most of their time at home.

While husbands' extramarital relationships were a public secret, wives sought to maintain their extramarital relationships in complete secrecy and emphasized extramarital sexual relations as bringing them personal satisfaction. Wives with extramarital lovers sought to publicly maintain the appearance of monogamy to their husbands, as marriage brought social and economic security and respectability. Yet many wives who engaged in extramarital sexual relationships emphasized that they engaged a lover out of the desire to attain sexual fulfillment, expressing that sex with their husbands was inadequate. Biloghe Metou, a Fang woman living in the village of Okolassi, recounted that she got a lover when it became clear that her husband preferred his newly acquired second wife and spent more nights with the second wife than with her. She relayed, "At the time, I was still young, a beautiful young woman. As soon as a man saw you passing by, he said

Geographies of female respectability

'Where are you going, such a beautiful woman.' And this finished with him taking you away. I chose him because he was pleasing and, since he was a neighbor, we were already friendly with each other."[68] Isabelle Ntoutoume, who lived in Nkok, relayed:

> I was well with my husband; he did not beat me or insult me. Only he had a very bad way of organizing himself. He spent one month here, two weeks there, which obliged us to go with other men during his numerous absences. When he would spend one month elsewhere, we [wives] who were left said to each other that he was gone in search of other women, and in consequence, we too should take advantage to go out with other men. I did it discretely, without my husband and his family knowing. In my time, women never ran after men, we did not go to men's houses. It is he who came to find me in the night and he left while it was still night.[69]

Ntoutoume and Metou signaled that their husbands' having sex with other women to whom they were not married opened the door to their seeking out lovers other than their husbands. Neither woman wanted to divorce her husband, but to feel desired and experience a sense of companionship. Husbands expressed anxiety about the time that wives spent outside the conjugal home, worrying that those were the times when their wives were engaging in extramarital sex. Yet it was in these women's personal spaces, in their conjugal homes, their sleeping mats, under the cloak of night, where the chances were minimal that others would see them, and often with men whom they met in close proximity to the conjugal home, that they engaged in extramarital sexual relations. Reflecting on women of her generation in 1940s and 1950s Libreville, Maman Denise stated: "What woman can say that since they were born, they did not cheat on their husbands?"[70] Denise continued that married women had lovers over the course of their marital careers at varied junctures for motivations of personal pleasure, love, or to become pregnant if one's husband was sterile.

As recounted in the opening anecdote of this chapter, the discovery and public unveiling of a married woman's extramarital sexual relations unleashed a variety of struggles around sexuality and power. Upon discovery and confession, many husbands beat their wives, an acceptable punishment according to many.[71] There were limits to husbands' violence, though—a wife could ask for a divorce in the case of serious cruelty, and a husband who killed his wife could face prosecution.[72] Righting the wrong of women's adultery was a two-part process: the personal matter of a husband inflicting physical punishment on the woman's body, and the civil matter of a husband receiving material compensation from the lover. Family or community councils often resolved the public discovery of adultery, with the lover paying a fee to the husband before witnesses.[73] Over the course of the 1930s through the 1950s, public discourse about wayward wives and extramarital sex reached a crescendo. Colonial, missionary, and African political leaders sought to regulate women's sexuality and how men resolved conflict over sexual access to women in colonial courts.

ADULTERY AND CRIMINAL COURTS OF LAW

What constituted "adultery" as a legal, moral, and social concept was distinctively gendered. Adultery in the discourses of African and French political leaders in the post–World War II period was understood as the problem of married women's extramarital sexual liaisons.[74] Women's extramarital sex translated itself into a two-pronged problem for the colonial state: limiting the reproduction of future workers as well as the productivity of workers employed by French enterprises.[75] Colonial officials conceived of "the labor problem" that plagued the colonial economy as also stemming from Gabonese women's sexuality. Private businessmen and colonial civil servants perpetually complained that they could not recruit sufficient numbers of male wage laborers for colonial enterprises, nor was the existing workforce effective. African women's unrestrained sexuality contributed to conflict among men, disrupting a controllable workforce that was to be the foundation of a productive colony.[76] Male laborers who originated from outside the Estuary department often abandoned their work contracts to return to their regions of origin to resolve news of their wives leaving them for other men.[77] The increase in adultery, argued an administrator in the Estuary department in 1947, had led to the crystallization of the instability in families.[78]

Rather than regulating adultery as a civil matter between African men, French administrators sought to regulate African wives' adultery as a criminal act, a crime against the state, in which French judges directly punished wives rather than compensating husbands. French officials viewed the practice of the adultery fee as exacerbating occurrences of wives' extramarital sex, since some husbands were complicit in their wives' liaisons as a way to make money. A 1925 colonial proposal to regulate native marriage recommended that instances of adultery by wives be adjudicated by courts presided over by French officials.[79] In 1942 a gathering of missionaries and Estuary village chiefs proposed a decree that "no payment can be demanded for adultery.

Those who traffic in this way will be severely punished."[80] According to this proposal, French judges presiding over cases of adultery would not negotiate compensation for husbands, but would punish the lovers *and* wives with fines or prison. By 1946, the penal code for French Equatorial Africa listed adultery as a criminal offense under which both the wife and the lover could be fined and/or imprisoned. Judgments could include prison sentences from three months to two years, as well as fines of 100–2,000 francs to be paid to the court.[81] The French criminal code also attempted to prosecute male lovers for wives' adultery under the rubric of criminal infractions such as wife-kidnapping and charge wandering wives with administrative offenses.

The only surviving register of the first-degree criminal court of the Estuary covers February 1937 to February 1939.[82] Within these two years, the criminal court heard a total of forty-five cases, about 25 percent of which involved the prosecution of wives who had committed adultery, some of whom abandoned their marital homes in other regions to sojourn to Libreville with their lovers. Many of the records include one-paragraph transcriptions of litigants' testimony, making them a particularly rich body of source materials. Neighborhood chiefs in Libreville searched for the women and brought them before the criminal court at the behest of their husbands, or husbands directly petitioned the court. The second-degree court of the Estuary department, which also held jurisdiction for the prosecution of criminal charges, included three cases of women prosecuted for adultery as a crime between 1935 and 1939 for which there are registers.[83]

Husbands who testified before the court in cases of adultery emphasized the primary insult as being not just their wives' sexual relations with other men, but also that the women had abandoned their husbands' homes to live with their lovers and continued to do so in spite of their repeated requests for their wives to return. Such was the case of Ebare Mba, who brought criminal charges of adultery against his wife, Andona Ndong, and adultery and wife-kidnapping charges against her lover, Etienne Meyo. Mba charged that Ndong had abandoned him and their child in a village near Owendo four years earlier to live in concubinage with Meyo in Libreville. In bolstering his claim, Mba repeatedly emphasized that he had completed bridewealth payments for Ndong, thereby making him the only man who had rights over sexual access to her. Ndong's sexual indiscretion was not only a disservice to him, Mba charged, but she was a failed mother, and their child "regretted the absence of his mother." The court sentenced Ndong to five months in prison and ordered Meyo to compensate Mba 500 francs.[84] Husbands like Ndong brought their spouses and their lovers to court as a last resort. Charges were filed only after repeated attempts to get the wife through their own intervention, family councils, and the mediation of chiefs.[85] These criminal cases were occurrences in which husbands acknowledged the social death of their marriages and that their wives refused to reconcile.

There were some exceptions in which women who admitted to extramarital sex were not convicted of adultery; rather, the second court granted wives' requests of a divorce from their husbands so that they could marry their lovers. An unidentified wife from the village of Nzeng Ayong left her husband, Otogho Nguema, who was the village chief, to live in the home of her lover, Sindoung, in Libreville. She then sought refuge at the Sainte Marie Mission when Nguema arrived in Libreville to demand her return. Her lover offered to reimburse Ngeuma's bridewealth so that he could marry her. Nguema retorted in court, "I will kill him if he marries my wife. I will let him live if he doesn't." The wife did not deny the accusations of adultery in court hearings, but countered that she wanted a divorce on grounds that her husband was brutal. Based on witness testimony and evidence of physical wounds on her body, the judge convicted Nguema of assault, repeatedly stabbing his wife with a knife. Though the court condemned Sindoung to pay Nguema a fine of 250 francs for adultery, judges approved Sindoung's request to reimburse the wife's bridewealth and pronounced a divorce between her and Nguema.[86]

Criminal cases of adultery reveal the complex valences around which some wives engaged in extramarital sex, from affective factors to pragmatic and material motivations. One unidentified wife who was condemned to pay a 25-franc fine for adultery testified that engaging in extramarital sex allowed her to complete agricultural labor crucial to the maintenance of her household. Her husband worked as a cook in town, while she spent days and nights on the outskirts of town cultivating her husband's land.[87] The husband caught her and her lover when he paid a surprise visit to the plantation. She justified the affair by stating that her lover labored alongside her in the fields in the physically intensive work of agricultural production. With no access to the labor of dependents or kin, she alone was responsible for all the work and exchanged sex for a helping hand and companionship *en brousse*.

Other women hoped that their lovers would reimburse their current husbands' bridewealth, thereby facilitating a divorce, and marry them in turn. The case of Eboume Enong, sentenced to serve four months in prison for adultery, is particularly illustrative of how some wives rationalized their extramarital relations as a strategy to leave their current marriages and enter into better ones. Enong was convicted of adultery not because her husband brought her before the criminal court, but because she brought her lover

AFFECTIVE and PRAGMATIC motives for extramarital relationships

before the criminal court on the charge of "making a false promise of marriage that he did not honor." She testified:

> Antoine promised to marry me and [now] he does not want to marry me, to give the bridewealth money. I was his lover [*J'ai fait bon ami*] for six months without him giving me a penny. My husband beat me several times to try to get me to admit [my affair], but I denied it. Today, I've had enough. Antoine needs to be punished. Yes, I cheated on my husband and I deserve to be punished. But Antoine doubly deserves punishment since he cheated my husband and me.[88]

Outraged that Antoine testified in court that he had never even met her, Eboume argued that Antoine was to be punished not only for engaging in sexual relations with another man's wife, but also for not fulfilling the promise that illicit sex would turn into respectable matrimony. In addition to these few cases of adultery, wives who were in Libreville without their husbands were charged with other criminal offenses.

Wives' extramarital sexuality was also prosecuted via criminal offenses against the colonial state, such as: refusing to obey a summons to appear before a chief; being in the city without a pass from the colonial administrator in her home province; or public misconduct. In June and July of 1938, the particularly zealous Mpongwé judge-conciliator Raphael Bineni brought four married women of varied ethnicities before the court. Two of the women had been born in Libreville, while the other two originated from outside Libreville. All of these women were married, but had absconded from their conjugal homes to live with their lovers. Their husbands ostensibly sought out Bineni to force their return. Instead of turning themselves in, many of the wives took refuge either in the surrounding bush or in other neighborhoods in the city; one wife traveled to her mother's village to try to secure money for reimbursement of the bridewealth.[89] Bineni accused the women of the following two infractions: "disobeying a verbal or written summons from an authority carrying out an administrative or police function" and "being absent from the subdivision of origin for more than ten days without receiving a pass from the commander of the subdivision."[90] Each received a sentence of from ten to twelve days in prison.

In a particularly vehement statement, Bineni testified that a woman identified as Bilogho, who had abandoned her husband in northern Gabon, had engaged in "prostitution in the timber camps and provok[ed] many disputes." Bineni charged Bilogho with not having an identity card, not paying the mandatory head tax, and not possessing a leave pass to be away from her home province.[91] Bilogho represented danger to colonial administrators and chiefs in that she evaded familial and state control. Sexual relationships allowed her to earn cash that neither the colonial state nor her husband could access.

However illustrative cases of criminal prosecution may be, few women were summoned before criminal courts for adultery. Only a small number of Libreville's inhabitants sought the criminal prosecution of women's extramarital relationships. Monetary compensation negotiated by chiefs continued to be the public and legal avenue through which husbands sought to maintain their marriages and manhood by establishing that they had the rights to manage sexual access to their wives.

ADULTERY AS THEFT: MONETARY COMPENSATION

Demonstrating the unevenness of colonial rule in the capital city, the question of who would regulate African women's sexuality was one of contestation. The Pahouin Congress of 1947 sought to limit, not diminish, the fines women's lovers were to be assessed. Those present recommended that a first-time offender be assessed 500 francs and the recidivist 1,000 francs.[92] Women's adultery was not a legal condition for divorce, but an affront to be resolved between the husband and the lover, after which, ideally, the marriage would be maintained. By the 1950s, African delegates of the Territorial Assembly protested attempts by colonial officials to regulate adultery through the criminal prosecution of women. In these arguments, adultery was not an offense that automatically led to the end of the marriage, but a misdeed for which redemption could result in the maintenance of the marriage. One delegate warned that a woman whose husband had her placed in prison for adultery would leave her husband and seek a divorce upon her release and that the husband would lose a wife whom he loved and who had rendered him service.[93] Marriage was the most crucial relationship through which men cultivated social, political, and economic capital, elite African men argued, and husbands' individual power over their wives was to be maintained.[94]

Though the letter of colonial law dictated that French judges were to adjudicate cases of adultery as criminal offenses, courts presided over by chiefs were the most frequent legal venues in which wronged husbands sought recourse. Men brought complaints before the customary court presided over by African chiefs primarily seeking the return of their wives who had taken refuge with kin or lovers, in addition to monetary compensation from their wives' lovers. One registry that has survived in the archives is of the customary court for the department of Libreville, which encompassed the town and its rural suburbs. The registry covers the period of November 1950 through October 1954. Over the course of these four years, the court presided over thirty-seven cases involving the legal complaint of a married woman having engaged in sexual relations with someone other than her husband.[95] Almost all of the litigants were Fang, reflecting that 95 percent of the subdivision's inhabitants were of this ethnicity. The entry for each case identifies the names, ages, and villages or neighborhoods of residence of plaintiffs and defendants, as well as a brief one-paragraph summary of the case. This summary includes the plaintiff's charge, the defendant's response, if she or he contests the plaintiff's claims, and the decision taken by the tribunal. The brief summary of proceedings might include one or two sentences by the wife or woman in question. Some of the cases provide information on the context in which disputes were taking place, while other summaries detail only the plaintiff's complaint and the judge's decision. The summaries of many of the cases do not provide enough detail to ascertain the terms of the debates. These summaries merely state the monetary amount for which the plaintiff was suing, followed by the judge's decision to award or deny monetary compensation.[96]

Husbands went to customary courts seeking the chiefs' disciplining of their wives and to establish their manhood when faced by other men who had sex with their wives without their consent. For husbands presenting complaints of adultery against their wives' lovers, their objective was the confirmation of their marriages and their exclusive ability to manage sexual access to their wives. A wife did not play a major role in the proceedings of adultery cases. The legal dispute was between her husband and her lover.[97] Customary court hearings in Libreville represented an arena in which husbands could publicly restore their honor by having their wives' lovers admit to the affair and condemned to remit just monetary compensation. Case summaries usually consisted of the plaintiff's statement that the defendant had committed "adultery" or had "sexual relations" with the plaintiff's wife, the amount requested, and the judge's award.[98]

While the legal language and forum of adjudicating extramarital sex in customary courts did not formally recognize married women as active agents in determining the legality of sexual relations in which they engaged, the acts of women seeking out male sexual partners other than their husbands brought them into direct confrontation with the colonial legal system. Although husbands were identified as plaintiffs in nearly all of the cases before customary courts, what brought men to court was that their wives, or women they claimed as their wives, initiated the conjugal-sexual crisis by allegedly having had sex with other men. Even though Fang women appeared to be objects between groups of competing men, it was women's actions that precipitated the skirmishes. A wife taking on a lover challenged the notion that she had been "sold" to her husband and that she could not negotiate rights to her person and sexuality. Though a husband sought retribution from his wife's lover for adultery, it was the wife's engagement in extramarital sex that called into question the conceptualization that remittance of bridewealth and marriage granted husbands exclusive access to their wives' sexuality.

Compensation from the lover to the husband reinforced that husbands who had married women via the remittance of bridewealth "owned" their wives' bodies. By the time they made it to court, the parties had likely undertaken varied forums of kin- and community-based arbitration, and husbands approached courts likely because their desired outcomes of compensation or the return of their wives was unattained. Many cases indicated that some wives' extramarital relations had taken place over the course of several years. If a husband petitioned the court, he likely had a good case, given that he had tried other methods of individual, kin, and community intervention to receive compensation.

In all of the adultery cases heard from November 1950 through October 1954, the customary court ruled in favor of the husband and ordered the lover to pay a fine directly to the husband.[99] As outlined by the case of Nzé Meyo versus Bekale Nguema, the order to pay an adultery fee was punishment for "having admitted to having sexual relations with a woman who did not belong to you."[100] Between 1950 and 1955, fines varied from as low as 50 francs to the most commonplace amount of 500 francs to higher judgments of 5,000 francs. Lovers who had pursued an extramarital affair with a woman over several years, or had sexual relations with a woman in the conjugal home, were assessed a hefty fine of 2,500 to 5,000 francs.[101] The court also levied the higher fee of 5,000 francs on any lover who attempted to convince the wife to divorce her current husband and marry him.[102] Court transcribers used the phrases "to turn her head" or "give her a bad head" to describe the efforts by lovers to convince wives to transform extramarital sexual relations into legal marriages.[103]

Like the attendees of the Pahouin Congress, French officials attempted to regularize amounts of adultery compensation. In a 1955 document titled "Note for village and canton chiefs," Rougeot, an administrator in the Estuary department, critiqued that if there were a uniform rate for adultery fees, each chief could determine a ruling as he saw fit. He viewed the common award of 5,000–7,000 francs as excessive. He expressed the desire for the adultery fee to be limited to 1,000 francs for cases of "simple adultery," in which a wife spent one night away from her conjugal home, and 1,500–2,000 francs in the case of recidivists and when women spent several nights away from the conjugal home. Additionally, adultery applied only to cases in which the husband had not consented for his wife to have sex with another man and to cases in which the wife and her lover were caught in "flagrant délit."[104] Last, the note of advice stated, any confessions that wives made to indiscretions under the duress of beatings that they received from their husbands would not be admissible in court deliberations. The absence of court records that would detail adultery cases after 1955 does not allow the assessment of Gabonese and French judges' following these limits and definitions. The language used in the adjudication of adultery cases involving monetary compensation to husbands characterized adultery as an act of theft, and women as passive vessels being acted upon by lovers, thereby erasing the factor that women were usually complicit in seeking out and maintaining extramarital sexual relationships. With the pronouncement of the chief's ruling of adultery and a monetary fine before an audience, the husband could publicly confirm the integrity of his conjugal home in the face of another man's attempt to call it into question. These were the very conundrums of marriage, sex, and power between a husband, his wife, and her lover with which the chapter began.

CONCLUSION

Conceptions of and contestations over what it meant to be a respectable woman or man in the shifting urban environment emerged from how Fidèle, Pauline, Goyo, and Goyo's wife experienced sexual relationships. Historical actors inhabiting Libreville between 1930 and 1960 did not uniformly agree on the meanings of these terms. Normative ideas of female space as areas closed to public view and limited to homosocial spaces such as kitchens located behind houses, and of male space as the village-gathering square where visitors were received, gave way to a new type of space, heterosexual space. Locales such as the street, the market, and the bar-café were new sites where married and unmarried men and women gathered, entailing changing mores of male and female respectability. Daily life in Libreville unfolded along positions of monetary wealth and poverty, youth and seniority, respectability and ill repute, public space and home, and the possibility of mobility within these positions. Experiences of marital and extramarital sex permitted men and women alike to negotiate these subjectivities. State, kith and kin, and church attempted to regulate the sexual marketplace and control the circulation of sexual tender.

Anxieties about sexual experiences, expressed in differentiated terms by husbands, wives, colonial officials, and African political leaders, reflected the simultaneous rigidity and flexibility of factors shaping urban person-hood. Conflict over extramarital sex also demonstrated both the resiliency and the flexibility of the idea of marriage. Even given all of this flux over the meanings of marriage, sex within marriage, and extramarital sex, conjugality continued to be the metaphor with which historical actors measured their relationships, whether among persons of the same or of differing ethnicities or social statuses. Metaphors about marriage also defined new forms of relationships occurring across racial lines, between African women and European men. The next chapter will explore how these metaphors called into question racial boundaries of difference.

7 ⤿ "A Black Girl Should Not Be with a White Man"
Interracial Sex, African Women, and Respectability

On July 10, 1935, what was a rather mundane traffic infraction in Libreville led to a heated exchange that revealed broader contestations over sexuality, race, and African women's claims of respectability in Libreville.[1] A car driven by an African male chauffer made an illegal U-turn in the middle of a street in sight of the French police commissioner. The ensuing exchange took place between the police commissioner and the passenger, a female colonial subject. The confrontation is preserved in the written record because Michel Moutarlier, the French lover of the woman in question, wrote a letter of complaint to the governor of the colony. Moutarlier wrote to protest the "disrespectful manner" in which the commissioner treated "my wife and the mother of my children," whom he identified as Flavie Nguia.[2] Moutarlier recounted that the driver told the police officer that he had left his driver's permit at his residence. Nguia intervened to request that they be allowed to return home to the nearby village of Sibang to retrieve the documents. The commissioner, whom Moutarlier intimated was drunk at the time, verbally assaulted Nguia and threatened to arrest her. Nguia responded that the commissioner had no right to arrest her. She then sought refuge in city hall, where the mayor diffused the escalating situation by impounding the car and permitting Nguia and the driver to leave.[3] In response to Moutarlier's letter of complaint, the mayor of Libreville asked the commissioner to summarize his account of the encounter with Nguia.

The commissioner's report dismissed Moutarlier's portrayal of Nguia as a respectable wife and mother. According to the police commissioner, Nguia was "a native woman" —a French colonial subject, neither white nor a citizen, subject to native law, and of commiserate social and legal status. The commissioner relayed his encounter of Nguia as such:

> A native woman descended from the car without having been addressed by me, nor asked to speak about the infraction. She took me to the side and told me in a tone bereft of any politeness, "I am Madame Moutarlier." I responded to her that I had not addressed her, to lay off . . . and to not involve herself in matters that did not concern her, and especially, not in official matters, to claim an identity that she did not possess; that I knew full well, having examined her papers, that she was Flavie Nguia. She replied to me in a tone less and less polite that she was Madame Moutarlier, and that if I didn't know this, I would learn [of it] at my own risk. [I would ask you to] admonish the subject in question; I am used to these types of incidents [and] we should not give them more importance than they are worth, especially considering the source where they came from.[4]

To the police commissioner the traffic violation involved only him and the driver. The native woman before him was inconsequential. However, Nguia inserted herself into the exchange, claiming a legal conjugal relationship with a white Frenchman and that such a relationship accorded her rights in authorizing the movement of Moutarlier's employees and property. For the police officer, Nguia's being nonwhite and her *indigène* identity card belied the intimacy and legitimacy of the relationship she claimed to have with Moutarlier.

Nguia attempted to school the commissioner in the de facto code that had operated in Gabon in which the French accorded "native" companions, some of whom were black and some of whom were métisses, of white men with social respectability. Though increasingly frowned upon in metropolitan and elite colonial circles beginning after World War I, sexual-domestic relationships between African women and European men remained commonplace at the time of Nguia and the police commissioner's confrontation. Nearly all such unions involved women of Myènè ethnolanguage groups, particularly Mpongwé. Like the vast majority of such unions, the relationship between Nguia and Moutarlier was most likely not a marriage according to French law. In all probability, Nguia and Moutarlier were involved in a sexual-domestic partnership that lasted over several years while Moutarlier lived in Gabon working in the timber industry. Nevertheless, Nguia invoked her popularly regarded status in Libreville as "Madame Moutarlier," even if the identity card issued by the municipal administrators did not acknowledge her as such. Moreover, Moutarlier insisted that colonial officials recognize Nguia's birthing of his children and live-in arrangement as furnishing her recognition as his wife. The commissioner was unmoved, expressing the opinion that "native women" involved in interracial relationships were of dubious moral character and African social-legal standing.

Though the city's police commissioner in the 1935 encounter regarded Nguia as a "native woman," of dubious morality and low social and legal status, two years later she gained French citizenship. In 1937, Flavie Nguia's petition to a colonial court of French Equatorial Africa to be recognized as a French citizen was approved. The court acknowledged that Flavie Nguia was métis, the child of a presumed French or European (white) man who no longer resided in the colony and an Mpongwé mother.[5] In theory, avenues existed for African men and women to apply for French citizenship.[6] Yet relatively few African women could fulfill the criteria such as wage-labor employment, French education and language skills, and other qualifications outlined in French policies. The numbers of male and female Africans who attained French citizenship across French Equatorial Africa (FEA) and French Occidental (West) Africa (FOA) were relatively low over the course of the twentieth century. From 1912 to 1922, only one African person in FEA obtained French citizenship, and in 1944 the head of the judiciary service in FEA relayed that of the twelve million Africans in FOA, only 251 had obtained French citizenship.[7] A 1936 law, however, provided for métis to apply for French citizenship on the grounds of their presumed descent from a European father, even though the father remained "unknown" and had not legally recognized paternity. This law opened a new avenue for "native" women such as Nguia to gain citizenship. In this legal encounter with colonial administrators, initiated by Nguia, interracial sex increased her social-legal standing in the colonial society. Being born of her Mpongwé mother's relationship with a white man accorded her the status of French citizen in her adult life. French citizenship would ostensibly grant her access to French education, adjudication under French law, and permit her to traverse racialized boundaries of respectability and social status.[8]

Nguia invoked her associations with white men and her skin color to shape her status not only in regard to French colonial society, but also within African communities in Libreville. In April 1941, Samba Augustin, an Mpongwé man, wrote a letter to the colony's governor-general complaining of police mistreatment resulting from his public confrontation with Nguia, whom he referred to as Madame Moutarlier. In this confrontation, Nguia invoked her descent from a European father as well as her "marriage" to a European husband to bolster her challenge of Mpongwé gender hierarchies. A few days earlier, Augustin wrote, he was standing at the port when he overheard Nguia making disparaging comments in French about Charles de Gaulle. Libreville was wary of a French Empire divided between loyalty to Vichy and loyalty to de Gaulle. Less than six months before, Libreville had been embroiled in the internecine war among the French, the town subjected to aerial bombs and naval attacks by Free France forces to wrest control from the Vichy-led governor. The atmosphere in Libreville remained charged, with residents debating which side should hold their loyalty. Augustin admonished Nguia that she should be speaking in "their" language (Mpongwé) and that when the French solicited African opinions on politics they would "address the men, not women." For Augustin, she was essentially Mpongwé, and he sought to remind her of an ostensibly Mpongwé understanding of gender roles in which women could not publicly participate in political discussions. Nguia did not dispute that she was Mpongwé— people of European and Mpongwé descent in twentieth-century Gabon, even those who became French citizens, identified themselves as both Mpongwé and mixed race (métis). Yet Nguia emphasized that her status to speak publicly about politics was based on skin color. She rebuked Augustin that a black man (nègre) had no right to limit the speech of a métis woman. Days after the confrontation, Augustin encountered two Frenchmen in the market and one of them, presumably Mr. Moutarlier or another European husband, identified Augustin as the man "who insulted my wife." The Frenchmen assaulted Augustin until a police officer stopped the fight. Augustin complained that he was imprisoned for three months without a trial, while the two European men were let go with impunity.[9]

These public deliberations involving Flavie Nguia and colonial officials, private French citizens, and an elite African man demonstrate how the subjectivities and actions of African women shaped how colonial societies and African communities drew and redrew the boundaries of social respectability and identity in colonial Libreville. The catalyst for each verbal or physical confrontation was Nguia's claim that women's sexual-conjugal associations with European men afforded them social and legal privileges. Nguia claimed the identities of wife of a Frenchman, and daughter of a

racial hierarchy is play

Frenchman, or métis woman, to subvert colonial and gender hierarchies. French and African men attempted to define her social and legal status—wife, mother, daughter, native woman, and Mpongwé woman—for differing purposes of maintaining individual honor, social control, or the management of public political discourse.

This chapter examines how, from the 1930s to circa 1960, individual and collective African women such as Nguia utilized interracial sexual and domestic relationships to negotiate tenuous avenues of social, economic, and political mobility. In doing so, I turn away from the analysis of interracial relationships and African women's bodies through the lens of "the colonial gaze."[10] Recent research on interracial sex in colonial-era Africa has urged analysis of the dialectics of African and European racial thought.[11] Following Nguia's gaze as she navigates varied public spaces and institutions in Libreville demonstrates the porousness of racial, gender, and institutional boundaries in the heart of the colonial city. In the police report, the correspondence of a private French male citizen and an elite African man and court records are Nguia's claims to circulate in city streets and roadways, participate in public political debates, and obtain French citizenship.

By the 1930s, how and on what terms interracial unions occurred in colonial Libreville was based on negotiations and contestations among Mpongwé women and men and European men. In keeping with practices of previous generations, the remittance of bridewealth and the consent of heads of families to interracial unions meant Mpongwé viewed interracial relationships as legitimate marriages. Material resources and money from these unions provided women's families with social and economic capital to live as elites as economic and political fortunes shifted. However, black and mixed-race women who engaged in interracial unions embodied forms of urban female wealth, leisure, and social and legal status that came into conflict with colonial categories *and* gender norms within Libreville's multiethnic African communities. Women asserted a sense of individual respectability based on their monogamous relationships with European men, which allowed them access to money and imported luxury goods, as well as ownership of land and houses. Furthermore, métisses claimed their skin color as indicative of their superiority in comparison to other Africans and of their closeness to European culture. In varied forms, Mpongwé women asserted that this respectability furnished them the legitimacy to directly challenge racialized hierarchies of native versus white, as well as African men's conceptions that women were to play limited roles in the city's political and economic spheres. Such negotiations destabilized multiple hierarchies of

[Margin annotations: "use of racial identity to subvert gender hierarchy"; "PURPOSE"; "turning away from analysis through 'colonial gaze'"; "negotiations and contestations"; "agency?"; "internalized racial discourse"]

power—colonial, gender, and seniority. In turn, African communities and colonial societies in Gabon debated over "the métis problem" as a question of how to control African women's sexuality and socioeconomic and political power in the colonial capital city.

"MY PARENTS DID NOT 'GIVE' MY MOTHER TO A FRENCHMAN": BRIDEWEALTH, MARRIAGE, AND KIN IN THE BROKERAGE OF INTERRACIAL RELATIONSHIPS

Between 1930 and 1958, the numbers of white women in Gabon increased, but they remained in short supply. In 1931, women made up an estimated 29 percent of the European population in Gabon, and by 1958, this had increased to about 41 percent. However, the resurgence of the export of timber propelled European men of varied nationalities to travel to Gabon. Private businessmen and working-class whites (*petits blancs*) openly engaged in interracial relationships, at times facing ostracization from elite colonial circles.[12] Civil servants and European men of higher economic status engaged in interracial relationships with greater circumspection. Colonial state civil servants were subject to termination or reprimand if they publicly flaunted their relationships with African women; a municipal employee was expelled from Gabon in 1941 when he got into a verbal fight with his African companion in a bar and then the street after a night of drinking.[13] After World War II, the European partners of Mpongwé women were more often businessmen and adventurers rather than colonial civil servants.

Interracial unions persisted in the 1930s and after World War II, often along generational lines, as métis women entered relationships with European men as had their mothers. Gabon's total population was small compared to other colonies in Francophone Africa, yet the number of métis individuals was high given the low population density.[14] Authoring a 1938 study on métis in Gabon, a man named Saint-Blancart, who was an intern at the mayor's office, enumerated a total of 104 métisses over the age of sixteen in Libreville. Saint-Blancart listed seventy of them, with almost 70 percent noted as "living in concubinage" with European men.[15] In a 1939 report, the French doctor who headed the Hospital of Libreville estimated that there had been about fifteen hundred *unions libres* (domestic and sexual relationships) between white men and indigenous women in Gabon since 1900.[16] The employee further delineated the racial categorization of women in unions libres: 60 percent of them were métis, 30 percent were black, and 10 percent were quadroon. In a 1941 report on métis, the governor of Gabon wrote that out of a total population of 7,000 Africans in Libreville, there were

IMPACT OF CLASS ON BEHAVIOUR

550 métis men and women, of whom 325 were under the age of sixteen.[17] A 1946 census relayed that 73 percent of métis in Gabon lived in its two largest urban centers, Libreville and Port-Gentil.[18] Guy Lasserre speculated in his 1957 socioethnographic survey of Libreville that "Mpongwé have a monopoly on *métissage*," and that 700 of the town's 750 métis were Mpongwé.[19]

Contrary to accounts in European travel narratives of all Mpongwé women engaging in relationships with European men, it seems that over the course of the twentieth century, a relatively small number of Mpongwé women engaged in interracial sex. However, it does appear that a majority of métisses born of their mothers' encounters with European men engaged in interracial unions. Overall, the majority of Mpongwé women engaged in sexual and conjugal relationships with African men. Moreover, Mpongwé women in Libreville lived at varied socioeconomic levels and engaged in a range of economic activities, from agricultural production, housekeeping, and sewing to working in shops. After World War II, increased educational opportunities for women opened up employment as teachers and office workers.[20]

Though not all Mpongwé women engaged in interracial unions, African and European historical representations accorded significance to Mpongwé women's relationships with European men. Mission-educated young women were especially valued since they had learned at least rudimentary French and European housekeeping skills. Sister Marie-Germaine remarked in 1931 that "among the Mpongoués [*sic*], girls are hardly raised for other purposes than to be handed over to the vices of white men. It is the great suffering of missionaries and nuns in Libreville to witness their best pupils literally sold to Europeans each year."[21] Missionary alarm was so great that Marie Bidang, a Fang woman who attended a Catholic mission in the 1930s, relayed that the adage "A black girl should not go out with a white man" was integral to the curriculum. I asked Bidang to elaborate further on the meaning of this prohibition, probing her to specify if women of other ethnicities also pursued relationships with European men. Bidang further qualified, "Yes, it's true that the Myènè girls went out with whites, but us, we were so fearful of divine advice that we were afraid to disobey."[22]

Some oral interviews with Mpongwé men and women about their own, their mothers', or their grandmothers' interracial unions repeat a common trope of dutiful daughters engaging with the European men their kin chose for them. Some women in Libreville in the 1930s and 1940s selected whom they would marry, but a pattern across ethnic groups was that fathers or other male relatives entered into an agreement of marriage for female dependents, at times in keeping with women's wishes and at other times not seeking women's consent. Mpongwé women reported that they did not enter inter-racial relationships as acts of individual defiance, but rather through the ini-tiative and sanction of family patriarchs as in a marriage to an African man. Fathers, uncles, or senior male relatives initiated women's relationships with European men.[23] Some relationships, particularly with men who worked in the timber industry, could last for several years while the men were stationed in Gabon. Colonial personnel settled in Libreville for a two- to three-year cycle, and men who worked for private industries such as banking or trans-port may have settled there for a few months or years. That many Mpongwé women were involved with European men over the course of their child-bearing years resulted in limited marriage prospects for Mpongwé men. Male Mpongwé interviewees who came of age from the 1930s to the 1950s reported that they sought sexual relationships and marriages with women of other ethnic groups because family patriarchs of the Mpongwé women they sought to marry had earmarked them for European men.[24] Once involved with a European man, a female interviewee reflected, the inclination was to find another. One woman's account of how male family members facilitated serial interracial relationships in the 1930s and 1940s reflected this pattern:

> I had my first partner while I was at the house [of my uncle]. A white man, he was a soldier. Things worked like that. You found a boy, you stayed with him. A relative of mine introduced me to him. He [the relative] came to my house and said, "You do not have a boy and I prefer to give you to this boy. I want you to stay with this person here." The white man was looking for a girl to stay with him. Then we stayed together in his house and then he went to France. [A year later] I found a [French] policeman to take me to Port-Gentil, a white policeman. It is my cousin who gave me this white man.[25]

The woman in this particular account was métis and recounted that fami-lies preferred to partner métis women with European men. Male kin's bro-kering of interracial unions mirrored the authority of men to broker the marriages of female dependents if the women were marrying African men. White men were resident in Gabon for a finite period, entailing a series of new "husbands." Once engaged in one interracial union, this interviewee, and other Mpongwé women, entered into a series of kin-brokered inter-racial unions.[26] Such male-brokered interracial unions followed Mpongwé practices of the time in that the European suitor paid bridewealth to the Mpongwé bride's family. As a global market economy enveloped Libreville, marriage and women's reproductive and productive capacities were a sound social and material investment. Interracial unions yielded significant capital in the form of bridewealth from European men.

Interracial unions might have not been recognized as marriage under French law, but were legitimate in Mpongwé communities according to rites of bridewealth exchange and family consent. In her study on prostitutes and their clients in colonial Nairobi, Luise White refers to the relationships as "illegal marriage," given that the components of prostitutes' work— sexual intercourse, conversation, cooking food, and so on—were "legitimately available in marriage."[27] In Libreville, Mpongwé families viewed women in interracial relationships as wives, not prostitutes. For Mpongwé communities, these relationships, if consecrated with the consent of women's family heads and sealed with the exchange of bridewealth, were legitimate marriages. The families of the women asked that European men give them bridewealth, a remittance that continued to serve as a legal confirmation of marriage.[28]

Aligning young women with European men in Gabon allowed an opening for many families to tap into the circulation of cash in the precarious timber economy of the twentieth century. A 1939 report by a state-employed French doctor recorded that a European man gave an initial gift of 2,000–3,000 francs to the family of his Mpongwé wife.[29] Additionally, a European man might also give his Mpongwé wife about 500 francs per month as her own income. The report estimated that with the initial gift to a woman's family and the monthly allowance, a two-year interracial union might result in a total of 14,000 francs going to a woman and her family. Given extreme fluctuations in Gabon's timber economy, the cash payments of bridewealth and monthly allowances given by a European man to his Mpongwé companion allowed Mpongwé families to purchase necessities. With family acceptance and the remittance of bridewealth from the European suitor to the woman's family, Mpongwé communities regarded such relationships as marriages, and being married remained a key marker of women's respectability.

As discussed in previous chapters, women who came of age in Libreville after the 1930s relayed a normative ideal that marriage brought respect, and to be a respected woman, you had to be married.[30] For men as well, marriage remained an ideal that they aspired to in order to reach adulthood and fulfill ambitions of a prosperous and healthy life. Marriage confirmed respectability as it established that a woman was sexually moral, engaging in sexual exchanges with one man as opposed to the "vagabondage" of having sex with many different men.[31] Mpongwé women carried this collective advice of how respectable wives should behave into their relationships with

Impact of global market economy on Libreville

VIEW

legitimate marriages ✝✝

interracial relationships as a way to weather economic hardship

"NORMATIVE" IDEAL of female "respectability" established

European men. Mpongwé individuals' accounts of interracial unions ubiquitously refer to the roles of Mpongwé women in such unions as "wives." In interviews, I asked Mpongwé men and women if interracial unions were prostitution, as declared by Catholic missionaries and some colonial sources. Mpongwé women vehemently denied that those in long-term arrangements with white men practiced prostitution. Informants argued that prostitution was what was practiced where women stood in the streets waiting for a series of men to come solicit them.[32]

Mpongwé women's roles in the homes of Frenchmen resembled much those of a wife. In addition to sexual services, women in live-in interracial unions completed housekeeping duties, management of staff and budget, and varied duties of household maintenance.[33] Rosalie Antchandi recounted that family members advised her in departing her home of origin for that of her European husband that she had to carry herself as a married woman: "You had to learn how to stay with your husband as long as he is here. You also had to take care of him: wash his clothes, his socks, darn the linens, choose the colors of the clothes that he would wear to the timber-yard, iron the clothes. I had to demonstrate to my husband that I was not a dumb woman!"[34] Mpongwé women's relationships with Frenchmen, while temporary since most Frenchmen eventually repatriated back to France, received their families' approval as marriages sealed with the transfer and acceptance of bridewealth. With family acceptance and the remittance of bridewealth from the European suitor to the woman's family, Mpongwé communities regarded such unions as marriages, markers of collective Mpongwé prestige.

Other women were often instrumental in negotiating an Mpongwé woman's relationship with a European man, circumventing male kin's control over women's conjugal-sexual relationships. Newly arrived single European men sometimes asked the Myènè wives of other European men to find them partners.[35] When I asked how her grandparents came to the decision to "give" her mother to a Frenchman in the 1940s, a word that other interviewees had used to describe how they came to be with a European man, Catherine Okili, a métis woman, countered, "The parents did not 'give' my mother to a Frenchman."[36] Okili recounted that it was her mother's sisters who were instrumental in her mother's interracial relationship. The family had twelve daughters, and the younger daughters watched as the older daughters entered into marriages with Mpongwé men and died a few years later. Intra-Mpongwé marriage was difficult for a young bride, Okili stated, because they faced physical abuse at the hands of the mothers and sisters-in-law. The remaining sisters preferred that none of the rest of them marry at all. But when approached by a Frenchman who was seeking an Mpongwé companion, the sisters consented to her mother's marriage to him, as she would not have to contend with any female in-laws. Some women sought out interracial unions without any kin intervention, circumventing elder male and female kin's control over their persons.[37]

Furthermore, women who themselves had been involved in interracial unions sometimes sought interracial unions for their daughters. Victorine Smith recounted of the Frenchman with whom she lived for several years and had a child: "I would ride my bicycle to work. He saw me every day [from his office]. Every time I pedaled, he would look at me through his telescope. One day, when I had left for work, he talked to my mother: 'I see your daughter, she is grown, she has finished school, she is pleasing. Can you give her to me? I am here alone.' My mother accepted. She didn't want me to marry a Gabonese man because I was her only girl child."[38]

Smith's mother was a métisse, and Smith was born of her mother's relationship with a European man. In negotiating a union with a European man for her daughter, Smith's mother circumvented the authority of her brother, who may have been able to determine his niece's marriage.[39] That the European man would eventually leave Gabon to return to France was another factor that led Smith's mother to view such relationships as favorable. The son that Smith bore with her European husband stayed with her in Gabon once the man repatriated.[40] In addition to retaining custody of her son after her European husband's departure, Victorine Smith also became the owner of the cement home in which they lived. That interracial unions permitted some women material benefits would come to be a point of asymmetry within Mpongwé communities and between Mpongwé and other African communities.

PROPERTY, LEISURE TIME, MATERIAL GOODS, AND FRENCH CITIZENSHIP: AFRICAN WOMEN'S MOBILITY

The fault lines of conflict across gender and generational lines were revealed, however, as women in interracial unions accumulated individual wealth. By the 1930s, many Mpongwé women would come to be individual property owners of cement houses, an indicator and a source of wealth in the city's differentiated housing conditions. The number of female property owners is difficult to quantify given the nonexistence of municipal property documents. Like prostitutes in colonial Nairobi whose clients were African men, Mpongwé women's sexual and domestic labor for European men allowed them to independently accumulate property.[41] Mpongwé women were among the first Africans to own cement homes (cases en dur) like those of European inhabitants of Libreville.[42] As many of Libreville's African inhabitants lived in precarious structures made of tin, cartons, and any materials that they could salvage, a cement home was significant. Since European men purchased the plots of land on which the homes were built from the colonial state, some women acquired the land with the houses and leased spaces behind their homes for income.[43] Of the phenomena in which there were many female Mpongwé property owners, Joseph Lasseny Ntchoveré, an Mpongwé chief, surmised, "Before, the possibility of obtaining loans did not exist. Men constructed with their own means, while women, due to the fact that they lived with Europeans, succeeded in obtaining houses."[44] Benoit Messani, another chief, stated, "It's because in the beginning our men did not have sufficient means to construct a dwelling for [a] wife. So, women *preferred* to be courted by whites, live with whites because as recompense, if there was a child that was born, the white gave her a house."[45]

Sexual-domestic exchanges with European men allowed Myènè women access to clothing and leisure time that distinguished them from other African women in the Estuary region. Historically, the types of cloth that one wore in Central Africa conveyed differentiated status, and by the twentieth century Africans in Brazzaville and Libreville incorporated European fashions to create new forms of social distinction.[46] By the 1940s, Libreville residents of varied ethnicities had enough access to cash to purchase the cloth to tailor European-style dresses, pants, and shirts.[47] Yet status could still be delineated by the quality and style of European clothes that people wore. Guy Lasserre conveyed in 1957 that Myènè women in Libreville were distinguishable with luxury clothing—shoes, hosiery, dresses, and purses— that mirrored the clothing worn by bourgeois Frenchwomen.[48] Mpongwé women could differentiate themselves from other African women by the value of their clothing and accessories and by wearing shoes, an item that few women of other ethnicities could afford.[49] Being the wife of a European also meant for an Mpongwé woman that she did not have to engage in agricultural production, the primary economic activity of African women living in Libreville. Fang informants commented that Myènè women in Libreville did not do "dirty" work like growing and selling manioc because their European husbands gave them enough money to buy their food in the market.[50] For a woman to be able to buy her food in the market and not cultivate plots of land indicated prestige.[51]

In a time of food shortages and economic collapse during the Depression, women involved with European men continued to own and display symbols of prosperity. That Libreville's Mpongwé women did not conform to the image of what Europeans thought an African woman should look like is an aspect that troubled many a traveler. In his journey down the West African coast in 1931, a Belgian traveler writing under a pseudonym sarcastically conveyed of the Libreville women he witnessed purchasing food in the market:

> The majority of women wear dresses of delicate colors; salmon is the color that dominates. Several even wear stockings and shoes . . . high heels and walk in them in the forced manner of a peasant in Sunday's best. Each of these elegant ladies has her small handbag in false crocodile, her *"Tom Pouce"*; all of these articles are sent in series by *La Samartine* or *Galeries Lafayette*. More and more we spoil our Africa! Again, there are only these young half-worldly black women. . . . But no, here are two old mamas, dressed in identical silk-like puce colored dresses, who walk around with much grace, as if it was absolutely necessary to prominently display their rump and their breasts. Who would expect to find coquetry there?[52]

Mpongwé women, some of whom were likely métis and others black, engaged in the quotidian act of buying food at the city market and conspicuously wore dresses, shoes, and purses advertised in French department store catalogs. Not only was it young women who had access to European clothing and accessories, but it appeared that older women did as well. The observer, identifying himself as M. Van de la Noitte, contrasted the scene of the town market to villages around Libreville. An area a few kilometers away from Libreville offered the following view: "Many trees, many flowers, many birds. In a hut are women kneeling, talking among themselves and smoking a pipe. . . . Banana trees with frayed leaves, orange ficus, disheveled huts. Here, no negroes in shoes, high heels, bag in false crocodile."[53] The women, likely Fang or ethnicities other than Mpongwé, wore cloth wrapped around their bodies, lived in sparsely furnished huts, and were preparing to go work in their fields.

Interracial sex also offered the possibility of French citizenship to métisses. The 1936 Decree Establishing the Jural Status of Mixed Race Persons of FEA outlined that métis individuals whose European fathers had not legally recognized them (*métis non reconnus*) could apply for and be granted acknowledgment of French citizenship (*la qualité de français*).[54] In FEA, the primary factor for the recognition of French citizenship was *jus sanguinis*, establishing that the petitioner had a European father from factors including physical appearance, name, and education.[55] The 1936 law opened a new avenue for African women who were daughters of white men to gain citizenship. A 1937 letter from the legal prosecutor of FEA lists the names of métis who were granted French citizenship in 1936. Of the sixty-one métis to whom the FEA court granted recognition as French citizens from 1936 to 1937, nearly 50 percent were women.[56] A 1945 census of the city of Libreville provides more clues into the extent to which métis in Libreville had pursued French citizenship. The census conveyed that of the 938 people recognized as "European," a little over 60 percent of them, 588, were métis who had obtained European citizenship.[57] Though the census did not delineate the gender breakdown of métis citizens for that year, it is probable that a significant number were women.

Interracial unions persisted as European men and Mpongwé women sought out each other. Some women capitalized upon such relationships as a means to evade the control of elder Mpongwé men and women, elevate their standards of living, and retain exclusive custody of their children. However, African and colonial society alike viewed women in interracial relationships as problematic, as individuals whose wealth threatened social cohesion and whose transgressions of racial and gender boundaries called hierarchies of political power into question.

EFFORTS TO REGULATE INTERRACIAL SEX

By the 1930s, colonial society and state sought to shape the terrain of race, sex, and status in the colony and increasingly turned attention to the sexual-conjugal arrangements of métis women. A hardening of racial attitudes and views toward miscegenation in metropolitan France in the 1930s resulted in the colonial administration's attempts to temper the occurrence of black-white unions across French Africa.[58] In the midst of the Depression, French leaders and pronatalists were worried that French women were not giving birth to enough children and promoted fecundity as a nationalist act to fortify the nation. The rhetoric of white depopulation and fecundity was also evident in the colonies. In 1931, an anonymous Frenchwoman wrote to the newspaper L'Etoile de l'AEF complaining that the governor-general of FEA allowed only soldiers who were officers to bring their wives with them; rank-and-file soldiers served their terms of duty in the colonies separated from their wives, who remained in France. Under the name of Mathe X, the contributor wrote, "The general interest and future of the race is at stake. It is not in the moment where we are crying . . . for the French to have children that we should separate a family for two long years."[59] The writer equated sex between Frenchmen and women in the colonies to a patriotic act of sustaining the French nation. An anonymous respondent supported her letter and berated the stinginess of private businesses and the colonial state in limiting

[handwritten margin notes: miscegenation = the mixing of races through marriage/having children; ① she could go into a little more detail here. She doesn't convey the degree; ② ✱ there was more to it than just worries about low birth rates and nationalism]

the presence of white French wives in the colonies. A "Mr. de l'Etoile" maintained that France needed children more than any other European nation. Biological reproduction could not be assured if French husbands continued to complete three-year tours in Africa without their wives and returned home to France for only six months at a time. He elaborated:

> The white woman in the Congo must be allowed to come by her husband's side. We will never be able to fully animate our FEA if the woman, as elsewhere does not bring to us . . . all that makes her so her! Look at the children [living in the Congo] do they look sick? Young households will provide for future good work by producing good colonial [settlers], children who have spent several years here since childhood. Let's not lose any opportunity to make many "children of the FEA," to attract families here.[60]

These two letters berated the unaccompanied white male who migrated to a colony in FEA and obtained an African wife. The letter writers proposed the ideal French family in the colonies as male personnel living with white wives and their children, a model white nuclear family. A 1940 anonymous letter signed by an "exploitant forestier" based in Gabon further displayed the disdain with which some Frenchmen began to look at interracial sexual relationships. This document is in the archives of Catholic missionaries in Paris, and it is not clear who the intended recipient was or where the letter circulated. The man, identifying himself as R.F., wrote, "For a long time it was thought that Gabon's climate was insufferable. Today, living conditions have changed. . . . It is undeniable that the woman is an equalizing element that imposes regular habits, more severe behavior; she brings to the colonial official a comfort which suppresses, in part, a terrible illness which we call *la gabonite* the cause of many irregularity. In this line, the authorities should watch over good order and quickly eliminate all scandal." Countering the conception of FEA as unsuitable for white women and that women's presence detracted from the business of colonial rule, the letter writer asserted that the presence of women would, in fact, sustain the colonial project by fostering stable home lives for Frenchmen.[61]

In Libreville, colonial administrators sought to limit European-African interaction, decreasing the numbers of public spaces in which African women and European men could meet, particularly for casual sexual encounters they categorized as prostitution. A 1932 ordinance regulating the sale and consumption of alcohol decreed: "No liquor establishment can be opened to natives and Europeans at the same time."[62] The ordinance also decreed that no women, except for women inheriting their husbands' businesses, could own or manage a bar. In addition, no woman could be employed at a bar, except if she was related to the family of the owner. Outside of this exception, servers had to be men who were at least sixteen years old. In another ordinance, dance halls could not serve alcohol. Establishments that did serve alcohol were subject to a fine if they allowed dancing, shouting, or music.[63]

In 1942, two laws, one relating to the medical treatment of venereal disease in Libreville and Port-Gentil and another regulating prostitution in FEA, were introduced to a meeting of notables in Libreville.[64] French officials asked the council of notables for help in identifying prostitutes so the women could receive treatment for venereal diseases at colonial health centers. The council of notables acknowledged venereal diseases as a problem. Yet the meeting summary relayed the way in which attendees noted the particular manifestation of sex work in Libreville: "Prostitution as practiced in Europe or Dakar does not exist in Libreville. For the most part, women are discreetly invited to the home of the man wanting to have sexual relations with them or the man makes a *rendez-vous* to come to the woman's home. In all the cases, solicitations come from the man (European or native) and the woman obliges, thus making it difficult to carry out a total fettering out of prostitutes."[65] Echoing the distinction that Mpongwé women interviewees had made of prostitutes as being women who paraded on the street and solicited men directly, African men notables also differentiated the way in which sex for money in Libreville occurred away from public view, through discretely negotiated solicitations by European men, with sexual encounters taking place in women's homes. The council approved the measure that they would report women who were prostitutes to the police commissioner or the mayor for possible medical examination. Police records for Libreville are scarce in the archives, making it impossible to ascertain if such efforts were pursued beyond the 1942 meeting. Yet this discussion by African notables and French colonial administrators suggests that the city's poltical interests sought to curtail interracial sex.

Colonial thinking about "the problem" of interracial sex shifted between concern about the unregulated bodies of women who were the lovers of European men to moral obligation of the French to provide some measure of care to métis daughters. With the election of the left-wing Popular Front government in 1936, the French increasingly turned their attention to social policy and reform in Africa, and the status of métis, and particularly métisses, was a central topic of research and policy in FEA.[66] As had occurred decades earlier in other parts of the French Empire, in 1936, the colonial state in FEA took on a new role in its relationship with métis populations: that of a concerned and benevolent father to ensure the material comfort and moral well-being of métis children who had been "abandoned" by their European fathers.[67] Between 1937 and 1946, in major cities throughout FEA, state-run boarding schools/"orphanages" (*internat de métis*) were opened for métis children. However, even as the French granted the possibility of citizenship and social services to métis individuals, French colonial state and society sought to emphasize that métis were to remain members of African society, serving as intermediaries between Africans who were not citizens and the French.[68]

By the late 1930s, colonial officials emphasized that the "métis problem" was actually a "métisses problem." The surprise to colonial officials that métisses continued to seek out interracial relationships even as attitudes in colonial circles in Gabon began to disdain such relations was captured in Saint-Blancart's 1938 report "Enquête sur les métis."[69] The report was in response to a Francophone Africa–wide survey of métis (Enquête sur les métis). Saint-Blacart's report argued that the "métis problem" was a no longer an issue since the state had begun to allow métis to become French citizens. However, Saint-Blancart maintained, "French citizenship has not given these girls the most minute moral sense, which would prevent them from gliding down the dangerous slope towards prostitution."[70] Colonial officials argued that the perpetuation of interracial sex and *métissage* threatened not just colonial governance or racial distinctions, but also the reproduction of Mpongwé communities.[71] The solution, as proposed by colonial employees, social services agencies, missionaries, and African male notables, was to direct the moral education of métisses so that they would see their métis and African counterparts as desirable marriage partners.[72] A report by the Libreville director of the orphanage for métis girls relayed that the métisses continued to view "prostitution" with white men as their primary means of making a living, and that "there is a very serious undertaking to accomplish in bringing about a change in [their] conception of family life."[73]

Colonial representations of métis women as degenerate and immoral women who needed to be reintegrated into indigenous society propelled social policy in Gabon and FEA after the war. Subsequent FEA social initiatives for métis sought to provide for their education and placement in jobs, but also to provide loans to métis men so that they could have enough money for bridewealth to marry métis women.[74] In 1941, the proposed FEA-wide Ordinance Instituting the Protection of Métis of Free France included the directive that FEA should "take all dispositions toward preventing the prostitution of métis girls or women." The report implicitly defined all interracial relationships as "prostitution" since it was rare for Gabonese women and Frenchmen to marry according to French law. While there is no evidence that this 1941 proposal passed, in 1946 the postwar FEA administration did authorize the creation of a central committee specifically targeting métisses. The mandate stipulated that the committee would "exercise supervision over the residence hall of métis girls. To materially and morally safeguard [them] until the moment of their marriage."[75] The committee was to encourage the marriage of mixed-race women to African men. Yet, even as colonial officials, elite colonial circles, and elite African men frowned upon *métissage*, sexual-domestic partnerships between Mpongwé women and European men continued through independence.

SINGLEHOOD AND ELDER YEARS: REFLECTIONS OF MPONGWÉ WOMEN

While the decision by Mpongwé women and their families to enter into interracial unions might have indicated agency, unintended consequences of transformations in gender roles and social reproduction in Mpongwé communities followed. When I was in Gabon in 2001, I happened upon Victorine Smith, a métis Mpongwé woman who founded an organization of mostly métis women educated at Catholic missions who met to pray together. I interviewed some of these women. Born in the 1920s and 1930s, many had entered into their first interracial relationships in the 1940s, a few remaining with one man for as long as twenty years and others having several European husbands. Most of their European partners were private European citizens, foresters, bankers, and office staff employed by varied enterprises. One interviewee, Agnès Lucille Edwige Osenga Diyaye, summarized a feeling expressed by many women of the risks that they faced in engaging in these relationships. Her aunt lived with a European man, and she would spend summer vacations in their household. Reflecting upon her aunt's experiences, Diyaye relayed: "In the region at that time, there were many *exploitant forestiers*. It was also a time in which women wanted to leave their state of torpor, of submission. On the other side, there were the whites, symbols of modernism and of light. . . . Black women and white men who found themselves together each faced a certain number of risks on their side. However, there were a lot of girls who went out with whites."[76]

Diyaye emphasized that Gabon's racial climate had changed from the time of her mother. Living with a French forestier in an Estuary timber camp, her aunt sometimes faced the racism of his white friends who protested if she sat at the table during a meal with them. She felt humiliated in those moments. She managed her husband's household and had given birth to his child, yet she faced moments of unexpected and brutal rejection by whites.

While many of the women in the prayer group were elite, well-to-do, and respected members of their communities, in their elderly years, they remained single, unmarried women by choice, an oddity in a society in which the ideal remained marriage to an African man at some point of time in their adulthood. Victorine Smith exclaimed, "Look at us. Almost all of us are alone, not married in our old age."[77] They occupied a different position than Mpongwé women who had married other African men. Remaining in Libreville with her French banker husband with whom she lived for "years and years," Victorine Smith conveyed her reluctance to have a relationship with an African man. She lived in a union libre with a métis Mpongwé man for a few years after her French partner left. She reflected:

reflects a struggle for freedom, to navigate space, mobility without punishment

> A relationship with a white man is not at all like one with an African. The white man is nice, the black man never! I tried but it did not work. I left him. All of these [accusations like]: "Where are you going?" or "Where have you come from?" If you get angry, he beats you. Not me! The black man is jealous: "I saw you talking to someone!" I never thought of getting married. My mother told me: "I don't want you to marry. Your husband will beat you, he won't let you go out."[78]

While some women like Smith made a deliberate choice to not marry or live with an African man, most women conveyed that their single status was an unwanted state. After their European partners repatriated, some of the women had attempted to enter relationships with African men and to marry, yet felt taken advantage of because of their material wealth or because they did not want to adhere to the gender roles ascribed for African women in their societies. One woman, whom I will call Marie France per her wishes, elaborated on these conundrums, and her reflections are worth citing at length:

> French men took better care of me than African men. We went out to dance. There was the *cercle de métis* on Saturdays. When I lived with a white man, I did not think about living with an African. It was at the last moment, when there was no longer a white man, that I took a boy who worked at the hospital. He was with me until I found a policeman to take me to Port-Gentil, a white policeman.

PHOTO 7.1. Mpongwé women and French military personnel, ca. 1950s. (Photograph from the personal collection of Simone Agnoret Iwenga St. Denis, Libreville.)

Upon my return, I found the [Mpongwé] boy living with another girl. When he said we will continue our relationship, I said I could not, since I am alone and you have a wife. He had a métis wife like me. Me, I don't like being the second wife. After that, I had other boys, but one day I abandoned this. For myself, it was better to stay free, to take care of my needs, instead of working for people who did nothing for me. If you did not find a boy who wanted to marry you, were you going to force him? Women preferred to be married, but what if you did not find someone? [In marriage], you are well in your house, with a gentle man who takes care of you. You also take care of him. To trail about like this is not good. There are many women who trail about today. All of the girlfriends with whom I went to school are not married.[79]

France expressed her preference for her time with a Frenchman, articulating that in this relationship there was the leisure time and means to go dancing in the multiracial setting of the social clubhouse of the town's métis organization. Only when there were no longer any white men available for her to engage in a relationship with did she consider the possibility of being with an African man. France expressed the interest in marriage with an Mpongwé man, conceiving that marriage provided social and economic security and mutual support between husband and wife. A woman without

PHOTO 7.2. A métis woman and child, ca. 1950s. (Photograph from the personal collection of Benoit Messani Nyangenyona, Libreville.)

a husband was in a vulnerable position of having to earn money and provide for herself. However, she did not want to be someone's second wife, concluding that living in a polygynous household would incur too much rancor. Marie France engaged in sexual relationships with African men that she hoped would lead to marriage. Yet, at some point in time, she withdrew from the marriage and sexual market, concluding that it was better to remain single and concentrate her efforts on providing her own basic material needs.

Other women like Marie France also expressed their aspirations toward marriages to African men that they pursued in the 1950s and 1960s after their European partners had left. They conveyed disappointment at failed efforts at marriage, but eventual acceptance in their postmenopausal years of being single. One métis interviewee recounted:

> I wished for someone settled to marry, but I did not have this luck. This is why I fought for my sister to enter a marriage. I find marriage to be a source of security. You are with your husband and children. I found this to be better. For me, it is my work that interests me. But since I am a woman, there were [African] men who courted me, I went out with certain among them and each time I became pregnant, the generator left. At the end of the day, I did not find this to be in my interest. I left behind this life twenty years ago. Before I wanted to be married, but this is no longer the case. I am well with

myself and it does not bother me. I do what I want with my life and I am well like this.[80]

This interviewee owned and operated a laundry business, her shop occupying a busy location in the Glass neighborhood since the late 1950s and providing her with a comfortable income. Another informant recounted, "I had other friends (*bon amis*) in passing, but I never really found anyone who truly wanted to marry me. But this didn't really bother me. With these relationships, I didn't really expect anything, maybe to have children."[81] This interviewee expressed that becoming a mother was of greater interest to her than being someone's wife, and that motherhood was not contingent to marriage. She already had a child with a European partner and was constructing a household for her and her children. One woman recounted of another member of the métis women's prayer group, "After the Frenchman left, she had a Gabonese husband [for a few years], but she finished her life alone."[82]

Occasionally, some Mpongwé women who had been in relationships with European men during the colonial era did marry a Gabonese man through customary marriage rites. Simone Agnoret Iwenga St. Denis relished in narrating the account of her grandmother's "success story" in marrying an Mpongwé man who was as educated and civilized as she was:

> After being with a white man for some time, my grandmother met a Gabonese man who was employed by the colonial state. He had been living in Brazzaville, Congo, but his family asked him to return to Gabon to marry. He fell upon my grandmother. Even though she told him that she was fixed with a white man, he continued to be around her to the extent that the white man noticed. When the white man pointed this out to her family, she revealed that the Gabonese man wanted to marry her in spite of the fact that she lived with a white man.[83]

Upon the Frenchman's departure, the couple married. Yet narratives such as St. Denis's about her grandmother were rare in the accounts of métis women. As unmarried women, shifting moments of material wealth and social capital, as well as moments of material poverty and social insecurity, marked their lives.

While colonial officials and some African political leaders may have attempted to limit the prevalence of episodic and long-term interracial relationships over the course of the 1930s through 1960, these relationships were an established part of Mpongwé practice and of quotidian manifestation in Libreville. These unions and the efforts of Mpongwé women to raise their children created new households that altered the very fabric of Mpongwé social and biological reproduction. Tracing who was a "native wife" and how these relationships came about demonstrates the transformative impact of such relationships on the social, economic, and political landscape of the city. The negotiations and expectations that accompanied indigenous women's engagement in sexual-conjugal exchanges with European men reveal the multivalent "landscapes of power" operating in colonial Libreville.[54] Representations of and lived experiences of interracial sexual-domestic unions referred to by varied historical actors as "marriage," "*mariage à la mode gabonaise*," "concubinage," "debauchery," and "prostitution" reveal the contested terrain of what it meant to be a respectable African woman in twentieth-century colonial Libreville.

As colonial state and society attempted to control governance in Gabon, African women's involvement in interracial unions revealed cracks in the edifices of colonial rule and permeability of social-legal categories. Contestations over interracial unions also reflected struggles over hierarchies of race, gender, and generation among African communities. African women traversing racialized sexual boundaries destabilized colonial rule and hierarchies of power within African communities. Struggles among Gabonese communities about interracial sex and the gendered negotiations of colonial encounters revealed the polyvalent subjectivities of African communities in determining social and legal status in the shifting urban locale. The topography of race, sex, and gender in Libreville remained fraught with fissures as individuals, societies, and states attempted to demarcate sexual boundaries. Multivalent contestations around the fault lines of sex, race, and gender demonstrated the varied strategies with which African women negotiated colonial governance and how these strategies shaped colonial ideologies and contestations about status within African communities.

Conclusion

LIBREVILLE ORIGINATED, as did many cities in Africa, between the mid-nineteenth and early twentieth centuries. It was an example of an archetype that scholars have called "a colonial city." This new urban form was created by colonial societies to serve the dual purpose of an administrative capital and a site for the management of African labor and resource extraction.[1] However, as historians of Africa have shown, African residents made claims for social, political, and economic rights to the colonial city. African urbanites, for the most part male wage laborers, resisted the confines of the colonial city. Urban African men lived lives with dignity in the cramped housing and working conditions, cultivated hybrid expressions of popular culture and leisure time, and struggled for political and labor concessions that confounded colonial thought. In spite of the efforts of chiefs and colonial officials to expel and control them, small numbers of women migrated to cities and created economic niches in areas such as prostitution, beer brewing, and trading in foodstuffs. The imbalanced sex ratios, monetization, and the demoralizing framework of racism in colonial cities transformed African male-female relations. African men and women engaged with each other through the sexual market of prostitution and in fleeting informal marriages and antagonistic struggles for material resources. A small group of women and men established formal marriages through shifting articulations of customary, Christian, Muslim, and European legal rites and debated the contours of family life, respectability, religious faith, and emerging nationalist politics. In the late colonial period, male urbanites made demands for their rural wives to join them, laid claim to urban domestic life, and cities

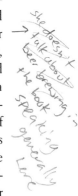

she doesn't talk about beer brewing. speaking generally here

217

rapidly expanded. This is the historiographical narrative of a typical colonial city. But Libreville was neither the archetypical colonial city intended by colonial officials nor the typical colonial city that historians have described. Rather, at its foundation, men and women in Libreville struggled to create a distinct model of a colonial city in Africa.

First, its poorest men demanded the right to conjugal, sexual, and domestic lives from the very first days of settlement. With the marriage mutiny, the town's African "subjects" rejected the failure of imagination in French efforts to establish the economic, political, and material infrastructures of the colonial city. In demanding wives, the former slave captives, among the poorest of Estuary residents, asserted aspirations to personhood and the capacity to articulate rights. Personhood in the town, the poor men asserted, necessitated emotional, sexual, social, and legal relationships with women. In the midst of the colonial city of Libreville, Mpongwé communities lived in small mixed rural-urban settlements marked by gender parity and shifting articulations of sexual economies as African and European strangers arrived on its shores and overland. The mutineers kidnapped women from these wealthier African communities neighboring the colonial city. Thus, the marriage mutiny was an episode of intra-African contestations—poor men versus wealthy men, newcomer versus autochthonous—in establishing the boundaries of belonging in the emerging town. This incident portends how intra-African hierarchies of wealth, ethnic differentiation, and changing understandings of manhood and womanhood would shape the fabric of urban life in the decades to come, far beyond the colonizer and colonized binary that scholars have deployed to frame the colonial city.

In many other African colonial cities, missionary representatives, colonial personnel, and African political leaders attempted to enact control over African urban life by keeping women, and therefore marriage and sex, out of the city. The denouement of the marriage mutiny in Libreville, with French civil and Catholic personnel consecrating the marriages of some of the former slave captives, illustrated how French and African power brokers would struggle to maintain control over the colonial city through managing the bodies and hearts of Libreville's African and European residents. In worrying about the "very dangerous" liaisons that could result if Libreville's newest residents remained unmarried, religious and political representatives were as much worried about sex between Africans and Europeans as intra-African sex outside of marriage. Interracial sex would remain prevalent in Libreville, belying the colonial city model of segregation between African and European neighborhoods, and therefore between black and white bodies. Racial boundaries and social and legal classifications proved to be porous in the very heart of the colonial city. This book's exploration of heterosexual relationships, and the policy debates and reform campaigns they generated, demonstrates the complex ways in which Libreville's varied inhabitants formulated the meanings of belonging and social and biological reproduction under changing historical and spatial conditions. As such, the story of marriage, sexuality, and urban life in Libreville reconfigures our understanding of several core themes in African colonial history.

Research in women's history across the continent of Africa has increased exponentially over the past three decades, and published works have established some canonical themes—transformations in marriage, childbearing, agricultural production, and migrancy and work in cities. Yet the history of women in Libreville complicates some of these foundational themes. The idea that the 1920s and 1930s witnessed the shutting down of the possibility of African women becoming urban migrants, what Diana Jeater calls the closing of the city as the "Pandora's box of female resistance," did not come to fruition.[2] As Teresa Barnes has demonstrated for the colonial city of Harare, there was no universal effort by colonial representatives and African men to prevent women from moving to Libreville.[3] More importantly, and in contrast to many colonial capital cities elsewhere in Africa, women in Libreville were not small in number, and, in fact, often reached or exceeded parity with men. Unlike other colonial cities, in other words, Libreville was not gendered "male." This quantitative and qualitative particularity compels an important rethinking of an all too common generalization in African history.

That life in Libreville afforded many women opportunities for social mobility, pleasure, and self-expression complicates our understanding of African women's urban experiences beyond the themes of marginalization, pain, and disorientation. Recent shifts in feminist scholarship have urged caution in scholars' conceptions of "woman" as a homogeneous category.[4] Women in Libreville were not homogeneous, but differentiated by ethnicity, access to education, conjugal status, legal standing, generation, and wealth. The presence of differentiated women in the town generated a sexual economy, parallel to and convergent with the expanding monetary economy. Townswomen and townsmen alike negotiated their socioeconomic status, sociality, and articulations of selfhood through the intimate relationships they were able to maintain or dissolve.

Women and men sought out marriage as a sound emotional, social, and material investment in the colonial city. Scholars of Africa have increasingly explored the meanings of the increased use of money in colonial Africa, the development of what Rachel Petrocelli calls in her research on Dakar a "local transactional culture" of urban economic life.[5] Convergent with the expansion of a monetary economy in Libreville, cash became the dominant component of bridewealth payments. The capacity of women as wives to facilitate social and biological reproduction was a motor of economic activity and sparked transactions over money—earning, saving, remitting, and borrowing—as well as the issuance of IOUs, indebtedness, theft, and wealth-accumulation. Men with female dependents could marry them off, with proceeds from bridewealth paying for the quotidian needs of urban and peri-urban households, such as taxes, food, and housing, and also allowing for some luxury items and services. Moreover, brides and female kin also sometimes received a portion of bridewealth payments, providing an avenue for women to access money and goods essential to city life. Men seeking to marry or remain married promised to pay the amounts demanded by women's kin, even in times of economic crisis when cash was scarce.

The convergences of the sexual and monetary economy also meant that many townsmen and townswomen could not or chose not to be married in certain moments of their lives. Historical actors negotiated changing terms of conduct and expectations for extramarital sexuality and domestic life. A number of African and European men who migrated to the Libreville region to tap into the timber economy remained unaccompanied by wives. They sought out African women for social and sexual companionship, remitting to women and/or their kin the cash and goods they had earned from wage labor in the colonial economy. Women's sexual and domestic labor was parallel to men's wage labor. Women also sought out lovers or husbands, to facilitate their own emotional, financial, and social needs. Colonial personnel were well aware of, and confounded by, the logics of an ever-changing sexual economy, which prevented them from ever fully maintaining social, political, or economic control over African women in the colonial city. Appreciating the ways in which Libreville residents bartered, conceptualized, and experienced sexual capital opens a new window onto everyday urban life.

Though research on African women has demonstrated the centrality with which anxieties about African women's sexuality, reproductive capacities, and legal rights were at the forefront of colonial thought, women seemed to have encountered colonial societies and states at a distance, mainly through the intermediary of African men or missionaries. The prevalence of sexual and domestic relationships between African women and white men in Libreville reveals the permeability of racial, gender, and spatial segregation in the colonial city. Some Mpongwé women cooked European men's food, maintained their homes, darned their socks, shared their beds, and bore mixed-race children. These interactions entailed African women entering the European city and white men traversing the African city. African women and white men interacted in public spaces of streets, halls, and bars, and intimate domestic spaces of bedrooms and kitchens, demonstrating the fictive nature of a white plateau and African villages. Scholars of interracial sex, intimacy, and empire in Asia and the Americas have debated how relationships between indigenous women and white men fluctuated between tense and tender ties, between confounding colonial governance and demonstrating colonial sexual violence.[6] These publications ask a common question: What does interracial sex tell us about the nature of colonial power?

In the preceding chapters, we have asked a different question: What do interracial sexual relationships tell us about the changing lives of African women and African conceptualizations of race and sexuality? The color of African women's skin and their relationships with white men as lovers, wives, or daughters shaped shifting hierarchies of generation, gender, and wealth in Libreville. Though interracial sexual relationships were continuous from nineteenth- to twentieth-century Libreville, the forms of such relationships and the negotiations that established them changed over time and encompassed shifting African and European mores. Oral and written sources reveal the contested tropes of respectable female sexuality and social standing over the course of women's lives from youth to elderhood.

African and mixed-race women in interracial relationships sometimes sustained the social and biological reproduction of colonial society. Like the educated and salaried West African women nurses and midwives uncovered in research by Pascale Barthélémy, some Mpongwé women were "agents of colonial power."[7] At other times, such women subverted colonial society, opening up access to wealth and increased social status for the women's extended kin groups. Through these sexual and domestic pathways, African women were often the intermediaries between colonial and African societies, voicing economic, legal, and political rights in the wake of colonial efforts to delineate the status of *indigène*. Moreover, interracial sex resulted in some individual women's access to material wealth and social capital. In asserting their identity of the distinct category of métis, some women obtained European legal status. These processes of mobility gave rise to kith and kin accusing them of greed and being morally suspect.

Writing about gender in African history has too often constituted either women's history or a history of men. *Conjugal Rights* has narrated a history of the changing processes of delineating womanhood *and* manhood, and thus sought to recast our understanding of the history of gender in Africa. Being a "man" in colonial Libreville was not a normative act of biology but negotiated along a spectrum of marital status, and sexuality, access to wealth, ethnic differentiation, and generation. "Men," this history of Libreville tells us, were never a unified category of historical actors in seemingly fixed categories: "elder men," "chiefs," "elite men," "young men," and "patriarchy." Juxtaposing men's and women's narratives of heterosexual relationships demonstrates the convergent and interdependent processes of "doing" gender. Relationships between men and women as lovers, spouses, siblings, parents and children, neighbors, and strangers reveal a more complex history of gender relationships in Africa than of men trying to control women through patriarchy and women trying to escape in order to maintain autonomy. The history of marriage and sexuality in Libreville is made up of the stories of how men and women engaged in a complex series of maneuvers, negotiations, and compromises as they attempted to actualize their visions of healthy and fulfilling lives in the changing forms of the city.

A growing body of scholars of Africa has questioned the idea of urbanization as a linear process and the crisis mode through which scholars have often analyzed urbanism in Africa. The expansion of cities in Africa has regularly been "othered" in books on global urban theory, with Africa as irrelevant or marginal to analysis of modern cities of the nineteenth and twentieth centuries.[8] As argued by Sarah Nuttall and Achille Mbembe in their edited volume on Johannesburg as "the premier African metropolis," scholars need to "allow space for the articulation of the originality of the African modern, its capacity to produce something new and singular, as yet unthought, and to find ways of accommodating this within our conceptual languages."[9] The expressions of urban becoming in Libreville through marriage and sexuality reveal the emotional, bodily, and spatial currents of how women *and* men experienced city life in ways that were the same and different from elsewhere in Africa and around the globe. In being both same and different, this biography of Libreville compels us to rethink our understanding of the practices and meanings of urbanism.

Historians of nineteenth- and twentieth-century cities around the world, such as Rio de Janeiro and São Paulo, London, Buenos Aires, Berlin, New York, and Ponce, have argued that practices and meanings of sexuality shaped the unfolding of ideas about politics, culture, space, and consumption in city life.[10] These themes have received little attention in African history.[11] As we have seen in the preceding chapters, townspeople in Libreville experienced and conceptualized sexuality alongside a continuum of affective and material factors. The varied sexual encounters that dotted the landscape of Libreville and its rural suburbs were a focal point through which its varied African and French inhabitants, men, women, youth, and elders, sought to shape the quotidian contours of city life, to fashion a heterosocial city in which residents could facilitate social and biological reproduction. The urban landscape congregated varied kinds of people and reshaped gender roles and boundaries. Life in the Libreville region provided new built environments in which men and women encountered each other. In varied spaces of Libreville, historical actors tendered sex to negotiate emotional and physical fulfillment, social status, material wealth, and power. The geography of Libreville was not determined by only the built environment, but by the movement of women's and men's bodies and expressions of eros. Sexual encounters operated in the interstices of and called into question seemingly fixed boundaries of male and female spaces, public and domestic, and legality and illegality. Tracing the history of the sentient bodies and lives of Libreville's residents, their wants, desires, and how historical actors rationalized and contested questions of how bodies mattered, reveals a history that is at once unique and universally human.

Notes

1. The French had yet to achieve political authority in the nascent colonial out-post. Though the British and French had declared the slave trade to be illegal, West-Central African societies continued to prosper from the clandestine transatlantic trade. European naval ships periodically patrolled the African Atlantic coast and seized ships with slave cargo. The French hoped that the liberated slaves would serve as an example of industrious agricultural production produced by free labor to Mpongwé and Gabonese communities that participated in the slave trade and practiced slavery. The French compelled the former captives to settle in Libreville with the threat of imprisonment on Gorée Island if they refused. Henry H. Bucher, "Liberty and Labor: The Origins of Libreville Reconsidered," *Bulletin de l'Institut Fondamental d'Afrique Noir*, 2nd series, 41, no. 3 (1979): 478–96; Annie Merlet, *Le pays des trois estuaires (1471–1900): Quatre siècles de relations extérieures dans les estuaires du Muni, de la Mondah, et du Gabon* (Libreville: Centre culturel français Saint-Exupéry, 1990), 89–90.

2. Archives Nationales du Sénégal (hereafter cited as ANS), 6G6, Compagnie du Gabon, Sénégal et Dépendances, Etat pour sévir à la décomposition de l'effectif de la population de Libreville, Le Commandant Martin, September 28, 1850.

3. ANS, 6G6, Compagnie du Gabon, Sénégal et Dépendances, Rapport sur l'attaque du plateau de Libreville, September 6, 1849.

4. Ibid.; Letter from le capitaine Commandant le comptoir Marin Commandant de Gorée, September 14, 1849.

5. I am inspired by Orlando Patterson's articulation of the "social death" of African-descended slaves in the Americas to mean the processes of natal alienation and

being denied as human by broader society. Patterson, *Slavery and Social Death: A Comparative Study* (Cambridge: Cambridge University Press, 1985), 75–82.

6. ANS, 6G6, Sénégal et Dépendances, Comptoir du Gabon, Commune de Libreville, Procès Verbal d'urgence pour le mariage des noirs de Loango (provenant du négrier de l'Eliza) habitants du village de Libreville au Gabon, October 6, 1849.

7. Lynn M. Thomas argues that "African political history must encompass the study of households, initiation, and marriage as well as overseas trade, imperialism, and international aid." Thomas, *Politics of the Womb: Women, Reproduction, and the State in Kenya* (Berkeley: University of California Press, 2003), 4.

8. Alfred Marshall, *Principles of Economics* (London: Macmillan, 1980), 1:1–2.

9. Barbara H. Rosenwein, "Worrying about Emotions in History," *American Historical Review* 107, no. 3 (2002): 821–45.

10. Barbara H. Rosenwein, "Problems and Methods in the History of Emotions," *Passions in Context* 1, no. 1 (2010): 10, http://www.passionsincontext.de/.

11. Historians and archaeologists of West and East Africa have demonstrated that some regions in the precolonial fifteenth and nineteen centuries exhibited urbanism. For examples, see page 11 of the introduction to as well as the essays in *Africa's Urban Past*, ed. David M. Anderson and Richard Rathbone (Portsmouth, NH: Heinemann, 2000), including Emmanuel Akyeampong, "'Wo pe tam won pe ba' (You Like Cloth but You Don't Want Children): Urbanization, Individualism, and Gender Relations in Colonial Ghana c.1900–39," 222–35.

12. John Parker, *Making the Town: Ga State and Society in Early Colonial Accra* (Portsmouth, NH: Heinemann 2000), xvii.

13. James Ferguson, *Expectations of Modernity: Myths and Meanings of Urban Life on the Zambian Copperbelt* (Berkeley: University of California Press, 1998), 25. Sarah Nuttall and Achille Mbembe also critique the "metanarrative of urbanization, modernization, and crisis" in research on contemporary African cities. Nuttall and Mbembe, eds., *Johannesburg: The Elusive Metropolis* (Durham, NC: Duke University Press, 2008), 5.

14. Phyllis M. Martin, *Leisure and Society in Colonial Brazzaville* (Cambridge: Cambridge University Press, 1995).

15. Frederick Cooper, ed., *Struggle for the City: Migrant Labor, Capital, and the State in Urban Africa* (Thousand Oaks, CA: Sage, 1983); Frederick Cooper, *On the African Waterfront: Urban Disorder and the Transformation of Work in Colonial Mombasa* (New Haven, CT: Yale University Press, 1987).

16. Frederick Cooper, *Decolonization and African Society: The Labor Question in French and British Africa* (Cambridge: Cambridge University Press, 1996); James R. Brennan, *Taifa: Making Nation and Race in Urban Tanzania* (Athens: Ohio University Press, 2012).

17. AbdouMaliq Simone, *For the City Yet to Come: Changing African Life in Four Cities* (Durham, NC: Duke University Press, 2004), 3.

18. Ibid., 118.

19. See, for example, Charles Van Onselen, *Studies in the Social And Economic History of Witwatersrand, 1886–1914* (New York: Longman, 1982); Van Onselen, *Chibaro: African Mine Labour in Southern Rhodesia, 1900–1933* (London: Pluto Press, 1976); Ferguson, *Expectations of Modernity,* 188; Frederick Cooper, *Decolonization and African Society;* Catherine Coquery-Vidrovitch, *The History of African Cities South of the Sahara: From the Origins to Colonization,* trans. Mary Baker (Princeton,

NJ: Markus Wiener, 2005); Bill Freund, *The African City: A History* (Cambridge: Cambridge University Press, 2007). Achille Mbembe and Sarah Nuttall critique that most studies of Johannesburg present the central figure as "the newly urban black man—his alienation, the transformation of his identity, the commodification of the past in the conflicting spaces of the city." While Mbembe and Nuttall seek to expand the realm of urban African studies beyond these themes of political economy, they do little to disrupt the conceptualization of men as the archetypal actors in African cities. Nuttall and Mbembe, *Johannesburg*, 11.

20. Kathleen Sheldon, ed., *Courtyards, Markets, City Streets: Urban Women in Africa* (Boulder, CO: Westview Press, 1996), 4.

21. Teresa Barnes, "Virgin Territory? Travel and Migration by African Women in Twentieth Century-Southern Africa," in *Women in African Colonial Histories*, ed. Jean Allman, Susan Geiger, and Nakanyike Musisi (Bloomington: Indiana University Press, 2002), 166–67.

22. Elizabeth Schmidt, "Race, Sex, and Domestic Labor: The Question of African Female Servants in Southern Rhodesia, 1900–1939," in *African Encounters with Domesticity*, ed. Karen T. Hansen (New Brunswick, NJ: Rutgers University Press,1992), 224; Karen T. Hansen, "Body Politics: Sexuality, Gender, and Domestic Service in Zambia," *Journal of Women's History* 2, no. 1 (1990): 120–41; Teresa Barnes and Everjoyce Win, *To Live a Better Life: An Oral History of Women in the City of Harare, 1930–70* (Harare: Baobab Books, 1982), 9; Luise White, *The Comforts of Home: Prostitution in Colonial Nairobi* (Chicago: University of Chicago Press, 1990); Belinda Bozzoli with the Assistance of Mmantho Nkotsoe, *Women of Phokeng: Consciousness, Life Strategy, and Migrancy in South Africa, 1900–1983* (Portsmouth, NH: Heinemann, 1991); Iris Berger, *Threads of Solidarity: Women in South African Industry, 1900–1980* (Bloomington: Indiana University Press, 1992); Claire C. Robertson, *Trouble Showed the Way: Women, Men, and Trade in the Nairobi Area, 1890–1990* (Bloomington: Indiana University Press, 1997); Iris Berger, "Feminism, Patriarchy, and African Women's History," *Journal of Women's History* 20, no. 2 (2008): 130–35; Iris Berger, "African Women's History: Themes and Perspectives," *Journal of Colonialism and Colonial History* 4, no. 1 (2003); Teresa Barnes, *"We Women Worked So Hard": Gender, Urbanization, and Social Reproduction in Colonial Harare, Zimbabwe, 1930–1956* (Portsmouth, NH: Heinemann, 1999); Iris Berger and E. Frances White, *Women in Sub-Saharan Africa: Restoring Women to History* (Bloomington: Indiana University Press,1999).

23. Dorothy L. Hodgson and Sheryl A. McCurdy, eds., *"Wicked Women" and the Reconfiguration of Gender in Africa* (Portsmouth, NH: Heinemann, 2001), 11.

24. Sean Redding, "South African Women and Migration in Umtata, Transkei, 1880–1935," in Sheldon, *Courtyards*, 44–46.

25. Judith A. Byfield, "Women, Marriage, Divorce and the Emerging Colonial State in Abeokuta (Nigeria), 1892–1904," in Hodgson and McCurdy, *Wicked Women*, 27–47.

26. See, for example, Elizabeth Schmidt, *Peasants, Traders, and Wives: Shona Women in the History of Zimbabwe, 1870–1939* (Portsmouth, NH: Heinemann, 1992); Margot Lovett, "Gender Relations, Class Formation, and the Colonial State in Africa," in *Women and the State in Africa*, ed. Jane L. Parpart and Kathleen A. Staudt (Boulder, CO: Lynne Rienner, 1989), 23–46.

27. Tabitha Kanogo, *African Womanhood in Colonial Kenya, 1900–1950* (Athens: Ohio University Press, 2005); Brett L. Shadle, *"Girl Cases": Marriage and Colonialism in Gusiiland, Kenya, 1890–1970* (Portsmouth, NH: Heinemann, 2006).

28. Sara Berry, *No Condition Is Permanent: The Social Dynamics of Agrarian Change in Sub-Saharan Africa* (Madison: University of Wisconsin Press, 1993); Brett L. Shadle, "'Changing Traditions to Meet Current Altering Conditions': Customary Law, African Courts and the Rejection of Codification in Kenya, 1930–60," *Journal of African History* 40, no. 3 (1999): 411–31; Rachel Jean-Baptiste, "Une Ville Libre? Marriage, Divorce, and Sexuality in Colonial Libreville, Gabon, 1849–1960" (PhD diss., Stanford University, 2005), 121–38; Rachel Jean-Baptiste, "'These Laws Should Be Made by Us': Customary Marriage Law, Codification and Political Authority in Twentieth-Century Colonial Gabon," *Journal of African History* 49, no. 2 (July 2008): 217–40.

29. Teresa Barnes, *We Women Worked So Hard*, 21–66; Robertson, *Trouble Showed the Way*, 100–101.

30. Jane L. Parpart, "The Household and the Mine Shaft: Gender and Class Struggles on the Zambian Copperbelt, 1926–64," *Journal of Southern African Studies* 13, no. 1 (1986): 36–56; Parpart, "Sexuality and Power on the Zambian Copperbelt, 1926–1964," in *Patriarchy and Class: African Women in the Home and the Workforce*, ed. Sharon B. Stichter and Jane L. Parpart (Boulder, CO: Westview Press, 1988), 141–60; Parpart, "'Where Is Your Mother?' Gender, Urban Marriage, and Colonial Discourse on the Zambian Copperbelt, 1924–1945," *International Journal of African Historical Studies* 27, no. 2 (1994): 241–71; Teresa Barnes, *We Women Worked So Hard*; Frederick Cooper, *Decolonization and African Society*.

31. Teresa Barnes, *We Women Worked So Hard*, 134–44; Robertson, *Trouble Showed the Way*, 102–3.

32. For example: Judith A. Byfield, *The Bluest Hands: A Social and Economic History of Women Dyers in Abeokuta (Nigeria) 1890–1940* (Portsmouth, NH: Heinemann, 2002); Abosede A. George, "Within Salvation: Girl Hawkers and the Colonial State in Development Era Lagos," *Journal of Social History* 44, no. 3 (2011): 837–59.

33. Jean Allman and Victoria Tashjian, *"I Will Not Eat Stone": A Women's History of Colonial Asante* (Portsmouth, NH: Heinemann, 2000), xxxvi–xxxvii.

34. Ibid., xxxvii.

35. Catherine Coquery-Vidrovitch, "Histoires des femmes d'Afrique," *Clio* 6 (1997): 7–13.

36. Odile Goerg, "Femmes africaines et pratique historique en France," *Politique Africaine* 72 (1998): 130–44; Anne Hugon, ed., *Histoire des femmes en situation coloniale: Afrique, Asie XXème siècle* (Paris: L'Harmattan, 2004); Odile Goerg, ed., *Perspectives historiques sur le genre en Afrique* (Paris: L'Harmattan, 2007).

37. Pascale Barthélémy, *Africaines et diplômées à l'époque coloniale, 1918–1957* (Rennes: Presses Universitaires de Rennes, 2010), 7.

38. Frederick Cooper, *Decolonization and African Society*, 266.

39. Lisa A. Lindsay, *Working with Gender: Wage Labor and Social Change in Southwestern Nigeria* (Portsmouth, NH: Heinemann, 2003), 22–23.

40. Barthélémy, *Africaines et diplômées*, 18–20.

41. Barbara M. Cooper, *Marriage in Maradi: Gender and Culture in a Hausa Society in Niger, 1900–1989* (Portsmouth, NH: Heinemann, 1997); Martin, *Leisure and Society*; Phyllis M. Martin, *Catholic Women of Congo-Brazzaville: Mothers and Sisters in Troubled Times* (Bloomington: Indiana University Press, 2009), esp. chap. 3, 67–92; Barthélémy, *Africaines et diplômées*, 14–15.

42. Georges Balandier, *Sociologie des Brazzaville noires* (Paris: Presses de la Fondation Nationale des Sciences Politiques, 1985), 1–10; Coquery-Vidrovitch, *History of African Cities*; Freund, *African City*, 85–86.

43. Allman, Geiger, and Musisi, *Women in African Colonial Histories*, 3.

44. Joan W. Scott, *Gender and the Politics of History* (New York: Columbia University Press, 1999), 28–50.

45. Scholarship on masculinity in Africa includes: T. Dunbar Moodie, *Going for Gold: Men, Mines, and Migration* (Berkeley: University of California Press, 1994); Carol Summers, "Mission Boys, Civilized Men, and Marriage: Educated African Men in the Missions of Southern Rhodesia, 1920–1945," *Journal of Religious History* 23, no. 1 (December 2002): 75–91; Stephan F. Miescher and Lisa A. Lindsay, *Men and Masculinities in Modern Africa* (Portsmouth, NH: Heinemann, 2002); Robert Morrell, ed., *Changing Men in Southern Africa* (Natal: University of Natal Press, 2001); Robert Morrell and Lahoucine Ouzgane, eds., *African Masculinities: Men in Africa from the Late Nineteenth Century to the Present* (New York: Palgrave Macmillan, 2005); Stephan F. Miescher, *Making Men in Ghana* (Bloomington: Indiana University Press, 2005); Lindsay, *Working with Gender*; Thomas V. McClendon, *Genders and Generations Apart: Labor Tenants and Customary Law in Segregation-Era South Africa, 1920s to 1940s* (Portsmouth, NH: Heinemann, 2002); Mark Hunter, *Love in the Time of AIDS: Inequality, Gender, and Rights in South Africa* (Bloomington: Indiana University Press, 2010).

46. Lindsay, *Working with Gender*, 12–13, 125.

47. Miescher, *Making Men in Ghana*, 2.

48. Frederick Cooper, *Decolonization*, 58–68.

49. Tsuneo Yoshikuni, *African Urban Experiences in Colonial Zimbabwe: A Social History of Harare before 1925* (Harare: Weaver Press, 2007), 81.

50. In his research on women in rural Kenya, Brett L. Shadle argues that scholars have paid an inordinate amount of attention to the small numbers of "runaway women" who left rural areas for cities. Such emphasis, he contends, leaves the impression that rural patriarchy "was irresistibly powerful, internally undifferentiated, and unshaken by instability." Shadle, *Girl Cases*, 11. However, studies such as Henrietta Moore and Megan Vaughan's work on gender and agricultural labor in Zambia have demonstrated that even with the emergence of the cash economy and male labor migration, women's agricultural production remained robust, and redistributive exchanges of food for labor gave women access to the cash economy. Moore and Vaughan, *Cutting Down Trees: Gender, Nutrition, and Agricultural Change in the Northern Province of Zambia, 1890–1990* (Portsmouth, NH: Heinemann, 1994). See especially chapter 3, "Relishing Porridge: The Gender Politics of Food," 46–78.

51. Marissa J. Moorman, *Intonations: A Social History of Music and Nation in Luanda, Angola, from 1945 to Recent Times* (Bloomington: Indiana University Press, 2008); Andrew Ivaska, *Cultured States: Youth, Gender, and Modern Style in 1960s Dar es Salaam* (Durham, NC: Duke University Press, 2011).

52. For more on the "othering" of sexuality in Africa, see Signe Arnfred, ed., *Re-Thinking Sexualities in Africa* (Uppsala: Nordic Africa Institute, 2004). For a critique of the AIDS paradigm, see Sheldon, *Courtyards*, 12; and Hunter, *Love in the Time of AIDS*, 1–18.

53. Luise White, *Comforts of Home*; Megan Vaughan, *Curing Their Ills: Colonial Power and African Illness* (Stanford, CA: Stanford University Press, 1991), esp. chap. 9, "Women, Wage Labor, and the Limits of Colonial Control," 221–28.

54. Thomas, *Politics of the Womb*.

55. Arnfred, *Re-Thinking Sexualities in Africa*.

56. For examples of this literature, see Megan Vaughan, "Syphilis and Sexuality," in *Curing Their Ills: Colonial Power and African Illness* (Stanford, CA: Stanford University Press, 1991), 129–55; Diana Jeater, *Marriage, Perversion and Power: The Construction of Moral Discourse in Southern Rhodesia, 1894–1930* (Oxford: Oxford University Press, 1993); Anne McClintock, *Imperial Leather: Race, Gender and Sexuality in the Colonial Contest* (New York: Routledge, 1994).

57. "African women represented the happy, 'primitive' state of pre-colonial Africa. It followed that when they stepped out of, or resisted, this role by becoming migrant workers themselves, they would become the object of a particularly heightened concern over social disintegration. In particular, the sexuality of African women only became a subject of distinct interest when it could no longer be contained by African men—when for instance, women moved to towns and cities as migrants, in their own right." Vaughan, *Curing Their Ills*, 22.

58. Jeater, *Marriage*, 195–96, 265.

59. Dorothy L. Hodgson and Sheryl A. McCurdy argue that marriage was "the primary locus of production, reproduction, consumption, distribution, and social control in societies, [and] becomes a key site of struggle in the context of economic and social transformations." Hodgson and McCurdy, *Wicked Women*, 7. Books on the history of marriage include: Kristin Mann, *Marrying Well: Marriage, Status, and Social Change among the Educated Elite in Colonial Lagos* (Cambridge: Cambridge University Press, 1985); Barbara M. Cooper, *Marriage in Maradi*; Shadle, *Girl Cases*; Allman and Tashjian, *I Will Not Eat Stone*.

60. Shadle, *Girl Cases*, 227.

61. Stephanie Newell, *The Forger's Tale: The Search for Odeziaku* (Athens: Ohio University Press, 2006), 10.

62. Jennifer Cole and Lynn M. Thomas, eds., *Love in Africa* (Chicago: University of Chicago Press, 2009). For additional arguments that love and emotional attachment have not received sufficient analysis in African history, see Kenda Mutongi, "'Dear Dolly's' Advice: Representations of Youth, Courtship, and Sexualities in Africa, 1960–1980," *International Journal of African Historical Studies* 33, no. 1 (2000): 1–23; Teresa Barnes, "Virgin Territory?," 166–67; Shadle, *Girl Cases*, xxx–xxxi.

63. Mark Hunter, "The Materiality of Everyday Sex: Thinking beyond Prostitution," *African Studies* 61, no. 1 (2002): 99–120.

64. John D'Emilio and Estelle B. Freedman, *Intimate Matters: A History of Sexuality in America* (Chicago: University of Chicago Press, 1997), xv.

65. Michel Foucault, *The History of Sexuality*, vol. 1, *An Introduction*, trans. Robert Hurley (New York: Pantheon, 1990), 8; Robert A. Padgug, "Sexual Matters: On Conceptualizing Sexuality in History," in *Passion and Power: Sexuality in History*, ed. Kathy Peiss and Christina Simmons (Philadelphia: Temple University Press, 1999), 22–23.

66. Stephen O. Murray and Will Roscoe, *Boy-Wives and Female Husbands: Studies of African Sexualities* (New York: Palgrave Macmillan, 2001); Arnfred, *Re-Thinking Sexualities*, 15; Marc Epprecht: *Hungochani: The History of a Dissident Sexuality in Southern Africa* (Montreal: McGill-Queen's University Press, 2004); Epprecht, *Heterosexual Africa? The History of an Idea from the Age of Exploration to the Age of AIDS* (Athens: Ohio University Press, 2008); Marc Epprecht and Charles Gueboguo,

eds., "New Perspectives on Sexualities in Africa," *Canadian Journal of African Studies / Revue Canadienne des Études Africaines* 43, no. 1 (2009): 1–7.

67. For an analysis of the interpretive lenses of queer theory, see Epprecht, *Hungochani*, 10–16.

68. Simone, *For the City Yet to Come*, 15.

69. David Spurr, *The Rhetoric of Empire: Colonial Discourse in Journalism, Travel Writing, and Imperial Administration* (Durham, NC: Duke University Press, 1993), 6.

70. Martin Chanock, *Law Custom and Social Order: The Colonial Experience in Malawi and Zambia* (Cambridge: Cambridge University Press, 1985); Terence Ranger, "The Invention of Tradition in Colonial Africa," in *The Invention of Tradition*, ed. Eric J. Hobsbawm and Terence Ranger (Cambridge: Cambridge University Press, 1983), 212.

71. Kristin Mann and Richard L. Roberts, *Law in Colonial Africa* (Stanford, CA: Stanford University Press, 1991).

72. Marcia Wright, "Justice, Women, and the Social Order in Abercorn, Northeastern Rhodesia, 1897–1903," in *African Women and the Law: Historical Perspectives*, ed. Margaret Jean Hay and Marcia Wright (Boston: Boston University African Studies Center, 1982), 33–50; Byfield, "Women, Marriage, Divorce," 27–46; Sean Hawkins, *Writing and Colonialism in Northern Ghana: The Encounter between the LoDagaa and "The World on Paper," 1892–1991* (Toronto: University of Toronto Press, 2002); Richard L. Roberts, *Litigants and Households: African Disputes and Colonial Courts in the French Soudan, 1895–1912* (Portsmouth, NH: Heinemann, 2005), chap. 6; Shadle, *Girl Cases*.

73. Roberts, *Litigants and Households*, 3.

74. Barbara M. Cooper, "Mediating Marriage: State Intrusion and Local Dispute Settlement," in *Marriage in Maradi*, 20–39.

75. Richard L. Roberts, "Text and Testimony in the *Tribunal de Première Instance*, Dakar, during the Early Twentieth Century," *Journal of African History* 31, no. 3 (November 1990): 447–63; Mann and Roberts, *Law in Colonial Africa*, 3.

76. ANG, Register 112, Afrique Equatoriale Française, Région de l'Estuaire, Registre des jugements, Tribunal Coutumier, Année 1950 Du 4 novembre 1950 au 1er Mai 1955 , Case 32, April 1, 1951; Rachel Jean-Baptiste, "'The Option of the Judicial Path': Disputes over Marriage, Divorce, and Extra-Marital Sex in Colonial Courts in Libreville, Gabon (1939–1959)," *Cahiers d'etudes africaines* 187–88 (2007): 643–70.

77. Sally Falk Moore, *Social Facts and Fabrications: "Customary" Law on Kilimanjaro, 1880–1980* (Cambridge: Cambridge University Press, 1986), 11.

78. Roberts, *Litigants and Households*, 9.

79. Nancy Rose Hunt, *A Colonial Lexicon of Birth Ritual, Medicalization, and Mobility in the Congo* (Durham, NC: Duke University Press, 1999), 23. For more on Africans and writing, see Hawkins, *Writing and Colonialism*.

80. K. David Patterson, "The Mpongwé and the Orungu of the Gabon Coast, 1815–1875: The Transition to Colonial Rule" (PhD diss., Stanford University, 1971), 12. For other discussions of primary sources for precolonial Gabonese sources, see Hubert Deschamps, *Traditions orales et archives au Gabon: Contribution à l'ethnohistoire* (Paris: Berger-Levrault, 1962); André Raponda-Walker, *Notes d'histoire du Gabon: Suivi de toponymie de l'estuaire Libreville et toponymie du Fernan-Vaz Port-Gentil* (Libreville: Raponda Walker, 1996); Joseph Ambouroué-Avaro, *Un peuple gabonais à l'aube de la colonisation: Le Bas-Ogowé au XIX siècle* (Paris: Karthala, 1981), 24–25.

81. Richard Adloff and Virginia Thompson, *The Emerging States of French Equatorial Africa* (Stanford, CA: Stanford University Press, 1960), 15.

82. Catherine Coquery-Vidrovitch, *Le Congo au temps des grandes compagnies concessionaires 1898–1930* (Paris: Mouton, 1972), 77.

83. François Charbonnier, ed., *Gabon, terre d'avenir* (Paris: Encyclopédie d'outremer, 1957); Anselme Nzoghe, "L'Exploitation forestière et les conditions d'exploitation des peuples de la colonie du Gabon de 1920 à 1940: Le travail forcé" (PhD diss., University de Provence, Aix-Marseille, 1984), 3–14.

84. French scholar Hubert Deschamps, who conducted research in Libreville as early as the 1960s, conveys that the city's archives were burned, either deliberately or accidentally, in a fire. Deschamps, *Traditions orales et archives au Gabon*.

85. Jan Vansina, *Oral Tradition: A Study in Historical Methodology*, trans. H. M. Wright (London: Transaction Publishers, 1965), 1–5.

86. Steven Feierman, *The Shambaa Kingdom: A History* (Madison: University of Wisconsin Press, 1974); David P. Henige, *The Chronology of Oral Tradition: Quest for a Chimera* (Oxford: Oxford University Press, 1974); Joseph C. Miller, ed., *The African Past Speaks: Essays on Oral Tradition and History* (Hamden, CT: Archon, 1980); James B. Webster, *Chronology, Migration, and Drought in Interlacustrine Africa* (New York: Holmes and Meier, 1978); Donald Moore and Richard L. Roberts, "Listening for the Silences," *History in Africa* 17 (1990): 319–25; Isabel Hofmeyr, "*We Spend Our Years as a Tale That Is Told*": Oral Historical Narrative in a South African Chiefdom (Portsmouth, NH: Heinemann, 1993).

87. Mary F. Smith, *Baba of Karo* (New Haven, CT: Yale University Press, 1953); Claire C. Robertson, *Sharing the Same Bowl: A Socioeconomic History of Women and Class in Accra, Ghana* (Ann Arbor: University of Michigan Press, 1990); Luise White, *Comforts of Home*, 21–28; Sarah Mirza and Margaret Strobel, eds., *Three Swahili Women: Life Histories from Mombasa, Kenya*, trans. Sarah Mirza and Margaret Strobel (Bloomington: Indiana University Press, 1989); Gracia Clark, *African Market Women: Seven Life Stories from Ghana* (Bloomington: Indiana University Press, 2010); John M. Chernoff, *Hustling Is Not Stealing: Stories of an African Bar Girl* (Chicago: University of Chicago Press, 2003); Susan N. G. Geiger, "Women's Life Histories: Method and Content," *Signs* 11, no. 2 (Winter 1986): 334–51.

88. Luise White, Stephan F. Miescher, and David William Cohen, eds., *African Words, African Voices: Critical Practices in History* (Bloomington: Indiana University Press, 2001), 15.

89. Luise White, "Telling More: Lies, Secrets, and History," *History and Theory* 39, no. 4 (December 2000): 11–22.

90. Bozzoli and Nkotsoe, *Women of Phokeng*, 6–13.

91. Marjorie Mbilinyi, "'I'd Have Been a Man': Politics and the Labor Process in Producing Personal Narratives," in *Interpreting Women's Lives: Feminist Theory and Personal Narratives*, ed. Personal Narratives Group (Bloomington: Indiana University Press, 1989), 204–27; Kirk Hoppe, "Whose Life Is It, Anyway? Issues of Representation in Life Narrative Texts of African Women," *International Journal of African Historical Studies* 26, no. 3 (1993): 623–36; Heidi Gengenbach, "Truth-Telling and the Politics of Women's Life History Research in Africa: A Reply to Kirk Hoppe," *International Journal of African Historical Studies* 27, no. 3 (1994): 619–27.

92. Luise White, "True Confessions," *Journal of Women's History* 15, no. 4 (Winter 2004): 144.

93. Stephan F. Miescher, "The Life Histories of Boakye Yiadom (Akasease Kofi of Abetifi, Kwawu): Exploring the Subjectivity and 'Voices' of a Teacher-Catechist in Colonial Ghana," in White, Miescher, and Cohen, *African Words*, 162–93; Miescher, *Making Men in Ghana*, 152.

94. Corinne A. Kratz, "Conversations and Lives," in White, Miescher, and Cohen, *African Words*, 142.

CHAPTER 1: SEXUAL ECONOMY IN THE ERA OF TRADE
AND POLITICS: THE FOUNDING OF LIBREVILLE,
1849–1910

1. K. David Patterson, *The Northern Gabon Coast to 1875* (Oxford: Oxford University Press, 1975), vii.

2. Jan Vansina, *Paths in the Rainforests: Toward a History of Political Tradition in Equatorial Africa* (Madison: University of Wisconsin Press, 1990), 11–16; Kairn A. Klieman, *"The Pygmies Were Our Compass": Bantu and Batwa in the History of Early West Central Africa, Early Times to c. 1900 C.E.* (Portsmouth, NH: Heinemann, 2003), xxv–xxxi.

3. Such research includes: K. David Patterson, *Northern Gabon Coast*; Henry H. Bucher, "The Village of Glass and Western Intrusion: An Mpongwé Response to American and French Presence in the Gabon Estuary: 1842–1845," *International Journal of African Historical Studies* 6, no. 3 (1973): 363–400; Bucher, "The Mpongwé of the Gabon Estuary: A History to 1860" (PhD diss., University of Wisconsin, 1977); Nicolas Métégué N'Nah, *Economies et Sociétés au Gabon dans la première moitie du dix-neuvième siècle* (Paris: L'Harmattan, 1979).

4. Guy Lasserre, "Libreville: Cité des eaux," in *Gabon, terre d'avenir*, ed. François Charbonnier (Paris: Encyclopédie d'outre-mer, 1957), 27–36.

5. Théophile Loungou-Mouele, "Le Gabon de 1910 à 1925: Les indices de la première guerre mondiale sur l'évolution politique, économique, et sociale" (PhD diss., Université de Provence, Centre d'Aix, 1984), 27–33.

6. Lasserre, "Libreville: Cité des eaux," 30.

7. Loungou-Mouele, "Le Gabon," 24–31.

8. K. David Patterson, *Northern Gabon Coast*, vii.

9. K. David Patterson, "The Mpongwé and the Orungu of the Gabon Coast, 1815–1875: The Transition to Colonial Rule" (PhD diss., Stanford University, 1971), 1; Henry H. Bucher, "The Mpongwé of the Gabon Estuary: A History to 1860" (PhD diss., University of Wisconsin, 1977); James F. Barnes, *Gabon: Beyond the Colonial Legacy* (Boulder, CO: Westview Press, 1992), 7–8.

10. The phrase *Myé né* literally means "I say that," signifying truth, clarity, or comprehensibility. Pasteur Teissères, *Méthode pratique pour apprendre l'Omyéné* (Paris: Société des Missions Evangéliques, 1957). Quoted in Annie Merlet, *Légendes et histoire des Myènès de l'Ogooué* (Libreville: Centre Culturel français Saint-Exupéry, 1990), 7.

11. Merlet, *Légendes et histoire*, 22.

12. Henry H. Bucher, "Mpongwé Origins: Historiographical Perspectives," *History in Africa* 2 (1975): 59–89; Joseph Ambouroué-Avaro, *Un peuple gabonais* à l'aube de la colonisation: Le Bas-Ogowé au XIX siècle (Paris: Karthala, 1981), 50–51.

13. Henry H. Bucher, "The Atlantic Slave Trade and the Gabon Estuary: The Mpongwé to 1860," in *Africans in Bondage: Studies in Slavery and the Slave Trade*;

Essays in Honor of Philip D. Curtin on the Occasion of the Twenty-Fifth Anniversary of African Studies at the University of Wisconsin, ed. Paul E. Lovejoy (Madison: University of Wisconsin Press, 1986), 137.

14. K. David Patterson, "Mpongwé and the Orungu," 42.

15. Ibid., 4.

16. Ambouroué-Avaro, *Un peuple gabonais,* 68–69.

17. K. David Patterson, "Mpongwé and the Orungu," 115.

18. Ibid., 70–73, 114–15; Bucher, "Mpongwé of the Gabon Estuary," 31; Ambouroué-Avaro, *Un peuple gabonais,* 69.

19. K. David Patterson, "The Vanishing Mpongwé: European Contact and Demographic Change in the Gabon River," *Journal of African History* 16, no. 2 (1975): 224.

20. Paul Du Chaillu, *Explorations and Adventures in Equatorial Africa* (London: Murray, 1861), 41; K. David Patterson, "Vanishing Mpongwé," 227.

21. Bucher, "Mpongwé of the Gabon Estuary"; K. David Patterson, "Mpongwé and the Orungu"; Annie Merlet, *Le pays des trois estuaries (1471–1900): Quatre siècles de relations extérieures dans les estuaires du Muni, de la Mondah, et du Gabon* (Libreville: Centre culturel français Saint-Exupéry, 1990).

22. Until the nineteenth century, neighboring Loango dominated the trade in slaves for the region. K. David Patterson, "Mpongwé and the Orungu," 43; Merlet, Légendes et histoire, 22–23.

23. K. David Patterson, "Mpongwé and the Orungu," 156.

24. Du Chaillu, *Explorations and Adventures,* 33–39.

25. Bucher, "Village of Glass," 377.

26. Alexis-Edouard Vignon, "Le comptoir français du Gabon, sur la côte occidentale d'Afrique," *Nouvelles Annales des Voyages* 4 (1856): 292–93; K. David Patterson, "Mpongwé and the Orungu," 120; Merlet, *Légendes et histoire,* 51.

27. Du Chaillu, *Explorations and Adventures,* 38–39; Marquis de Compiègne, *L'Afrique Equatoriale: Gabonais, pahouins, gallois* (Paris: Plon, 1875), 189–90.

28. Albert Bushnell, letter, January 1, 1855, American Board of Commissioners for Foreign Missions. Volume 2: West Africa Letters of Presbyterian Missionaries, 1840–1852.

29. K. David Patterson, "Mpongwé and the Orungu," 117–18.

30. Ibid., 121.

31. Ibid.

32. John A. Ballard, "The Development of Political Parties in French Equatorial Africa" (PhD diss., Fletcher School of Law and Diplomacy, Tufts University, 1963), 24.

33. Henry Bucher Papers (hereafter cited as HBP), Princeton Theological Seminary: Paul Marie Victor Barret, *La Sénégambie et Guinée—La région gabonaise. L'Afrique Occidentale, la nature et l'homme noir,* vol. 2 (Paris: Challamel, 1888), 144–45.

34. Jeremy M. Rich, *A Workman Is Worthy of His Meat: Food and Colonialism in the Gabon Estuary* (Lincoln: University of Nebraska Press, 2007), 28–29.

35. Joseph-Henri Neu, "Etudes gabonaises: Le pays et les habitants," *Annales Apostoliques* 4 (October 1886): 132–33; Bucher, "Atlantic Slave Trade," 150; Vansina, *Paths in the Rainforests,* 71–100.

36. Vansina, *Paths in the Rainforests,* 71–100.

37. Du Chaillu, *Explorations and Adventures,* 59.

38. Ibid., 41.

39. Barret, *La Senégambie*, 146–47.

40. Archives Nationales du Gabon (hereafter cited as ANG), William Walker Papers Box 1, file 5, William Walker, "Mpongwé Laws or Customs," n.d.; Barret, *La Sénégambie*, 146–47.

41. An example of such an interpretation is that argued by Henry H. Bucher, who contends that customary marriage regulations "reinforced two basic realities in Mpongwé society: the customary dominance over women by men . . . and the control of the older men over the wealth, power, and productivity of the younger ones." Bucher, "Mpongwé of the Gabon Estuary," 80.

42. Archives Générales des Pères de Saint-Esprit de Chevilly-Larue (hereafter cited as CSSP), Box 148, Père Henri-Joseph Neu, *Le Gabon*, ca. late nineteeth century, 117; HBP, Capitaine Ricard, "Notes sur le Gabon," *Revue Coloniale* 14 (1855): 258; ANG, Walker, "Mpongwé Laws or Customs."

43. Henri Trilles, *Chez les Fang, ou quinze années de séjour au Congo français* (Lille: Desclée, De Brouwer, 1912), 259; Barret, *La Sénégambie*, 147.

44. ANG, Walker, "Mpongwé Laws or Customs"; Barret, *La Sénégambie*, 148–49.

45. HBP, Ricard, "Notes sur le Gabon," 258; Vignon, "Le comptoir français," 295; Bucher, "Atlantic Slave Trade," 148.

46. Bucher, "Atlantic Slave Trade," 140.

47. Barret, *La Sénégambie*; Du Chaillu, *Explorations and Adventures*; William Hutton, *A Voyage to Africa: Including a Narrative of an Embassy to One of the Interior Kingdoms, in the Year 1820* (London: Longman, Hurst, Rees, Orme, and Brown, 1821), 122.

48. HBP, Ricard, "Notes sur le Gabon"; Vignon, "Le comptoir français," 293–94.

49. CSSP, 211.3b, Folder 1, Monseigneur Père Marie le Berre, *Notes diverses sur les mariages indigènes*, n.d.

50. Ibid.

51. Ibid.

52. HBP, Ricard, "Notes sur le Gabon," 258.

53. CSSP, Neu, *Le Gabon*, 120–21.

54. Ibid.

55. Ibid., 1.

56. K. David Patterson, "Mpongwé and the Orungu," 45; K. David Patterson, "Vanishing Mpongwé," 227–28; Bucher, "Mpongwé of the Gabon Estuary," 186.

57. Joseph Lasseny Ntchoveré, interview by author, Libreville, March 2, 2002.

58. Barret, *La Sénégambie*, 149; Compiègne, *L'Afrique Equatoriale*, 192.

59. Owen White, "Miscegenation in French West Africa," in *Children of the French Empire: Miscegenation and Colonial Society in French West Africa, 1895–1960* (Oxford: Oxford University Press, 1999), 7–32.

60. Willem Bosman, *A New and Accurate Description of the Coast of Guinea* (London: Cass, 1698), 406.

61. Hutton, *Voyage to Africa*, 112; Paul Gaffarel, *Les colonies françaises* (Paris: Librairie Germer Baillière, 1899), 148.

62. Charles Castellani, *Les femmes au Congo* (Paris: Flammarion, 1898), 35–40.

63. Père Le Jeune, *Au Congo: La situation faite à la femme et la famille* (Paris: Augustin Challamel, 1900), 483.

64. K. David Patterson, "Vanishing Mpongwé," 229.

65. Bucher, "Mpongwé of the Gabon Estuary," 186.

66. Jeremy M. Rich, "'Une Babylone Noire': Interracial Unions in Colonial Libreville, c. 1860–1914," *French Colonial History* 4 (2003): 145.

67. CSSP, 211.4a6, Rapport sur la Communauté et la Mission de Sainte Marie, March 1, 1860.

68. George E. Brooks, *Eurafricans in Western Africa: Commerce, Social Status, Gender, and Religious Observance from the Sixteenth to the Eighteenth Century* (Athens: Ohio University Press, 2003); Hilary Jones, *The Métis of Senegal: Urban Life and Politics in French West Africa* (Bloomington: Indiana University Press, 2013).

69. Two women who were involved in interracial unions are mentioned in nineteenth-century missionary sources as having amassed individual wealth. Rich, *Une Babylone Noire*, 159–61.

70. Patterson argues that a compilation of statistics demonstrates that the Mpongwé population (including slaves) was reduced from 6,000 to 3,000. K. David Patterson, "Vanishing Mpongwé," 226.

71. Ibid., 221–22.

72. Christopher Chamberlin, "The Migration of the Fang into Central Gabon during the Nineteenth Century: A New Interpretationn," *International Journal of African Historical Studies* 11, no. 3 (1978): 421.

73. Pierre Alexandre and Jacques Binet, *Le groupe dit pahouin: Fang—Boulou—Beti* (Paris: Presses Universitaires de France, 1958); Chamberlin, "Migration of the Fang," 421; Métégué N'Nah, Économies et sociétés au Gabon; Ambouroué-Avaro, *Un Peuple gabonais*; Elikia Mbokolo, *Noirs et blancs en Afrique Équatoriale: Les sociétés côtières et la pénétration française, vers 1820–1874* (Mouton: Ecole Hautes Etudes en Sciences Sociales, 1981); Nicolas Métégué N'Nah, *Lumière sur points d'ombre: Contribution à la connaissance de la société gabonaise* (Langres: Guéniot, 1984); John M. Cinnamon, "The Long March of the Fang: Anthropology and History in Equatorial Africa" (PhD diss., Indiana University, 1998); Florence Bernault, "Dévoreurs de la nation: Le mythe des invasions Fang au Gabon," in *Etre étranger et migrant en Afrique au vingtième siècle*, ed. Catherine Coquery-Vidrovitch and Issiaka Mandé (Paris: L'Hamarttan, 2003), 169–88.

74. Christopher J. Gray, *Colonial Rule and Crisis in Equatorial Africa: Southern Gabon, ca. 1850–1940* (Rochester, NY: University of Rochester Press, 2002), 32; Chamberlin, "Migration of the Fang," 429–56.

75. Merlet, *Le pays des trois estuaires*, 61.

76. Bucher, "Mpongwé of the Gabon Estuary"; Richard Adloff and Virginia Thompson, *The Emerging States of French Equatorial Africa* (Stanford, CA: Stanford University Press, 1960), 5–6.

77. Albert Bushnell, correspondence, May 24, 1857, American Board of Commissioners for Foreign Missions, Volume 2: West Africa Letters of Presbyterian Missions, 1840–1852; Compiègne, *L'Afrique Equatoriale*, quoted in Victor Largeau, *Encyclopédie pahouine, Congo français: Éléments de grammaire et dictionnaire français-pahouin* (Paris: Leroux, 1901), 31.

78. Compiègne, *L'Afrique Equatoriale*, 189–90.

79. Gray, *Colonial Rule*, 35.

80. Alexandre and Binet, *Le groupe dit pahouin*, 44–49.

81. Largeau, *Encyclopédie pahouine*, 22.

82. Alexandre and Binet, *Le groupe dit pahouin*, 45–46.

83. Ibid., 45.

84. Largeau, *Encyclopédie pahouine*, 22.

85. Chamberlin, "Migration of the Fang."

86. Largeau, *Encyclopédie pahouine*, 11–12.

87. Compiègne, *L'Afrique Equatoriale*, 158; Largeau, *Encyclopédie pahouine*, 14.

88. Largeau, *Encyclopédie pahouin*, 12–13.

89. Rich, *Workman Is Worthy*, 54–55.

90. Chamberlin, "Migration of the Fang," 449.

91. C. Cuny, "De Libreville au Cameroun," *Bulletin de la Société de Géographie* 7, no. 17 (1896): 340; Raymond Mayer, *Histoire de la famille gabonaise* (Libreville: Centre Culturel Français Saint-Exupéry, 2002), 200–203.

92. A. Nguema Allogo, "Esquisse d'un historique de la dot chez les fang," *Revue gabonaise d'etudes politiques, economique, et juridiques* 7 (1981): 32.

93. Ibid., 32.

94. Largeau, *Encyclopédie pahouine*, 83.

95. Ibid., 331; Trilles, *Chez les Fang*, 258; Juline Endamne, interview by author, Paris, France, May 5, 2004.

96. Alexandre and Binet, *Le groupe dit pahouin*, 52–53.

97. Compiègne, *L'Afrique Equatoriale*, 168–69.

98. Léon Mba, "Essai de droit coutumier pahouin," in *Ecrits ethnographiques* (Libreville: Raponda Walker, 2001), 82.

99. Maurice Delafosse, Dr. Poutrin, and Monseigneur Le Roy, *Enquête coloniale dans l'Afrique française occidentale et équatoriale sur l'organisation de la famille indigène, les fiançailles, le mariage avec une esquisse générale des langues de l'Afrique* (Paris: Société d'Edition géographiques, maritime et colonial, 1930), 528–29.

100. Largeau, *Encyclopédie pahouine*, 331.

101. Compiègne, *L'Afrique Equatoriale*, 157.

102. Delafosse, Poutrin, and Le Roy, *Enquête coloniale dans l'Afrique française.*

103. If the wife died as a result of these trials, however, the husband was to compensate her family for her death. Largeau, *Encyclopédie pahouine*, 84.

104. Ibid., 81.

105. Ibid., 495–96.

106. Largeau stresses the seriousness of this act. If the wife assented, without saying anything, she would go to a garden and extract a young flower from a banana plant. She would pound it with powder from a red tree to make a paste and call her husband over. Before witnesses, she would throw the paste into the ocean, signifying that the malediction had been lifted. Largeau, *Encyclopédie Pahouine*, 439.

107. Alexandre and Binet, *Le groupe dit pahouin*, 55.

108. Ibid.

109. Largeau, *Encyclopédie pahouine*, 332.

110. République du Gabon, *Libreville: Capitale rénovée* (Paris: Société Internationale d'Etudes et de Réalisations Africaines, 1979), 5.

111. Thomas J. Hutchinson, *Ten Years' Wanderings among the Ethiopians: With Sketches of the Manners and Customs of the Civilized and Uncivilized Tribes, from Senegal to Gaboon* (London: Hurst and Blackett, 1861), 252.

112. The most important French trading house was Pilastre du Havre, while the British firms included Hatton and Cookson, John Holt, Cooper and Company, and the German firm of Wurmer. Compiègne, *L'Afrique Equatoriale*, 199.

113. Adloff and Thompson, *Emerging States*, 13; Catherine Coquery-Vidrovitch, *Le Congo au temps des grandes compagnies concessionaires 1898–1930* (Paris: Mouton, 1972).

114. Adloff and Thompson, *Emerging States*, 15; Coquery-Vidrovitch, *Le Congo*.

CHAPTER 2: PLANNING, PROTEST, AND PROSTITUTION: LIBREVILLE IN THE ERA OF TIMBER, 1910–1929

1. Such research includes: Nicolas Métégué N'Nah, *Domination coloniale au Gabon: Les combattants de la première heure, 1839–1920* (Paris: L'Hamarttan, 1981); Christopher J. Gray, *Colonial Rule and Crisis in Equatorial Africa: Southern Gabon, ca. 1850–1940* (Rochester, NY: University of Rochester Press, 2002); Gilchrist Anicet Nzenguet Iguemba, *Colonisation, fiscalité et mutations au Gabon, 1910–1947* (Paris: L'Hamarttan, 2005).

2. Giles Sautter, *De l'Atlantique au fleuve Congo: Une géographie du sous-peuplement, République du Congo, République Gabonaise* (Paris: Centre d'Etudes Africaines, 1966); C. Félix Pambo-Loueya, "La colonie du Gabon de 1914 à 1939: Étude economique et sociale" (PhD diss., Université de Paris VII, 1980), 60; Gray, *Colonial Rule*, 150–51; Rich, *A Workman Is Worthy*, chap. 4, "Famine in the Gabon Estuary, 1914–1930," 64–85.

3. For further discussion of Gabon's contributions to the French war effort, see Colette Dubois, "Le prix d'une guerre: Deux colonies pendant la première guerre mondiale (Gabon—Oubangui-Chari, 1911–1923)" (PhD diss., Aix-en-Provence, Université de Provence, 1985).

4. Georges Balandier, *The Sociology of Black Africa: Social Dynamics in Central Africa*, trans. Douglas Garman (New York: Praeger, 1970), 166.

5. Georges Bruel, *La France equatoriale africaine: Le pays, les habitants, la colonisation, les pouvoirs public* (Paris: Larose, 1935), 436–39.

6. Actions that could incur punishment under the *indigénat* included: refusal to execute administrative orders, display of ill will in their execution, refusal to give information, failure to declare a change of address, failure to register with the administration while traveling, and "public statements, speeches, chants, or any other manifestations tending to weaken respect for French authority or its European representatives." John A. Ballard, "The Development of Political Parties in French Equatorial Africa" (PhD diss., Fletcher School of Law and Diplomacy, Tufts University, 1963), 39.

7. Gray, *Colonial Rule*, 205.

8. Ballard, "Development of Political Parties," 15–16.

9. Dubois, "Le prix d'une guerre," 43–48.

10. Théopile Loungou-Mouele, "Le Gabon de 1910 à 1925: Les indices de la première guerre mondiale sur l'évolution politique, économique, et sociale" (PhD diss., University of Aix-Marseille, 1984), 56.

11. There were thirty-seven different administrator-mayors between 1910 and 1950. Ballard, "Development of Political Parties," 14, 27.

12. *Journal official du Gabon*, "Arrêté reconnaissant des chefs indigènes dans le secteur de Libreville," September 1, 1906, 273.

13. Ballard, "Development of Political Parties," 27.

14. Bruel, *La France équatoriale africaine*, 455–56.

15. Richard Adloff and Virginia Thompson, *The Emerging States of French Equatorial Africa* (Stanford, CA: Stanford University Press, 1960), 254.

16. Dubois, "Le prix d'une guerre," 53; Florence Bernault, *Démocraties ambiguës en Afrique centrale: Congo-Brazzaville, Gabon, 1940–1965* (Paris: Karthala, 1996), 33; Clotaire Messi Me Nang, "Les travailleurs des chantiers forestiers du Gabon: Hybridité et invisibilité d'une culture ouvrière, 1892–1962" (PhD diss., Université de Paris I, 2007), 55–57.

17. Jane I. Guyer, "Colonial Situations in Long-Term Perspective: The Value of Beti Bridewealth," in *Money Matters: Instability, Values, and Social Payments in the Modern History of West African Communities*, ed. Jane I. Guyer (Portsmouth, NH: Heinemann, 1995), 117.

18. Messi Me Nang, "Les travailleurs," 56.

19. Ibid., 60–61.

20. Rich, *Workman Is Worthy*, 17.

21. In 1910, Gabon exported 51,000 tons of okoumé, but by 1913 this number had tripled to 150,668 tons. After the slump of World War I, a high of 305,000 tons were exported in 1927. Gray, *Colonial Rule*, 150; Pambo-Loueya, "La colonie du Gabon," 60; Balandier, *Sociology of Black Africa*, 166; Sautter, *De l'Atlantique au fleuve Congo*, 768, 853.

22. Anselme Nzoghe, "L'Exploitation forestière et les conditions d'exploration des peuples de la colonie du Gabon de 1920 à 1940: Le travail forcé" (PhD diss., Université de Provence, Aix-Marseille, 1984), 158.

23. Archives Nationales du Gabon (hereafter cited as ANG), Microfilm Reel 51MI421, Rapport Annuel 1921; Centre d'Archives d'Outre Mer (hereafter cited as CAOM), AEF/GGAEF/4 1 D37, Situation de la Colonie à la fin de 1931; Dubois, "Le prix d'une guerre," 79–80.

24. Nzoghe, "Exploitation forestière," 140–60.

25. Ibid., 162.

26. Ibid., 159–60.

27. Messi Me Nang, "Les travailleurs," 108–10.

28. Christopher J. Gray and Francois Ngolet, "Lambaréné, *Okoumé*, and the Transformation of Labor along the Middle Ogooué (Gabon), 1870–1945," *Journal of African History* 40, no. 1 (1998): 90–100; Balandier, *Sociology of Black Africa*, 166.

29. Loungou-Mouele, "Le Gabon," 384.

30. Gray and Ngolet, "Lambaréné," 101.

31. Ibid., 98.

32. Nzoghe, "L'Exploitation forestière," 159–60.

33. Ibid., 187.

34. Messi Me Nang, "Les travailleurs," 172.

35. A report in 1922 from the northern town of Oyem recorded that of 175 men recruited for a timber camp, 30 died in the first month of working. Balandier, *Sociology of Black Africa*, 169. See also Bernault, *Démocraties ambiguës*, 53; Gray and Ngolet, "Lambaréné," 90–100.

36. Messi Me Nang, "Les travailleurs," 171–72.

37. Nzoghe, "L'Exploitation forestière," 196.

38. Adloff and Thompson, *Emerging States*, 346.

39. Ballard, "Development of Political Parties," 27.

40. ANG, Microfilm Reel 51-MI-57, Rapport Annuel, 1932.

41. Years missing because colonial officials did not collect demographic data every year. ANG, Microfilm Reel 51-MI-25. Rapport Annuel 1912; Archives Générales des Pères de Saint-Esprit de Chevilly-Larue (hereafter cited as CSSP), Box 667, Journal of St. Pierre, January 12, 1912; ANG, Microfilm Reel 51MI401. Rapport d'Ensemble sur la Situation de la Colonie et les Evènements de la Guerre en 1916; ANG, Microfilm Reel 51MI411. Rapport Annuel 1918; CAOM, AEF/GGAEF: 4 (1) D 28, Rapport Annuel 1924; 4 (1) D 33, Rapport du Quatrième Trimestre, 1927; 4(1) D 35, Rapport Annuel du 1929; Loungou-Mouele, "Le Gabon," 449.

42. Loungou-Mouele, "Le Gabon," 330; Rich, *Workman Is Worthy*, 66–67.

43. Gray, *Colonial Rule*, 153.

44. Rich, *Workman Is Worthy*, 1–12; Gray, *Colonial Rule*, 161.

45. Loungou-Mouele, "Le Gabon," 299.

46. Ibid., 317–19.

47. Ibid., 320–21.

48. Ibid., 449–51.

49. Patrick Ceillier, Saint-Malo, France. Also published in Patrick Ceillier and Jean-Émile Mbot, *À Libreville, c'était hier* (Libreville: Editions du Luto, 2002), 35.

50. CSSP, Box 677, Journal de la communauté de Sainte Marie, June 5, 1907.

51. Gabrielle M. Vassal, *Life in French Congo* (London: Unwin, 1925), 18–19.

52. Ibid.

53. Frederick W. H. Migeod, *Across Equatorial Africa* (London: Cranton, 1923), 16–17.

54. CSSP, Box 677, Gabon *Journal de Vicariat*, 1911–1918, January 21, 1912; ANG: Microfilm Reel 51-MI-40-1, Rapport d'Ensemble sur la Situation de la Colonie et les Evènements de la Guerre en 1916; Microfilm Reel 51MI421, Rapport Annuel 1921.

55. ANG, Microfilm Reel 51-MI-40-1, Rapport d'Ensemble sur la Situation de la Colonie et les Evènements de la Guerre en 1916.

56. CSSP, Boite 677, *Journal de la Communauté de St. Pierre*, April 1911.

57. Archives de la Maison Mère des soeurs de Castres Bleues du Gabon, Box 105, "Aperçu de l'œuvre des sœurs de l'Immaculée Conception à Libreville," n.d.

58. Vassal, *Life in French Congo*, 18–19.

59. Migeod, *Across Equatorial Africa*, 16.

60. Longou-Mouele, "Le Gabon," 144.

61. ANG, Microfilm Reel 51MI401, Rapport Annuel de la Commune de Libreville 1924.

62. ANG, Microfilm Reel 51MI55, Rapport Annuel du 1928.

63. Patrick Ceillier, Saint-Malo, France. Also published in Ceillier and Mbot, *À Libreville*, 110.

64. ANG, Microfilm Reel 51-MI-40-1, Rapport d'Ensemble sur la Situation de la Colonie et les Evènements de la Guerre en 1916.

65. ANG, 1826, Fichier Sous Série 1E, Résumé des Rapports Mensuels, April 15, 1914.

66. Patrick Ceillier, Saint-Malo, France. Also published in Ceillier and Mbot, *À Libreville*, 110.

67. Migeod, *Across Equatorial Africa*, 25.

68. Ibid., 17–18.

69. Joseph Blache, *Vrais noirs et vrais blancs d'Afrique du vingtième siècle* (Orléans: Caillette, 1922), 204–5.

70. Migeod, *Across Equatorial Africa*, 17.

71. ANG, Microfilm Reel 51MI26, Annual Report 1913.

72. CSSP, Boite 677, *Journal de la Communauté de St Pierre*, June 9, 1912.

73. ANG, Microfilm Reel 51MI25, *Rapport Mensuel du Mai, 1912.*

74. CSSP, Boite 677, *Journal de la Communauté de St. Pierre*, June 9, 1912.

75. ANG, Microfilm Reel 51MI25, Rapport Mensuel June 2012.

76. Ballard, "Development of Political Parties," 67–68.

77. Ibid., 110–12.

78. *L'Echo Gabonais*, 1922–1924; *La Voix Coloniale*, 1924–1928; ANG, Microfilm Reel 51MI51, Rapport Annuel 1924.

79. Microfilm Reel 51MI421, Rapport Annuel 1921; ANG, Microfilm Reel 51MI51, Hygiène Urbaine, Comité Consultatif, Rapport Annuel 1924.

80. Maurice Rondet-Saint, *Dans notre empire noir* (Paris: Société d'Editions, 1929), 64–65.

81. Vassal, *Life in French Congo*, 18–19.

82. Migeod, *Across Equatorial Africa*, 11–14.

83. Ibid., 13.

84. Sara Berry, "Hegemony on a Shoestring: Indirect Rule and Farmers' Access to Resources," in *No Condition Is Permanent: The Social Dynamics of Agrarian Change in Sub-Saharan Africa* (Madison: University of Wisconsin Press, 1993), 22–42. Other scholars have also dismantled the notion of the hegemonic colonial state. See Frederick Cooper, *Decolonization and African Society: The Labor Question in French and British Africa* (Cambridge: Cambridge University Press, 1996).

85. Catherine Coquery-Vidrovitch, *Le Congo au temps des grandes compagnies concessionnaires 1898–1930* (Paris: Mouton, 1972), 86.

86. Guy Lasserre, *Libreville: La ville et sa région* (Paris: Colin, 1958), 201–2.

87. Ibid., 198–99.

88. Père Le Jeune, *Au Congo: La situation faite à la femme et la famille* (Paris: Augustin Challamel, 1900), 500.

89. CAOM, AEF/GGAEF/5D44,Letter 57, Letter from the Governor of Gabon to the Governor of FEA, March 12, 1914.

90. ANG, Microfilm Reel 51MI26, Political Report, City of Libreville, March 1915.

91. CSSP, 4J1.5a, Letter from Louis Matrou, Vicariat Apostolique du Gabon to Propagande de la Foi, December 22, 1915.

92. Georges Balandier, *Ambiguous Africa: Cultures in Collision*, trans. Helen H. Weaver (New York: Pantheon, 1966), 179.

93. Robert H. Milligan, *The Fetish Folk of West Africa* (New York: Revell, 1912), 42.

94. Vassal, *Life in French* Congo, 18.

95. Maurice Delafosse, Dr. Poutrin, and Monseigneur Le Roy, *Enquête coloniale dans l'Afrique française occidentale et équatoriale sur l'organisation de la famille indigène, les fiançailles, le mariage* (Paris: Société d'Edition géographiques, maritime et colonial, 1930), 494–95.

96. Simone Agnoret Iwenga St. Denis, interview by author, Libreville, February 8, 2002.

97. France Renucci, *Souvenirs de femmes au temps des colonies* (Paris: Balland, 1988), 171–77.

98. Ibid., 175.

99. By the twentieth century, Mpongwé in Libreville had already taken to eating increased amounts of imported food. Rich, *Workman Is Worthy*, 86–106.

100. Luise White, *The Comforts of Home: Prostitution in Colonial Nairobi* (Chicago: University of Chicago Press, 1990).

101. Milligan, *Fetish Folk*, 50–52; Blache, *Vrais noirs et vrais blancs*, 199–204.

102. Blache, *Vrais noirs et vrais blancs*, 200.

103. CSSP, Box 677, Journal de la communauté de St. Marie, December 28 1908.

104. Delafosse, Poutrin, and Le Roy, *Enquête coloniale*, v.

105. Albert Londres, *Terre d'ébène: La traite des noirs* (Paris: Le Serpent à Plumes, 1929), 222.

106. Alexandre Le Roy, *La désorganisation de la famille africaine* (Paris: Soye, 1903), 843.

107. CAOM, AEF/GGAEF/3D4, Mission d'Inspection des Colonies, Colonie de l'AEF Moyen-Congo et Gabon, Lettre de la déléguée Angélique Bouyé Dinga à M. l'Inspecteur Général, November 24, 1919.

108. Ibid.

109. Migeod, *Across Equatorial Africa*, 15–16.

110. ANG, Microfilm Reel 51MI26, Rapport Annuel 1913.

111. Delafosse, Poutrin, and Le Roy, *Enquête coloniale*, 525.

112. Quoted in Loungou-Mouele, "Le Gabon," 325.

113. ANG, 577, Lettre des habitants de la Subdivision de Lambaréné à M. le Lieutenant Gouverneur du Gabon, June 20, 1921.

114. Ibid.

115. Londres, *Terre d'ébène*, 233–37.

116. Migeod, *Across Equatorial Africa*, 16.

117. ANG, Microfilm Reel 51MI26: Rapport du 1er Trimestre 1911; Rapport Annuel 1913.

118. CAOM, AEF/GGAEF/5D53, Procès-verbal: Berland René, Administrateur Adjoint des Colonies, avons interrogé comme suit et en commun: Okenegué Stanislas, Chef du Village d'Oréti et Barnabé Anghile, Chef du Village Nkadoua, Fait à la Mairie de Libreville, April 11, 1922.

119. CAOM, AEF/GGAEF/5D53, Circonscription de l'Estuaire et Commune de Libreville: Situation Politique. Ravitaillement Libreville, January 1922.

120. Ibid.

121. Ibid.

122. Rachel Jean-Baptiste, "'A Black Girl Should Not Be with a White Man': Sex, Race, and African Women's Social and Legal Status in Colonial Gabon, c. 1900–1946," *Journal of Women's History* 22, no. 2 (Summer 2010): 56–82.

123. Judith Van Allen argued that women who organized protests in Nigeria were attempting to retain avenues of political power and protest that women had in precolonial times but lost with the implementation of indirect rule. Van Allen, "'Aba Riots' or Igbo 'Women's War'? Ideology, Stratification, and the Invisibility of Women," in *Women in Africa: Studies in Social and Economic Change*, ed. Nancy J. Hafkin and Edna G. Bay (Stanford, CA: Stanford University Press, 1976), 59–85.

124. ANG, Microfilm Reel 51MI411, Rapport Annuel of 1918.

125. Adloff and Thompson, *Emerging States*, 346; Gray, *Colonial Rule*, 153.

126. Quoted in Loungou-Mouele, "Le Gabon," 360.

127. J. L. Faure and Justin Gordart, *La vie aux colonies: Préparation de la femme à la vie colonial* (Paris: Larose, 1938), 277.

128. Nancy Rose Hunt, "Noise over Camouflaged Polygamy, Colonial Morality Taxation, and a Woman-Naming Crisis in Belgian Africa, " *Journal of African History* 32, no. 3 (1991): 471–94.

129. ANG, Microfilm Reel 51-MI-25, Annual Report 1912, CSSP, 2D60.2a4, Mariage Indigène, Rapport Avril 1923; CSSP, 5b1.10b3, document 1, Rapport de M. Rolland, Professeur à la Faculté de droit de Paris, sur les conflits de coutumes, présenté plénière du 30 juin 1927; Delafosse, Poutrin, and Le Roy, *Enquête coloniale*, 528.

130. Delafosse, Poutrin, and Le Roy, *Enquête Coloniale*, 496.

131. CSSP, 5b1.10b2, 18, Notes sur le projet de réglementation de mariage indigène, September 11, 1921; CSSP, 5b1.10b2, 12, Rapport de Père Bouvier "En Voyage dans l'Abanga," March 15, 1925.

132. Thomas, *Politics of the Womb*, 11.

133. For the most comprehensive analysis of the French colonial legal system in Francophone Africa, but FOA in particular, see Richard L. Roberts, *Litigants and Households: African Disputes and Colonial Courts in the French Soudan, 1895–1912* (Portsmouth, NH: Heinemann, 2005).

134. Martin Chanock, *Law, Custom and Social Order: The Colonial Experience in Malawi and Zambia* (Cambridge: Cambridge University Press, 1985), 192–216.

135. ANG, Microfilm Reel 51- MI421, Rapport Annuel 1921.

136. CSSP, 5b1.10b2, 18, Notes sur le Project de réglementation de mariage indigène, September 11, 1921.

137. CSSP, 5b1.10b2, 17, Mariage Indigène au Gabon, Simples Notes et Desiderata, Travaux de Mgr. Matrou, V.A. du Gabon, n.d., ca. 1920s.

138. CSSP, 5b1.10b2, 18, Notes sur le projet de réglementation de mariage indigène, September 11, 1921; CSSP, 5b1.10b2, 17, Mariage indigène au Gabon, Simples Notes et Desiderata, Travaux de Mgr. Matrou, no date, ca. 1925.

139. CAOM, AEF/GGAEF/5D56, Projet de réglementation du mariage indigène, January 20, 1925.

140. CSSP, 5b1.10b2, 15, Projet de réglementation du mariage indigène, January 1, 1922.

141. CAOM, AEF/GGAEF/5D56, Projet de réglementation du mariage indigène, January 20, 1925.

142. CSSP, 5b1.10b2, 15, Projet de Réglementation du mariage indigène, January 1, 1922. In the 1922 document, bridewealth was to be limited to Fang near the coastal regions to between 300 and 400 francs and for those in the interior to 150 francs. For patrilineal groups other than the Fang, bridewealth limits were much smaller, between 100 and 150 francs. For matrilineal groups throughout the colony, bridewealth varied between 30 and 100 francs.

143. The 1925 document distinguished between coastal and interior regions—400 francs for coastal regions and 250 francs worth of goods or cash for the interior. CSSP, 5b1.10b2, 14, Mariage Indigène au Gabon: Simples Notes et desiderata, no date.

144. Wives who abandoned their husbands' homes and wives who committed adultery could be subject to imprisonment. Divorce would be allowed only in the case of a husband's impotence, habitual misconduct by the wife, and the conviction of the husband for more than fives years in prison. CSSP, 5b1.10b2, 15, Projet de Réglementation du mariage indigène, January 1, 1922.

145. CAOM, AEF/GGAEF/5D56, Letter 109, Lettre du M. GG de l'AEF a M. les Lieutenant Gouverneurs du Gabon a LBV, July 19, 1922.

146. CSSP, 5b1.10b2, 17, Mariage Indigène au Gabon, Simples Notes et Desiderata, Travaux de Mgr. Matrou, V.A. du Gabon, n.d., ca. 1925; AEF, GGAEF, 5D56, Note reacting to the Projet d'arrête règlement les mariages indigènes au Gabon, February 14, 1925.

CHAPTER 3: MIGRATION AND GOVERNANCE: THE EXPANSION OF LIBREVILLE

1. Archives Nationales du Gabon (hereafter cited as ANG), Microfilm Reel 51-MI-75, Rapport politique du deuxième semestre, Département de l'Estuaire; ANG, H 172, Région Sanitaire de l'Estuaire, Rapport Trimestriels, 1938–1956, Démographie, Rapport Annuel, 1944, April 26, 1945; ANG, H 172, Région Sanitaire de l'Estuaire, Rapport Trimestriels, 1938–1956, Démographie, Rapport Annuel, 1945, July 19, 1946; ANG, 44, Région de l'Estuaire, Rapport Politique pour l'Année 1947; ANG, 1644, Groupe Mobile de Recensement, Situation du Recensement de Libreville. Compte-rendu à M. le Président du Conseil, Maire de Libreville, September 20, 1958.

2. ANG, Microfilm Reel 51-MI-66-1, Lettre de l'inspecteur des Affaires Administratives au Gouverneur de l'AEF, February 9, 1938.

3. Giles Sautter, *De l'Atlantique au fleuve Congo: Une géographie du sous-peuplement, République du Congo, République Gabonaise* (Paris: Centre d'Etudes Africaines, 1966), 768.

4. Centre d'Archives d'Outre Mer (hereafter cited as CAOM), AEF/GGAEF/4(1) D 37, Situation de la Colonie à la fin de 1931; Anselme Nzoghe, "L'Exploitation forestière et les conditions d'exploitation des peuples de la colonie du Gabon de 1920 à 1940: Le travail forcé" (PhD diss., Université de Provence, Aix-Marseille, 1984), 256.

5. ANG, Microfilm Reel 51-MI-57, Rapport Annuel, 1932.

6. ANG, Rapport Annuel, 1932; ANG, Microfilm Reel 51-MI-60, Rapport Annuel du Département de l'Estuaire, 1934; ANG, Carton 578, Situations Générales, Faits Importants, Commune de Libreville; ANG, Microfilm Reel 51-MI-64-1, Rapport du Deuxième Semestre de l'Année, 1936; ANG, Microfilm Reel 51-MI-66-1, Rapport Politique du Premier Semestre de l'Estuaire, 1937.

7. CAOM, Situation de la Colonie, 1931.

8. ANG, Microfilm Reel 51-MI-59, Rapport Ensemble de l'Année, 1933.

9. ANG, 2DA (I) 10, Rapport Trimestriel, Troisième Trimestre, Circonscription de l'Estuaire, Subdivision de Libreville, 1934.

10. ANG, 4(1) D44, Rapport du Deuxième Semestre, Département de Woleu-Ntem, 1936.

11. ANG, Rapport Politique du Deuxième Semestre, 1937.

12. ANG, Microfilm Reel 51-MI-66-2, Rapport Politique du Deuxième Semestre, 1937.

13. Not all colonial representatives concurred with reports of Mpongwé disappearance. The previous governor in 1932 stated that reports of the Mpongwé vanishing had been exaggerated: "The Mpongwé most certainly are not increasing, but they continue to live in affluence, very separate from the bottom of the Pahouin population." ANG, Microfilm Reel 51-MI-57, Rapport Annuel, 1932; ANG, Microfilm Reel 51-MI-64-1, Rapport du Deuxième Semestre, 1936; ANG, Microfilm Reel 51-MI-66-1, Rapport Politique du Premier Semestre de l'Estuaire, 1937.

14. ANG, 2DA (1)10, Rapport Politique Semestriel Deuxième Semestre 1938, Département de l'Estuaire.

15. Richard Adloff and Virginia Thompson, *The Emerging States of French Equatorial Africa* (Stanford, CA: Stanford University Press, 1960), 363.

16. Ibid.

17. Nzoghe, "L'Exploitation forestière," 194–95.

18. Ibid., 259.

19. About 1,198 people in the Estuary region were engaged in one-year labor contracts, and 542 people held contracts for less than one year. Nzoghe, "L'Exploitation forestière," 259.

20. Frederick Cooper, *Decolonization and African Society: The Labor Question in French and British Africa* (Cambridge: Cambridge University Press, 1996), 50–51.

21. ANG, Sous Série 1E, Carton 406, Affaires Civiles, Rapport en Conseil d'Administration, Présentation d'un projet d'arrêté fixant le taux de l'impôt de capitation dans la colonie du Gabon pour l'année 1931, October 17, 1930.

22. ANG, Microfilm Reel 51-MI-57, Rapport Annuel de la Colonie, 1932; ANG, Microfilm Reel 51-MI-60, Rapport Annuel du Département de l'Estuaire, 1934; ANG, Microfilm Reel 51-MI-64-1, Rapport du Deuxième Semestre, 1936; ANG, Microfilm Reel 51-MI-66-1, Rapport Politique du Premier Semestre de l'Estuaire, 1937; ANG, Sous Série 1E, 578, Situations Générales, Faits Importants, Commune de Libreville, 1938.

23. ANG, Microfilm Reel 51-MI-57, Rapport Annuel, 1932; ANG, Microfilm Reel 51-MI-66-1, Rapport Politique, 1937; ANG, Microfilm Reel 51-MI-64-1, Rapport du Deuxième Semestre, 1936; ANG, 2DA (1)5, Rapport Politique Semestriel Premier semestre 1939, Département de l'Estuaire, Subdivision de Libreville, July 22, 1939.

24. ANG, Microfilm Reel 51-MI-57, Annual Report of 1932.

25. ANG, Microfilm Reel 51-MI-59, Rapport d'Ensemble de l'Année 1933.

26. AEF/GGAEF/4D138, Annual Report of 1932.

27. Ibid.

28. AEF/GGAEF/4D138, Letter from M. the Lieutenant Governor of Gabon to the Governor of AEF, Rapport du Quatrième Trimestre 1932, November 2, 1932.

29. CAOM, AEF/GGAEF/41D38, Annual Report of 1932.

30. ANG, Microfilm Reel 51-MI-59, Rapport d'Ensemble de l'Année 1933.

31. ANG, Microfilm Reel 51-MI-74-1, Rapport Politique du premier Trimestre, 1938 du Département de L'Estuaire.

32. AEF/GGAEF/4D138, Letter from M. the Lieutenant Governor of Gabon to the Governor of AEF, November 2, 1932.

33. ANG, Microfilm 51-MI-62-1, Department of the Estuary, Rapport du Deuxième Trimestre.

34. The original writings of Léon likely are in the possession of descendants who have not made them available for public access.

35. Only one-sixteenth of the entire French Empire followed Free France, with FEA being the largest single block of colonies. In addition to FEA, the New Hebrides, French Oceana, French India, and New Caledonia were the only colonial territories to follow de Gaulle in 1940. Others followed FEA's example between 1940 and 1944. Eric T. Jennings, *Vichy in the Tropics: Pétain's National Revolution in Madagascar, Guadeloupe, and Indochina, 1940–1944* (Stanford, CA: Stanford University Press, 2001), 10–12.

36. A drastic reduction from 232,000 tons in 1938 to 140,000 tons in 1939, to a low of 10,000 tons in 1942; the okoumé market continued to limp along at 36,500 tons toward the war's conclusion in 1945. Léon Modest Nnang Ndong, "Le Gabon dans la deuxième guerre mondiale: L'effort de guerre, indices économiques et sociaux" (PhD diss., Université Panthéon-Sorbonne, 2011), 175.

37. Ibid., "Le Gabon," 160–65.

38. Ibid., 179.

39. Ibid., 137–39.

40. Ibid., 189.

41. Frederick Cooper, *Decolonization*, 267.

42. Jean L. Trocbain, "Les études poursuivies par l'Institut d'études centrafricaines depuis sa création sur le territoire de la République du Congo," *Bulletin Institut d'Etudes Centrafricaines* 19–20 (1960): 127–88.

43. Guy Lasserre, *Libreville: La ville et sa région* (Paris: Colin, 1958).

44. Henrietta L. Moore and Megan Vaughan, *Cutting Down Trees: Gender, Nutrition, and Agricultural Change in the Northern Province of Zambia, 1890–1990* (Portsmouth, NH: Heinemann, 1994).

45. Nnang Ndong, "Le Gabon," 207.

46. Ibid.

47. Ibid., 208–9.

48. René Bascou-Brescane, Étude des conditions de vie à Libreville, 1961–1962 (Paris: Secrétariat d'État aux affaires étrangères chargé de la coopération, 1962), 8.

49. Nnang Ndong, "Le Gabon," 210; François Charbonnier, *Gabon, terre d'avenir* (Paris: Encyclopédie d'outre-mer, 1957), 73.

50. Lasserre, *Libreville*, 207–9.

51. Fernand Grébert, *Au Gabon: L'Afrique Equatoriale Française* (Paris: Sociétés des Missions Evangéliques, 1948), 7–8.

52. Lasserre, *Libreville*, 207–9.

53. ANG, Microfilm Reel 51-MI-7: Rapport Politique Semestriel Deuxième Semestre 1939, Département de l'Estuaire, Subdivision de Libreville, July 22, 1939; Rapports du 2eme Semestre de l'Estuaire, 1942; Rapport politique du deuxième semestre, Département de l'Estuaire; ANG, H 172: Région Sanitaire de l'Estuaire, Rapport Trimestriels, 1938–1956, Démographie, Rapport Annuel, 1944, April 26, 1945; Région Sanitaire de l'Estuaire, Rapport Trimestriels, 1938–1956, Démographie, Rapport Annuel, 1945, July 19, 1946; ANG, H 17, Région Sanitaire de l'Estuaire Rapports Trimestriels 1938–1956, Démographie années diverses, Département Sanitaire de l'Estuaire; Rapport Annuel, 1945, ANG, 44, Région de l'Estuaire, Rapport Politique pour l'Année 1947; ANG, 1644, Groupe Mobile de Recensement, Situation du Recensement de Libreville. Compte-rendu à M. le Président du Conseil, Maire de Libreville, Septembre 20, 1958; Lasserre, *Libreville*, 239; Forence Bernault, *Démocraties ambiguës en Afrique centrale: Congo-Brazzaville, Gabon, 1940–1965* (Paris: Karthala, 1996), 56.

54. ANG 2DA (I) 5, Rapport Politique Semestriel, 2me Semestre 1944, Département de l'Estuaire, Subdivision de Libreville; ANG, 2DA (I) 5, Rapport Politique Semestriel, 2eme Semestre 1947, Département de l'Estuaire, Subdivision de Libreville; ANG, 2DA (I) 5, Rapport Politique Semestriel, 2eme Semestre 1948, Département de l'Estuaire, Subdivision de Libreville; Archives Générales des Pères de Saint-Esprit de Chevilly-Larue (hereafter cited as CSSP), 4J1.11b3, Population du Vicariat de Libreville, 1955.

55. Lasserre, *Libreville*, 199–200.

56. Rachel Jean-Baptiste, "Une Ville Libre? Marriage, Divorce, and Sexuality in Colonial Libreville, Gabon, 1849–1960" (PhD diss., Stanford University, 2005), 159–63.

57. ANG, Microfilm Reel 51-MI-75, Rapport politique du deuxième semestre, Département de l'Estuaire; ANG, H 172, Région Sanitaire de l'Estuaire, Rapport Trimestriels, 1938–1956, Démographie, Rapport Annuel, 1944, April 26, 1945; ANG, H 172, Région Sanitaire de l'Estuaire, Rapport Trimestriels, 1938–1956, Démographie, Rapport Annuel, 1945, July 19, 1946; ANG, 44, Région de l'Estuaire, Rapport Politique pour l'Année 1947; ANG, 1644, Groupe Mobile de Recensement, Situation du Recensement de Libreville. Compte-rendu à M. le Président du Conseil, Maire de Libreville, September 20, 1958.

58. Lasserre, *Libreville*, 218.

59. ANG, Microfilm Reel 51-MI-75, Rapport Politique du Premier Semestre 1939, Département de l'Ogoouée-Maritime.

60. Charbonnier, *Gabon*, 78.

61. Lasserre, *Libreville*, 238.

62. ANG, 2DA(I)16, Sondage Démographique dans le District de Libreville, Dans le District de Libreville, étude réalisée par Marcel Soret de l'Institut d'Etudes à M. le Chef de Région de l'Estuaire, April 25, 1957.

63. Lasserre, *Libreville*, 233.

64. Bascou-Brescane, *Etude des Conditions*, 9.

65. Lasserre, *Libreville*, 307–8; CSSP 4J1.11b3, Circulaire 3, 1957, Sainte Marie de Libreville, November 18, 1957.

66. CSSP, 4J1.11b3.

67. Charbonnier, *Gabon*, 91–92.

68. ANG, H172, Santé, Démographie, Département Sanitaire de l'Estuaire, Rapport Annuel, 1944.

69. ANG, Microfilm Reel 2DA(I) 5, Rapport Politique Semestriel, 2eme Semestre 1947, Département de l'Estuaire, Subdivision de Libreville.

70. Laurent Bastiani, *Enquête su la sex-ratio, 1951–1955* (Brazzaville: Haut-commissariat de l'Afrique équatoriale française, Groupe d'études des comptes économiques, Service de la Statistique General, 1956), 1.

71. Laurent Bastiani, *Inventaire des ressources humaines de l'Afrique Equatoriale Française* (Brazzaville: Haut-commissariat de l'Afrique équatoriale française, Groupe d'études des comptes économiques, Service de la Statistique General, 1956).

72. Lasserre, *Libreville*, 235.

73. ANG, 810, Note Concernant L'Etat Civil Africain, May 1947; ANG, 4015, Georges Balandier, Institut d'Etudes Centre Africaines, "Rapports Préliminaires de la Mission d'Information Scientifique en Pays Fang," March 20, 1949.

74. ANG, 2DI, Etude sommaire des populations de la Subdivision de Libreville par rapport au milieu géographique, January 27, 1945.

75. John A. Ballard, "The Development of Political Parties in French Equatorial Africa" (PhD diss., Fletcher School of Law and Diplomacy, Tufts University, 1963), 20.

76. Lasserre, *Libreville*, 28–30.

77. Débats de L'Assemblé Territoriale du Gabon, "Première Session Ordinaire 1954 du 15 Mars au 2 Avril," 262.

78. Lasserre, *Libreville*, 32.

79. ANG, 2DA(I) 5, Rapport Politique Semestriel, 2eme Semestre 1944, Département de l'Estuaire, Subdivision de Libreville.

80. Fidèle-Marcellin Allogho-Nkoghe, "Politique de la ville et logique d'acteurs a la recherche d'alternatives d'aménagement pour les quartiers informels de Libreville" (PhD diss., Université de Montpellier III, 2006), 62.

81. Débats de L'Assemblé Territoriale du Gabon, "Première Session Ordinaire 1955 du 10 Mars au 15 Avril," April 14, 1955, p. 120; Lasserre, *Libreville*, 16–17.

82. ANG, Microfilm Reel 51-MI-57, Rapport Annuel 1932. For criminal hearings on vagabondage, see Cases 4, 21, 24, 25, and 32 in ANG, Register 82, Registre du Tribunal du premier degré de la Commune de Libreville, Jugements rendus en matière répréssive années, 1937–1939.

83. Débats, April 14, 1955, 120.

84. Ibid.

85. Lasserre, *Libreville*, 33.

86. Ibid., 262–64.

87. Nnang Ndong, "Le Gabon," 213.

88. Nzoghe, "L'Exploitation forestière," 79; Nnang Ndong, "Le Gabon," 135.

89. Nnang Ndong, "Le Gabon," 232.

90. Georges Balandier, *Ambiguous Africa: Cultures in Collision*, trans. Helen H. Weaver (New York: Pantheon, 1966), 179.

91. Ibid.

92. Lasserre, *Libreville*, 30–33.

93. Ibid., 2.

94. Ibid., 30–33.

95. Bascou-Brescane, *Etude des conditions*, 1.

96. Lasserre, *Libreville*, 41–42, 119.

97. Ibid., 42–44.

98. Bascou-Brescane, *Etude des Conditions*, 29.

99. Ibid., 40.

100. Lasserre, *Libreville*, 183.

101. Bascou-Brescane, *Etude des Conditions*, 101–2.

102. Ibid., 101–3.

103. Ibid., 108–9.

104. Collection of Patrick Ceillier. Also published in Patrick Ceillier and Jean-Émile Mbot, À *Libreville, c'était hier* (Libreville: Editions du Luto, 2002), 124.

105. Lasserre, *Libreville*, 2–3.

106. Ibid., 275–76.

107. Ibid., 278–79.

108. Bascou-Brescane, *Etude des Conditions*, 75.

109. Jean-Baptiste, "Une Ville Libre," 231–32.

110. Charbonnier, *Gabon*, 115.

111. Ibid., 80.

112. Ibid., 90.

113. Karen T. Hansen, *Distant Companions: Servants and Employers in Zambia, 1900–1985* (Ithaca, NY: Cornell University Press, 1989), 3.

114. Russell Warren Howe, *Theirs the Darkness* (London: Jenkins, 1956), 17.

115. Charbonnier, *Gabon*, 185.

116. Bastiani, *Enquête sur la sex-ratio*, 2.

117. Ballard, "Development of Political Parties," 87.

118. Ibid., 185–92.

119. Ibid., 27.

120. Ibid., 193–96.

121. Ibid., 348.

CHAPTER 4: THE BRIDEWEALTH ECONOMY: MONEY AND RELATIONSHIPS OF AFFINITY

1. Archives Nationales du Gabon (hereafter cited as ANG), Répertoire des Collections de Registres Divers, Code 104, Régions de l'Estuaire, Tribunal du Deuxième degré du département de l'Estuaire, Jugements rendus en matière répressive numéros 338 du 19 mars 1935 au 26 août 1939, Case 3, 1935.

2. ANG, Jugements rendus en matière répressive numéros 338 du 19 mars 1935 au 26 août 1939, Case 3, 1935.

3. Ibid.

4. Honorine Ngou, *Mariage et Violence dans la société traditionelle fang au Gabon* (Paris: L'Hamarttan, 2007), 15–29. For more on domestic violence across Africa, see *Domestic Violence and the Law in Colonial and Postcolonial Africa*, ed. Emily S. Burrill, Richard L. Roberts, and Elizabeth Thornberry (Athens: Ohio University Press, 2010).

5. For a similar case of murder and violence, see ANG Répertoire des Collections de Registres Divers, Code, Région de l'Estuaire, Tribunal du Deuxième degré du département de l'Estuaire, Jugements rendus en matière répressive, Case 39, August 24, 1939 and Case 14, February 18, 1941.

6. Archives Générales des Pères de Saint-Esprit de Chevilly-Larue (hereafter cited as CSSP), 4J1.5a, Box 175, Dossier A, V, Letter from Mgr Adam to Propagande de la foi, July 20, 1899; CSSP, 5B1.10b2, Louis Martrou, Notes sur le projet de réglementation du mariage indigène, November 8, 1921; ANG 4016, Michel Julien Faguinovery, Notable Galoa et exploitant-forestier à M. le Gouverneur Général de l'AEF s/c de M les chefs de la subdivision de Lambaréné, du département de l'Ogoée maritime, et de l'administration supérieur du Gabon, June 22, 1932; Père Gilles Sillard, interview by author, Chevilly-Larue, France, July 18, 2001; Gregory Minsta, interview by author, Libreville, December 14, 2001.

7. Gregory Minsta, interview by author, Libreville, December 14, 2001.

8. I use the terms "tense and tender" as invoked by Ann Stoller to mean the analysis of "the broad-scale dynamics of rule and the intimate domains of implementation." Stoler, "Tense and Tender Ties: The Politics of Comparison in North American History and (Post) Colonial Studies," *Journal of American History* 88, no. 3 (December 2001): 831.

9. A. R. Radcliffe-Brown and C. Daryll Forde, eds., *African Systems of Kinship and Marriage* (Oxford: Oxford University Press,1950), 46–47.

10. Ibid., 48.

11. John L. Comaroff, ed., introduction to *The Meaning of Marriage Payments* (New York: Academic Press, 1980), 1–48.

12. Ibid., 33.

13. See Barbara M. Cooper, "Women's Worth and Wedding Gift Exchange in Maradi, Niger, 1907–89," *Journal of African History* 36, no. 1 (1995): 121–40; Barbara M. Cooper, *Marriage in Maradi: Gender and Culture in a Hausa Society in Niger,*

1900–1989 (Portsmouth, NH: Heinemann, 1997), 90–110; Sara C. Mvududu, *Lobola: Its Implications for Women's Reproductive Rights* (Harare: Weaver Press, 2002), 10.

14. Colin Murray, "High Bridewealth, Migrant Labour and the Position of Women in Lesotho," *Journal of African Law* 21, no. 1 (1977): 79–96.

15. Guyer, "Colonial Situations," 121–22; Brett L. Shadle, *"Girl Cases": Marriage and Colonialism in Gusiiland, Kenya, 1890–1970* (Portsmouth, NH: Heinemann, 2006), 102–14.

16. Shadle, *Girl Cases*, 106–7.

17. Jean Allman and Victoria Tashjian, *"I Will Not Eat Stone": A Women's History of Colonial Asante* (Portsmouth, NH: Heinemann, 2000), 70–71.

18. Barbara M. Cooper, *Marriage in Maradi*, 100–101.

19. Guyer, "Colonial Situations," 120–21.

20. [[TK msp 152]]

21. The cash component of bridewealth did increase in other regions in Africa, but in the postcolonial period. For the case of Cameroon, see Guyer, "Colonial Situations," 122.

22. Lynn Schler, "The Strangers of New Bell: Immigration, Community and Public Space in Colonial Douala, Cameroon, 1914–1960" (PhD diss., Stanford University, 2001), 153–54.

23. Lynn Schler, *The Strangers of New Bell: Immigration, Public Space and Community in Colonial Douala, Cameroon, 1914–1969* (Pretoria: Unisa Press, 2008), 63.

24. For more on the concept of wealth in people, see Jan Vansina, *Paths in the Rainforests: Toward a History of Political Tradition in Equatorial Africa* (Madison: University of Wisconsin Press, 1990), 77; Jane I. Guyer, "Wealth in People, Wealth in Things—Introduction," *Journal of African History* 36, no. 1 (1995): 83–90.

25. Jane I. Guyer, "Colonial Situations in Long-Term Perspective: The Value of Beti Bridewealth," in *Money Matters: Instability, Values, and Social Payments in the Modern History of West African Communities*, ed. Jane I. Guyer (Portsmouth, NH: Heinemann, 1995), 115.

26. Older Fang informants also insisted that every man and woman was married in pre-1960 Libreville. Interviews by author: Jean Ebale Mba, Libreville, February 28, 2002; Mme. Mbele, Libreville, May 10, 2002.

27. Thérèse Biloghe, interview by author, Libreville, April 17, 2002.

28. Moise Meyo Mobiang, interview by author, Libreville, March 1, 2002.

29. Guyer, "Colonial Situations," 121.

30. Sylvain Mve Mba, interview by author, Okolassi, December 12, 2001.

31. CSSP, 4J1.mb3, Circulaires et Lettres Mgr Jérôme Adam, Libreville, 1948, Bulletin du Gabon, Janvier-Février-Mars 1948, Relevés du Questionnaire 1947–1948.

32. Interviews by author, Libreville: Marc Luc Iwenga, January 30, 2002; Okolassi: Pauline Essola, November 21, 2001; Sylvain Mve Mba, December 12, 2001; Ntoum: Emmanuel Ongone Bikeigne, May 4, 2002.

33. Benoit Messani, interview by author, Libreville, March 5, 2002.

34. Marie Bidang, interview by author, Ntoum, June 1, 2002.

35. Myènè Avekaza, interview by author, Libreville, November 21, 2001.

36. Tabitha Kanogo, *African Womanhood in Colonial Kenya, 1900–1950* (Athens: Ohio University Press, 2005), 51.

37. Joseph Lasseny Ntchoveré, interview by author, Libreville, April 16, 2002.

38. Thérèse Biloghe, interview by author, Libreville, April 17, 2002.

39. Madame Messani, interview by author, Libreville, March 7, 2002.

40. Ibid.

41. Benoit Messani, interview by author, Libreville, March 5, 2002.

42. Marie Appia Remondo, interview by author, Libreville, December 14, 2001.

43. Guyer, "Colonial Situations," 122.

44. Albertine Ntsame Ndong, interview by author, Okolassi, November 7, 2001.

45. Léotine Nseghe, interview by author, Okolassi, November 7, 2001.

46. Bernadette Angone, interview by author, Okolassi, November 21, 2001.

47. Ibid.

48. Myènè Avekaza, interview by author, Libreville, November 21, 2001.

49. Ibid.

50. Moise Meyo Mobiang, interview by author, Libreville, April 15, 2001.

51. David Edou Ntoutoume, interview by author, Ntoum, March 3, 2001; Martin Nguema, interview by author, Okolassi, November 28, 2001.

52. Emmanuel Ongone Bikeigne, interview by author, Ntoum, May 15, 2002.

53. Sylvain Meve Mba, interview by author, Okolassi, December 4, 2001.

54. Marie Solange Bikie, interview by author, Ntoum, April 2, 2002.

55. Emilie Minkue, interview by author, Okolassi, November 14, 2001.

56. David Edou Ntoutoume, interview by author, Ntoum, March 3, 2001.

57. ANG, 146, Lettre de chef Félicien Endanne to the Chef de l'Estuaire à Libreville, Situation de la rareté de l'argent a créé au point de vue des dots à la crise économique, 1931–1933, July 19, 1931.

58. Ibid.

59. ANG, 146, Lettre du Chef de la subdivision de Libreville de l'Estuaire du Nord (Kango) à M le chef de la circonscription de l'Estuaire à Libreville, Subdivision de l'Estuaire Nord, Septembre 4, 1931.

60. ANG, Microfilm Reel 51-MI-58-7, Lettre du Gouverneur-Général de l'AEF à Monsieur le Lieutenant Gouverneur du Gabon, July 4, 1933.

61. Ibid.

62. ANG, Microfilm Reel 51-MI-57, Annual Report, 1932.

63. ANG, 156, Sous Série 1E: Politique Indigène, Procès Verbal des Réunions du Conseil des Notables tenue les 20 et 21 Mars 1933 a Lambaréné, March 20–March 31, 1933.

64. ANG, 2DA (I) 10, Circonscription de l'Estuaire, Subdivision de Libreville, Rapport trimestriel, Quatrième trimestre 1932.

65. ANG, 146, Sanction de Police Administrative, Colonie du Gabon, Circonscription de l'Estuaire, Subdivision de Cocobeach, September 4, 1931. It also appears that the bridewealth fraud (*escroquerie de la dot*) was a crime prosecuted in the largely Fang region of Woleu-Ntem. A 1936 trimester report relayed that of six cases heard by the criminal court of that region in January and February, three men were convicted of escroquerie, which involved prison terms of six months. ANG, Microfilm 51-MI-63-1, Région du Gabon, Département de l'Estuaire, Rapport du Deuxième Trimestre de l'Année 1936, August 28, 1936.

66. CSSP, Boite 271, Dossier B, III, Gilbert Obembe, "Marigae chez les Mpongoué," n.d. This was likely an article that appeared in an AEF newspaper or a Catholic missionary annal in the 1930s, since the newspaper clipping is in a dossier of documents, collected by Monsignor Tardy, related to marriage in Gabon from 1930 to 1933.

67. ANG 4016, Michel Julien Faguinovery, June 22, 1932.

68. Ibid.

69. CSSP, 2D60.2a4, Document 1, "Mariage Indigène," Mgr. Martrou, Evêque du Gabon, au Governeur, April 1923.

70. ANG, Microfilm Reel 51-MI-58-7, Lettre du Gouverneur Général de l'AEF à Monsieur le Lieutenant Gouverneur du Gabon, July 4, 1933.

71. CSSP, 2D60.1b2, Le Chef de Canton Léon Mba de la zone urbaine de Libreville à Monsieur le Révérend Père Defrnould supérieur de la Mission Catholique de Sainte Marie, November 20, 1930; ANG, 146, Lettre du Chef de la Subdivision de Libreville de l'Estuaire du Nord (Kango) à M. le Chef de la circonscription l'Estuaire a Libreville, September 4, 1931; ANG, Microfilm Reel 51-MI-57, Annual Report of 1932; ANG,88, Registres des Jugements en Matière Civile, Tribunal Indigène du premier degré, Subdivision de Libreville, Case 34, May 30, 1936; ANG, Microfilm Reel 51-MI-64-2, Note Pour M. le Chef de la Subdivision, Président de la Subdivision, Président du Tribunal Indigène de premier Degré de LBV, Réponses du Chef de Subdivision, November 26, 1936; ANG, Microfilm Reel 51-MI-64-2, AEF, Région du Gabon, Justice Indigène, Tribunal, Procès-Verbal. November 26, 1936; ANG, 88, Registres des Jugements en Matière Civile, Tribunal Indigène du 1er degré, Subdivision de Libreville, Case 5, February 13, 1937.

72. ANG, 104, Région de l'Estuaire, Tribunal du deuxième degré du Département de l'Estuaire. Libreville. Jugement rendus en matière Répressive #'s 338 du 19 mars 1935 ay 26 aout 1939: Case 19, May 20, 1937; Case 11, May 30,1937; Case 34, December 13, 1937; Case 20, June 9, 1938; ANG, 2DA (I) 11, Région de l'Estuaire. Justice Civil Indigène. Les Affaires Opposant les Individus Traitées au Tribunal du 1er degré de la Subdivision de Libreville, May 9, 1939; ANG, 2DA(I)5, Rapport Politique Semestriel, Deuxième Semestre, Département de l'Estuaire, Subdivision de Libreville, 1938; ANG, 1916, Procès Verbaux des Séances du Conseil Représentatif du Gabon, March 15, 1950; Centre d'Archives d'Outre Mer (hereafter cited as CAOM), AEF / GGAEF/5D56, Lettre du Gouverneur Chef du Territoire du Gabon à M. le GG de l'AEF, February 27, 1947; JC Bobeyeme, "La jeunesse fang," Journal AEF, December 12, 1947, CAOM, AEF/ GGAEF/5D56, Lettre du l'Inspecteur Général du Travail de l'AEF à M. le Directeur des Affaires Politiques et Sociales, December 13, 1947; ANG, 91, Registres des Jugements en Matière Civile, Registres des Audiences Publiques Conciliation, Commune de Libreville, July 9, 1956; Léon Mba, "Discours Prononcé à Port-Gentil par le Président de la République," in Bulletin Quotidien de l'Agence Gabonaise d'Information, Bulletin Spécial (Libreville, 1963), 4; interviews by author in Okolassi: Léontine Nseghe, November 7, 2001; Emilie Minkue, November 14, 2001; Achey Oyeng, November 14, 2001; Martine Ada Ndong, November 21, 2001; Pauline Essola, November 21, 2001; Sylvain Mve Mba, December 4, 2001; Agathe Marcelle Iwenga, January 13, 2002; interviews by author in Libreville: Raphaël Sala, February 14, 2002; Ella Ntoutoume, February 17, 2002; Bernadette Angone, February 21, 2002; Jeanne Antoinette Ella, March 27, 2002; Céline Escola Ntoutoume, March 28, 2002; Thérèse Biloghe, April 17, 2002; Antoinette Awuta, June 5, 2002; interviews by author in Ntoum: David Edou Ntoutoume, April 2, 2001; Marie Solange Bikie, April 2, 2002.

73. CSSP, 5b1.10b2, 18, Notes sur le projet de réglementation de mariage indigène, September 11, 1921; CSSP, 5b1.10b2, 12, Rapport de Père Bouvier, "En Voyage dans l'Abanga," March 15, 1925; CSSP, 2D60.1b2, Le Chef de Canton Léon Mba de la zone urbaine de Libreville à Monsieur le Révérend Père Defranould supérieur de la

Mission Catholique de Sainte Marie, November 20, 1930; ANG, 146, Lettre du Chef de la Subdivision de Libreville de l'Estuaire du Nord (Kango) à M. le Chef de la circonscription l'Estuaire a Libreville, September 4, 1931; ANG, Microfilm Reel 51-MI-57, Annual Report of 1932; ANG,88, Registres des Jugements en Matière Civile, Tribunal Indigène du 1er degré, Subdivision de Libreville, Case 34, May 30, 1936; ANG, Microfilm Reel 51-MI-64-2, Note Pour M. le Chef de la Subdivision, Président de la Subdivision, Président du Tribunal Indigène de 1er Degré de LBV, Réponses du Chef de Subdivision, November 26, 1936; ANG, Microfilm Reel 51-MI-64-2, AEF, Région du Gabon, Justice Indigène, Tribunal, Procès-Verbal. November 26, 1936; ANG, 88, Registres des Jugements en Matière Civile, Tribunal Indigène du 1er degré, Subdivision de Libreville, Case 5, February 13, 1937; ANG, 104, Région de l'Estuaire, Tribunal du deuxième degré du Département de l'Estuaire. Libreville. Jugement rendus en matière Répressive #'s 338 du 19 mars 1935 ay 26 aout 1939, Case 19, May 20, 1937; ANG, 104 Répertoire des Collections de Registres Divers. Archives Générales, Case 11, May 30,1937; ANG, 104, Brochure entité Répertoire des Collections de Registres Divers. Archives Générales, Case 34, December 13, 1937; ANG, 104, Région de l'Estuaire, Tribunal du 2eme degré du Département de l'Estuaire, Libreville, Jugement rendus en matière Répressive #'s 338 du 19 mars 1935 ay 26 aout 1939, Case 20, June 9, 1938; ANG, 2DA (I) 11, Région de l'Estuaire. Justice Civil Indigène. Les Affaires Opposant les Individus Traitées au Tribunal du 1er degré de la Subdivision de Libreville, May 9, 1939; ANG, 2DA(I)5, Rapport Politique Semestriel, Deuxième Semestre, Département de l'Estuaire, Subdivision de Libreville, 1938; ANG, 1916, Procès Verbaux des Séances du Conseil Représentatif du Gabon, March 15, 1950; 1950; CAOM, AEF/GGAEF/ 5D56, Lettre du Gouverneur Chef du Territoire du Gabon à M. le GG de l'AEF, February 27, 1947; JC Bobeyeme, "La jeunesse fang," *Journal AEF*, December 12, 1947, CAOM, AEF/GGAEF/5D56, Lettre de l'Inspecteur Général du Travail de l'AEF à M. le Directeur des Affaires Politiques et Sociales, December 13, 1947; Léon Mba, "Discours Prononcé à Port-Gentil par le Président de la République," *Bulletin Quotidien de l'Agence Gabonaise d'Information, Bulletin Spécial* (Libreville, 1963): 4; ANG, 91, Registres des Jugements en Matière Civile, Registres des Audiences Publiques Conciliation, Commune de Libreville, July 9, 1956; oral interviews by author in Okolassi: Léotine Nseghe, November 7, 2001; Emilie Minkue, November 14, 2001; Achey Oyeng, November 14, 2001; Martine Ada Ndong, November 21, 2001; Pauline Essola, November 21, 2001; Sylvain Mve Mba, December 4, 2001; Agathe Marcelle Iwenga, January 13, 2002; oral interviews by author in Libreville: Raphaël Sala, February 14, 2002; Ella Ntoutoume, February 17, 2002; Bernadette Angone, February 21, 2002; Jeanne Antoinette Ella, March 27, 2002; Céline Escola Ntoutoume, March 28, 2002; Thérèse Biloghe, April 17, 2002; Antoinette Awuta, June 5, 2002; oral interviews by author in Ntoum: David Edou Ntoutoume, April 2, 2001; Marie Solange Bikie, April 2, 2002.

74. CAOM, AEF/GGAEF5D56, Lettre du l'Inspecteur Général du Travail de l'AEF à M. le Directeur des Affaires Politiques et Sociales, December 13, 1947; Rufin Didzambou, "Les migrations de salariat au Gabon de 1843 à 1960: Processus et incidences" (PhD diss., Université de Lille II, 1995), 78–79; Clotaire Messi Me Nang, "Les travailleurs des chantiers forestiers du Gabon: Hybridité et invisibilité d'une culture ouvrière, 1892–1962" (PhD diss., Université de Paris I, 2007), 176.

75. Guyer, "Colonial Situations," 124–25.

76. Shadle, *Girl Cases*, 106.

77. Fore more on the cost of living in Libreville, see Guy Lasserre, *Libreville: La ville et sa région* (Paris: Colin, 1958); Jeremy M. Rich, *A Workman Is Worthy of His Meat: Food and Colonialism in the Gabon Estuary* (Lincoln: University of Nebraska Press, 2007).

78. Félix Éboué, *Politique indigène de L'Afrique Equatoriale Française* (Brazzaville: Imprimerie officielle de l'Afrique Equatoriale Française, 1941).

79. Elikia Mbokolo, "French Colonial Policy in Equatorial Africa in the 1940s and 1950s," in *The Transfer of Power in Africa*, ed. Prosser Gifford and William R. Louis (Hartford, CT: Yale University Press, 1982), 199.

80. John A. Ballard, "The Development of Political Parties in French Equatorial Africa" (PhD diss., Fletcher School of Law and Diplomacy, Tufts University, 1963), 30–31.

81. Frederick Cooper, *Decolonization and African Society: The Labor Question in French and British Africa* (Cambridge: Cambridge University Press, 1996), 175.

82. Ibid., 2–5; Lisa A. Lindsay, *Working with Gender: Wage Labor and Social Change in Southwestern Nigeria* (Portsmouth, NH: Heinemann, 2003), 105–26.

83. Frederick Cooper, *Decolonization and African Society*, 2.

84. ANG, Sous Série 1E, 1514/C.I, Letter from Jean-Hilaire Aubame, Député du Gabon, à Monsieur le Haut-Commissaire de la République Gouverneur Général de l'AEF, February 24, 1949.

85. CAOM: AEF/GGAEF5D256, Lettre du Gouverneur Général de l'AEF, Messieurs les Gouv. Chefs de Territoire, September 7, 1950; AEF/GGAEF5D256, Lettre du Ministre de la France d'Outre-Mer Nicolay à M le GG de l'AEF, April 17, 1951; AEF/GGAEF5D256, Etudes sur la Dot, Fait pour le Conseil coutumier: Propositions de M. Kwame Maurice, Président Général et Fondateur du CCA, Assesseur prés le tribunal coutumier de Poto-Poto, August 3, 1951.

86. CAOM, FM/1ffpol/2150/3, Note sur le Problème des Dots pour le haut-commissaire et par délégation Le délégué de l'AEF à Paris, date illegible.

87. Ibid.

88. CAOM, FM/1affpol/2150/3, Note pour M. le Délégué à Paris du haut-commissaire de la République en AEF du Direction des Affaires Politique, February 8, 1950.

89. CAOM, AEF/GGAEF5D256, Avant Propos de Décret, April 17, 1951.

90. CAOM, Avant Propos de Décret, April 17, 1951.

91. Débats de l'Assemblé Territoriale du Gabon, Session Ordinaire, 25 Avril–17 Mai 1952; Assemblée Territoriale du Gabon, May 2, 1952.

92. Ibid.

93. Ibid.

94. Ibid.

95. Débats de l'Assemblé Territoriale du Gabon, Session Ordinaire, 25 Avril–17 Mai 1952; Assemblée Territoriale du Gabon, May 8, 1952.

96. Ibid.

97. Débats de l'Assemblé Territoriale du Gabon, Session Ordinaire, 25 Avril–17 Mai 1952; Assemblée Territoriale du Gabon, May 14, 1952.

98. Jeanne Maddox Toungara, "Changing the Meaning of Marriage: Women and Family Law in Côte D'Ivoire," in *African Feminism: The Politics of Survival in Sub-Saharan Africa*, ed. Gwendolyn Mikell (Philadelphia: University of Pennsylvania Press, 1997), 55–57.

99. Barbara M. Cooper, *Marriage in Maradi*, 16.

100. Shadle, *Girl Cases*, 111–14.

101. La Fondation du Général de Gaulle, arrêté 1021 du 17 Décembre 1940, Marriage Loans for Natives of FEA, Law Number 1.021 that appeared in January 1, 1941, edition of the *Journal official*. ANG, 115, Letter from Governor-General Laurentie to M. le Chef du Territoire du Gabon, 116/APAG, March 15, 1942.

102. Aix, AEF/GGAEF5D56, Letter 95/APAG, Lettre du GG de L'AEF à M. Les Chefs de Territoire de Brazzaville, Libreville, Bangui, Port Lamy, August 25, 1941.

103. For more on Vichy-controlled French West Africa, see Ruth Ginio, *French Colonialism Unmasked: The Vichy Years in French West Africa* (Lincoln: University of Nebraska Press, 2006),161–72. For an analysis of Vichy colonial policies elsewhere in the French Empire, see Eric T. Jennings, *Vichy in the Tropics: Pétain's National Revolution in Madagascar, Guadeloupe, and Indochina, 1940–1944* (Stanford, CA: Stanford University Press, 2001).

104. ANG, 810, Letter from the Gouverneur Général du territoire du Gabon à M le chef du département de l'Estuaire, March 13, 1942.

105. CAOM, AEF/GGAEF5D256, Arrêté Instituant le prêt aux mariage et attribuant compétence en la matière au Gouverneurs Chefs de Territoires, August 30, 1950.

106. ANG, 115, Letter from the Gouverneur p.i. Chef du Territoire du Gabon aux Messieurs les chef du département, December 1941.

107. ANG, 810, Letter from the Gouverneur Général du territoire du Gabon à M le chef du département de l'Estuaire, August 31, 1942.

108. Ibid.; ANG, 115, Letter from the Gouverneur p.i. Chef du Territoire du Gabon aux Messieurs les chef du département, November 17, 1945.

109. ANG, 870, Sous Série 1E, Demandes de Prêts aux Mariages, 1942, 1945, 1946, 1947, AG/84, Le Gouverneur, chef du territoire du Gabon à Monsieur le Gouverneur Général de l'AEF, January 26, 1942.

110. ANG 870, Sous Série 1E, Prêts aux mariages 1942–45–46, L'administrateur des colonies N. Sadoul, Chef du Département du Djouah à Monsieur le Gouverneur des Colonies, Chef du Territoire du Gabon, January 7, 1942.

111. ANG 870, Sous Série 1E, Prêts aux mariages 1942–45–46, L'administrateur des colonies N. Sadoul, Chef du Département du Djouah à Monsieur le Gouverneur des Colonies, Chef du Territoire du Gabon, March 4, 1942.

112. ANG, 870, Sous Série 1E, Demandes de Prêts aux Mariages, 1942, 1945, 1946, 1947, Le Gouverneur, chef du territoire du Gabon à Monsieur le chef du département du Djouah, Aide aux jeunes célibataires désirant se marier, March 14, 1942.

113. ANG 870, Sous Série 1E, Prêts aux marriages 1942–45–46, Le Gouverneur, chef du territoire du Gabon à Monsieur de le chef du département de la Nyanja, January 24, 1942.

114. ANG, 870, Sous Série 1E, Demandes de Prêts aux Mariages, 1942, 1945, 1946, 1947, Le Gouverneur, chef du territoire du Gabon a Monsieur le gouverneur Général de l'Afrique Equatoriale française, January 26, 1942; ANG, 870, Sous Série 1E, Demandes de Prêts aux Mariages, 1942, 1945, 1946, 1947, Territoire du Gabon ANG, Territoire du Gabon, Département de l'Estuaire, Extrait des décision, Dossier prêts aux mariage, April 28, 1943; ANG, 870, Prêts aux Mariages, La Fondation du Général de Gaulle, arrêté 1021 du 17 Décembre 1940, December 12, 1946; ANG, 690, Sous Série 1E, Demandes de prêts aux mariages année 1947, n.d.

115. ANG, 870, Sous Série 1E, Demandes de Prêts aux Mariages, 1942, 1945, 1946, 1947, Le Gouverneur des colonies, chef du territoire du Gabon à Monsieur le Gouverneur général de l'Afrique Equatoriale française, February 1942.

116. CAOM, FM /1affpol/2150/3, Prêt aux mariage, date illegible.

117. Registres des Jugements en Matière Civile, Registres des Audiences Publiques Conciliation, Commune de Libreville, July 9, 1956; interviews by author in Okolassi: Léotine Nseghe, November 7, 2001; Emilie Minkue, November 14, 2001; Achey Oyeng, November 14, 2001; Pauline Essola, November 21, 2001; Sylvain Mve Mba, December 4, 2001; interviews by author in Libreville: Raphaël Sala, February 14, 2002; Ella Ntoutoume, February 17, 2002; Thérèse Biloghe, April 17, 2002; Antoinette Awuta, June 5, 2002; interviews by author in Ntoum: David Edou Ntoutoume, April 2, 2001; Marie Solange Bikie, April 2, 2002.

118. ANG 870, Sous Série 1E, Prêts aux mariages 1942–45–46, Donation de Gaulle, le chef du bureau de l'administration général, January 19, 1942.

119. ANG, 870, Letter 46, Lettre du Chef du Département de l'Estuaire à M. le Gouverneur, Chef du Territoire du Gabon, January 26, 1945.

120. ANG, 870, Sous Série 1E, Demandes de Prêts aux Mariages, 1942, 1945, 1946, 1947, Télégramme-Lettre, APAG/592 Le Gouverneur Général à Monsieur le Gouverneur du Gabon, November 28, 1948; ANG, 870, Sous Série 1E, Demandes de Prêts aux Mariages, 1942, 1945, 1946, 1947, AG/1143, Le gouverneur, chef du territoire du Gabon (M. Assier de Pompignan) a M. le Gouverneur Général AEF, December 21, 1942.

121. ANG, 870, Letter 3 269, l'Administrateur-Maire de Libreville à Monsieur le Gouverneur, Chef du territoire du Gabon, April 4, 1946.

122. ANG, 690, Demandes de prêts aux mariages années 1947, Henri Ango, Dessinateur aide-topographe en service aux travaux publics a Libreville à Monsieur le Gouverneur des colonies, chef du territoire dur Gabon, sous couverture de M. l'ingénieur du chef du service des travaux publics au Gabon, February 17, 1947.

123. ANG, 690, Demandes de prêts aux mariages années 1947, Henri Ango, Dessinateur en service aux travaux publics a Monsieur le Gouverneur, chef du territoire du Gabon, s/c de Monsieur le chef du service des travaux publics au Gabon, August 7, 1947.

124. ANG, 690, Demandes de prêts aux mariages années 1947, Letter 1132/APS, Le Gouverneur des colonies, chef de la territoire du Gabon à monsieur le chef du service des travaux publics du Gabon, September 12, 1947. For example, see the application of Gilbert Obiang, who worked as a nurse in Libreville. ANG, Sous Série 1E, 174, Affaires Concernant les Demandes de Prêts aux mariages, Décision, Affaires Sociales 62/ AS, January 3 1952; ANG, Sous Série 1E, 174, Affaires Concernant les Demandes de Prêts aux mariages, Décision, Affaires Sociales 62/ AS, January 14, 1952.

125. ANG, 690, Demandes de prêts aux mariages années 1947, Letter 686/TP, En Retour à M. le Gouverneur, Chef du Territoire du Gabon, October 22, 1947.

126. Other successful applications that year included: ANG, 690, Demandes de prêts aux mariages années 1947, Affaires Politiques 1302/APS, Décision Alphonse Rendjogo, Libreville, November 27, 1947; ANG, 690, Demandes de prêts aux mariages années 1947, Affaires Politiques 766/APS, Décision Paul Taty, July 10, 1947.

127. David W. Cohen, "Pim's Doorway," in *The Combing of History* (Chicago: University of Chicago Press, 1994), 112–47.

CHAPTER 5: JURISPRUDENCE: MARRIAGE AND DIVORCE LAW

1. Archives Nationales du Gabon (hereafter cited as ANG), 2DA(I)5. Rapport Politique Semestriel, deuxième semestre 1938, Département de l'Estuaire, Subdivision de Libreville.

2. ANG, 4015, Georges Balandier, Institut d'Etudes Centre Africaines. *Rapports Préliminaires de la Mission d'Information Scientifique en Pays Fang*, January 24, 1949–March 20, 1949.

3. Centre d'Archives d'Outre Mer (hereafter cited as CAOM), AEF/GGAEF/4ID47, Rapport Politique du Premier Semestre de l'Ogouée-Maritime, 1939; ANG, 51-MI-65-2, Rapport politique du premier semestre de l'Estuaire, Etat d'Esprit des Populations, Subdivision de Kango, 1943; ANG, Sous Série 1E, Territoire du Gabon, Région de l'Estuaire, Rapport Politique du 1947.

4. CAOM, AEF/GGAEF/5D56, Note pour M. le Gouverneur Général au Sujet de la Note de M. le Médecin Général concernant la Politique sociale de l'indigène, July 26, 1942; CAOM, AEF/GGAEF/5D56, Lettre 20, Circulaire du Gouverneur Général de l'AEF aux M. les Gouverneurs Chefs de Territoire, February 5, 1946.

5. CAOM, AEF/GGAEF/4ID47, Rapport Politique du Premier Semestre de l'Ogouée-Maritime, 1939; ANG, 51-MI-65-2, Rapport Politique du Gabon 1947.

6. The question of women's choice in marriage was also at the center of colonial debates on marriage law in FOA. Marie Rodet, "Gender, Customs, and Colonial Law in French Sudan, 1918–1939," *Cahiers d'etudes africaines* 47, nos. 187–88 (2007): 583–602.

7. As early as 1897, the colonial administration in Gabon decreed that all of the colony's inhabitants were subject to the rule of law in courts administered by colonial officials. Silvère Ngoundos Idourah, *Colonisation et confiscation de la justice en Afrique: L'administration de la justice au Gabon, Moyen-Congo, Oubangui-Chari et Tchad de la création des colonies à l'aube des indépendances* (Paris: L'Harmattan, 2001), 219.

8. The same can be said for FOA, in which the majority of civil cases heard by colonial courts involved questions about marriage. Marie Rodet, "Continuum of Gendered Violence: The Colonial Female Desertion as a Customary Criminal Offense, French Soudan, 1900–1949," in *Domestic Violence and the Law*, ed. Emily S. Burrill, Richard L. Roberts, and Elizabeth Thornberry (Athens: Ohio University Press, 2010), 74–93.

9. ANG, Microfilm Reel 51-MI-21, Rapport Trimestriel pour le Quatriéme Trimestre 1909.

10. ANG, Microfilm Reel 51-MI-25, Rapport Annuel 1912.

11. Idourah, *Colonisation et confiscation*, 241.

12. ANG, Microfilm Reel 51-MI-60, Rapport Annuel du Département de l'Estuaire 1934. ANG, Microfilm Reel MI-651, Inspection des Affaires Administratives. Rapport d'Ensemble sur la Vérification du Département de l'Estuaire et de la Commune Mixte de Libreville, 1940.

13. Idourah, *Colonisation et confiscation*, 242.

14. ANG, Sous Série 2D(I)10, Circonscription de l'Estuaire, Subdivision de Libreville, Rapport Trimestriel, Quatrième Trimestre 1934. The law of 1936 reorganizing native justice specified, "In civil and commercial matters, the attempt at conciliation is obligatory. Village and tribal chiefs are invested with the power to reconcile parties who solicit them with their litigation when the parties are composed of members of their jurisdiction. If a chief is not available, a native assessor of the court of the first degree will suffice. The agreement reached upon in the presence of the conciliator and parties acquires authority of an agreement when written according to the law of the 29 September 1920." *Journal Officiel de l'Afrique Equatoriale Française*, May 13, 1937.

15. Burrill, Roberts, and Thornberry, introduction to *Domestic Violence and the Law*, 14.

16. AEF/GGAEF/4D138, Annual Report of 1932.

17. ANG, Microfilm Reel 51MI57, Letter 819, Lettre de Monsieur le Lieutenant Gouverneur du Gabon au Gouverneur Générale de l'AEF, November 2, 1932.

18. CAOM, AEF/GGAEF/41D38, Annual Report of 1932.

19. CAOM, AEF/GGAEF/ 5D56, "Coutumes Galoases, Pahouines, Akelaises."

20. AEF, GGAEF/ 5D56/ Projet d'arrêté: Règlementant le mariage indigène en pays fang, 1936.

21. ANG, Microfilm Reel 51MI57, Annual Report 1932.

22. ANG, Sous Série 1E, Politique Indigène, Procès-Verbal des Réunions du Conseil des Notables Tenues les 20 et 21 Mars a Lambaréné, March 21, 1933; ANG, Microfilm Reel 51-MI-63-1, Région du Gabon, Département de l'Estuaire. Rapport du 2eme Trimestre, de l'Année 1936, August 28, 1936; ANG, Microfilm Reel MI-651, Inspection des Affaires Administratives. Rapport d'Ensemble sur la Vérification du Département de l'Estuaire et de la Commune Mixte de Libreville, 1940.

23. ANG, Microfilm Reel 51-MI-64-2, Lettre de la population indigène Mariée (Libreville) a M. le Gouverneur General de l'AEF, August 8, 1936.

24. ANG, Microfilm Reel 51MI641, Notes de l'Inspecteur des Affaires Administratives. Enquête sur le Commandement dans la Subdivision de Kango, October 22, 1936.

25. ANG, Microfilm Reel 51MI641, Enquête sur le Commandement dans la Subdivision de Kango, October 22, 1936.

26. Ibid.

27. Ibid.

28. Sous Série 1E, 132, Nso Nze chef de Canton de l'Abanga Samkita à Ntoum à M. Le Chef de la Subdivision de Ndjolé à Monsieur l'Administrateur des Colonies, Chef du département de l'OgoouéMaritime à PortGentil, June 23, 1939.

29. Ibid.

30. Biologhe Metou, interview by author, Okolassi, November 21, 2001.

31. CAOM, AEF/GGAEF/4(1)D44, Note pour le Président du Tribunal Indigène de premier degré de Libreville, November 26, 1936.

32. Léon Mba, "Essai de droit coutumier pahouin," in Ecrits ethnographiques (Libreville: Raponda Walker, 2001), 50.

33. ANG, Mircofilm Reel 51MI641, Lettre de l'Administrateur en Chef Soalhat, Inspecteur des Affaires Administratives à M. le Gouverneur Général de l'AEF, December 12, 1936.

34. CAOM, AEF/GGAEF/4(1)D44, Note le Président du Tribunal Indigène de premier degré de Libreville, November 26, 1936; ANG, Microfilm Reel 51-MI-64-2, Letter 34, Gouvernement Général de l'AEF, Affaires Politiques et Administration Générale, Notes sur l'Inspection de la Subdivision de Libreville, Le Directeur des Affaires Politique et de l'Administration Générale, January 21, 1937.

35. Sean Hawkins, "'The Woman in Question': Marriage and Identity in the Colonial Courts of Northern Ghana, 1907–1954," in Women in African Colonial Histories, ed. Jean Allman, Susan Geiger, and Nakanyike Musisi (Bloomington: Indiana University Press, 2002), 118.

36. CAOM, AEF/GGAEF/4(1)D44, Note pour le Président du Tribunal Indigène de premier degré de Libreville, November 26, 1936.

37. Ibid.

38. ANG, Microfilm Reel 51-MI-64-2, Lettre des Assesseurs MASSAMBA et Ndende Jean-Baptiste à M. e Gouverneur de l'AEF, s/c de Messieurs le Maire de la Commune et le Lieutenant Gouverneur du Gabon, December 30, 1936.

39. ANG, Microfilm Reel 51-MI-64-2, Lettre des Assesseurs MASSAMBA et Ndende, December 30, 1936.

40. CAOM AEF/GGAEF/4(1)D44, Note pour Président du Tribunal Indigène de premier degré de Libreville, November 26, 1936.

41. In a defensive response to the investigation, administrators in the subdivision retorted: "The commander of the subdivision does his best to check up on the legal disputes submitted to the conciliators, but he cannot claim to instruct and mediate all the civil conflicts himself. If all matters decided by the conciliators were to be looked over as outlined in the law of the 20 September 1920, he wouldn't have any time to do his work." In CAOM, AEF/GGAEF/4(1)D44, Note pour le Président du Tribunal Indigène de premier degré de Libreville, November 26, 1936; ANG, Microfilm Reel 51MI642, Observations Auxquelles a Donné Lieu L'inspection de la Subdivision de LBV par M. Soalhat, Inspecteur des Affaires Administratives du Gabon. Vérification de la Tenue des Registres et Carnets Prévus par les Règlements et Instructions, December 2, 1936.

42. Barbara M. Cooper, *Marriage in Maradi: Gender and Culture in a Hausa Society in Niger, 1900–1989* (Portsmouth, NH: Heinemann, 1997), 14–15.

43. Félix Éboué, *Politique Indigène de L'Afrique Equatoriale Française* (Brazzaville: Imprimerie officielle de l'Afrique Equatoriale Française, 1941), 20–21.

44. ANG, 51-MI-65-2, Bulletin de Renseignements Politiques, "Tribunaux Coutumier," September 25, 1946.

45. ANG, Microfilm 51-MI-65-2, Bulletin de Renseignements Politiques, September 1946.

46. CAOM, AEF/GGAEF/5D56, Documentation sur le Mariage Africain en AEF, July 10, 1950.

47. CAOM, AEF/GGAEF/5D56, Circulaire du GG de l'aef aux M. les Gouverneurs Chefs de Territoire, Libreville, Bangui, FortLamy, et Brazzaville, February 5, 1946.

48. CAOM, AEF/GGAEF/5D56, Letter 391, Lettre du GG de l'aef aux Messieurs les Chefs de Territoire Gabon, Moyen-Congo, OubanguiChari, July 6, 1948.

49. ANG, 146, Letter 418, Lettre de L'Administrateur des Colonies, H. Tastevin, Chef de la Circonscription de l'Estuaire à M. Le Chef de la Subdivision de Libreville, June 27, 1944.

50. Gaston Rapotchombo, *Hommage à Léon Mba* (Libreville: Ministère de l'Information, des Postes et Télécommunications de la République gabonaise 1970), 62–66, 75–107.

51. Dominique Etoughe, *Justice indigènee et essor du droit coutumier au Gabon: La contribution de Léon M'ba, 1924–1938* (Paris: L'Harmattan, 2007), 27–28.

52. Mba, "Essai de droit coutumier," 75.

53. Ibid., 76–77.

54. Ibid.

55. Florence Bernault, *Démocraties ambiguës en Afrique centrale: Congo-Brazzaville, Gabon, 1940–1965* (Paris: Karthala, 1996), 217.

56. Etoughe, *Justice indigène*, 118–19.

57. Archives Générales des Pères de Saint-Esprit de Chevilly-Larue (hereafter cited as CSSP), 2D60.2a4, Document 1, Mariage Indigène, April 1923 Report by Monseigneur Martrou, Evêque de Gabon to the Governor.

58. CSSP, 2D60.3A1, "La Pauvre Femme Africaine" article Monseigneur Tardy in les *Annales des Pères du SaintEsprit*, Janvier 1936.

59. CSSP, 2D60.2a4 Document 5, Projet de Règlement des mariages entre indigènes de race Fang, Article XIII, October 1942.

60. CSSP, Projet de Règlement, Article XIII, October 1942.

61. ANG, 51-MI-65-2, Bulletin de Renseignements Politiques, "Consultation par Race," September 25, 1946.

62. CSSP, 2D60.2a4, Congres pahouin de Mitzic, 1.

63. Ibid., 3.

64. CAOM, AEF/GGAEF/5D56, Six Veux du Conseil Représentatif du Gabon sur la Question de la taxe sur les polygames, Regnault, Président de l'Assemblé, May 1947.

65. Georges Balandier, *The Sociology of Black Africa: Social Dynamics in Central Africa*, trans. Douglas Garman (New York: Praeger, 1970), 199.

66. CSSP, 2D60.2a4, *Congrès Pahouin de Mitzic*, 4.

67. Ibid., 3.

68. AIX, AEF/GGAEF/15D1, Conseil Représentatif du Gabon, ProcèsVerbal, March 24, 1948.

69. Assemblée Territoriale du Gabon, Séance du 14 Mai 1952, Mariage Devant le Chef de Canton.

70. ANG, Conseils et Assemblées, 1916, Procès Verbaux des Séances du Conseil Représentatif du Gabon, March 15, 1960; ANG, Conseils et Assemblés, 1916, Procès Verbaux des Séances du Conseil Représentatif du Gabon, March 2, 1952; Assemblée Territoriale du Gabon, Séance du 2 Mai 1952, Débats de l'Assemblée Territoriale du Gabon, Session Ordinaire 25 Avril–17 Mai 1952; Assemblée Territoriale du Gabon, Séance du 8 Mai 1952, Débats de l'Assemblée Territoriale du Gabon, Session Ordinaire 25 Avril–17 Mai 1952; Assemblée Territoriale du Gabon, Séance du 14 Mai 1952, Débats de l'Assemblée Territoriale du Gabon, Session Ordinaire 25 Avril–17 Mai 1952.

71. Assemblée Territorial du Gabon, Débats de l'Assemblée Territorial du Gabon, Session Ordinaire, April 25–May 17 1952, May 8, 1952.

72. Assemblée Territorial du Gabon, Débats de l'Assemblée Territorial du Gabon, Session Ordinaire, April 25–May 17, 1952, May 14, 1952.

73. Assemblée Territorial du Gabon, May 14, 1952.

74. Ibid.

75. ANG: Register 91,City of Libreville, Conciliation Hearings, January 1956 to November 1957; Register 112, Afrique Equatoriale Française, Région de l'Estuaire, Registre des Jugements, Tribunal Coutumier, November 4, 1950, to May 1, 1955; Register 116, Région de l'Estuaire. District de Libreville. Tribunal du premier degré et deuxième degré, 1956–1959.

76. Céline Essola Ntoutoume, interview by author, Libreville, March 28, 2002.

77. ANG: Register 91, City of Libreville, Conciliation Hearings, January 1956 to November 1957; Register 112, Afrique Equatoriale Française, Région de l'Estuaire, Registre des Jugements, Tribunal Coutumier, November 4, 1950, to May 1, 1955; Register 116, Région de l'Estuaire. District de Libreville. Tribunal du premier dégré et deuxième degré, 1956–1959.

78. Rodet, "Continuum of Gendered Violence," 82–87.

79. For example, see ANG, Register 91, Henri George Obame versus Monique Mekang, November 4, 1957.

80. ANG, Register 91, Jean Bernard Ngoua versus Marie Lucienne, November 11, 1957.

81. For a similar case, see ANG, Register 112: Case 19, February 1, 1951.

82. ANG, Register 107: Appeal 3, Toussaint Dowet-Pither versus Emilienne Gondjout, May 23, 1949.

83. ANG, 2DA(I)11, Région de l'Estuaire, Justice Civil Indigène, Les Affaires Opposant les Individus Traitées au Tribunal du Premier Degré de la Subdivision de Libreville, Jean-Baptiste Asse Bekale vs. Bekale Mba, May 5, 1939.

84. Mba, "Essai de droit coutumier," 73–74.

85. ANG, Lettre du Gouverneur Général de l'Afrique Equatorial Française à Monsieur le Chef du Territoire du Gabon, Libreville, 116/APAG, March 13, 1942.

86. Register 116: Augustin Mougangue versus Pauline Babina, June 7, 1958.

87. ANG, Register 107: Case 1, October 10, 1950, Pauline Matanga versus Antoine Figuereido.

88. See also the following cases in which the second-degree court reversed decisions by the first-degree court and judged that relationships were either formal engagements or marriages that entailed the reimbursement of goods or cash to the plaintiff. ANG, Register 116: Vincent Waga versus Cathérine Betoe, November 11, 1959; Maurice Ntoutoume versus Mlle. Marie Christine, October 31, 1959.

89. ANG, Register 112: Case 60, February 9, 1952.

90. ANG, Register 107: Affaire Nguema Mba, Rapt de femme, Case 36, May 10, 1949.

91. ANG, Register 112: Case 9, January 1951; Case 37, May 15, 1951; Case 59, February 3, 1952; January 1953; Case 113, June 15, 1953; Case 114, June 16, 1953; Case 126, December 12, 1953; Case 128, March 16, 1954; Case 169, November 16, 1954.

92. ANG, Register 116: Gabriel Nguema versus Christine Debani, April 11, 1959; Joseph Tamba versus Flonorine Mobonassi, November 28, 1959; Georges Mombo versus Marie Essime Moeye, February 2, 1960.

93. Jean Allman and Victoria Tashjian, "I Will Not Eat Stone": A Women's History of Colonial Asante (Portsmouth, NH: Heinemann, 2000), 66–68.

94. ANG, Register 116: Appel jugement de tribunal du premier degré de Libreville, Jean François Bekale versus Essonne Obone, November 22, 1957.

95. ANG, Register 112: Case 13, January 16, 1951; Case 31, April 16, 1951; Case 42, July 9, 1951; Case 45, October 16, 1951; Case 69, May 31, 1952; Case 76, June 30, 1952; Case 83, December 2, 1952; Case 134, January 1954.

96. ANG, Register 112: Case 134, January 15, 1954.

97. ANG, Register 107: Case 1, Eyang Emane versus Philippe Mouloungui, April 16, 1948.

98. M. Auganeur, "L'enfant dans la famille gabonaise," Bulletin de la Sociétés des Recherches Congolaises 3 (1923):15–21.

99. Ibid., 17; Mba, "Essai de droit coutumier," 88–89.

100. Louise Tati, née Délicat, interview by author, Libreville, December 9, 2002.

101. ANG, Register 106: Affaire Mba Meyo tentative de correction d'assesseur indigènes, Jugements 50 du 18 septembre 1941. ANG, Register 116: Appel Jugements 140 du 5/29/57 du tribunal du premier degré de Libreville, January 3, 1958; Appel Jugements du 4/4/58 du tribunal du premier degré de Libreville, July 7, 1958; El Hadj Mhamadou Bekale Ignace (perhaps the father, brother, or uncle of the wife) versus Louis Obame Nang, November 15, 1959; Ekomie Omoghe versus Paul Nkoghe Mba, April 4, 1959.

102. ANG, 2DA(I)11, Jean-Baptiste Asse Bekale versus Mba Bekale, May 19, 1939. ANG, Register 116: Appel Jugements du Tribunal premier degré Commune de Libreville: Bekale Ignace El Hadj Mhamadou versus Louis Obame Nang, November

15, 1957; Nzé Mba versus Justin Bekale, April 11, 1959; ANG, Register 116: Paul Emane Richard versus Juliette Eto, January 4, 1957; El Hadj Mhamadou Bekale Ignace versus Louis Nang Obame, November 15, 1957; Paul Bekale versus Mme. Bekale Marie Louise Condja, January 1, 1958.

103. ANG, Register 91, Tribunal Indigène de Premier Degré, Registres des Audiences Publique Conciliation, Commune de Libreville, Joseph Ngoua versus MarieThérèse Betoe, August 6, 1956.

104. Ibid.

105. ANG, Register 116: Joseph Ngoua versus MarieThérèse Betoe, December 7, 1956.

106. ANG, Register 116: Paul Bekale versus Condja Marie Louise Bekale, January 3, 1958.

107. ANG, Register 116: Appel du jugement par défaut du tribunal du premier degré de la commune de Libreville, Eyang Emane versus Philippe Mouloungui, July 9, 1958.

108. ANG, Register 116: Appel jugement 201 du 10/13/60 du tribunal du premier degré Commune de Libreville, Vincent Mathurin Nguema versus Jeanne Anguenzoune, March 12, 1960; Appel Jugements 66 du 3/11/60, Cécile Atonet et son père versus Jean Matthieu Effame, April 23, 1960; Appel Jugements 93, Tribunal du Premier degré de Libreville, Delphine Obame Ekombeng et son père Michel Biloghe Obame versus Michel Bitom Bitée, June 25, 1960.

109. ANG, Register 107: Affaire Augustin Mbava contre Ndoutoune Edzang, Jugement d'appel numéro 1 du 13 janvier 1949; ANG, Register 116: Appel du tribunal de droit local district de Libreville, April 11, 1961, Paul Abogho versus Jean Martin Etonghe, December 23, 1961.

110. ANG, Register 107: Affaire Augustin Mbava contre Ndoutoune Edzang, Jugement d'appel numéro 1 du 13 janvier 1949.

111. Hawkins, "Woman in Question," 133.

CHAPTER 6: "FAIRE BON AMI" (TO BE GOOD FRIENDS):
SEX, PLEASURE, AND PUNISHMENT

1. Archives Nationales du Gabon (hereafter cited as ANG), 107, Tribunal Indigène du 2eme Dégrée, Registres des jugements en matière répressive, Région de l'Estuaire, Jugement 35 du 28 Novembre 1944 rendu sur citation, Affaire Tsiangani Pauline, Ndongo Fidèle, Ndoti François, Mayossa Kango, Moudaka, Bilola, Moukamba, Samba, Rébellion, November 28, 1944.

2. The same legal conceptions of adultery held true across sub-Saharan Africa in the twentieth-century colonial period. See, for example, in Ghana and Kenya: Jean Allman and Victoria Tashjian, "I Will Not Eat Stone": A Women's History of Colonial Asante (Portsmouth, NH: Heinemann, 2000); Brett L. Shadle, "Girl Cases": Marriage and Colonialism in Gusiiland, Kenya, 1890–1970 (Portsmouth, NH: Heinemann, 2006); Sean Hawkins, "'The Woman in Question': Marriage and Identity in the Colonial Courts of Northern Ghana, 1907–1954," in Women in African Colonial Histories, ed. Jean Allman, Susan Geiger, and Nakanyike Musisi (Bloomington: Indiana University Press, 2002), 116–43.

3. ANG, 107, Tribunal Indigène du 2eme Dégrée, Affaire Tsiangani Pauline.

4. Guy Lasserre, Libreville: La ville et sa région (Paris: Colin, 1958), 212.

5. For more on working conditions and an analysis of workers' complaints, see Clotaire Messi Me Nang, "Les travaillerus des chantiers forestiers du Gabon: Hybridité et invisibilité d'une culture ouvrière, 1892–1962" (PhD diss., Université de Paris I, 2007), 261–72.

6. Benoit Messani Nyangenyona, interview by author, Libreville, March 7, 2002.

7. Sexual relations between wage laborers in timber camps and married women from surrounding villages set off cycles of violent exchanges between men in villages and labor camps. A series of such incidents in the village of Nzeng Ayong in 1932 unleashed an investigation followed by the colony's governor: ANG, 571, Fichier Sous Série 1E, Lettre de N'Nguema Otogho, Chef du village de Nzeng Ayong, faisant élection du fonction du chef du Département de la Haute Bé à M. le Gouverneur du Gabon, s/c de M. l'Administrateur-Maire, November 30, 1932; ANG, 571, Fichier Sous Série 1E, Lettre l'Administrateur en Chef des Colonies, Assier de Pompignan Chef de la Circonscription de l'Estuaire à M. le Lieutenant Gouverneur du Gabon, Requêtes et Réclamations Indigènes, 1929–1948, December 12, 1932.

8. African and French political leaders argued that husbands often deliberately profited from the adultery fees, either encouraging their wives to have sexual relations with other men to extract the money or turning a blind eye to such relations until they needed cash. ANG, 1916, Sous Série 1E: Conseils et Assemblées, Procès Verbaux des Séances du Conseil Représentatif du Gabon, Venue des Femmes de Travailleurs sur Les Chantiers Forestiers, March 15, 1950.

9. Sarah Nuttall and Achille Mbembe, eds., *Johannesburg: The Elusive Metropolis* (Durham, NC: Duke University Press, 2008), 7.

10. Mary Weismantel, *Cholas and Pishtacos: Stories of Race and Sex in the Andes* (Chicago: University of Chicago Press, 2001), 50–53.

11. Frederick Cooper coins the term "geography of experience" based on Mamdou Diouf's call for Africanists to develop new concepts of geography other than colonial categories. See Frederick Cooper, "Africa's Pasts and Africa's Historians," *African Sociological Review* 3, no. 2 (1999): 15–16; Mamadou Diouf, "Des historiens et des histoires, pourquoi faire? L'Historiographie africaine entre l'Etat et les Communautés," *African Sociological Review* 3, no. 2 (1999): 106–9.

12. [[TK]]

13. Sylvain Mve Mba, interview by author, Okolassi, December 12, 2001.

14. Thérèse Biloghe, interview by author, Libreville, April 17, 2002; Pauline Essola, interview by author, Okolassi, November 21, 2001.

15. Marc Luc Iwenga, interview by author, Libreville, January 30, 2002.

16. Marie Solange Bikie, interview by author, Ntoum, January 15, 2002.

17. Lasserre, *Libreville*, 259.

18. Biologhe Metou, interview by author, Okolassi, November 21, 2001.

19. Interviews by author in Okolassi: Albertine Ntsame Ndong, November 7, 2001; Léotine Nseghe, November 7, 2001.

20. Interviews by author in Okolassi: Albertine Ntsame Ndong, November 7, 2001; Osette Ayetebe Obame, November 21, 2001; interviews by author in Libreville: Josette Moussirou Sickout, January 17, 2002; Céline Escola Ntoutoume, March 28, 2002.

21. Assogho Obiang, interview by author, Okolassi, December 4, 2001.

22. David Edou Ntoutoume, interview by author, Ntoum, April 2, 2001.

23. Léon Mba, "Essai de droit coutumier pahouin," in *Ecrits ethnographiques* (Libreville: Raponda Walker, 2001), 70; Anonymous 4, interview by author, Libreville,

April 7, 2002; Albertine Ntsame Ndong, interview by author, Okolassi, November 7, 2001.

24. Albertine Ntsame Ndong, interview by author, Okolassi, November 7, 2001.

25. Albertine Andone Essono, interview by author, Libreville, June 4, 2002.

26. Raphaël Sala, interview by author, Libreville, February 14, 2002.

27. Benoit Messani Nyangenyona, interview by author, Libreville, March 5, 2002; Martin Nguema, interview by author, Okolassi, November 28, 2001.

28. Jean Francois Mba Ntoutoume, interview by author, Nkok, March 6, 2002.

29. Raphaël Sala, interview by author, Libreville, February 14, 2002.

30. Martin Nguema, interview by author, Okolassi, November 28, 2001.

31. Jean Francois Mba Ntoutoume, interview by author, Nkok, March 6, 2002.

32. Anonymous 12, interview by author, Libreville, February 2, 2002.

33. Martin Nguema, interview by author, Okolassi, November 28, 2001.

34. Sylvain Mve Mba, interview by author, Okolassi, Decmber 4, 2001.

35. Archives Générales des Pères de Saint-Esprit de Chevilly-Larue (hereafter cited as CSSP), Box 4J1.5a. Louis Matrou to Propagande de la Foi, extract from *Vicariat Apostolique du Gabon*, December 22, 1915; CSSP, 2D60.2a4, Mariage Indigène, Rapport Avril 1923; CSSP, 5b1.10b3, document 1, Rapport de M. Rolland, Professeur à la Faculté de droit de Paris, sur les conflits de coutumes, présenté plénière du 30 juin 1927.

36. CSSP, 2D60.2a4, Document 12, Extrait de Lettre Haut Commissaire Cornut Gentille à Monsieur Durant-Beville, Conseiller de la République, March 5, 1928.

37. ANG, 1916, Sous Série 1E: Conseils et Assemblées, Procès Verbaux des Séances du Conseil Représentatif du Gabon, Venue des Femmes de Travailleurs sur Les Chantiers Forestiers, March 15, 1950.

38. CSSP, 5b1.10b8.

39. The same is true for other regions in Africa, such as Botswana. Arnfred, *Re-Thinking Sexualities*, 23.

40. Achey Oyeng, interview by author, Okolassi, November 14, 2001.

41. Raphaël Sala, interview by author, Libreville, February 14, 2002.

42. ANG, Register 82, Registre des collections divers, Région de l'Estuaire, Registre du Tribunal du premier degré de Libreville, Jugements rendus en matière repressive, Années 1937–1939, Case 82.

43. Catherine Okili, interview by author, Libreville, January 22, 2002.

44. Yvonne Tchicot, interview by author, Libreville, December 11, 2002; Céline Escola Ntoutoume, interview by author, Libreville, March 28, 2002.

45. Mme. Messani, interview by author, Libreville, March 2, 2002.

46. Agathe Marcelle Iwenga, interview by author, Libreville, January 13, 2002.

47. Simone Agnoret Iwenga St. Denis, interview by author, Libreville, March 6, 2002.

48. Sharon Marcus, *Apartment Stories: City and Home in Nineteenth-Century Paris and London* (Berkeley: University of California Press, 1999), 13.

49. Teresa Barnes and Everjoyce Win, *To Live a Better Life: An Oral History of Women in the City of Harare*, 1930–70 (Harare: Baobab Books, 1982), 67–77.

50. Maman Denise, interview by author, Okolassi, November 14, 2001.

51. Interviews by author: Albertine Ntsame Ndong, Okolassi, November 7, 2001; Marie-Hélène Mengue, Ntoum, April 17, 2002; Biologhe Metou, Okolassi, November 21, 2001; Assogho Obiang, Okolassi, December 4, 2001.

52. Interviews by author: Assogho Obiang, Libreville, April 17, 2002; Marlyse, Nkok, March 6, 2002; Anonymous 4, Libreville, April 7, 2002.

53. Sylvain Mve Mba, interview by author, Okolassi, December 4, 2001.

54. Gregory Minsta, interview by author, Libreville, May 23, 2002.

55. Interviews by author: Emmanuel Ongone Bikeigne, Ntoum, May 15, 2002; David Edou Ntoutoume, Ntoum, March 3, 2001; Jean Ebale Mba, Libreville, February 28, 2002; Jean Francois Mba Ntoutoume, Nkok, March 6, 2002.

56. Gregory Minsta, interview by author, Libreville, May 23, 2002.

57. ANG, 2DI, Etude sommaire des populations de la Subdivision de Libreville par rapport au milieu géographique, January 27, 1945.

58. ANG, Microfilm Reel 51-MI-66-2, Rapport Politique du Deuxième Semestre, 1937.

59. Sylvain Mve Mba, interview by author, Okolassi, December 4, 2001.

60. Ibid.

61. Ibid.

62. Jean Ebale Mba, interview by author, Libreville, January 25, 2002.

63. Mengue's husband, Bourobo Pambo, expelled his wife that night from their marital home, threatened to ask her family for the reimbursement of bridewealth and a divorce, and husband and wife agreed that she would take refuge at the male nurse's house since they were both angry. Bourobo asked for his wife to return the next day and she went back to their marital home. Days later, Mengue asked Bourobo if she could return to the nurse's home to retrieve a basket she had forgotten there. Bourobo thought she spent too long at the nurse's house and had not returned home in a timely manner, so he suspected that Mengue had had sex with the nurse. Bourobo appeared at the nurse's house with a knife in hand and punched him. ANG, 939, Fichier Sous Série 1E, Administration Générale, Requêtes 1936, Procès-verbaux, February 11, 2010.

64. Agathe Marcelle Iwenga, interview by author, Libreville, January 13, 2002.

65. Thérèse Biloghe, interview by author, Libreville, April 17, 2002.

66. Simone Agnoret Iwenga St. Denis, interview by author, Libreville, March 6, 2002.

67. Céline Ntoutoume Escola, interview by author, Libreville, March 28, 2002.

68. Biologhe Metou, interview by author, Okolassi, November 21, 2001.

69. Isabelle Ntoutoume, interview by author, Nkok, December 12, 2001.

70. Maman Denise, interview by author, Okolassi, November 14, 2001.

71. Mba, "Essai de droit coutumier," 76; interviews by author: Victorine Smith, Libreville, December 9, 2002; Maman Denise, Okolassi, November 14, 2001; Assogho Obiang, Okolassi, December 4, 2001.

72. Mba, "Essai de droit coutumier," 77.

73. Biologhe Metou, interview by author, Okolassi, November 21, 2001.

74. ANG, Microfilm Reel 51-MI-7, Rapport Politique Semestriel, 2ème Semestre 1946, Département de l'Estuaire, Subdivision de Libreville; ANG, Microfilm Reel 51-MI-7, Rapport Politique Semestriel, 2ème Semestre 1946, Département de l'Estuaire, Subdivision de Libreville.

75. ANG, H172, Santé, Démographie, Département Sanitaire de l'Estuaire. Rapport Annuel, 1944. ANG, Microfilm 51-MI-66-2, Rapport Politique du Deuxième Trimestre de l'Estuaire 1937; ANG, Fichier Sous Série 1E, Carton 629, Registre des Délibérations du Conseil des Notables, Département du Djouah, September 8, 1938.

76. Maurice Delafosse, Dr. Poutrin, and Monseigneur Le Roy, *Enquête coloniale dans l'Afrique française occidentale et équatoriale sur l'organisation de la famille indigène, les fiançailles, le mariage avec une esquisse générale des langues de l'Afrique* (Paris: Société d'Edition géographiques, maritime et colonial, 1930), 528.

77. ANG, 2DA(I)5. Rapport Politique Semestriel, 2ème Semestre 1938, Département de l'Estuaire, Subdivision de Libreville.

78. ANG, Microfilm 51-MI-65-2, Rapport Politique du Gabon 1947, Evolution des Coutumes, 1.

79. COAM, AEF/GGAEF/5D56, Projet d'arrêté Règlement les Mariages Indigènes au Gabon, January 20, 1925.

80. CSSP, 2D60.2a4, Document 5, Projet de règlement des mariages entre Indigènes de race Fang, Article 11.

81. ANG, 2686, Lettre du Procureur Général, Chef du Service Judicaire de l'aef aux Messieurs les Chefs de Territoire du Gabon, du Moyen-Congo, de l'Oubangui-Chari, et du Tchad, June 26, 1946; CAOM, AEF/GGAEF/5D56, Lettre du Chef du Département de Pool (Congo) à M. le GG, chargé de l'Administration du Territoire du MoyenCongo, Référence: Lettre 20 AP.2 du 5 février 1946 au sujet des Divorces Indigènes April 4, 1947.

82. ANG, Répertoire des Collections de Registres Divers, Registre 82.

83. ANG, Répertoire des Collections de Registres Divers, Registre 104, Région de l'Estuaire, Tribunal du Deuxième degré du département de l'Estuaire, Libreville, Jugement rendus en matière répressive, 338 du mars 1935 au 26 août 1939, Case 20, December 16, 1935; Case 40, September 9, 1937; and Case 2, March 3, 1938.

84. ANG, Registre 82, Case 30, July 21, 1938.

85. See also ANG, Registre 82, Case 4, January 14, 1939.

86. See also ANG, Registre 82, Case 17, May 5, 1938.

87. ANG, Registre 82, Case 17, May 5, 1932; Case 4, January 14 1939.

88. ANG, Registre 82, Case 17, May 5, 1932; Case 39, October 18, 1938.

89. ANG, Registre 82, Case 22, June 30, 1938; Case 26, July 15, 1938; Case 28, July 21, 1938; Case 29, July 21, 1938.

90. ANG, Registre 82, Case 22, June 30, 1938; Case 26, July 15, 1938; Case 28, July 21, 1938; Case 29, July 21, 1938.

91. ANG, Registre 82, Case 29, July 21, 1938.

92. CSSP, 2D60.2a4, *Congrès Pahouin de Mitzic*, 1.

93. ANG, Assemblée Territoriale du Gabon, Débats de l'Assemblée Territoriale du Gabon, Session Ordinaire 25 Avril 17, Séance du 14 Mai 1952, May 14, 1952.

94. ANG, Assemblée Territoriale du Gabon, Séance du 14 Mai 1952, Débats de l'Assemblée Territorial du Gabon, Session Ordinaire 25 Avril 17 a Mai 1952.

95. ANG, Register 112, Afrique Equatoriale Française, Région de l'Estuaire, Registre des jugements, Tribunal Coutumier, Année 1950 Du 4 novembre 1950 au 1er Mai 1955.

96. ANG, Register 112, Registre des jugements, Tribunal Coutumier. See, for example, Case 11, January 4 1951; Case 23, February 2, 1951; Case 24, February 2, 1951; Case 28, May 15, 1951; Case 148, June 15, 1954.

97. The same was true for other areas in Africa, such as Ghana. Allman and Tashjian, *I Will Not Eat Stone*, 172.

98. ANG, Register 112, Registre des jugements, Tribunal Coutumier. For examples, see Case 46, October 15, 1951; Case 63, March 15, 1952; Case 98, February 1, 1953; Case 129, January 15, 1954, ANG, Register 112, Registre des jugements, Tribunal Coutumier.

99. ANG, Register 112, Registre des jugements, Tribunal Coutumier. 1950: Case 2, November 5; Case 5, December 2; Case 6, December 15. 1951: Case 10, January 4; Case 18, February 1; Case 25, February 2; Case 46, October 15; Case 47, October 16; Case 50, November 13. 1952: Case 63, March 15; Case 67, April 15; Case 70, Mai 31; Case 88, December 2. 1953: Case 90, January 5; Case 91, January 5; Case 98, February 1; Case 108, April 16; Case 114, June 16. 1954: Case 129, January 15; Case 130, January 15; Case 133, February 3; Case 143, April 1; Case 145, May 1; Case 150, October 1; Case 161, October 15; Case 164, October 24; Case 169, December 1. ANG, Register 112, Registre des jugements, Tribunal Coutumier.

100. ANG, Register 112, Registre des jugements, Tribunal Coutumier. Case 133, February 3, 1954.

101. ANG, Register 112, Registre des jugements, Tribunal Coutumier. See Case 6, December 15, 1950; Case 63, March 15, 1952; Case 98, February 1, 1953; Case 145, May 1, 1954.

102. ANG, Register 112, Registre des jugements, Tribunal Coutumier. Case 91, January 5, 1953; Case 98, February 1, 1953; Case 108, April 16, 1953; Case 145, May 1 1953.

103. ANG, Register 112, Registre des jugements, Tribunal Coutumier. See Case 5, December 2, 1950; Case 67, April 15, 1952; Case 161, October 15, 1954.

104. ANG, 2DAI8, Archives du District de Libreville, Justice 1948–1964, Note pour les chefs de village et de canton, re: les juges coutumiers, district de Libreville, March 21, 1955.

CHAPTER 7: "A BLACK GIRL SHOULD NOT BE WITH A WHITE MAN": INTERRACIAL SEX, AFRICAN WOMEN, AND RESPECTABILITY

1. Archives Nationales du Gabon (hereafter cited as ANG), 927, Lettre de Michel Moutarlier, Exploitation Forestier à M. L'Administrateur Supérieur, July 27, 1935.

2. Ibid.

3. Ibid.

4. ANG, 927, Renseignements à M. Le Chef du Département de l'Estuaire du Commissaire de Police, July 28, 1935.

5. "Décret du 15 Septembre 1936 fixant le statut des métis nés en AEF de parents demeurés légalement inconnus," *Journal Officiel de la République Française* 220, September 19, 1936; Centre d'Archives d'Outre Mer (hereafter cited as CAOM), AEF/GGAEF/5D44, "Application du Décret du 15 Septembre 1936," February 13, 1937.

6. Yet, as argued by Alice Conklin, over the course of the interwar years, "skin color became a decisive marker of Frenchness," and the French government limited avenues for Africans to obtain citizenship. Conklin, "Redefining 'Frenchness': Citizenship, Race Regeneration, and Imperial Motherhood in France and West Africa, 1914–40," in *Domesticating the Empire: Race, Gender, and Family Life in French and Dutch Colonialism*, ed. Julia Clancy-Smith and Frances Gouda (Charlottesville: University of Virginia Press, 1989), 69.

7. CAOM, fm1/affpol/2125/2, Note sur la réorganization des évolués, cityonité, métis, January 10, 1944. John A. Ballard, "The Development of Political Parties in

French Equatorial Africa" (PhD diss., Fletcher School of Law and Diplomacy, Tufts University, 1963), 30.

8. In spite of some being French citizens, *métis* across Francophone Africa complained that they could not access the same employment, health, and education resources as white citizens living in Africa. CAOM/GGAEF/5D44, Association des l'Amicale des métis de l'AEF, Letter from Amicale des Métis de l'AEF of Brazzaville to M. Marius Moutet, Ministère de la France d'Outre Mer in Paris, July 2, 1946; Letter from the Amicale des Métis du Gabon to the Governor General de l'AEF, November 1, 1947. CAOM, Fm, 1affpol/3406/6, Letter from le Président Nicolas Rigonaux de l'Union des Eurafricains of French West Africa to M. Le Ministre de la France d'Outre Mer, Letter 32, February 2, 1949.

9. ANG, 927, Letter from Samba Augustin Demeurant à la Montaigne Sainte à M. Le Gouverneur Général, April 6, 1941.

10. Most research on interracial sex, *métissage*, and colonialism has focused on European discourses and representations. A sample of this literature includes: Anne McClintock, *Imperial Leather: Race, Gender and Sexuality in the Colonial Contest* (New York: Routledge, 1994); Antoinette Burton, ed., *Gender, Sexuality and Colonial Modernities* (London: Routledge, 1999); Jock McCulloch, *Black Peril, White Virtue: Sexual Crime in Southern Rhodesia, 1902–1935* (Bloomington: Indiana University Press, 2000); Jean Gelman Taylor, *The Social World of Batavia: European and Eurasian in Dutch Asia* (Madison: University of Wisconsin Press, 2001); Conklin, "Redefining 'Frenchness' "; Ann L. Stoler, "Rethinking Colonial Categories: European Communities and the Boundaries of Rule," *Comparative Studies in Society and History* 31, no. 1 (January 1989): 134–61; Stoler, "Making Empire Respectable: The Politics of Race and Sexual Morality in 20th-Century Colonial Cultures," *American Ethnologist* 16, no. 4 (November 1989): 634–60; Stoler, *Carnal Knowledge and Imperial Power: Race and the Intimate in Colonial Rule* (Berkeley: University of California Press, 2002).

11. Heidi Gengenbach, " 'What My Heart Wanted': Gendered Stories of Early Colonial Encounters in Southern Mozambique," in *Women in African Colonial Histories*, ed. Jean Allman, Susan Geiger, and Nakanyike Musisi (Bloomington: Indiana University Press, 2002), 29; Guilia Barrera, "Colonial Affairs: Italian Men, Eritrean Women, and the Construction of Racial Hierarchies in Colonial Eritrea (1885–1941)" (PhD diss., Northwestern University, 2002); Carina E. Ray, "Policing Sexual Boundaries: The Politics of Race in Colonial Ghana" (PhD diss., Cornell University, 2007); Christopher Joon-Hai Lee, "The 'Native' Undefined: Colonial Categories, Anglo-African Status, and the Politics of Kinship in British Central Africa, 1929–38," *Journal of African History* 46, no. 3 (2005): 455–78; Carina E. Ray, " 'The White Wife Problem': Sex, Race, and the Contested Politics of Repatriation to Interwar British West Africa," *Gender and History* 21, no. 3 (2009): 628–46; Hilary Jones, *The Métis of Senegal: Urban Life and Politics in French West Africa* (Bloomington: Indiana University Press, 2013).

12. Guy Lasserre, *Libreville: La ville et sa région* (Paris: Colin, 1958), 245–46.

13. ANG, 927, Lettre du Commissaire de Police à M. le Chef de la Sûreté, July 21, 1941.

14. A 1938 census of métis in French West Africa recorded a total of 3,437 métis. However, historian Owen White estimates the numbers to be larger, from 3,500 to 4,500. Owen White, *Children of the French Empire: Miscegenation and Colonial Society in French West Africa, 1895–1960* (Oxford: Oxford University Press, 1999), 2–3.

15. CAOM, AEF/GGAEF/5D44, "Enquête sur les Métis," February 15, 1938.

16. CAOM, AEF/GGAEF/5D44, Letter from Le Médecin Capitaine Soulage, Médecin-Chef du Département Sanitaire de L'Estuaire à M. Le Médecin des Services Sanitaire et Médicale de l'AEF, March 1, 1939.

17. CAOM, AEF/GGAEF/5D44, Letter 159, RE: Des *Métis*, from the Governor of Gabon to the Governor of French Equatorial Africa, February 21, 1941.

18. Cited in Florence Bernault, *Démocratie ambiguës en Afrique centrale: Congo-Brazzaville, Gabon, 1940–1965* (Paris: Karthala, 1996), 61.

19. Lasserre, *Libreville*, 243.

20. Agathe Marcelle Iwenga, interview by author, Libreville, January 13, 2002.

21. Marie-Germaine, *Le Christ au Gabon* (Louvain: Museum Lessianum, 1931), 90.

22. Marie Bidang, interview by author, Ntoum, June 1, 2002.

23. Interviews by author in Libreville: Anonymous 3, January 5, 2002; Simone Agnoret Iwenga St. Denis, February 8, 2002; Rosalie Antchandie, June 6, 2002.

24. Interviews by author in Libreville: Adrien Gustave Anguilet, February 2, 2002; Benoit Messani Nyangenyona, March 7, 2002; Joseph Lasseny Ntchoveré, March 2, 2002; Myènè Avekaza, April 27, 2002.

25. Anonymous 3, interview by author, Libreville, January 5, 2002.

26. Interviews by author in Libreville: Anonymous 3, January 5, 2002; Antoinette Awuta, June 5, 2002.

27. Luis White, *The Comforts of Home: Prostitution in Colonial Nairobi* (Chicago: University of Chicago Press, 1990), 11, 224.

28. Interviews by author in Libreville: Anonymous 1, June 10, 2002; Rosalie Antchandie, June 6, 2002; Victorine Smith, December 11, 2002.

29. CAOM, AEF/GGAEF/5D44, Letter from Le Médecin Capitaine Soulage. March 1, 1939.

30. Thérèse Biloghe, interview by author, Libreville, April 17, 2002.

31. Simone Agnoret Iwenga St. Denis, interview by author, Libreville, February 8, 2002.

32. Anonymous 2, interview by author, Libreville. March 29, 2002.

33. Victorine Smith, interview by author, Libreville, December 11, 2002.

34. Rosalie Antchandie, interview by author, Libreville, June 6, 2002.

35. Interviews by author in Libreville: Agathe Awuta, June 5, 2002; Rosalie Antchandie, June 6, 2002.

36. Catherine Okili, interview by author, Libreville, January 20, 2002.

37. Agnès Lucille Edwidge Osenga Diyaye, interview by author, Libreville, January 15, 2002.

38. Victorine Smith, interview by author, Libreville, December 11, 2002.

39. M. Auganeur, "L'enfant dans la famille gabonaise," *Bulletin de la Sociétés des Recherches Congolaises* 3 (1923): 15.

40. Victorine Smith, interview by author, Libreville, December 11, 2002.

41. Luise White, *Comforts of Home*, 79–125.

42. Lasserre, *Libreville*, 245; Victorine Smith, interview by author, Libreville, December 29, 2002.

43. Victorine Smith, interview by author, Libreville, December 11, 2002.

44. Joseph Lasseny Ntchoveré, interview by author, Libreville, March 2, 2002.

45. Benoit Messani, interview by author, Libreville, March 5, 2002.

46. Phyllis M. Martin, *Leisure and Society in Colonial Brazzaville* (Cambridge: Cambridge University Press, 1995); Jeremy M. Rich, "Civilized Attire: Dress, Cultural

Change and Status in Libreville, Gabon, ca. 1860–1914," *Cultural and Social History* 2, no. 2 (2005): 189–214.

47. See photos in Lasserre, *Libreville*, 86–87.

48. Lasserre, *Libreville*, 243.

49. Anonymous 4, interview by author, Libreville, April 7, 2002.

50. Jean Ebale Mba, a Fang man who moved to Libreville in the 1930s, reflected, "At the time, the Myènè were the principal purchases. I have to tell you that they did not like to go into the bush." Jean Ebale Mba, interview by author, Libreville, February 28, 2002.

51. Maman Denise, interview by author, Okolassi, November 14, 2001; interviews by author in Libreville: Victorine Smith, December 11, 2002; Agathe Awunta, June 1, 2002.

52. M. Van de la Noitte, "Impressions d'Escale: Libreville," *L'Etoile de l'AEF*. 2/14/1931, p. 7. CAOM. FM, 1affpol/3097.

53. Ibid.

54. Across the French Empire from the 1920s through the 1930s, new laws outlined that métis whose French *or* European fathers had not legally recognized them could apply for and be granted French citizenship (*la qualité de citoyen français*). Stoler, "Rethinking Colonial Categories," 134–61; Stoler, *Carnal Knowledge*; Owen White, *Children of the French Empire*; Emmanuelle Saada, *Les enfants de la colonie: Les métis de l'Empire français entre sujétion et citoyenneté* (Paris: La Découverte, 2007); Saada, *Empire's Children: Race, Filiation, and Citizenship in the French Colonies*, trans. Arthur Goldhammer (Chicago: University of Chicago Press, 2012).

55. Elsewhere in the French Empire, métis's moral character could also determine whether or not judges granted their petitions for citizenship. CAOM, AEF/GGAEF/5D44, "Service Judiciare de l'AEF, Application du Décret du 15 Septembre 1936 Fixant le Statut des Métis en AEF, Circulaire 203/PG à M. les Procureurs de Brazzaville, Libreville, Bangui, February 13, 1947.

56. CAOM, AEF/GGAEF/5D44, Letter from the Procureur Général, October 20, 1937.

57. ANG, H 172, Région Sanitaire de l'Estuaire, Rapport Trimestriels 1938–1956, Démographie, Département Sanitaire de l'Estuaire, Rapport Annuel, 1945.

58. For parallel shifts in French West Africa see, Owen White, "Miscegenation in French West Africa," in *Children of the French Empire*, 7–32.

59. CAOM, FM. 1affpol/3097, Letter by Mathe X, *L'Etoile de l'AEF*, March 28, 1931, p. 10.

60. CAOM, FM. 1affpol/3097, M. G. de l'Etoile. "La Femme Blanche en AEF: Une Requête de Bon Ton," *L'Etoile AEF*, March 28, 1931, p. 15.

61. Archives Générales des Pères de Saint-Esprit de Chevilly-Larue (hereafter cited as CSSP), 4J1.6a1, R.F. in Libreville, Exploitant Forestier, "Le Gabon et son avenir," October 10, 1940, 4.

62. ANG, Sous Série 1, Police et Prison, 2302, Arrêté règlement la Police des débits de boisson dans la colonie, December 30, 1932.

63. Ibid.

64. CAOM, AEF/GGAEF/6Y1, Conseil des Notables, Estuaire, Procès-verbaux du Conseil des Notables Indigènes, 1937–1935, September 28, 1942.

65. Ibid.

66. Ghislaine Lydon, "Women, Children and the Popular Front's Mission of Inquiry in French West Africa," in *French Colonial Empire and the Popular Front: Hope and*

Disillusion, ed. Tony Chafer and Amanda Sackur (London: Palgrave Macmillan, 1999), 170–87; Elikia Mbokolo, "French Colonial Policy in Equatorial Africa in the 1940s and 1950s," in *The Transfer of Power in Africa*, ed. Prosser Gifford and William R. Louis (New Haven, CT: Yale University Press, 1982), 173–210.

67. For a more detailed examination of discourses of abandonment and métis in the French Empire, see Owen White, *Children of the French Empire*.

68. Mutual aid societies of métis across French West and Equatorial Africa similarly encouraged métisse women to marry African men. Rachel Jean-Baptiste, "'Miss Eurafrica': Men, Women's Sexuality, and Métis Identity in Late Colonial French Africa, 1945–1960," *Journal of the History of Sexuality* 20, no. 3 (September 2011): 568–93.

69. CAOM, fm/1affpol/2125, dossier 2, Problème de Métis, AEF, 1936.

70. CAOM, AEF/GGAEF/5D44, Enquête no. 4, M. Saint-Blancart, Elève-Administrateur des colonies en service a la Mairie de Libreville, Enquête sur les Métis, February 15, 1938.

71. In other African regions during colonial rule, perceptions of population crises propelled colonial states and African elites toward attempts to manage sexual behavior. Carol Summers, "Intimate Colonialism: The Imperial Production of Reproduction in Uganda, 1907–1925," *Signs* 16, no. 4 (1991): 787–807; Nancy Rose Hunt, "'Le bébé en brousse': European Women, African Birth Spacing, and Colonial Intervention in Breast Feeding in the Belgian Congo," *International Journal of African Historical Studies* 21, no. 3 (1988): 401–32; Nancy Rose Hunt, "Domesticity and Colonialism in Belgian Africa: Usumbura's *Foyer Social*, 1946–1960," *Signs* 15, no. 3 (1988): 447–74; Dorothy L. Hodgson and Sheryl A. McCurdy, *"Wicked Women" and the Reconfiguration of Gender in Africa* (Portsmouth, NH: Heinemann, 2001); Lynn M. Thomas, *Politics of the Womb: Women, Reproduction, and the State in Kenya* (Berkeley: University of California Press, 2003).

72. Sisters of Saint Joseph de Cluny who ran a boarding school for métisses in Brazzaville argued that it was difficult to get the girls to accept to marry an African man. CAOM, AEF/GAEF/5D44, Letter 493, the Chef du Territoire du Moyen Congo to the Governor General of French Equatorial Africa, re: Assistance au Mineurs Métis in Response to the Governor's Circulaire 143/Ap.3, August 17, 1943.

73. CAOM, AEF/GGAEF/5D44, Letter from Le Directeur de l'Ecole Urbaine de Libreville à M. Le Directeur de l'Enseignement, February 8, 1939.

74. CAOM, AEF/GGAEF/5D44, Edict Instituting the Work of the Protection of *Métis* of Free French Equatorial Africa, May 1941.

75. CAOM, AEF/GGAEF/5D44, Arétée portant création d'un comité de patronage des enfants métis de l'AEF, April 10, 1946.

76. Agnès Lucille Edwige Osenga Diyaye, interview by author, Libreville, January 15, 2002.

77. Victorine Smith, interview by author, Libreville, December 31, 2002.

78. Victorine Smith, interview by author, Libreville, December 9, 2002.

79. Marie France, interview by author, Libreville, January 5, 2002.

80. Anonymous 2, interview by author, Libreville, June 9, 2002.

81. Rosalie Antchandie, interview by author, Libreville, June 6, 2002.

82. Catherine Okili, interview by author, Libreville, January 22, 2002.

83. Simone Agnoret Iwenga St. Denis, interview by author, Libreville, February 8, 2002.

84. I use the term "landscapes of power" as utilized and defined by Richard L. Roberts to mean asymmetrical social relations, the agency with which men and women actively engaged with colonial institutions, and "the uneven nature of the terrain that men and women traversed in order to accomplish their goals." Roberts, *Litigants and Households: African Disputes and Colonial Courts in the French Soudan, 1895–1912* (Portsmouth, NH: Heinemann, 2005), 19–21.

CONCLUSION

1. For more on "the colonial city" as an archetype, see Bill Freund, *The African City: A History* (Cambridge: Cambridge University Press, 2007), 76–82; Mamadou Diouf, "(Re)Imagining an African City: Performing Culture, Arts, and Citizenship in Dakar (Senegal), 1980–2000," in *The Spaces of the Modern City: Imaginaries, Politics, and Everyday Life,* ed. Gyan Prakash and Kevin M. Kruse (Princeton, NJ: Princeton University Press, 2008), 348.

2. Diana Jeater, *Marriage, Perversion, and Power: The Construction of Moral Discourse in Southern Rhodesia, 1894–1930* (Oxford: Oxford University Press, 1993), 259.

3. Teresa Barnes, *"We Women Worked So Hard": Gender, Urbanization, and Social Reproduction in Colonial Harare, Zimbabwe, 1930–1956* (Portsmouth, NH: Heinemann, 1999).

4. For more on class differentiation among African women and the need for careful analysis of the term "feminism," see Abosede A. George, "Feminist Activism and Class Politics: The Example of the Lagos Girl Hawker Project," *Women's Studies Quarterly* 35, nos. 3–4 (2007): 128–43.

5. Rachel Petrocelli, "City Dwellers and the State: Making Modern Urbanism in Colonial Dakar, 1914–1944" (PhD diss., Stanford University, 2011), see chap. 9, "Managing Money: Saving and Spending in the City."

6. Ann L. Stoler, "Tense and Tender Ties: The Politics of Comparison in North American History and (Post) Colonial Studies," *Journal of American History* 88, no. 3 (December 2001): 829–65; Ramón A. Gutiérrez, "What's Love Got to Do with It?" *Journal of American History* 88, no. 3 (December 2001): 866–69.

7. Pascale Barthélémy, *Africaines et diplomées à l'époque coloniale, 1918–1957* (Rennes: Presses Universitaires de Rennes, 2010), 283.

8. See, for example, John R. Short, *Urban Theory: A Critical Assessment* (New York: Routledge, 2006).

9. Sarah Nuttall and Achille Mbembe, eds., *Johannesburg: The Elusive Metropolis* (Durham, NC: Duke University Press, 2008), 9; Phil Hubbard, *Cities and Sexualities* (New York: Routledge, 2012).

10. Christine Stansell, *City of Women: Sex and Class in New York, 1789–1860* (Chicago: University of Chicago Press, 1987); Timothy J. Gilfoyle, *City of Eros: New York City, Prostitution, and the Commercialization of Sex, 1790–1920* (New York: Norton, 1992); Donna J. Guy, *Sex and Danger in Buenos Aires: Prostitution, Family, and Nation in Argentina* (Lincoln: University of Nebraska Press, 1992); Judith R. Walkowitz, *City of Dreadful Delight: Narratives of Sexual Danger in Late-Victorian London* (Chicago: University of Chicago Press, 1992); Eileen J. Suárez Findlay, *Imposing Decency: The Politics of Sexuality and Race in Puerto Rico, 1870–1920* (Durham, NC: Duke University Press, 1999); James N. Green, *Beyond Carnival: Male Homosexuality in*

Twentieth-Century Brazil (Chicago: University of Chicago Press, 2001); Hubbard, *Cities and Sexuality.*

11. Exceptions include: Jeater, *Marriage*; Megan Vaughan, *Curing Their Ills: Colonial Power and African Illness* (Stanford, CA: Stanford University Press, 1991); Luise White, *The Comforts of Home: Prostitution in Colonial Nairobi* (Chicago: University of Chicago Press, 1990).

Bibliography

ORAL INTERVIEWS CITED

Angone, Bernadette. Libreville, February 21, 2002; Okolassi, November 21, 2001.
Anguilet, Adrien Gustave. Libreville, February 2, 2002.
Anonymous 1. Libreville, June 10, 2002.
Anonymous 2. Libreville, March 29, 2002; June 9, 2002.
Anonymous 3. Libreville, January 5, 2002.
Anonymous 4. Libreville, April 7, 2002.
Anonymous 12. Libreville, February 2, 2002.
Antchandie, Rosalie. Libreville, June 6, 2002.
Avekaza, Myènè. Libreville, November 21, 2001; April 27, 2002.
Awunta, Agathe. Libreville, June 1, 2002.
Awuta, Antoinette. Libreville, June 5, 2002.
Bidang, Marie. Ntoum, June 1, 2002.
Bikeigne, Emmanuel Ongone. Ntoum, May 4, 15, 2002.
Bikie, Marie Solange. Ntoum, January 15, 2002; April 2, 2002.
Biloghe, Thérèse. Libreville, April 17, 2002.
Denise, Maman. Okolassi, November 14, 2001.
Diyaye, Agnès Lucille Edwige Osenga. Libreville, January 15, 2002.
Ella, Jeanne Antoinette. Libreville, March 27, 2002.
Endamne, Juline. Paris, France, May 5, 2004.
Essola, Pauline. Okolassi, November 21, 2001.
Essono, Albertine Andone. Libreville, June 4, 2002.
France, Marie. Libreville, January 5, 2002.
Iwenga, Agathe Marcelle. Libreville, January 13, 2002; Okolassi, January 31, 2002.
Iwenga, Marc Luc. Libreville, January 30, 2002.
Marlyse. Nkok, March 6, 2002.
Mba, Jean Ebale. Libreville, January 25, 2002; February 28, 2002.
Mba, Sylvain Mve. Okolassi, December 4, 12, 2001.

Mbele, Mme. Libreville, May 10, 2002.
Mengue, Marie-Hélène. Ntoum, April 17, 2002.
Messani, Mme. Libreville, March 2, 7, 2002.
Metou, Biologhe. Okolassi, November 21, 2001.
Minkue, Emilie. Okolassi, November 14, 2001.
Minsta, Gregory. Libreville, December 14, 2001; May 23, 2002.
Mobiang, Moise Meyo. Libreville, April 15, 2001; March 1, 2002.
Ndong, Albertine Ntsame. Okolassi, November 7, 2001.
Ndong, Martine Ada. Okolassi, November 21, 2001.
Nguema, Martin. Okolassi, November 28, 2001.
Nseghe, Léotine. Okolassi, November 7, 2001.
Ntchoveré, Joseph Lasseny. Libreville, March 2, 2002; April 16, 2002.
Ntoutoume, Céline Escola. Libreville, March 28, 2002.
Ntoutoume, David Edou. Ntoum, March 3, 2001; April 2, 2001.
Ntoutoume, Ella. Libreville, February 17, 2002.
Ntoutoume, Isabelle. Nkok, December 12, 2001.
Ntoutoume, Jean Francois. Nkok, March 6, 2002.
Nyangenyona, Benoit Messani. Libreville, March 7, 2002.
Obame, Osette Ayetebe. Okolassi, November 21, 2001.
Obiang, Assogho. Libreville, April 17, 2002; Okolassi, December 4, 2001.
Okili, Catherine. Libreville, January 20, 22, 2002.
Olivera, Antoinette Mikidou. Libreville, December 9, 2002.
Oyeng, Achey. Okolassi, November 14, 2001.
Remondo, Marie Appia. Libreville, December 14, 2001.
Sala, Raphaël. Libreville, February 14, 2002; Ntoum, February 15, 2002.
Sickout, Josette Moussirou. Libreville, January 17, 2002.
Sillard, Père Gilles. Chevilly-Larue, France, July 18, 2001.
Smith, Victorine. Libreville, December 9, 11, 29, 31, 2002.
St. Denis, Simone Agnoret Iwenga. Libreville, February 8, 2002; March 6, 2002.
Tati, Louise, née Délicat. Libreville, December 9, 2002.
Tchicot, Yvonne. Libreville, December 11, 2002.

ARCHIVES CONSULTED

Archives de la Maison Mère des Soeurs de Notre-Dame de l'Immaculée Conception de Castres (Soeurs Bleues). Libreville, Gabon.
Archives des Soeurs de Notre-Dame de l'Immaculée Conception de Castres (Soeurs Bleues). Rome, Italy.
Archives Général de la Congrégation des Pères du Saint-Esprit (Spiritans) (CSSP). Chevilly-Larue, France.
Archives Nationales de Gabon (ANG). Libreville, Gabon.
Archives Nationales du Sénégal (ANS). Dakar, Senegal.
Centre d'Archives d'Oture Mer (CAOM). Aix-en-Provence, France.
Henry Bucher Papers (HBP). Princeton Theological Seminary, Princeton, New Jersey.
Houghton Library, American Board of Commissioners for Foreign Missions Archives. Harvard University, Cambridge, Massachusetts.

Adloff, Richard, and Virginia Thompson. *The Emerging States of French Equatorial Africa*. Stanford, CA: Stanford University Press, 1960.

Akyeampong, Emmanuel. "'Wo pe tam won pe ba' (You Like Cloth but You Don't Want Children): Urbanization, Individualism, and Gender Relations in Colonial Ghana, c.1900–39." In Anderson and Rathbone, *Africa's Urban Past*, 222–35.

Alexandre, Pierre, and Jacques Binet. *Le groupe dit pahouin: Fang—Boulou—Beti*. Paris: Presses Universitaires de France, 1958.

Allman, Jean, Susan Geiger, and Nakanyike Musisi, eds. *Women in African Colonial Histories*. Bloomington: Indiana University Press, 2002.

Allman, Jean, and Victoria Tashjian. *"I Will Not Eat Stone": A Women's History of Colonial Asante*. Portsmouth, NH: Heinemann, 2000.

Allogho-Nkoghe, Fidèle-Marcellin. "Politique de la ville et logique d'acteurs à la recherche d'alternatives d'aménagement pour les quartiers informels de Libreville." PhD diss., Université de Montpellier III, 2006.

Allogo, A. Nguema. "Esquisse d'un historique de la Dot chez les fang." *Revue gabonaises d'etudes politiques, economique, et juridiques* 7 (1981): 32–42.

Ambouroué-Avaro, Joseph. *Un peuple gabonais à l'aube de la colonisation: Le Bas-Ogowé au XIX siècle*. Paris: Karthala, 1981.

Anderson, David M., and Richard Rathbone, eds. *Africa's Urban Past*. Portsmouth, NH: Heinemann, 2000.

Anicet Nzenguet Iguemba, Gilchrist. *Colonisation, fiscalité et mutations au Gabon, 1910–1947*. Paris: L'Harmattan, 2005.

Arnfred, Signe, ed. *Re-Thinking Sexualities in Africa*. Uppsala: Nordic Africa Institute, 2004.

Assemblée Territoriale du Gabon. Débats de l'Assemblée Territoriale du Gabon. Session Ordinaire, 25 Avril–17 Mai 1952.

Auganeur, M. "L'enfant dans la famille gabonaise." *Bulletin de la Sociétés des Recherches Congolaises* 3 (1923): 15–21.

Balandier, Georges. *Ambiguous Africa: Cultures in Collision*. Translated by Helen H. Weaver. New York: Pantheon, 1966.

———. *Sociologie des Brazzaville noires*. Paris: Presses de la Fondation Nationale des Sciences Politiques, 1985.

———. *The Sociology of Black Africa: Social Dynamics in Central Africa*. Translated by Douglas Garman. New York: Praeger, 1970.

Ballard, John A. "The Development of Political Parties in French Equatorial Africa." PhD diss., Fletcher School of Law and Diplomacy, Tufts University, 1963.

Barnes, James F. *Gabon: Beyond the Colonial Legacy*. Boulder, CO: Westview Press, 1992.

Barnes, Teresa. "Virgin Territory? Travel and Migration by African Women in Twentieth-Century Southern Africa." In Allman, Geiger, and Musisi, *Women in Colonial African Histories*, 164–90.

———. *"We Women Worked So Hard": Gender, Urbanization, and Social Reproduction in Colonial Harare, Zimbabwe, 1930–1956*. Portsmouth, NH: Heinemann, 1999.

Barnes, Teresa, and Everjoyce Win. *To Live a Better Life: An Oral History of Women in the City of Harare, 1930–70*. Harare: Baobab Books, 1982.

Barrera, Guilia. "Colonial Affairs: Italian Men, Eritrean Women, and the Construction of Racial Hierarchies in Colonial Eritrea (1885–1941)." PhD diss., Northwestern University, 2002.

Barret, Paul Marie Victor. *La Sénégambie et Guinée—La région gabonaise. L'Afrique occidentale, la nature et l'homme noir.* Paris: Challamel, 1888.

Barthélémy, Pascale. *Africaines et diplômées à l'époque coloniale, 1918–1957.* Rennes: Presses Universitaires de Rennes, 2010.

Bascou-Brescane, René. *Etude des conditions de vie à Libreville, 1961–1962.* Paris: Secrétariat d'État aux affaires étrangères chargé de la cooperation, 1962.

Bastiani, Laurent. *Enquête sur la sex-ratio, 1951–1955.* Brazzaville: Haut-commissariat de l'Afrique équatoriale française, Groupe d'études des comptes économiques, Service de la Statistique General, 1956.

———. *Inventaire des ressources humaines de l'Afrique equatoriale française.* Brazzaville: Haut-commissariat de l'Afrique équatoriale française, Groupe d'études des comptes économiques, Service de la Statistique General, 1956.

Berger, Iris. "African Women's History: Themes and Perspectives." *Journal of Colonialism and Colonial History* 4, no. 1 (2003).

———. "Feminism, Patriarchy, and African Women's History." *Journal of Women's History* 20, no. 2 (2008): 130–35.

———. *Threads of Solidarity: Women in South African Industry, 1900–1980.* Bloomington: Indiana University Press, 1992.

Berger, Iris, and E. Frances White. *Women in Sub-Saharan Africa: Restoring Women to History.* Bloomington: Indiana University Press, 1999.

Bernault, Florence. *Démocraties ambiguës en Afrique centrale: Congo-Brazzaville, Gabon, 1940–1965.* Paris: Karthala, 1996.

———. "Dévoreurs de la nation: Le mythe des évasions Fang au Gabon." In *Etre étranger et migrant en Afrique au vingtième siècle*, edited by Catherine Coquery-Vidrovitch and Issiaka Mandé, 169–88. Paris: L'Harmattan, 2003.

Berry, Sara. *No Condition Is Permanent: The Social Dynamics of Agrarian Change in Sub-Saharan Africa.* Madison: University of Wisconsin Press, 1993.

Blache, Joseph. *Vrais noirs et vrais blancs d'Afrique au vingtième siècle.* Orléans: Caillette, 1922.

Bosman, Willem. *A New and Accurate Description of the Coast of Guinea, Divided into the Gold, the Slave, and the Ivory Coasts: Containing a Geographical, Political and Natural History of the Kingdoms and Countries; with a Particular Account of the Rise, Progress and Present Condition of All the European Settlements upon That Coast.* London: Cass, 1698.

Bozzoli, Belinda, and Mmantho Nkotsoe. *Women of Phokeng: Consciousness, Life Strategy, and Migrancy in South Africa, 1900–1983.* Portsmouth, NH: Heinemann, 1991.

Brennan, James R. *Taifa: Making Nation and Race in Urban Tanzania.* Athens: Ohio University Press, 2012.

Brooks, George E. *Eurafricans in Western Africa: Commerce, Social Status, Gender, and Religious Observance from the Sixteenth to the Eighteenth Century.* Athens: Ohio University Press, 2003.

Bruel, Georges. *La France equatoriale africaine: Le pays, les habitants, la colonisation, les pouvoirs publics.* Paris: Larose, 1935.

Bucher, Henry H. "The Atlantic Slave Trade and the Gabon Estuary: The Mpongwé to 1860." In *Africans in Bondage: Studies in Slavery and the Slave Trade; Essays* in Honor of Philip D. Curtin on the Occasion of the Twenty-Fifth Anniversary of African Studies at the University of Wisconsin, edited by Paul E. Lovejoy, 136–54. Madison: University of Wisconsin Press, 1986.

——. "Liberty and Labor: The Origins of Libreville Reconsidered." Bulletin de l'Institut Fondamental d'Afrique Noir, 2nd series, 41, no. 3 (1979): 478–96.

——. "The Mpongwé of the Gabon Estuary: A History to 1860." PhD diss., University of Wisconsin, 1977.

——. "Mpongwé Origins: Historiographical Perspectives." History in Africa 2 (1975): 59–89.

——. "The Village of Glass and Western Intrusion: An Mpongwé Response to the American and French Presence in the Gabon Estuary: 1842–1845." International Journal of African Historical Studies 6, no. 3 (1973): 363–400.

Burrill, Emily S., Richard L. Roberts, and Elizabeth Thornberry, eds. Domestic Violence and the Law in Colonial and Postcolonial Africa. Athens: Ohio University Press, 2010.

Burton, Antoinette, ed. Gender, Sexuality and Colonial Modernities. London: Routledge, 1999.

Byfield, Judith A. The Bluest Hands: A Social and Economic History of Women Dyers in Abeokuta (Nigeria), 1890–1940. Portsmouth, NH: Heinemann, 2002.

——. "Women, Marriage, Divorce and the Emerging Colonial State in Abeokuta (Nigeria),1892–1904." In Hodgson and McCurdy, Wicked Women, 27–47.

Castellani, Charles. Les femmes au Congo. Paris: Flammarion, 1898.

Ceillier, Patrick, and Jean-Émile Mbot. À Libreville, c›était hier. Libreville: Editions du Luto, 2002.

Chamberlin, Christopher. "The Migration of the Fang into Central Gabon during the Nineteenth Century: A New Interpretation." International Journal of African Historical Studies 11, no. 3 (1978): 429–56.

Chanock, Martin. Law, Custom and Social Order: The Colonial Experience in Malawi and Zambia. Cambridge: Cambridge University Press, 1985.

Charbonnier, François, ed. Gabon, terre d'avenir. Paris: Encyclopédie d'outre-mer, 1957.

Chernoff, John M. Hustling Is Not Stealing: Stories of an African Bar Girl. Chicago: University of Chicago Press, 2003.

Cinnamon, John M. "The Long March of the Fang: Anthropology and History in Equatorial Africa." PhD diss., Indiana University, 1998.

Clark, Gracia. African Market Women: Seven Life Stories from Ghana. Bloomington: Indiana University Press, 2010.

Cohen, David W. The Combing of History. Chicago: University of Chicago Press, 1994.

Cole, Jennifer, and Lynn M. Thomas, eds. Love in Africa. Chicago: University of Chicago Press, 2009.

Comaroff, John L., ed. The Meaning of Marriage Payments. New York: Academic Press, 1980.

Compiègne, Marquis de. L'Afrique Equatoriale: Gabonais, pahouins, gallois. Paris: Plon, 1875.

Conklin, Alice L. "Redefining 'Frenchness': Citizenship, Race Regeneration, and Imperial Motherhood in France and West Africa, 1914–40." In Domesticating the Empire: Race, Gender, and Family Life in French and Dutch Colonialism, edited by Julia Clancy-Smith and Frances Gouda, 65–83. Charlottesville: University of Virginia Press, 1998.

Cooper, Barbara M. *Marriage in Maradi: Gender and Culture in a Hausa Society in Niger, 1900–1989*. Portsmouth, NH: Heinemann, 1997.

———. "Women's Worth and Wedding Gift Exchange in Maradi, Niger, 1907–89." *Journal of African History* 36, no. 1 (1995): 121–40.

Cooper, Frederick. "Africa's Pasts and Africa's Historians." *African Sociological Review* 3, no. 2 (1999): 1–29.

———. *Decolonization and African Society: The Labor Question in French and British Africa*. Cambridge: Cambridge University Press, 1996.

———. *On the African Waterfront: Urban Disorder and the Transformation of Work in Colonial Mombasa*. New Haven, CT: Yale University Press, 1987.

———, ed. *Struggle for the City: Migrant Labor, Capital, and the State in Urban Africa*. Thousand Oaks, CA: Sage, 1983.

Coquery-Vidrovitch, Catherine. "Histoire des femmes d'Afrique." *Clio* 6 (1997): 7–13.

———. *The History of African Cities South of the Sahara: From the Origins to Colonization*. Translated by Mary Baker. Princeton, NJ: Markus Wiener, 2005.

———. *Le Congo au temps des grandes compagnies concessionnaires 1898–1930*. Paris: Mouton, 1972.

Cuny, C. "De Libreville au Cameroun." *Bulletin de la Société de Géographie* 7, no. 17 (1896): 340–45.

Delafosse, Maurice, Dr. Poutrin, and Monseigneur Le Roy. *Enquête coloniale dans l'Afrique française occidentale et équatoriale sur l'organisation de la famille indigène, les fiançailles, le mariage avec une esquisse générale des langues de l'Afrique*. Paris: Société d'Edition géographiques, maritime et colonial, 1930.

D'Emilio, John, and Estelle B. Freedman. *Intimate Matters: A History of Sexuality in America*. Chicago: University of Chicago Press, 2007.

Deschamps, Hubert. *Traditions orales et archives au Gabon: Contribution à l'ethnohistoire*. Paris: Berger-Levrault, 1962.

Didzambou, Rufin. "Les migrations de salariat au Gabon de 1843 à 1960: Processus et incidences." PhD diss., Université de Lille II, 1995.

Diouf, Mamadou. "Des historiens et des histoires, pourquoi faire? L'Historiographie africaine entre l'Etat et les Communautés." *African Sociological Review* 3, no. 2 (1999): 99–128.

———. "(Re)Imagining an African City: Performing Culture, Arts, and Citizenship in Dakar (Senegal), 1980–2000." In *The Spaces of the Modern City: Imaginaries, Politics, and Everyday Life*, edited by Gyan Prakash and Kevin M. Kruse, 346–73. Princeton, NJ: Princeton University Press, 2008.

Dubois, Colette. "Le prix d'une guerre: Deux colonies pendant la première guerre mondiale (Gabon—Oubangui-Chari, 1911–1923)." PhD diss., Aix-en-Provence, Université de Provence, 1985.

Du Chaillu, Paul Belloni. *Explorations and Adventures in Equatorial Africa*. London: Murray, 1861.

Éboué, Félix. *Politique indigène de L'Afrique Equatoriale Française*. Brazzaville: Imprimerie officielle de l'Afrique Equatoriale Française, 1941.

Epprecht, Marc. *Heterosexual Africa? The History of An Idea from the Age of Exploration to the Age of AIDS*. Athens: Ohio University Press, 2008.

———. *Hungochani: The History of a Dissident Sexuality in Southern Africa*. Montreal: McGill-Queen's University Press, 2004.

Epprecht, Marc, and Charles Gueboguo, eds. "New Perspectives on Sexualities in Africa." *Canadian Journal of African Studies / Revue Canadienne des Études Africaines* 43, no. 1 (2009): 1–7.

Etoughe, Dominique. *Justice indigène et essor du droit coutumier au Gabon: La contribution de Léon M'ba, 1924–1938.* Paris: L'Harmattan, 2007.

Falk Moore, Sally. *Social Facts and Fabrications: "Customary" Law on Kilimanjaro, 1880–1980.* Cambridge: Cambridge University Press, 1986.

Faure, J. L., and Justin Godart. *La vie aux colonies: Préparation de la femme à la vie coloniale.* Paris: Larose, 1938.

Feierman, Steven. *The Shambaa Kingdom: A History.* Madison: University of Wisconsin Press, 1974.

Findlay, Eileen J. Suárez. *Imposing Decency: The Politics of Sexuality and Race in Puerto Rico, 1870–1920.* Durham, NC: Duke University Press, 1999.

Ferguson, James. *Expectations of Modernity: Myths and Meanings of Urban Life on the Zambian Copperbelt.* Berkeley: University of California Press, 1998.

Foucault, Michel. *The History of Sexuality.* Vol. 1, *An Introduction.* Translated by Robert Hurley. New York: Pantheon, 1990.

Freund, Bill. *The African City: A History.* Cambridge: Cambridge University Press, 2007.

Gaffarel, Paul. *Les colonies françaises.* Paris: Librairie Germer Baillière, 1899.

Geiger, Susan N. G. "Women's Life Histories: Method and Content." *Signs* 11, no. 2 (Winter 1986): 334–51.

Gengenbach, Heidi. "Truth-Telling and the Politics of Women's Life History Research in Africa: A Reply to Kirk Hoppe." *International Journal of African Historical Studies* 27, no. 3 (1994): 619–27.

———. "'What My Heart Wanted': Gendered Stories of Early Colonial Encounters in Southern Mozambique." In Allman, Geiger, and Musisi, *Women in African Colonial Histories,* 19–47.

George, Abosede A. "Feminist Activism and Class Politics: The Example of the Lagos Girl Hawker Project." *Women's Studies Quarterly* 35, nos. 3–4 (2007): 128–43.

———. "Within Salvation: Girl Hawkers and the Colonial State in Development Era Lagos." *Journal of Social History* 44, no. 3 (2011): 837–59.

Gilfoyle, Timothy J. *City of Eros: New York City, Prostitution, and the Commercialization of Sex, 1790–1920.* New York: Norton, 1992.

Ginio, Ruth. *French Colonialism Unmasked: The Vichy Years in French West Africa.* Lincoln: University of Nebraska Press, 2006.

Goerg, Odile. "Femmes africaines et pratique historique en France." *Politique Africaine* 72 (1998): 130–44.

———, ed. *Perspectives historiques sur le genre en Afrique.* Paris: L'Harmattan, 2007.

Gray, Christopher J. *Colonial Rule and Crisis in Equatorial Africa: Southern Gabon, ca. 1850–1940.* Rochester, NY: University of Rochester Press, 2002.

Gray, Christopher J., and Francois Ngolet. "Lambaréné, *Okoumé* and the Transformation of Labor along the Middle Ogooué (Gabon), 1870–1945." *Journal of African History* 40, no. 1 (1999): 87–107.

Grébert, Fernand. *Au Gabon: L'Afrique Equatoriale Française.* Paris: Sociétés des Missions Evangéliques, 1948.

Green, James N. *Beyond Carnival: Male Homosexuality in Twentieth-Century Brazil.* Chicago: University of Chicago Press, 2001.

Gutiérrez, Ramón A. "What's Love Got to Do with It?" *Journal of American History* 88, no. 3 (December 2001): 866–69.

Guy, Donna J. *Sex and Danger in Buenos Aires: Prostitution, Family, and Nation in Argentina*. Lincoln: University of Nebraska Press, 1992.

Guyer, Jane I. "Colonial Situations in Long-Term Perspective: The Value of Beti Bridewealth." In *Money Matters: Instability, Values, and Social Payments in the Modern History of West African Communities*, edited by Jane I. Guyer, 113–32. Portsmouth, NH: Heinemann, 1995.

——. "Wealth in People, Wealth in Things—Introduction." *Journal of African History* 36, no. 1 (1995): 83–90.

Hansen, Karen T. "Body Politics: Sexuality, Gender, and Domestic Service in Zambia." *Journal of Women's History* 2, no. 1 (1990): 120–41.

——. *Distant Companions: Servants and Employers in Zambia, 1900–1985*. Ithaca, NY: Cornell University Press, 1989.

Hawkins, Sean. "'The Woman in Question': Marriage and Identity in the Colonial Courts of Northern Ghana, 1907–1954." In Allman, Geiger, and Musisi, *Women in African Colonial Histories*, 116–43.

——. *Writing and Colonialism in Northern Ghana: The Encounter between the LoDagaa and "The World on Paper," 1892–1991*. Toronto: University of Toronto Press, 2002.

Henige, David P. *The Chronology of Oral Tradition: Quest for a Chimera*. Oxford: Oxford University Press, 1974.

Hodgson, Dorothy L., and Sheryl A. McCurdy, eds. *"Wicked Women" and the Reconfiguration of Gender in Africa*. Portsmouth, NH: Heinemann, 2001.

Hofmeyr, Isabel. *"We Spend Our Years as a Tale That Is Told": Oral Historical Narrative in a South African Chiefdom*. Portsmouth, NH: Heinemann, 1993.

Hoppe, Kirk. "Whose Life Is It, Anyway? Issues of Representation in Life Narrative Texts of African Women." *International Journal of African Historical Studies* 26, no. 3 (1993): 623–36.

Howe, Russell Warren. *Theirs the Darkness*. London: Jenkins, 1956.

Hubbard, Phil. *Cities and Sexualities*. New York: Routledge, 2012.

Hugon, Anne, ed. *Histoire des femmes en situation coloniale: Afrique, Asie XXème siècle*. Paris: L'Harmattan, 2004.

Hunt, Nancy Rose. *A Colonial Lexicon of Birth Ritual, Medicalization, and Mobility in the Congo*. Durham, NC: Duke University Press, 1999.

——. "Domesticity and Colonialism in Belgian Africa: Usumbura's *Foyer Social*, 1946–1960." *Signs* 15, no. 3 (1990): 447–74.

——. "Le bébé en brousse": European Women, African Birth Spacing, and Colonial Intervention in Breast Feeding in the Belgian Congo." *International Journal of African Historical Studies* 21, no. 3 (1988): 401–32.

——. "Noise over Camouflaged Polygamy, Colonial Morality Taxation, and a Woman-Naming Crisis in Belgian Africa." *Journal of African History* 32, no. 3 (1991): 471–94.

Hunter, Mark. *Love in the Time of AIDS: Inequality, Gender, and Rights in South Africa*. Bloomington: Indiana University Press, 2010.

——. "The Materiality of Everyday Sex: Thinking beyond 'Prostitution.'" *African Studies* 61, no. 1 (2002): 99–120.

Hutchinson, Thomas J. *Ten Years' Wanderings among the Ethiopians: With Sketches of the Manners and Customs of the Civilized and Uncivilized Tribes, from Senegal to Gaboon.* London: Hurst and Blackett, 1861.

Hutton, William. *A Voyage to Africa: Including a Narrative of an Embassy to One of the Interior Kingdoms, in the Year 1820.* London: Longman, Hurst, Rees, Orme, and Brown, 1821.

Idourah, Silvère Ngoundos. *Colonisation et confiscation de la justice en Afrique: L'administration de la justice au Gabon, Moyen-Congo, Oubangui-Chari et Tchad de la création des colonies à l'aube des indépendances.* Paris: L'Harmattan, 2001.

Ivaska, Andrew. *Cultured States: Youth, Gender, and Modern Style in 1960s Dar es Salaam.* Durham, NC: Duke University Press, 2011.

Jean-Baptiste, Rachel. "'A Black Girl Should Not Be with a White Man': Sex, Race, and African Women's Social and Legal Status in Colonial Gabon, c. 1900–1946.'" *Journal of Women's History* 22, no. 2 (Summer 2010): 56–82.

———. "'Miss Eurafrica': Men, Women's Sexuality, and Métis Identity in Late Colonial French Africa, 1945–1960." *Journal of the History of Sexuality* 20, no. 3 (September 2011): 568–93.

———. "'The Option of the Judicial Path': Disputes over Marriage, Divorce, and Extra-Marital Sex in Colonial Courts in Libreville, Gabon (1939–1959)." *Cahiers d'etudes africaines* 187–88 (2007): 643–70.

———. "'These Laws Should Be Made by Us': Customary Marriage Law, Codification and Political Authority in Twentieth-Century Colonial Gabon." *Journal of African History* 49, no. 2 (July 2008): 217–40.

———. "Une Ville Libre? Marriage, Divorce, and Sexuality in Colonial Libreville, Gabon, 1849–1960." PhD diss., Stanford University, 2005.

Jeater, Diana. *Marriage, Perversion, and Power: The Construction of Moral Discourse in Southern Rhodesia, 1894–1930.* Oxford: Oxford University Press, 1993.

Jennings, Eric T. *Vichy in the Tropics: Pétain's National Revolution in Madagascar, Guadeloupe, and Indochina, 1940–1944.* Stanford, CA: Stanford University Press, 2001.

Jones, Hilary. *The Métis of Senegal: Urban Life and Politics in French West Africa.* Bloomington: Indiana University Press, 2013.

Kanogo, Tabitha. *African Womanhood in Colonial Kenya, 1900–1950.* Athens: Ohio University Press, 2005.

Klieman, Kairn A. *"The Pygmies Were Our Compass": Bantu and Batwa in the History of Early West Central Africa, Early Times to c. 1900 C.E.* Portsmouth, NH: Heinemann, 2003.

Kratz, Corinne A. "Conversations and Lives." In White, Miescher, and Cohen, *African Words,* 127–61.

Largeau, Victor. *Encyclopédie pahouine, Congo français: Éléments de grammaire et dictionnaire français-pahouin.* Paris: Leroux, 1901.

Lasserre, Guy. "Libreville: Cité des eaux." In Charbonnier, *Gabon.*

———. *Libreville: La ville et sa région.* Paris: Colin, 1958.

Lee, Christopher Joon-Hai. "The 'Native' Undefined: Colonial Categories, Anglo-African Status and the Politics of Kinship in British Central Africa, 1929–38." *Journal of African History* 46, no. 3 (2005): 455–78.

Le Jeune, Père. *Au Congo: La situation faite à la femme et la famille.* Paris: Challamel, 1900.

Le Roy, Alexandre. *La désorganisation de la famille africaine*. Paris: Soye, 1903.

Lindsay, Lisa A. *Working with Gender: Wage Labor and Social Change in Southwestern Nigeria*. Portsmouth, NH: Heinemann, 2003.

Little, Kenneth. *African Women in Towns: An Aspect of Africa's Social Revolution*. London: CUP Archive, 1977.

Londres, Albert. *Terre d'ébène: La traite des noirs*. Paris: Le Serpent à Plumes, 1929.

Loungou-Mouele, Théophile. "Le Gabon de 1910 à 1925: Les indices de la première guerre mondiale sur l'évolution politique, économique, et sociale." PhD diss., Université de Provence, Centre d'Aix, 1984.

Lovett, Margot. "Gender Relations, Class Formation, and the Colonial State in Africa." In *Women and the State in Africa*, edited by Jane L. Parpart and Kathleen A. Staudt, 23–46. Boulder, CO: Lynne Rienner, 1989.

Lydon, Ghislaine. "Women, Children and the Popular Front's Mission of Inquiry in French West Africa." In *French Colonial Empire and the Popular Front: Hope and Disillusion*, edited by Tony Chafer and Amanda Sackur, 170–87. London: Palgrave Macmillan, 1999.

Mann, Kristin. *Marrying Well: Marriage, Status, and Social Change among the Educated Elite in Colonial Lagos*. Cambridge: Cambridge University Press, 1985.

Mann, Kristin, and Richard L. Roberts. *Law in Colonial Africa*. Stanford, CA: Stanford University Press, 1991.

Marcus, Sharon. *Apartment Stories: City and Home in Nineteenth-Century Paris and London*. Berkeley: University of California Press, 1999.

Marie-Germaine. *Le Christ au Gabon*. Louvain: Museum Lessianum, 1931.

Marshall, Alfred. *Principles of Economics*. Vol. 1. London: Macmillan, 1980.

Martin, Phyllis M. *Catholic Women of Congo-Brazzaville: Mothers and Sisters in Troubled Times*. Bloomington: Indiana University Press, 2009.

——. *Leisure and Society in Colonial Brazzaville*. Cambridge: Cambridge University Press, 1995.

Mayer, Raymond. *Histoire de la famille gabonaise*. Libreville: Centre Culturel Français Saint-Exupéry, 2002.

Mba, Léon. "Discours Prononcé à Port-Gentil par le Président de la République." *Bulletin Quotidien de l'Agence Gabonaise d'Information, Bulletin Spécial*. Libreville, 1963.

——. "Essai de droit coutumier pahouin." In *Ecrits ethnographiques*. Libreville: Raponda Walker, 2001.

Mbilinyi, Marjorie. "'I'd Have Been a Man': Politics and the Labor Process in Producing Personal Narratives." In *Interpreting Women's Lives: Feminist Theory and Personal Narratives*, edited by Personal Narratives Group, 204–27. Bloomington: Indiana University Press, 1989.

Mbokolo, Elikia. "French Colonial Policy in Equatorial Africa in the 1940s and 1950s." In *The Transfer of Power in Africa*, edited by Prosser Gifford and William R. Louis, 173–210. New Haven, CT: Yale University Press, 1982.

——. *Noirs et blancs en Afrique Équatoriale: Les sociétés côtières et la pénétration française, vers 1820–1874*. Mouton: Ecole Hautes Etudes en Sciences Sociales, 1981.

McClendon, Thomas V. *Genders and Generations Apart: Labor Tenants and Customary Law in Segregation-Era South Africa, 1920s to 1940s*. Portsmouth, NH: Heinemann, 2002.

McClintock, Anne. *Imperial Leather: Race, Gender and Sexuality in the Colonial Contest.* New York: Routledge, 1994.

McCulloch, Jock. *Black Peril, White Virtue: Sexual Crime in Southern Rhodesia, 1902–1935.* Bloomington: Indiana University Press, 2000.

Merlet, Annie. *Légendes et histoire des Myéné de l'Ogooué.* Libreville: Centre culturel français Saint-Exupéry, 1990.

———. *Le pays des trois estuaires (1471–1900): Quatre siècles de relations extérieures dans les estuaires du Muni, de la Mondah, et du Gabon.* Libreville: Centre culturel français Saint-Exupéry, 1990.

Messi Me Nang, Clotaire. "Les travailleurs des chantiers forestiers du Gabon: Hybridité et invisibilité d'une culture ouvrière, 1892–1962." PhD diss., Université de Paris I, 2007.

Métégué N'Nah, Nicolas. *Domination coloniale au Gabon: Les combattants de la première heure, 1839–1920.* Paris: L'Harmattan, 1981.

———. *Economies et Sociétés au Gabon dans la première moitié du dix-neuvième siècle.* Paris: L'Harmattan, 1979.

———. *Lumière sur points d'ombre: Contribution à la connaissance de la société gabonaise.* Langres: Gueniot, 1984.

Miescher, Stephan F. "The Life Histories of Boakye Yiadom (Akasease Kofi of Abetifi, Kwawu): Exploring the Subjectivity and 'Voices' of a Teacher-Catechist in Colonial Ghana." In White, Miescher, and Cohen, *African Words, African Voices,* 162–93.

———. *Making Men in Ghana.* Bloomington: Indiana University Press, 2005.

Miescher, Stephan F., and Lisa A. Lindsay. *Men and Masculinities in Modern Africa.* Portsmouth, NH: Heinemann, 2002.

Migeod, Frederick W. H. *Across Equatorial Africa.* London: Cranton, 1923.

Miller, Joseph C. *The African Past Speaks: Essays on Oral Tradition and History.* Hamden, CT: Archon, 1980.

Milligan, Robert H. *The Fetish Folk of West Africa.* New York: Revell, 1912.

Mirza, Sarah, and Margaret Strobel, eds. *Three Swahili Women: Life Histories from Mombasa, Kenya.* Translated by Sarah Mirza and Margaret Strobel. Bloomington: Indiana University Press, 1989.

Moodie, T. Dunbar. *Going for Gold: Men, Mines, and Migration.* Berkeley: University of California Press, 1994.

Moore, Donald, and Richard L. Roberts. "Listening for the Silences." *History in Africa* 17 (1990): 319–25.

Moore, Henrietta L., and Megan Vaughan. *Cutting Down Trees: Gender, Nutrition, and Agricultural Change in the Northern Province of Zambia, 1890–1990.* Portsmouth, NH: Heinemann, 1994.

Moorman, Marissa J. *Intonations: A Social History of Music and Nation in Luanda, Angola, from 1945 to Recent Times.* Bloomington: Indiana University Press, 2008.

Morrell, Robert, ed. *Changing Men in Southern Africa.* Natal: University of Natal Press, 2001.

Morrell, Robert, and Lahoucine Ouzgane, eds. *African Masculinities: Men in Africa from the Late Nineteenth Century to the Present.* New York: Palgrave Macmillan, 2005.

Murray, Colin. "High Bridewealth, Migrant Labour and the Position of Women in Lesotho." *Journal of African Law* 21, no. 1 (1977): 79–96.

Murray, Stephen O., and Will Roscoe. *Boy-Wives and Female Husbands: Studies in African Sexualities*. New York: Palgrave Macmillan, 2001.

Mutongi, Kenda. "'Dear Dolly's' Advice: Representations of Youth, Courtship, and Sexualities in Africa, 1960–1980." *International Journal of African Historical Studies* 33, no. 1 (2000): 1–23.

Mvududu, Sara C. *Lobola: Its Implication for Women's Reproductive Rights*. Harare: Weaver Press, 2002.

Neu, Joseph-Henri. "Etudes gabonaises: Le pays et les habitants." *Annales Apostoliques* 4 (October 1886): 125–41.

Newell, Stephanie. *The Forger's Tale: The Search for Odeziaku*. Athens: Ohio University Press, 2006.

Ngou, Honorine. *Mariage et violence dans la société traditionnelle fang au Gabon*. Paris: L'Harmattan, 2007.

Nnang Ndong, Léon Modeste. *L'effort de guerre dans l'Afrique: Le Gabon dans la deuxième guerre mondiale 1939–1947*. Paris: L'Harmattan, 2001.

———. "Le Gabon dans la deuxième guerre mondiale: L'effort de guerre, indices économiques et sociaux." PhD diss., Université Panthéon-Sorbonne, 2011.

Nuttall, Sarah, and Achille Mbembe, eds. *Johannesburg: The Elusive Metropolis*. Durham, NC: Duke University Press, 2008.

Nzoghe, Anselme. "L'Exploitation forestière et les conditions d'exploitation des peuples de la colonie du Gabon de 1920 à 1940: Le travail forcé." PhD diss., Université de Provence, Aix-Marseille, 1984.

Padgug, Robert A. "Sexual Matters: On Conceptualizing Sexuality in History." In *Passion and Power: Sexuality in History*, edited by Kathy Peiss and Christina Simmons, 14–31. Philadelphia: Temple University Press, 1999.

Pambo-Loueya, C. Félix. "La colonie du Gabon de 1914 à 1939: Étude economique et sociale." PhD diss., Université de Paris VII, 1980.

Parker, John. *Making the Town: Ga State and Society in Early Colonial Accra*. Portsmouth, NH: Heinemann, 2000.

Parpart, Jane L. "The Household and the Mine Shaft: Gender and Class Struggles on the Zambian Copperbelt, 1926–64." *Journal of Southern African Studies* 13, no. 1 (1986): 36–56.

———. "Sexuality and Power on the Zambian Copperbelt, 1926–1964." In *Patriarchy and Class: African Women in the Home and the Workforce*, edited by Sharon B. Stichter and Jane L. Parpart, 141–60. Boulder, CO: Westview Press, 1988.

———. "'Where Is Your Mother?' Gender, Urban Marriage, and Colonial Discourse on the Zambian Copperbelt, 1924–1945." *International Journal of African Historical Studies* 27, no. 2 (1994): 241–71.

Patterson, K. David. "The Mpongwé and the Orungu of the Gabon Coast, 1815–1875: The Transition to Colonial Rule." PhD diss., Stanford University, 1971.

———. *The Northern Gabon Coast to 1875*. Oxford: Oxford University Press, 1975.

———. "The Vanishing Mpongwé: European Contact and Demographic Change in the Gabon River." *Journal of African History* 16, no. 2 (1975): 217–38.

Patterson, Orlando. *Slavery and Social Death: A Comparative Study*. Cambridge: Cambridge University Press, 1985.

Petrocelli, Rachel. "City Dwellers and the State: Making Modern Urbanism in Colonial Dakar, 1914–1944." PhD diss., Stanford University, 2001.

Radcliffe-Brown, A. R., and C. Daryll Forde, eds. *African Systems of Kinship and Marriage*. Oxford: Oxford University Press, 1950.

Ranger, Terence. "The Invention of Tradition in Colonial Africa." In *The Invention of Tradition*, edited by Eric J. Hobsbawm and Terence Ranger, 211–62. Cambridge: Cambridge University Press, 1983.

Raponda-Walker, André. *Notes d'histoire du Gabon: Suivi de toponymie de l'estuaire Libreville et toponymie du Fernan-Vaz Port-Gentil*. Libreville: Raponda Walker, 1996.

Rapotchombo, Gaston. *Hommage à Léon Mba*. Libreville: Ministère de l'Information, des Postes et Télécommunications de la République gabonaise, 1970.

Ray, Carina E. "Policing Sexual Boundaries: The Politics of Race in Colonial Ghana." PhD diss., Cornell University, 2007.

——. "'The White Wife Problem': Sex, Race, and the Contested Politics of Repatriation to Interwar British West Africa." *Gender and History* 21, no. 3 (2009): 628–46.

Redding, Sean. "South African Women and Migration in Umtata, Transkei, 1880–1935." In Sheldon, *Courtyards*, 31–46.

Renucci, France. *Souvenirs de femmes au temps des colonies*. Paris: Balland, 1988.

République du Gabon. *Libreville: Capitale rénovée*. Paris: Société Internationale d'Etudes et de Réalisations Africaines, 1979.

Rich, Jeremy M. "Civilized Attire: Dress, Cultural Change and Status in Libreville, Gabon, ca. 1860–1914." *Cultural and Social History* 2, no. 2 (2005): 189–214.

——. "'Une Babylone Noire': Interracial Unions in Colonial Libreville, c. 1860–1914." *French Colonial History* 4 (2003): 145–69.

——. *A Workman Is Worthy of His Meat: Food and Colonialism in the Gabon Estuary*. Lincoln: University of Nebraska Press, 2007.

Roberts, Richard L. *Litigants and Households: African Disputes and Colonial Courts in the French Soudan, 1895–1912*. Portsmouth, NH: Heinemann, 2005.

——. "Text and Testimony in the *Tribunal de Première Instance*, Dakar, during the Early Twentieth Century." *Journal of African History* 31, no. 3 (November 1990): 447–63.

Robertson, Claire C. *Sharing the Same Bowl! A Socioeconomic History of Women and Class in Accra, Ghana*. Ann Arbor: University of Michigan Press, 1990.

——. *Trouble Showed the Way: Women, Men, and Trade in the Nairobi Area, 1890–1990*. Bloomington: Indiana University Press, 1997.

Rodet, Marie. "Continuum of Gendered Violence: The Colonial Female Desertion as a Customary Criminal Offense, French Soudan, 1900–1949." In Burrill, Roberts, and Thornberry, *Domestic Violence and the Law in Colonial and Postcolonial Africa*, 74–93.

——. "Gender, Customs, and Colonial Law in French Sudan, 1918–1939." *Cahiers d'etudes africaines* 47, nos. 187–88 (2007): 583–602.

Rondet-Saint, Maurice. *Dans notre empire noir*. Paris: Société d'Editions, 1929.

Rosenwein, Barbara H. "Problems and Methods in the History of Emotions." *Passions in Context* 1, no. 1 (2010): 1–32. http://www.passionsincontext.de/.

——. "Worrying about Emotions in History." *American Historical Review* 107, no. 3 (2002): 821–45.

Saada, Emmanuelle. *Empire's Children: Race, Filiation, and Citizenship in the French Colonies*. Translated by Arthur Goldhammer. Chicago: University of Chicago Press, 2012.

———. *Les enfants de la colonie: Les métis de l'empire français entre sujétion et citoyen-
neté*. Paris: La Découverte, 2007.
6Schler, Lynn. "The Strangers of New Bell: Immigration, Community and Public
Space in Colonial Douala, Cameroon, 1914–1960. " PhD diss., Stanford University,
2001.
———. *The Strangers of New Bell: Immigration, Public Space and Community in
Colonial Douala, Cameroon, 1914–1960*. Pretoria: Unisa Press, 2008.
Schmidt, Elizabeth. *Peasants, Traders, and Wives: Shona Women in the History of
Zimbabwe, 1870–1939*. Portsmouth, NH: Heinemann, 1992.
———. "Race, Sex, and Domestic Labor: The Question of African Female Servants in
Southern Rhodesia, 1900–1939." In *African Encounters with Domesticity*, edited by
Karen T. Hansen, 221–41. New Brunswick, NJ: Rutgers University Press, 1992.
Scott, Joan W. *Gender and the Politics of History*. New York: Columbia University
Press, 1999.
Shadle, Brett L. " 'Changing Traditions to Meet Current Altering Conditions': Customary
Law, African Courts and the Rejection of Codification in Kenya, 1930–60."
Journal of African History 40, no. 3 (1999): 411–31.
———. "*Girl Cases*": *Marriage and Colonialism in Gusiiland, Kenya, 1890–1970*.
Portsmouth, NH: Heinemann, 2006.
Sheldon, Kathleen, ed. *Courtyards, Markets, City Streets: Urban Women in Africa*.
Boulder, CO: Westview Press, 1996.
Short, John R. *Urban Theory: A Critical Assessment*. New York: Routledge, 2006.
Simone, AbdouMaliq. *For the City Yet to Come: Changing African Life in Four Cities*.
Durham, NC: Duke University Press, 2004.
Smith, Mary F. *Baba of Karo*. New Haven, CT: Yale University Press, 1953.
Spurr, David. *The Rhetoric of Empire: Colonial Discourse in Journalism, Travel Writing,
and Imperial Administration*. Durham, NC: Duke University Press, 1993.
Stansell, Christine. *City of Women: Sex and Class in New York, 1789–1860*. Chicago:
University of Chicago Press, 1987.
Stoler, Ann L. *Carnal Knowledge and Imperial Power: Race and the Intimate in
Colonial Rule*. Berkeley: University of California Press, 2002.
———. "Making Empire Respectable: The Politics of Race and Sexual Morality in
20th-Century Colonial Cultures." *American Ethnologist* 16, no. 4 (November 1989):
634–60.
———. "Rethinking Colonial Categories: European Communities and the Boundaries
of Rule." *Comparative Studies in Society and History* 31, no. 1 (January 1989): 134–61.
———. "Tense and Tender Ties: The Politics of Comparison in North American History
and (Post) Colonial Studies." *Journal of American History* 88, no. 3 (December
2001): 829–65.
Summers, Carol. "Intimate Colonialism: The Imperial Production of Reproduction in
Uganda, 1907–1925." *Signs* 16, no. 4 (Summer 1991): 787–807.
———. "Mission Boys, Civilized Men, and Marriage: Educated African Men in the
Missions of Southern Rhodesia, 1920–1945." *Journal of Religious History* 23, no. 1
(December 2002): 75–91.
Taylor, Jean Gelman. *The Social World of Batavia: European and Eurasian in Dutch
Asia*. Madison: University of Wisconsin Press, 2001.
Thomas, Lynn M. *Politics of the Womb: Women, Reproduction, and the State in Kenya*.
Berkeley: University of California Press, 2003.

Toungara, Jeanne Maddox. "Changing the Meaning of Marriage: Women and Family Law in Côte D'Ivoire." In *African Feminism: The Politics of Survival in Sub-Saharan Africa*, edited by Gwendolyn Mikell, 53–76. Philadelphia: University of Pennsylvania Press, 1997.

Trilles, Henri. *Chez les Fang, ou quinze années de séjour au Congo français*. Lille: Desclée, De Brouwer, 1912.

Trocbain, Jean L. "Les études poursuivies par l'Institut d'études centrafricaines depuis sa création sur le territoire de la République du Congo." *Bulletin Institut d'Etudes Centrafricaines* 19–20 (1960): 127–88.

Van Allen, Judith. "'Aba Riots' or Igbo 'Women's War'? Ideology, Stratification, and the Invisibility of Women." In *Women in Africa: Studies in Social and Economic Change*, edited by Nancy J. Hafkin and Edna G. Bay, 59–85. Stanford, CA: Stanford University Press, 1976.

Van Onselen, Charles. *Chibaro: African Mine Labour in Southern Rhodesia, 1900–1933*. London: Pluto Press, 1976.

———. *Studies in the Social and Economic History of Witwatersrand, 1886–1914*. New York: Longman, 1982.

Vansina, Jan. *Oral Tradition: A Study in Historical Methodology*. Translated by H. M. Wright. London: Transaction Publishers, 1965.

———. *Paths in the Rainforests: Toward a History of Political Tradition in Equatorial Africa*. Madison: University of Wisconsin Press, 1990.

Vassal, Gabrielle M. *Life in French Congo*. London: Unwin, 1925.

Vaughan, Megan. *Curing Their Ills: Colonial Power and African Illness*. Stanford, CA: Stanford University Press, 1991.

Vignon, Alexis-Edouard. "Le comptoir français du Gabon, sur la côte occidentale d'Afrique." *Nouvelles annales des voyages* 4 (1856): 281–302.

Walkowitz, Judith R. *City of Dreadful Delight: Narratives of Sexual Danger in Late-Victorian London*. Chicago: University of Chicago Press, 1992.

Webster, James B. *Chronology, Migration, and Drought in Interlacustrine Africa*. New York: Holmes and Meier, 1978.

Weismantel, Mary. *Cholas and Pishtacos: Stories of Race and Sex in the Andes*. Chicago: University of Chicago Press, 2001.

White, Luise. *The Comforts of Home: Prostitution in Colonial Nairobi*. Chicago: University of Chicago Press, 1990.

———. "Telling More: Lies, Secrets, and History." *History and Theory* 39, no. 4 (December 2000): 11–22.

———. "True Confessions." *Journal of Women's History* 15, no. 4 (Winter 2004): 142–44.

White, Luise, Stephan F. Miescher, and David W. Cohen, eds. *African Words, African Voices: Critical Practices in Oral History*. Bloomington: Indiana University Press, 2001.

White, Owen. *Children of the French Empire: Miscegenation and Colonial Society in French West Africa, 1895–1960*. Oxford: Oxford University Press, 1999.

Wright, Marcia. "Justice, Women, and the Social Order in Abercorn, Northeastern Rhodesia, 1897–1903." In *African Women and the Law: Historical Perspectives*, edited by Margaret Jean Hay and Marcia Wright, 33–50. Boston: Boston University African Studies Center, 1982.

Yoshikuni, Tsuneo. *African Urban Experiences in Colonial Zimbabwe: A Social History of Harare before 1925*. Harare: Weaver Press, 2007.

Index

extramarital sexual relationships, *(cont'd)*
resulting from, 173; as prevalent, 163;
reduced fertility and morbidity attributed
to, 68–69; sexual economy of women's,
71–72; standards for, 181–82; women seek
to find new husband through, 156. *See
also* adultery
Faguinovery, Michel Julien, 114
family size, 86
famine, 51, 52, 81
Fang, Estuary. *See* Estuary Fang
farming. *See* agriculture
FEA. *See* French Equatorial Africa (FEA)
Ferguson, James, 5–6
flirting, 173, 175
food shortages, 51, 52, 66–67, 68, 205
forced labor: African *forestiers* not allowed
to pay cash in lieu of, 64–65; chiefs
in enforcement of, 48; demographic
decline due to, 68; in extraction of
forest products, 43; Fang elude efforts to
extract, 56, 77; from schoolgirls, 54
Foucault, Michel, 14
France, Marie, 212–14
Free French, 81, 82, 124, 197, 245n35
French citizenship, 196, 206–7, 210, 267n6,
270n54
French Equatorial Africa (FEA): African
family size in, 86; bridewealth loan fund
in, 124–33; centralized control sought
by, 43, 46–47, 52; Decree Establishing
the Jural Status of Mixed Race Persons
of 1936, 206–7; Free French control, 81,
82, 124, 245n35; Frenchwomen in, 59,
199; importing laborers, 94–95; Institute
for Central African Studies research on,
82; Mandel Decree of 1939, 145, 149, 157;
métis as concern in, 209–10; Mpongwé
ask for Gabon to be autonomous from,
58; Ordinance Instituting the Protection
of Métis of Free France proposal of
1941, 210–11; planned communities in,
90; salaried workers in, 94; sex ratio in,
85–86; timber industry in, 48. *See also*
Gabon
furniture, 92, 110
Gabon: administration division of, 46, 47;
attempt to curtail African economic
autonomy, 62, 64; colonial consolidation,
1910–1929, 45–50; concessionary system
in, 42; ethnic groups in, 26; lack of
scholarly attention to early history of, 23;
okoumé wood industry, 44, 48–50, 51,
52, 64, 71, 76, 239n21; political parties,
95; population decline in twentieth

century, 45, 68; postcolonial state as
autocratic, 18; rivers of, 26; road network
of, 90; sources for precolonial history of,
17–18; topography of, 25–26; violence of
colonial rule in, 42–43. *See also* Estuary
region
"Galoas, Pahouin, and Akélais Customs"
(1933), 139–40
gardens, 38, 91, 94
Geiger, Susan, 9
gender: in African history, 6–12; contestation
of roles, 24; convergent and
interdependent processes in, 221–22;
equal ratio in Libreville, 24; in Fang
division of labor, 37–38; as fluid, 9;
gendering of the African worker, 9;
gendering men, 10; hierarchies, 45,
59, 197, 198, 218; interracial sexual
relationships disrupt relations of,
65; negotiation of roles, 31; seen as
synonymous with women, 9. *See also*
men; women
Georges, King, 28
Glass, King, 28, 30
Glass neighborhood, 85, 89, 92
Gondjout, Paul, 122, 150
Gray, Christopher, 49
Guyer, Jane, 103, 104, 108, 117
Hawkins, Sean, 143
heterosexuality: changes in relationships, 4,
24; as not normative, 14–15; systems of
feeling in, 12. *See also* sexuality
Hodgson, Dorothy L., 7, 230n59
homosexuality: men deny, 170; seen as un-
African, 15
houses, 54, 56, 62, 91–93, *93*, 204–5
Howe, Russell, 94
Hunt, Nancy Rose, 17
identity cards, 84, 188, 195, 196
Idourah, Silvère Ngoundos, 137
imported goods: in bridewealth, 2, 31, 38, 39,
40, 100, 106; food, 29, 76, 92; increasing
prices for, 52, 76; Libreville's residents
consume, 53–54; Libreville's trade in, 21,
56; Mpongwé wealth in, 29, 62, 76; status
indicated by, 30; wives traded for, 33;
women in interracial sexual relationships
have access to, 198; women's sexual labor
in acquiring, 62
impotence, 32, 170
indigénat, 46, 238n6
infant mortality, 68, 86
Institute for Central African Studies, 82
interracial sexual relationships, 194–216;
benefits for women in, 207; bridewealth

Moore, Henrietta, 82, 229n50
Moore, Sally Falk, 16–17
Moorman, Marissa J., 12
motherhood, 177, 215
Mpongwé, 25–35; access to formal education by, 29, 53, 58; agriculture of, 29; attempts to turn men to agriculture, 66; Catholics' view of, 35; clans, 26; clothing of, 53–54, 205; on customary law commission, 69; decentralized control in, 28; ethnic change in Libreville, 75, 83; European cultural norms adopted by, 53–55; on Fang as not city people, 89; Fang eclipse, 27, 36, 37, 77, 83, 244n13; Fang women seek divorces before Mpongwé chiefs, 143–44; girls' activities, 54; houses, 54, 92; interracial relationships between white men and women of, 2, 3, 24, 33–35, 45, 59–67, 195, 198, 199–216, 220–21; laziness attributed to, 55, 63, 66; Libreville site ceded by, 1; in Libreville's population, 53; Ligue des Droits de l'Homme of, 58; as managers of European factories, 36; marital status by ethnicity and gender in Libreville, 1944, 87; marriage among, 30–31; men as civil servant clerks, 48, 53; men in timber industry, 50; métis among, 200; as middlemen in European trade, 24, 26, 28–29, 35, 36, 37; mothers' influence on women, 61; as patrilineal, 26; percentage of women unmarried in 1918, 60; poisoning as means of social control among, 65; political organization of, 27–28; political voice of women among, 45, 63, 67, 197; polygamy among, 179; population by 1880s, 28; population decrease in mid-nineteenth century, 35; resist being categorized as natives, 57–58; settlement in Estuary region, 27; in slave trade, 28, 29, 30; tenuous marital ties among, 31–32; urban planning opposed by, 57, 89; wedding receptions among, 114
Musisi, Nakanyike, 9
Myènès: attempt to curtail economic autonomy of, 64; clothing of, 205; Estuary Fang eclipse, 77; in interracial sexual relationships, 59, 195, 203, 205; in Libreville's population, 53; as middlemen in European trade, 28, 36; monetization of bridewealth among, 108; in Professional Association of African Native Employees, 58; settle on Gabon coasts, 26. See also Mpongwé

Native Social Policy (Éboué), 119
Ndong, Albertine Ntsame, 108
Newell, Stephanie, 14
Ngolet, Francois, 49
Ngou, Honorine, 98
Nguema, Martin, 171, 172
Nguia, Flavie, 194–98
Nkolo, Edidie, 19
Nkotsoe, Mmantho, 19
Nnang Ndong, Léon Modest, 83
Nseghe, Léotine, 108–9
Ntchoveré, Joseph Lasseny, 33, 105, 205
Ntoutoume, David Edou, 111–12
Ntoutoume, Isabelle, 184
Ntoutoume, Jean Francois Mba, 170
Nuttall, Sarah, 165, 222, 227n19
Nyangenyona, Benoit Messani, 164, 169
Obame, Thanguy, 19
Obembe, Gilbert, 114
Ogooué region, 29
Okili, Catherine, 175, 203
okoumé wood. See timber industry
oral histories, 18–20
Ordinance Instituting the Protection of Métis of Free France (1941), 210–11
Oyeng, Achey, 173
Padgug, Robert A., 14
Pahouin Congress (1947), 148–49, 157, 189, 191
Parker, John, 5
Patterson, K. David, 23, 29, 35
Patterson, Orlando, 225n5
Petrocelli, Rachel, 219–20
poisoning, 65
political parties, 95
polygamy: by big men, 30; bridewealth loan fund requires renunciation of, 124, 126, 130; Catholic Church's view of, 70, 104; customary law recognizes, 148; decline of, 179; divorce in, 148; by ethnic group, 179; among Fang, 52, 63, 179; girlfriends replace, 179; as indicator of wealth and status, 179; among Mpongwé, 179; prostitution in polygamous marriages, 172–73; women reject after interracial relationships, 214
Poutrin, Dr., 68
Professional Association of African Native Employees, 58, 95
prostitution, 171–76; bridewealth associates marriage with, 115; colonial administrators' and missionaries' views on, 172–73; distinguishing factor of, 175; as economic niche for women, 217; by Fang women, 45, 63–64; as illegal, 172; interracial sexual relationships seen as,

opportunity in, 71; Libreville population affected by, 51, 52; Libreville's port affected by, 77; monetization of bridewealth and, 100; Myènè autonomy limited in, 64; post–World War II surge in, 81, 83; prostitution in, 172, 188; sexual activity in camps, 162–65, 263n6; World War II and, 81–82, 246n36

transportation, 91

"trust system" of trade, 34

urban life: African urbanization, 222–23; African women and men in shaping in, 4; the body as unit of analysis of, 165; in colonial cities, 217–19; marriage in shaping ideas about, 4, 5, 6; migration to cities after World War II, 7–8; personhood in, 218; precolonial African urbanism, 9, 226n11; transition from precolonial city-state to colonial city, 5; urban Africa, 5–6; urban becoming versus urbanization, 5–6; women's freedom in, 139

urban planning, 57–59, 75, 82, 89–90

vagabonds, 78, 90, 202

vagrancy, 90

Valentin-Smith, Governor, 125, 128

Van Allen, Judith, 242n123

Van de la Noitte, M., 206

Vansina, Jan, 18, 30

Vassal, Gabrielle, 53, 54, 58, 60

Vaughan, Megan, 13, 82, 229n50

La Voie Coloniale (newspaper), 58

wage labor: adultery seen as disrupting workers, 185; African versus European conceptions of, 6; for bridewealth payments, 102, 111–12, 122; bridewealth prices compared with wages, 116–18; city life and increased freedom for, 138; in colonial cities, 217; as economy of exploitation, 49; intersection of sexual economy with, 9; labor agitation and unions, 11, 95; male litigants in colonial courts employed in, 151; men migrate to Estuary region for, 11; only legal wife to receive husband's wages, 182; recruiting laborers, 94–95; as requirement for bridewealth loan fund, 128, 129, 130; seen as temporary, 112; in timber industry, 49–50, 76, 77, 81; transforming migratory groups into, 96; types of, 94; women and, 7, 8, 164, 166; women's sexual and domestic labor compared with, 220

water supply, 92

Weismantel, Mary, 165

White, Luise, 10, 12, 19, 202

White, Owen, 33

wife kidnapping, 39, 40, 109, 152–53, 186

witchcraft, 41, 79, 147

women: in African urbanism, 6–12; in agriculture, 11, 29, 30, 37–38, 56, 66, 77, 93–94, 166–67, 205, 229n50; in bridewealth negotiation, 101; bridewealth portion for, 108; choice of husbands, 11, 130, 145, 156, 157, 200; colonial currency empowers, 124; colonial officials on conjugal rights of, 136; colonial representations of, 230n57; desert their marriages, 153; divorce attributed to debauchery of, 123; divorce sought by, 32, 139, 141–44; dress, 54, 93; economic activities of, 93–94; economic niches for, 217; education for girls, 30, 45, 54, 86, 177, 200, 211; in extramarital sexual relationships, 32–33, 41, 124, 135, 147, 152, 156, 178, 183–85; in Fang division of labor, 37–38; fixed in rural areas, 7; Frenchwomen in French Equatorial Africa, 59, 199; gender seen as synonymous with, 9; good, 171, 172; husbands permit them sexual relationships with other men, 32–33, 39, 263n8; imported goods consumed by, 54; as intermediaries between colonial and African societies, 221; interracial sexual relationships between European men and Mpongwé, 2, 3, 24, 33–35, 45, 59–67, 194–216; Libreville marriage mutiny of 1849, 1–3, 11, 218; in Libreville's population, 50, 51, 52, 78, 84; as litigants in colonial courts, 143, 151–52; marital status by ethnicity and gender in Libreville, 1944, 87; Mba's "Essay on Fang Customary Law" on, 147; mediated encounters with colonial society, 220; men seek control over, 7, 23; mothers' influence on Mpongwé, 61; as motor of economic activity, 220; Mpongwé and Fang compared, 56–57; Mpongwé girls' activities, 54; percentage of Mpongwé women unmarried in 1918, 60; physical pleasure of, 174, 183–84; political voice of Mpongwé, 45, 63, 67, 197; power in Mpongwé society, 30; prepubescent brides, 31, 39, 69, 139; promiscuity of, 173, 174; as property, 161; property and wealth acquired through interracial relationships, 45, 62–63, 66, 67; restrictions on, 8, 11, 166–68; runaway, 229n50; seen as predatory, 170–71; sex-